MISHNAH'S DIVISION OF AGRICULTURE

Program in Judaic Studies
Brown University
BROWN JUDAIC STUDIES
Edited by
Jacob Neusner,
Wendell S. Dietrich, Ernest S. Frerichs,
Alan Zuckerman

Project Editors (Project)

David Blumenthal, Emory University (Approaches to Medieval Judaism)
Ernest S. Frerichs, Brown University (Dissertations and Monographs)
Lenn Evan Goodman, University of Hawaii (Studies in Medieval Judaism)
William Scott Green, University of Rochester (Approaches to Ancient Judaism)
Ivan Marcus, Jewish Theological Seminary of Americas
(Texts and Studies in Medieval Judaism)
Marc L. Raphael, Ohio State University (Approaches to Judaism in Modern Times)
Jonathan Z. Smith, University of Chicago (Studia Philonica)

Number 79

MISHNAH'S DIVISION OF AGRICULTURE
A History and Theology of *Seder Zeraim*

by
Alan J. Avery-Peck

MISHNAH'S DIVISION OF AGRICULTURE
A History and Theology of *Seder Zeraim*

by
Alan J. Avery-Peck

Scholars Press
Chico, California

MISHNAH'S DIVISION OF AGRICULTURE
A History and Theology of *Seder Zeraim*

by

Alan J. Avery-Peck

Library of Congress Cataloging in Publication Data

Avery-Peck, Alan J. (Alan Jeffery), 1953–
  Mishnah's Division of agriculture.

  (Brown Judaic studies ; no. 79)
  Bibliography: p.
  Includes index.
  1. Mishnah. Zera'im—Commentaries. 2. Agricultural
laws and legislation (Jewish law). I. Title. II. Series.
BM506.Z83A94 1985 296.1'2307   85–10782
ISBN 0–89130–888–1 (alk. paper)
ISBN 0–89130–889–X (pbk. : alk. paper)

Printed in the United States of America
on acid-free paper

FOR
JACOB NEUSNER

TABLE OF CONTENTS

                          ix

PREFACE

The Mishnaic Division of Agriculture presents the early rabbis' sustained consideration of a theological issue of central concern to the nascent rabbinic movement. The problem concerns how Israelites are to maintain and implement laws that derive from the Biblical understanding of a mutual relationship between God and the people of Israel. The rabbis, that is, inherited Scripture's perspective that the land of Israel is a special possession of God, given to the Israelite nation so that the people might grow food for sustenance. Since God owns the land and through it provides for the nation, a share of the land's crops must be paid back to God. This payment, in the form of tithes and other agricultural offerings, is made through the Temple's officials and others who have a special claim for divine help. The same notion of God's ownership of the land explains Scripture's insistence that the land be used only in ways commensurate with the holiness of its owner. The Biblical agricultural laws thus focus upon the idea of God as master of the land of Israel and of the Temple priests and Levites as God's appointed representatives on earth.

Yet Mishnah's rabbis live in a period in which the outward signs of God's rule over and care for the people and land of Israel no longer exist and in which the priesthood itself has lost its cultic function. For, in 70 C.E., the Temple was destroyed and Israelites lost control over the land. Then, in the war of 133-135, their messianic attempt to regain sovereignty through military might failed, leaving portions of the land burned and barely capable of producing food for the people. In light of this, the validity of Scripture's claims and the importance of its rules could hardly be self-evident. In responding to this theological problem, the Division of Agriculture represents one central facet of the program of rectification construed by Mishnah's authorities. It expresses the meaning the agricultural requirements are to have in the time of Mishnah's farmers.

The division's first claim is simply that the rules legislated by Scripture continue to be in force over the people of Israel. The rabbis detail in specific terms how Israelites are to plant, harvest and eat the produce of the land of Israel, so as to carry out their part of the original agreement with God. By taking this approach, the early rabbis claim that, despite what the events of history seem to indicate, God still owns the land of Israel and through it takes special care of the Israelite nation. Only in light of these facts should Scripture's prohibitions and tithing requirements still have effect.

In the division before us, however, Mishnah's rabbis do more than rehearse Scripture's agricultural restrictions and tithing laws. For as we shall see, their outwardly conservative approach masks the recognition that things indeed have changed since the time when the Temple stood. The rabbis choose this division as a context for speaking about specific problems brought about by the destruction of the Temple. These problems concern the mode of sanctification to apply within the Israelite world now that the Temple-cult no longer exists. In light of this larger problem, rabbinic consideration of the topic of agriculture focuses upon the fact that, because of the land's divine ownership, the crops it produces are capable of sanctification. Mishnaic treatment of the agricultural law therefore acknowledges that, in planting, Israelites come into contact with and control holiness. In this, their powers and responsibilities parallel those of the priests who once ministered at the altar of the Jerusalem-Temple.

Speaking in the period after the destruction of the Temple, the Mishnaic Division of Agriculture thus describes the rabbinic understanding of the relationship between the people of Israel and their God, as that relationship is formalized through the Israelites' treatment of their holy land and their handling of the produce that derives from it. The point of the division is that, even though the Temple has been destroyed, holiness still abides within the Israelite nation. Whereas once it was controlled by priests who ministered at the altar, now it is manipulated by common Israelites who assume the responsibility to grow and consume food in accordance with God's law. With the Temple destroyed and the land defiled, Israelites themselves become the symbol of the continuing presence of God and of God's blessings upon the land. In granting these powers to Israelites, Mishnah's authorities suggest an approach to the issue of sanctification appropriate to their own time and unlike that of any prior Judaic thinking.

This study sets out to evaluate this rabbinic theology of sanctification first of all by delineating the intellectual history of the Mishnaic Division of Agriculture. It outlines, that is to say, which of Mishnah's rules derive from early in the development of the law and which come from later periods. By isolating the state of the law in each of Mishnah's major periods of development, we can recognize the evolving concerns of the early rabbinic movement and can determine the meaning that the agricultural law had for those who, in the first centuries, legislated concerning it. The meaning is drawn along two grids.

1) Mishnah is the end product of approximately two hundred years of deliberation among early rabbinic authorities. Mishnah therefore does not contain a single monolithic perspective upon the proper implementation--let alone the purpose and meaning--of the agricultural law. Later authorities provided the systematic framework within which the earlier materials they chose to preserve are to be interpreted. Even so, as this study will show, we still have access to the larger legal perspectives of those earlier generations of authorities. In detailing the particular contributions and understandings of authorities in each of the major periods in the development of the law, this study allows evaluation of the intellectual underpinnings and development of nascent rabbinic Judaism.

2) Comparison of the ideas of the several generations of Mishnaic authorities indicates that, while we have evidence of the changing perspectives of each generation of authorities, Mishnah's final formulators and redactors have included in this division a quite unitary set of issues and legal concerns. The Division of Agriculture is redacted as a sustained essay about the particular issue I have pointed out, that of sanctification. Along with delineating, to the extent possible, the perspectives of each generation of authorities, I therefore clarify the meaning and intent of the Division of Agriculture as a redacted whole.

This study thus has two goals, determination of the contribution to the Division of Agriculture of each generation of Mishnaic authorities and evaluation of the significance of the division as a completed whole speaking in the second century. These goals are met, first, by a rule-by-rule analysis of the division's laws. Found in Chapters Two through Eleven, this analysis 1) indicates the legal or conceptual foundation that supports each law and 2) determines each legal statement's historical provenance. With this information in hand I begin interpretation of each stratum in the development of the law and of the history of the division's law as a whole. The former evaluation appears in Chapters Twelve, Thirteen and Fourteen, which summarize the state of the law before 70 and in Yavnean and Ushan times, and which suggest the meaning of each period's law within its own historical circumstances. The latter is accomplished in the concluding chapter, which suggests the implications of the historical development of the law for our understanding of nascent rabbinic Judaism.

In order to allow informed reading of the law-by-law analyses of each tractate, found in the long middle section of this book, the first chapter describes the meaning of the Division of Agriculture as a redacted whole. It does this by isolating the focus of each of the division's tractates and, on this basis, by ascertaining the legal and theological point of the complete division. Better to evaluate the point of the division, this first chapter also relates the law of the Division of Agriculture to its Scriptural foundations and compares the focus of this rabbinic writing with that of other contemporary writing on the topic of agriculture.

The introduction describes in detail the purpose and methods of this study and indicates its relationship to and dependence upon existing scholarship on Mishnah as a whole and the Division of Agriculture in particular.

Professor Martin Jaffee, of the University of Virginia, patiently read and extensively commented on the entire manuscript. Marty and I were together when, as students at the Hebrew University and then at Brown University, we worked on commentaries to individual tractates of the Division of Agriculture. In conversations as fellow graduate students and since then by telephone, in letters and at conferences, Marty has constantly contributed to this project. I alone am responsible for this book's shortcomings. But I thank Martin Jaffee for his help, which has made this study much better than it otherwise could have been.

Professor Gary Porton, of the University of Illinois, offered intellectual guidance and moral support during the years in which this study was researched and written. His encouragement and advice are constant sources of strength, his friendship always a source of joy. For these things I thank him.

This book is dated on the occasion of the swearing in of my wife, Lisa J. Avery-Peck, to the Louisiana State Bar. It thus marks for both of us the conclusion of several years of hopes, aspirations and arduous work, and signifies the beginning, of course, of new projects and adventures. I offer Lisa my gratitude for her willingness to share these things with me.

For a decade Professor Jacob Neusner has guided and taught me, selflessly given me of his time and, as an added gift, has offered me his warm and nurturing friendship. I can thank him only by giving back in a small way that which in important ways is his to begin with. Dedication of this book thanks Jacob Neusner for all that he has done for me through his generosity as a teacher and friend and through his example as a scholar and a mensch.

Alan J. Avery-Peck

New Orleans, Louisiana
October 5, 1984
Erev Yom Kippur, 5745

ABBREVIATIONS AND BIBLIOGRAPHY

Aberbach	= Aberbach, Moses, The Roman-Jewish War (66-70 A.D.): Its Origins and Consequences (London, 1966).
Ah.	= Ahilot
Albeck	= Albeck, H., The Six Orders of the Mishnah (Hebrew) (Jerusalem and Tel Aviv, 1957).
Albeck, Mabo	= Albeck, H., Mabo LaMishnah (Jerusalem and Tel Aviv, 1959).
Allon	= Allon, G., "On The Social History of Palestine in the Days of the Mishnah" (Hebrew) in Tarbiz XXI (1951).
Ar.	= Arakhin
Aruch	= Kohut, Alexander, ed., Aruch Completum, 8 vols., (Vienna, 1878-1892; second ed., 1926).
[Avery-]Peck, Alan	= [Avery-]Peck, Alan, The Priestly Gift in Mishnah: A Study of Tractate Terumot (Chico, 1981).
A.Z.	= Abodah Zarah
b.	= Babli, Babylonian Talmud, cited by tractate and folio number of ed. Romm (Vilna, 1886); ben, "son of" as in Simeon b. Gamaliel.
B.B.	= Baba Batra
Bek.	= Bekhorot
Ber.	= Berakhot
Bert	= Obadiah b. Abraham of Bertinoro, Mishnah commentary in Romm ed. of Mishnah (Vilna, 1908, and reprints).
Bes.	= Besah
Bik.	= Bikkurim
B.M.	= Baba Mesia
B.Q.	= Baba Qamma

Brooks   = Brooks, Roger, Support for the
                                  Poor in the Mishnaic Law of
                                  Agriculture: Tractate Peah
                                  (Chico, 1983).

Cato, Agriculture   = Marcus Porcius Cato, On
                                  Agriculture, tr. William Davis
                                  Hooper [Loeb Classical Library],
                                  (London, 1933).

Clark   = Clark, Kenneth W., "Worship in the
                                  Jerusalem Temple after A.D. 70,"
                                  in New Testament Studies 6 (July,
                                  1960), pp. 269-80.

Davies   = Davies, W.D., The Territorial
                                  Dimension of Judaism (Berkeley,
                                  1982).

Dem.   = Demai

Dt.   = Deuteronomy

Ed.   = Eduyyot

Eissfeldt   = Eissfeldt, Otto, Erstlings und
                                  Zehnten im Alten Testament
                                  (Leipzig, 1917).

Epstein, Mabo'   = Epstein, Jacob Nahum Halevi, Mabo'
                                  lenosah hammishnah [Prolegomenon
                                  to the Text of the Mishnah], 2
                                  vols., (Jerusalem & Tel Aviv,
                                  1948, second edition, 1964).

Epstein, Mebo'ot   = Epstein, Jacob Nahum Halevi,
                                  Mebo'ot Lesifrut hatanna'im
                                  [Prolegomena to the Tannaitic
                                  Literature] ed. Ezra Z. Melamed
                                  (Jerusalem and Tel Aviv, 1957).

Erub.   = Erubin

Ex.   = Exodus

Essner, "Orlah"   = Essner, Howard, "Mishnah Tractate
                                  ^cOrlah: Translation and
                                  Commentary," in W.S. Green, ed.,
                                  Approaches to Ancient Judaism.
                                  Vol. III (Chico, 1981), pp. 105-
                                  148.

Feliks, Agriculture   = Feliks, Yehudah, Agriculture in
                                  Palestine in the Period of the

Mishna and Talmud (Hebrew)
(Jerusalem and Tel Aviv, 1963).

Feliks, Plant World   = Feliks, Yehudah, The Plant World
of the Bible (Hebrew) (Tel Aviv,
1957).

Finley   = Finley, Moses I., The Ancient
Economy (Berkeley, 1973).

Frank   = Frank, Tenney, Economic Survey of
Ancient Rome. Vol. V. Roman Italy
and the Empire (Baltimore, 1940).

Gen.   = Genesis

Git.   = Gittin

GRA   = Elijah b. Solomon Zalmon, Mishnah
commentary in Romm. ed. of
Mishnah.

Green, Joshua   = Green, William, The Traditions of
Joshua Ben Hananiah (Leiden, 1981).

Green, "Rabbinism"   = Green, William, "Reading the
Writing of Rabbinism," in Journal
of the American Academy of
Religion 51:2, June, 1983, pp.
191-206.

Guthrie   = Guthrie, H. H., Jr., "Tithe," in
Interpreters Dictionary of the
Bible, vol. 3, pp. 654-655.

Guttman   = Guttman, Alexander, "The Problem
of the Anonymous Mishnah," in
Hebrew Union College Annual 16,
1941, pp. 137-155.

Haas   = Haas, Peter J., A History of the
Mishnaic Law of Agriculture:
Tractate Maaser Sheni (Chico,
1980).

Hag.   = Hagigah

Hal.   = Hallah

Havivi   = Havivi, Abraham, "Mishnah Hallah
Chapter One: Translation and
Commentary," in William S. Green
ed., Approaches to Ancient
Judaism. Vol. III, (Chico, 1981),
pp. 149-184.

Hor.   = Horayot
Hul.   = Hullin
Jaffee   = Jaffee, Martin, Mishnah's Theology
                                of Tithing: A Study of Tractate
                                Maaserot (Chico, 1981).
Jastrow   = Jastrow, Marcus, A Dictionary of
                                the Targumim, the Talmud Babli and
                                Yerushalmi, and the Midrashic
                                Literature, 2 vols., (New York,
                                1895-1903; repr. New York, 1975).
JE   = The Jewish Encyclopedia, 12 vols.,
                                (New York and London, 1901, 1906;
                                repr. New York, 1975).
Kasovsky, Mishnah   = Kasovsky, C. Y., Thesaurus
                                Mishnae: Concordantiae verborum
                                etc., 4 vols., (Tel Aviv, 1957,
                                rev. 1967).
Kasovsky, Tosefta   = Kosovsky, C. Y., Thesaurus
                                Thosephthae: Concordantiae
                                verborum etc., 6 vols.,
                                (Jerusalem, 1932-1961).
Kel.   = Kelim
Ker.   = Keritot
Ket   = Ketubot
Kil.   = Kilaim
Lev.   = Leviticus
Levine   = Levine, Lee, "The Causes of 66-70
                                C-E," Judaism, XX:2, 1971, pp.
                                244-248.
Lieberman, "Greek"   = Lieberman, Saul, "How Much Greek
                                in Jewish Palestine?" in Biblical
                                and Other Studies (Brandeis
                                University, Texts and Studies I),
                                pp. 123-141; reprinted in Fischel,
                                H., ed., Essays in Greco-Roman and
                                Related Talmudic Literature (Ktav,
                                1977), pp. 325-343.
Lieberman, Hellenism   = Lieberman, Saul, Hellenism in
                                Jewish Palestine (New York, 1950).

Lieberman, TK   = Lieberman, Saul, Tosefta Ki-fshuta:
                         A Comprehensive Commentary on the
                         Tosefta, I. Order Zera^{c}im, 2 vols.,
                         (New York, 1955).

Lieberman, TZ   = Lieberman, Saul, ed., The Tosefta
                         According to Codex Vienna with
                         Variants from Codex Erfurt,
                         Genizah MSS. and Editio Princeps,
                         I. The Order of Zera^{c}im (New
                         (York, 1955).

Low, Flora   = Low, Immanuel, Die Flora der
                         Juden, 4 vols., (Vienna and
                         Leipzig, 1926).

MacCulloch   = MacCulloch, J. A., "Tithes" in
                         Encyclopedia of Religion and
                         Ethics, ed., James Hastings
                         (New York, 1924), Vol. XII, pp.
                         347-350.

Maimonides   = Kitab es-Siraj (Mishnah
                         Commentary); in standard editions
                         of the Mishnah.

Mak.   = Makkot

Makh.   = Makhshirin

Mandelbaum   = Mandelbaum, Irving, A History of
                         The Mishnaic Law of Agriculture:
                         Kilayim (Chico, 1982).

Mantel   = Mantel, Hugo, "The Causes of the
                         Bar Kokhba Revolt," Jewish
                         Quarterly Review (1968) LVIII:3,
                         pp. 224-242, LVIII:4, pp. 274-296.

Me.   = Meilah

Meg.   = Megillah

Men.   = Menahot

Mid.   = Middot

Miq.   = Miqvaot

Morris   = Morris, Colin, The Discovery of
                         the Individual: 1050-1200 (New
                         York, 1972).

M.Q.   = Moed Qatan

MR   = Mishnah Rishonah. Ephraim Isaac
                         of Premysla, Mishnah commentary

	(1882), in standard editions of Mishnah.
M.S.	= Maaser Sheni
MS	= Meleket Shelomoh. Solomon b. Joshua Adeni, Mishnah commentary, in standard editions of Mishnah.
MS.	= manuscript
Naz.	= Nazir
Ned.	= Nedarim
Neg.	= Negaim
Nelson	= Nelson, Benjamin, "Eros, Logos, Nomos, Polis: Their Changing Balances and the Vicissitudes of Communities and Civilizations," in Allan W. Eister, ed., Changing Perspectives in the Scientific Study of Religion (New York, 1974), pp. 85-111.
Neusner, Appointed Times	= Neusner, Jacob, A History of the Mishnaic Law of Appointed Times, 5 vols., (Leiden, 1981).
Neusner, Damages	= Neusner, Jacob, A History of the Mishnaic Law of Damages, 5 vols., (Leiden, 1982).
Neusner, Development	= Neusner, Jacob, Development of a Legend: Studies in the Traditions Concerning Yohanan ben Zakkai (Leiden, 1970).
Neusner, Eliezer	= Neusner, Jacob, Eliezer ben Hyrcanus: The Tradition and the Man, 2 vols., (Leiden, 1973).
Neusner, Holy Things	= Neusner, Jacob, A History of the Mishnaic Law of Holy Things, 6 vols., (Leiden, 1978-79).
Neusner, Judaism	= Neusner, Jacob, Judaism: The Evidence of the Mishnah (Chicago, 1981).
Neusner, Life	= Neusner, Jacob, A Life of Yohanan ben Zakkai (Leiden, 1962; second edition, completely revised, 1970).

Neusner, Modern Study   = Neusner, Jacob, ed., The Modern
Study of the Mishnah (Leiden,
1973).

Neusner, Pharisees   = Neusner, Jacob, The Rabbinic Traditions about the Pharisees before
70, 3 vols., (Leiden, 1971).

Neusner, Piety   = Neusner, Jacob, From Politics to
Piety: The Emergence of Pharisaic
Judaism (Second Edition, Ktav,
1979).

Neusner, Purities   = Neusner, Jacob, A History of the
Mishnaic Law of Purities, 22
vols., (Leiden, 1974-1977).

Neusner, Women   = Neusner, Jacob, A History of the
Mishnaic Law of Women, 5 vols.,
(Leiden, 1979-80).

Neusner, Tosefta   = Neusner, Jacob, The Tosefta
Translated from the Hebrew,
5 vols., (New York, 1977-1981).

Neusner, "Transcendence"   = Neusner, Jacob, "Transcedence
and Worship Through Learning,"
in Journal of Reform Judaism
25:2 (1978), pp. 15-29.

Newman   = Newman, Louis, The Sanctity of the
Seventh Year: A Study of Mishnah
Tractate Shebiit (Chico, 1983).

Nid.   = Nid.

Num.   = Numbers

Oppenheimer, Am Ha-Aretz   = Oppenheimer, Aharon, The Am Ha-
Aretz (Leiden, 1977).

Oppenheimer, "First Tithe"   = Oppenheimer, Aharon, "Hafrasat
Ma^{c}aśer Riśo'n: Halakhah
lema^{c}aśeh bitqufat bayit šeni,"
in Benjamin DeVries Memorial
Volume (Jerusalem, 1968), pp.
970-983.

Oppenheimer, "Terumot"   = Oppenheimer, Aharon, "Terumot and
Ma'aserot," in Encyclopedia
Judaica, Vol. 15, pp. 1025-28.

Or.   = Orlah

Pe.   = Peah

Pes.   = Pesahim
Porton, "Dispute"   = Porton, Gary G., "The Artificial
                                Dispute: Ishmael and Aqiba," in
                                Jacob Neusner, ed., Judaism,
                                Christianity and other Greco-Roman
                                Cults (Leiden, 1975), pp. 18-29.
Porton, Ishmael   = Porton, Gary G., The Traditions of
                                Rabbi Ishmael, 4 vols., (Leiden,
                                1976-1980).
Primus   = Primus, Charles, Aqiva's Contri-
                                bution to the Law of Zeraim
                                (Leiden, 1977).
Qid.   = Qiddushin
Qin.   = Qinnim
R.   = Rabbi
Radding   = Radding, Charles M., "Evaluation
                                of Medieval Mentalities: A
                                Cognative-Structural Approach,"
                                in The American Historical Review
                                83:3 (June, 1978), pp. 557-597.
R.H.   = Rosh Hashshanah
Rostovtzeff   = Rostovtzeff, Mikhail, The Social
                                and Economic History of the
                                Hellenistic World, 3 vols.
                                (Oxford, 1941).
Rouse   = Rouse, W. H. D., "Tithes (Greek)"
                                in Encyclopedia of Religion and
                                Ethics, ed., James Hastings, (New
                                York, 1924), Vol. XII, pp. 350-351.
Sacks-Hutner   = The Mishnah with Variant Readings,
                                Order Zera^{c}im, 2 vols.; edited by
                                Nissan Sacks, at the Institute for
                                the Complete Israeli Talmud, Joshua
                                Hutner, director, (Jerusalem,
                                1972-75).
Safrai, "Judaea"   = Safrai, S., "The Status of
                                Provincia Judaea after the
                                Destruction of the Second Temple,"
                                in Zion XXVII (1962).
Safrai, "Sabbatical"   = Safrai, S., "The Practical Im-
                                plementation of the Sabbatical

Year after the Destruction of the
Second Temple," (in Hebrew) in
Tarbiz XXV-XXVI, 1966.

Sambursky   = Sambursky, S., _The Physics of the
                               Stoics_ (London, 1959).

Sarason, _Demai_   = Sarason, Richard S., _A History of
                               the Mishnaic Law of Agriculture:
                               A Study of Tractate Demai, Part
                               One_ (Leiden, 1979).

Sarason, "_Zeraim_"   = Sarason, Richard S., "Mishnah and
                               Scripture: Preliminary
                               Observations on the Law of
                               Tithing in _Sedar Zeraim_," in W.S.
                               Green, ed., _Approaches to Ancient
                               Judaism, Vol. II_ (Chico, 1980),
                               pp. 81-96.

Schafer   = Schafer, Peter, "The Causes of the
                               Bar Kokhba Revolt," in Jakob
                               Petuchowski and Ezra Fleischer,
                               eds., _Studies in Aggadah, Targum
                               and Jewish Liturgy in Memory of
                               Joseph Heinemann_ (Jerusalem,
                               1981), pp. 74-94.

Schiffman, _Sectarian Law_   = Schiffman, Lawrence H., _Sectarian
                               Law in the Dead Sea Scrolls_
                               (Chico, 1983).

Shurer-Vermes-Millar   = Shurer, Emil, _The History of the
                               Jewish People in the Age of Jesus
                               Christ_, rev. ed. by G. Vermes and
                               F. Millar, Vol. I (Edinburgh,
                               1973).

Sens   = Samson b. Abraham of Sens,
                               Mishnah commentary in Romm edition
                               of Babylonian Talmud.

Shab.   = Shabbat
Shav.   = Shabuot
Sheb.   = Shebiit
Sheq.   = Sheqalim
Smallwood   = Smallwood, E. Mary, _The Jews Under
                               Roman Rule: From Pompey to
                               Diocletian_ (Leiden, 1976).

Smith   = Smith, Morton, "Palestinian
                                     Judaism in the First Centuries,"
                                     in Moshe Davis, ed., Israel: Its
                                     Role in Civilization (New York,
                                     1956), pp. 67-81.
Snaith   = Snaith, N. A., Leviticus and
                                     Numbers (London, 1967).
Sot.   = Sotah
Strack   = Strack, Hermann, Introduction to
                                     the Talmud and Midrash
                                     (Philadelphia,   reprint: 1959).
Suk   = Sukkah
T.   = Tosefta
Ta.   = Taanit
Tam.   = Tamid
Tem.   = Temurah
Ter.   = Terumot
Theophrastus, Enquiry   = Theophrastus, Enquiry into Plants,
                                     tr. Sir Arthur Hart, 2 vols.,
                                     [Loeb Classical Library], (London,
                                     1916).
Toh.   = Tohorot
T.Y.   = Tebul Yom
TYT   = Tosepot Yom Tob. Yom Tob Lippmann
                                     Heller, Mishnah commentary, in
                                     standard editions of Mishnah.
Uqs.   = Uqsin
Urbach, "Charity"   = Urbach, Ephraim E., "Political and
                                     Social Tendencies in Talmudic
                                     Concepts of Charity" (in Hebrew),
                                     in Zion XVI (1951), pp. 1-27.
Varro, Agriculture   = Varro, Marcus Terentius, On
                                     Agriculture, tr. William Davis
                                     Hooper [Loeb Classical Library],
                                     (London, 1933).
Vermes, Scrolls   = Vermes, Geza, The Dead Sea Scrolls
                                     in English (Harmondsworth, 1968).
Weiner   = Weiner, David, "A Study of Mishnah
                                     Tractate Bikkurim, Chapter Three,"
                                     in W. S. Green, ed., Approaches to
                                     Ancient Judaism. Vol. III (Chico,
                                     1981), pp. 89-104.

Wenig   = Wenig-Rubenstein, Margaret, "A
                                    Commentary on Mishnah-Tosefta Bik-
                                    kurim, Chapters One and Two," in
                                    W. S. Green, ed., Approaches to
                                    Ancient Judaism. Vol. III (Chico,
                                    1981), pp. 47-88.
White, Bibliography   = White, K. D., A Bibliography of
                                    Roman Agriculture (Reading, 1970).
White, Farming   = White, K. D., Roman Farming
                                    (Ithaca, 1970).
y.   = Yerushalmi, Palestinian Talmud.
Yad.   = Yadayyim
Yeb.   = Yebamot
Yom.   = Yomah
Y.T.   = Yom Tob
Zab.   = Zabbim
Zeb.   = Zebaḥim
Zuckermandel   = Zuckermandel, Moses Samuel,
                                    Tosephta, based on the Erfurt and
                                    Vienna Codices, with Parallels
                                    and Varients (Trier, 1881-82;
                                    revised edition with supplement
                                    by Saul Lieberman, Jerusalem,
                                    reprint: 1970).

TRANSLITERATIONS

א	= '		ל	= l
ב	= b		ם, מ	= m
ג	= g		ן, נ	= n
ד	= d		ס	= s
ה	= h		ע	= c
ו	= w		ף, פ	= p
ז	= z		ץ, צ	= ṣ
ח	= ḥ		ק	= q
ט	= ṭ		ר	= r
י	= y		שׁ	= š
כ, ך	= k		שׂ	= ś

ת = t

Transliterations represent the consonantal structure of the
Hebrew word, with no attempt made to vocalize. I do not
distinguish between the spirantized and non-spirantized forms of
b, g, d, k, p, and t. Verbal roots are indicated by
capitalization, e.g., TRM. When, on occasion, a word is
vocalized, the following notation is used:

       a = qamaṣ, pataḥ   i = ḥiriq

      ei = ṣere-yod   o = ḥolem, ḥolem ḥaser,

       e = ṣere, segol, vocal shewa   qamaṣ qaṭan

              u = šuruq, qubbuṣ

Quiescent shewa is not represented. Proper names and commonly
used words are reproduced in their more frequent English usage,
e.g., Eleazar, Mishnah, etc.

INTRODUCTION

This volume focuses upon a narrowly historical question. Examining the Mishnaic Division of Agriculture, it asks which of Mishnah's rules and ideas derive from early stages of rabbinic thinking about the topic of agriculture and which rules come from later periods in the formation of Mishnaic law. This study thus works to describe the historical development of the ideas contained in one of Mishnah's six major divisions. It identifies the theoretical underpinnings of the Mishnaic law of agriculture, focuses upon the intermediate stages in which those foundations were developed and, finally, describes how those ideas were put to use in the creation of the completed document before us.

The purpose of these analyses is to understand the meaning of Mishnah's law for those who, in the first centuries, created it. As we shall see, this law is not primarily the end product of long centuries during which agricultural practices and customs evolved within the Israelite nation. The Division of Agriculture, rather, is the creation of several small groups of individuals, organized in academies, who began working on this topic shortly before the destruction of the Jerusalem-Temple in 70 C.E. and who completed their deliberations in the late second century. This means that in order to understand the laws contained in this division, we must isolate the contributions of these individual academies. In this way we hope clearly to understand the perspectives and attitudes of the founders of rabbinic Judaism.

Isolating the ideas of each individual generation of Mishnaic authorities allows us to carry out two important steps in interpreting the division before use.

1) Delineating each generation's approach to the law of agriculture facilitates recognition of that generation's understanding of the relationship between Israel and its God. For in the view of Mishnah's rabbis, that relationship is formalized in the Israelites' fulfillment of special obligations that revolve around their planting, harvesting and consuming the produce of the land of Israel. By identifying the attitude of each generation of authorities we may, further, interpret their thought in light of the particular historical environment in which they carried out their legal deliberations. In this

1

respect, this volume intends to contribute to our understanding of the social and political, as well as the theological, roots of rabbinic Judaism.

2) Isolating the ideas of each generation of authorities does more than distinguish the contributions to the Mishnaic Division of Agriculture of the different rabbinic academies. It further allows us to point out the larger agendum of issues that, as we shall see, is established early in the formation of the law and that is systematically explored in each of the strata of the law before us. As a result of the historical analysis carried out here, we therefore derive a clear picture of the concerns and meaning of the Division of Agriculture as a whole while at the same time delineating the history of ideas that brought it to the shape in which it stands before us today.

A characterization of each generation's thought appears at the end of this volume, in chapters devoted to the state of the law before 70, in Yavneh and during Ushan times. The significance of the conceptual history of the law, viewed whole, then is examined in the final conclusions. These concluding studies, however, depend upon detailed analyses that allow us to discern the historical development of the law contained in this division. These are found in the long middle section of this book, in which I take up in turn each of the tractates in this division so as to ascertain the historical provenance of the laws it contains. Let me now describe the method by which this historical evaluation is carried out.

I begin by dividing each tractate into its constituent thematic units--agglomerates of law concerning a single topic or expressing a single legal theory.[1] Within these units, I list separately the rules and legal statements assigned to each of the three identifiable periods of early rabbinic law, before 70 and the periods of Yavneh and Usha.[2] This listing provides a rough chronology of Mishnah's law and therefore allows us initially to characterize the main issues and understandings of each period.

Two questions attract our attention at this point. The important one concerns how to ascertain that what is attributed to a specific authority actually derives from the historical period in which he was active. The second question concerns the dating of Mishnah's anonymous laws.

To verify a statement's provenance in a particular period I begin by delineating the legal theory that stands behind the

statement.[3] In this way I can discern the logical or factual
dependence of that statement upon other laws assigned either to
its same period or to other generations of authorities. The
point is to see, for instance, whether or not what is assigned
to a Yavnean 1) is consistent with other Yavnean opinions, 2)
takes up ideas assigned to individuals who lived before 70 and/or
3) serves as a basis for laws attributed to Ushans. If the
statement under consideration meets one or more of these
criteria, there is good reason to assume that it indeed derives
from the middle, Yavnean, stratum in the development of the law.
If, by contrast, what is assigned to an authority known to have
been active before 70 assumes facts or legal theories that, while
unknown to Yavneans, are commonplace at Usha, we must assume that
the attribution is pseudepigraphic. The statement presumably
derives from Ushan times, along with the other laws that share
its thematic concerns or conceptual perspective.

One alternative to the assumptions based here upon the
logical connections between laws in Mishnah's several strata may,
I believe, be quickly rejected. This is to assume that the final
generation of Mishnaic authorities created the whole elaborate
system of law before us, assigning to the names of past
generations ideas representing the logical steps towards the
final approach to the law that they established. This
alternative explanation is shown to be very unlikely by the
consistent pattern of legal growth evidenced in this division and
in the rest of Mishnah. It is difficult to believe that the
intricate legal developments depicted here are all the result of
the calculated Ushan and post-Ushan use of pseudepigraphy.[4]

It is unlikely that the final generation of Mishnaic
authorities invented the whole weaving of law found in the
Mishnah. Still, the basis for my claim to interpret the
significance of the law for each generation of Mishnaic masters
must be clearly explained. This is for two reasons.

1) While the laws in the division derive from over a period
of close to two hundred years, the literary character of the
division as a whole results from the work of only a single
generation of Mishnaic formulators. This is clear from the fact
that all of the laws before us are phrased in a small number of
highly stylized and formalized linguistic patterns. These
literary conventions appear in the anonymous rules and in the
mouths of the division's named authorities, early and late. The
work of formulation presumably was carried out at a single time,

by those rabbinic masters, primarily Ushans, who represent the final generation of cited authorities.[5]

2) The individuals who gave linguistic expression to antecedent materials also chose which of those available laws would be preserved in the Mishnah. The Yavnean and pre-Yavnean materials before us thus have not been selected for transmission by their own authors, in conformity with their particular theory of what must be said on the topic of agriculture. Rather, they were saved by later redactors who chose to use specific materials in light of their own conceptions of what the Division of Agriculture should and should not represent.

The selection and reformulation of antecedent materials by later authorities means that the Division of Agriculture, along with the Mishnah as a whole, is a product of and expresses the meaning intended by its final formulators and redactors. This fact limits what we can know about earlier authorities' thinking. Since we do not have access to all that Yavneans, for instance, said, or to how they would have said it, we cannot claim to isolate and interpret a Yavnean system of agricultural law. This does not, however, preclude interpretation of the Yavnean legal perspective in general and, through evaluation of that perspective, delineation of the significance for Yavneans of their legal deliberations. This is as follows.

The Yavnean and pre-Yavnean materials in this division all reflect a single theory of law, a theory quite distinct from that which stands behind the division's Ushan materials. This study therefore moves behind the larger framework of the division as a redacted whole, so as to take seriously the legal attitude that early rules consistently portray. I do not claim to know all that the earlier authorities said, and I certainly cannot envision how the Division of Agriculture would have looked had they, instead of later authorities, formulated and redacted it. Yet these early masters' attitude towards the law, revealed in the sizable body of materials that has been preserved, constitutes important evidence for how the first generations of Mishnah's authorities imagined their role as legislators. This attitude therefore serves to make manifest their understanding of how the covenant relationship between God and the people of Israel should, through human legal activity, unfold.

To summarize: The method employed here both indicates the likelihood that a legal idea derives from the period of the

authority to which it is assigned and provides an initial
characterization of the legal theories of each generation of
authorities. In doing this, it isolates the meaning of Mishnah's
materials on two levels: first, for the generation of
authorities that created each individual law, and then for those
who created of these antecedent materials the document that
stands before us today.

The approach used here allows me to discern the historical
provenance of most of the Division of Agriculture's anonymous
statements. These anonymous rules are reviewed after I have
evaluated the attributed materials and drawn a sketch of the
state of the law in each period.[6] Comparison with the assigned
laws allows determination--on the basis of legal and factual
content--of the period from which the anonymous materials must
derive. An important result of this analysis is to show that,
in the vast majority of cases, the anonymous materials found in
the Division of Agriculture are congruent in issue and approach
with the latest attributed laws. Anonymous rules in no case
suggest basic premises or facts upon which later legal developments depend. This disproves the still repeated notion of past
generations of scholars that at least certain of Mishnah's
anonymous rules contain this document's most ancient ideas.[7]

The method employed here allows delineation and verification
of the historical development of Mishnaic legal thinking on the
topic of agriculture. It must be clear however that this method,
which focuses upon the ideational content of Mishnah's statements, proves only that what is assigned to a particular
authority could, or could not, have been said in the period
during which that rabbi was active. This method cannot however
prove that a statement actually was made by the authority to whom
Mishnah attributes it. While such confirmation would be
important in the advancement of rabbinic biography, I envisage no
method that would allow proof along these lines.[8] I can only
point out the general result of this study, that Yavnean and
Ushan materials uniformly meet the test of authentication to
which I submit them. This highlights in a general way the
viability of Mishnah's attributions. Only in several cases do
Mishnah's statements fail the test used here. These are rules
that, while assigned to the Houses of Hillel and Shammai, assumed
to have been active in the period before 70, appear instead to
have been created by rabbis working in Ushan times. The

implications of this pseudepigraphic assigning of laws to early authorities are discussed in Chapter Twelve.

This study is limited in one other way that bears mention. My history of Mishnaic law is detailed in only three major stages, representing, as I have said, the rabbinic masters who lived before 70 and in the academies at Yavneh and Usha. I am not able, however, to propose a finer delineation, showing the development of legal thinking within each of these periods. The reason is that Mishnah itself does not provide a more detailed discrimination among its materials. All authorities who worked, for instance, at Yavneh engage in conversation with all other rabbis from that same period. The same is the case for the rabbis who worked in Ushan times. Mishnah's stratification of its authorities into three periods, and the concomitant commonality of ideas within each of these periods, precludes the discerning of finer distinctions in the growth of Mishnah's agricultural law.[9]

The results of the law-by-law evaluation of the tractates are summarized in introductions to each tractate and to its individual thematic units. These introductions serve to describe the tractate as a whole, to point to the aspect of its topic taken up for extended analysis and to indicate the specific legal theory proposed by each generation of authorities to resolve that legal issue. These introductions are placed before the rules they evaluate to allow informed reading of my detailed discussions of those individual laws.

After the systematic examination of the Division of Agriculure's law has been carried out, final conclusions are possible. Found at the end of this volume, these are of two types.

First, Chapters Twelve, Thirteen and Fourteen systematize what the previous discussions have shown about the state of the law before 70 and in the periods of Yavneh and Usha. These chapters allow us to see what was thought about the agricultural requirements in each of the periods in question. On that basis I point out the legal philosophy developed in each period and move ahead to relate this approach to the law to the particular historical situation in which that generation lived.

Second, with evaluations of each of the three stages of the law in hand, I draw conclusions concerning the historical development of rabbinic thinking about the topic of agriculture

in general. What do we learn about Mishnah's rabbis and about
the program of nascent rabbinic Judaism from the growing legal
agendum of the Division of Agriculture? By answering this
question I contribute to our understanding of the Mishnah as a
historical document that reveals the philosophy of rabbinic
Judaism's earliest authorities.

Intelligent reading of the specifics of the division's laws,
discussed in Chapters Two through Eleven, is facilitated by the
overview of the system of agriculture as a whole, found in
Chapter One. In that Chapter I review the topic and contents of
each of Mishnah's tractates so as to identify the larger program
of inquiry to which they contribute. Examination in this same
context of the division's Scriptural roots and of contemporary
parallels in the Greco-Roman writings on agriculture allow the
reader to see clearly the content and focus of the Mishnaic law
before us.

By this point it should be clear that this study takes
seriously the documentary limits of Mishnah's Division of
Agriculture. I assume, that is to say, that the statement
Mishnah's rabbis wished to make concerning the topic of
agriculture is made within the literary context of the tractates
in this division. I therefore do not refer to laws concerning
agriculture found outside of Mishnaic Division of Agriculture,
whether they appear elsewhere in Mishnah or in later rabbinic
documents. Other than Mishnah itself, the only document to which
I refer in the course of this study is the Tosefta. The Tosefta
serves the purposes of this study insofar as its attributions
support conclusions concerning the provenance of certain of
Mishnah's laws already derived from an analysis of Mishnah alone.
A large scale evaluation of the attitudes and legal theories
concerning agriculture found in the Tosefta--or the Talmudim--
would be an important contribution towards our understanding of
the growth of rabbinic Judaism. Such analysis however is beyond
the scope of this volume, which claims only to interpret the
Mishnaic law of agriculture.

This study does not refer to Tractate Berakhot which, while
found in the Division of Agriculture, has no apparent substantive
or ideational relationship to the other tractates of this
division. The question of why Tractate Berakhot, on the
liturgical life of the Israelite nation, has been placed in this
division, and indeed at the beginning of the Mishnah as a whole,
is beyond the scope of this study.

The analyses undertaken in this volume depend upon recently published commentaries to each of the tractates of the Division of Agriculture. I refer specifically to the work of R. Brooks (Peah), R. Sarason (Demai), I. Mandelbaum (Kilaim), L. Newman (Shebiit), M. Jaffee (Maaserot), P. Haas (Maaser Sheni), A. Havivi (Hallah), H. Essner (Orlah), M. Wenig and D. Weiner (Bikkurim) and to my own work on Tractate Terumot. These commentaries are all distinguished from past exegesis of this division by their attention to the theoretical concerns that underlie Mishnah's law and by their insistence that identification of these concerns flow from literary and thematic evaluation of the tractate viewed as an integral whole. These studies thus propose to locate the meaning that the law had for the rabbis who promulgated it, not for the later generations that received and interpreted it in light of their own concerns and needs.[10] By initiating the systematic interpretation of Mishnah's tractates viewed as literary wholes, and by locating the issues of mind that stand behind Mishnah's rules and disputes, these studies make possible my own evaluation of the logical relationships among this division's diverse rules.

A second intellectual debt must also be acknowledged. I refer to Jacob Neusner's interpretations of the tractates in Mishnah's other five divisions and to his pioneering studies of the history of the law contained in those other orders. In his studies of Mishnah, Professor Neusner sets a new agendum for the interpretation of early rabbinic literature. This program of inquiry, to a great extent completed in Professor Neusner's own scholarship on Mishnah, calls for evaluation of the historical development and meaning of Mishnaic law. This study takes up the challenge that Professor Neusner's work on Mishnaic law presents, applying to the Division of Agriculture questions and methods that he used in evaluating Mishnah's other divisions.

By carrying out for the Division of Agriculture the type of study that Dr. Neusner conducted for Mishnah's five other divisions, this volume completes the first rule-by-rule delineation of the historical growth and meaning of all Mishnaic law. As a result, for the first time, discussions of early rabbinic history have access to the specific legal perspectives of each period of Mishnah's formation. At the same time, the present volume moves beyond the original agendum of issues proposed by Neusner. He emphasized 1) the question of the

veracity of Mishnah's attributions and of the provenance of the
anonymous statements and 2) the meaning of each of Mishnah's
divisions as redacted wholes.   Completion of the latter task is
marked by his study, Judaism: The Evidence of the Mishnah.   His
work on Mishnah's other five divisions has answered the first
question, proving the general trustworthiness of all attributions
except those to authorities who lived before 70.   Neusner
likewise has shown that anonymous rules consistently represent
the thought of late rabbinic masters.   For both of the questions
Neusner posed, this study provides the corresponding evidence of
the Division of Agriculture, to which Neusner did not have
access.   With his studies completed, however, this volume
concentrates less upon proof of the historical assignments of
Mishnah's laws and more upon the issue of what the specific
developments in Mishnaic legal thinking teach about the formation
and early growth of rabbinic Judaism.   In particular, in the
concluding chapters of this study I examine the historical
context for the legal developments of each of the Division of
Agriculture's generations of authorities and compare the
ideational development of Mishnaic law with the growth of other
legal systems.   In this way I both take up and carry forward the
program of inquiry proposed by Neusner.

The debt to past scholarship of any study of Mishnah
obviously goes deeper than studies carried out in the past
fifteen years.   My use of traditional as well as modern
commentaries and other secondary sources is indicated in the
bibliography.   These references serve in a general way to reflect
the continuing dependence of the present generation of students
of the rabbinic literature upon past exegesis, including the
traditional commentaries published in the margins of standard
printings of the Mishnah and the Talmuds and more recent
interpretations, published both in traditional and secular
contexts.   These works of interpretation share the quest for the
meaning of Mishnah's law, providing the set of exegetical
potentials from which the historian ultimately must choose.   They
therefore stand at the base of all historical interpretation and
reconstruction.

PART I

THE MISHNAIC SYSTEM OF AGRICULTURE

CHAPTER ONE

THE MISHNAIC DIVISION OF AGRICULTURE

I. The Topic of the Division of Agriculture

The Division of Agriculture details the proper modes in which Israelites are to plant, harvest, process and eat the crops that they grow for sustenance upon the land of Israel. For Mishnah these matters concern, first, how Israelites are to fulfill their responsibility to pay from the produce certain agricultural tithes. These taxes support the poor of the community of Israel and contribute to the maintenance of the priests and Levites who serve in the Temple in Jerusalem. Within the Division of Agriculture, this requirement to separate tithes leads to a wide range of topical concerns. In addition to describing each of the major tithes and providing rules for their separation,[1] Mishnah's authorities discuss how the holy tithes are to be prepared for consumption and provide details of how Israelites are to make certain that they do not eat produce from which these tithes have not been separated at all.[2]

The Division of Agriculture does not, however, concern simply the payment of agricultural tithes. Within the Israelite understanding of the world certain other limitations, known from Scripture and described in detail in the Division of Agriculture, restrict the Israelites' use of the land. Israelites, that is to say, must plant and harvest their fields according to specified norms. These norms hold that crops must be arranged in the field in ways that prevent certain species from growing together. Other rules preclude the consumption of fruit from a tree's first three bearing years. Mishnah even regulates the year to year permissibility of carrying out agricultural activities alto-gether, restricting, for instance, the planting and harvesting of crops in the seventh year of the sabbatical cycle.[3] The division as a whole thus takes up the wide range of concerns that devolve upon both the production and consumption of food in the Israelite world.

The wide range of topics discussed here, taken directly from Scripture, must not prevent us from seeing the single point of the division as a whole. For seen as a unity, this division's diverse topical interests in fact reflect a single perspective that its authors bring to their work on this theme. For

13

Mishnah's rabbis, the agricultural laws outline how Israelites
are to maintain and use a land that ultimately is the special
possession of God. To do this, Israelites must correctly use the
land in all facets of the production of food. First, they must
plant, cultivate and harvest their crops in ways that accord with
the character of the land's divine ownership. Once the food of
the land is ready for consumption they must further pay
agricultural tithes. This payment releases the lien upon the
food held by God, who, by providing the land, earns a share in
the crop. Mishnah's rabbis thus do not understand the payment of
tithes simply to be a method of maintaining the Temple-cult or of
supporting the needy of their community. Nor do they understand
the other regulations that control use of the land to fulfill
only general agricultural, social or economic functions (e.g.,
the possible agricultural value of allowing the land to lie
fallow once every seven years). Mishnah's authorities, rather,
see in these regulations descriptions of how Israelites are to
use their land in accordance with the specific nature of God's
creation of the universe and in keeping with God's special
relationship with the people and land of Israel.[4]

While, on the surface, Mishnah speaks of the payment of farm
taxes and the implementation of idiosyncratic agricultural
taboos, we see that, within the larger frame of the division as a
whole, these regulations phrase an overarching understanding of
the character of the world and of the place of the Israelite
nation within that universe. As Mishnah's authorities know from
Scripture, because, in creating the world, God rested on the
seventh day, so the land of Israel, the possession of God, must
be allowed to rest each seventh year.[5] Since, when creating the
world, God carefully distinguished each and every discrete
species of plant, so in planting their fields, Israelites must be
careful not to plant together different species, which would
eradicate the distinction established by God.[6] And because crops
that grow upon the land of Israel partake of the bounty of God's
land, they are bonded to God and may not be eaten until God's
interest in them has been satisfied, through payment of
heave-offering and tithes.[7]

In all, the Division of Agriculture describes what
Israelites must know not simply to grow produce and run their
economy, but, more important, to carry out their production and
consumption of food under the terms of sanctity, originally

described in Scripture, in which God created the world. The laws given here thus comprise one central aspect of the larger rabbinic agendum for the Israelite nation in the first centuries. These laws show in concrete terms how Israelites are to live their lives in holiness and describe how they may forge a world that conforms to the state of perfection in which God originally created the universe.

II.   Rabbinic and Greco-Roman Writing on Agriculture

To begin to make sense of the concerns of the division before us, we must locate the larger contexts within which the rabbinic interest in agriculture is rooted. While the Scriptural foundations for the agricultural law will be explored in detail in the following section of this introduction, it is important to begin with the evidence contemporary with Mishnah's own authors. For we shall find that, indeed, the rabbinic interest in agriculture is in keeping with larger trends in the Greco-Roman world in which the Mishnaic rabbis lived. Beginning as early as the time of Hesiod, plant and animal husbandry was a topic of great concern for ancient writers, who dealt at length with the use of the land in the production of food. Important representatives of this genre are the Greek and Latin writings of Theophrastus (4th century B.C.E.), Cato (2nd century B.C.E.), Varro (1st century C.E.) and Pliny (1st century C.E.). Indicative of the importance of this topic in the Greco-Roman world is the list, at Varro I.1.7-9, of fifty Greek and Latin authors on agriculture known to Varro. Columella (I.1.7) likewise is familiar with many writings on this topic.[8]

Before we move ahead to examine the comparison between the Mishnaic and the Greek and Latin writings, we must be clear that these Greco-Roman works provide the only other systematic writings of Mishnah's own period with which we can compare the rabbinic Division of Agriculture. The contemporary Judaic literatures, by contrast, show little interest in this topic. The Dead Sea community engaged in communal meals (see Schiffman, Sectarian Law, pp. 191-201), and all of its food was prepared in accordance with strictly regulated procedures. Yet the available texts do not concern themselves with the specifics of how this food was to be grown and prepared for consumption. Observance of agricultural laws as a matter of piety actually was made light of within the early Christian community, as is clear from the degradation of Pharisees as indivduals who "tithe dill and cummin but have neglected the weightier matters of the law, justice, mercy and faith."[9] The early Christians thus produced no sustained writing on agriculture or on the meaning of Scripture's agricultural rules (or, indeed, on any other Pentateuchal commandments). Within the Judaic context of the first centuries, then, the rabbinic movement alone saw in Scripture's agricultural law a topic for systematic analysis. This means, as I said, that for purposes of contemporary comparison, we must leave the Judaic context entirely.

Contrary to what we might expect, however, comparison with the Greek and Latin works on agriculture does not serve to point out the extent to which the Israelite community of the first centuries participated in the Hellenistic culture and scientific economy of its time. The comparison points out, rather, the extent to which the Israelite community of the first centuries maintained ideals developed in its Scriptural heritage, but failed to concentrate upon contemporary developments in either technological or literary concerns. For in the Greek world, by the time of Aristole and Theophrastus, agriculture had been seen primarily as a matter of science, a technical subject to be approached through observation and to be written about 1) in terms of profit and loss, just as were other business concerns, or, 2) from a scientific perspective, as in the case of Theophrastus' botanical writings. In Xenophon's Oeconomicus, written some 600 years before Mishnah, we already find a guidebook for household and farm management.[10] Among scientific works, Theophrastus' Historia Plantarum and De Causis Plantarum initiated the work of systematic botany. In the middle of the second century B.C.E. Cato transferred the subject of agriculture into the Latin speaking world, writing practical guides for farming and the organization and management of estates producing wine and olive oil (White, p. 19). The first book of Varro's De Re Rustica covers the topics of 1) terrain and soil, 2) staff and equipment, 3) techniques of cultivation and 4) the yearly agricultural calender, such that "all the processes of cultivation from sowing-time to harvest are clearly described" (White, p. 23). The most systematic and complete work on agriculture is that of Columella, completed in the first century, that is, close to the period in which Mishnah's authorities worked. He covers all aspects of scientific plant and animal husbandry and the economic management of an estate. In the time of Mishnah's framers, Pliny produced his vast encyclopedia. In Books Seventeen and Eighteen he speaks in detail about arboriculture and agriculture. Books Twelve through Sixteen as well deal with trees (White, pp. 28-29).

While this list of authors and their contributions could be greatly extended, it should already be sufficient to indicate the preoccupation of Roman literary culture with the topic of agriculture and to characterize the topics about which the Greco-Roman authors wrote. This survey makes clear the very different attitudes that the rabbinic and Greco-Roman authors had concerning the topic of agriculture. When the Greco-Roman writers spoke of farming, their concerns revolved around the contemporary sciences of plant-husbandry, botanical classification and land management. This is not to argue that, in the Greco-Roman world at large, the planting and harvesting of crops was not a matter of important religious concern. To the contrary, we know from certain sources about the agricultural celebrations and the rituals that pertained to the production of food. Obviously, agricultural deities were of preeminent importance in Greco-Roman religion. The point, however, is that, whatever importance these activities had in the lives of common people, they were taken for granted as aspects of everyday life. They were a separate subject, referred to in inscriptions and transmitted from generation to generation, but were not deemed worthy of sustained intellectual attention.[11]   Greco-Roman writers did not for the most part trouble themselves with what they regarded as the superstitions that surrounded the common folk's agricultural habits. They concerned themselves rather with the science and economics of food production and processing.

By contrast to the Greco-Roman authors, when Mishnah's rabbis think about agriculture, they consider solely matters of non-empirical significance. Their discussion of what should or should not be done in the planting, harvesting and processing of crops is not determined by economic and agricultural reality. It reflects rather the Israelites' perception of the existence of a deity who owns the land and who enhances or withdraws its fruitfulness depending upon the people's fulfillment of his particular desires. Surely Israelite farmers in the first centuries learned and used contemporary methods of plant-husbandry, adopted the tools used by the Greeks around them and through plant-science attempted to improve the production of their fields.[12] From the perspective of Mishnah's own authors, however, these are not the matters of importance in the successful production of food. What counts according to Mishnah's rabbis is the Israelites' observance of the divine laws that assure the presence of God's blessing upon the produce of the land of Israel.

While the rabbinic and Greco-Roman authors present two very different approaches to the topic of agriculture, we must be clear that they share a single goal, the improved productivity of the land and the enhanced quality of the crops. Just as Greek and Latin authors presented their scientific studies so as to allow improved food production, so the rabbis of Mishnah understood observance of the laws they presented as the means of assuring the safety of the people of Israel within its land, of promoting the fruitfulness of the ground and of assuring the quality of the crops produced. This attitude is stated explicitly by Simeon b. Eleazar, of the final generation of Mishnaic masters. Mishnah Sotah 9:13 and Tosefta Maaser Sheni 5:30 read:

> R. Simeon b. Eleazar says, "[Failure to keep the produce in a state of cultic] cleanness removed the flavor and aroma [from the food] and [failure to separate] tithes removed the plumpness and abundance."

The same extended passage in Tosefta Maaser Sheni draws out Mishnah's understanding of the relationship between the separation of tithes and the prosperity that, in the Hebrew Bible, God promises the Israelite nation. Dt. 6:11-12 refers to "houses full of good things, which you [Israelites] did not [yourselves] fill, and cisterns hewn out, which you did not hew, and vineyards and olive trees, which you did not plant." Scripture concludes that "when you [Israelites] eat and are full, then take heed lest you forget the Lord, who brought you out of Egypt." Tosefta Maaser Sheni 5:28 makes explicit its understanding that, through the separation of tithes, Israelites thank God for this prosperity and assure that God's goodness will continue to be available. Thus the passage states that "all agriculture offerings are [given] in response to [the number of God's] gifts [to the Israelite nation]."

The comparison between the Greco-Roman and rabbinic writers thus shows two different paths to a single desired result. This comparison further makes clear the unique character, in Mishnah's own day, of the rabbinic handling of the topic of agriculture. Surely, in light of the character of Mishnah and the rabbinic movement as a whole, we cannot be surprised that Mishnah's authorities focus upon Scriptural ideas and that they fail to speak of matters of science. Still, what we have seen here does have important implications for our larger understanding of the early rabbinic movement and its relationship to the Hellenistic philosophical and cultural world in which it grew.[13] This importance is in tempering the claims that have been made concerning the similarity between the earliest rabbis and the contemporary Greek thinkers. As Morton Smith, among others, has argued, the rabbinic movement exhibited numerous traits familiar from Hellenistic culture. Speaking specifically of the Pharisees, Smith states:

> Not only was the theory of the Pharisaic school that of a school of Greek philosophers, but so were its practices. Its teachers taught without pay, like philosophers; they attached to themselves particular disciples who followed them around and served them, like philosophers; they looked to gifts for support, like philosophers; they were exempt from taxation, like philosophers; they were distinguished in the street by their walk, speech, and peculiar clothing, like philosophers; and finally--what is after all the meat of the matter--they discussed the questions philosophers discussed and reached the conclusions philosophers reached (Smith, p. 81).

Smith's conclusion, based upon later sources' description of the appearance of the rabbis and on parallels pointed out by many scholars between rabbinic exegetical terminology and methods, points to one certain aspect of the formation of the rabbinic movement in the first centuries. As Smith suggests, Hellenistic philosophy certainly contributed to the overall social style of the rabbinic estate and influenced certain of the methods they used and even questions they probed. Yet, when we examine closely the actual concerns of the Greco-Roman and rabbinic writings on a single topic, we see the essential discontinuity between the rabbis and other contemporary intellectuals. The content and focus of rabbinic thought and the interests of Greco-Roman authors writing on the topic at hand simply do not correspond. The Division of Agriculture as a statement of rabbinic theology thus has as its primary context not the contemporary Hellenistic world in which the rabbis lived, but, as we shall see in a moment, in the world of Scripture that these rabbis inherited from Israelite antiquity.[14]

The rabbinic departure from the concerns of their own time will have important implications in the conclusion of this chapter, when we examine the meaning of the Division of Agriculture within the context of the first centuries. That analysis, however, depends upon our first locating the real foundation of the division before us. We therefore must turn away from the Hellenistic writers who so far have taken our attention. We look now instead at the Hebrew Scriptures, which, in the Division of Agriculture, the rabbinic authorities rework and develop. For the facts and interests of Scripture provide the primary foundation for all that Mishnah's authors do with the topic of agriculture.

III. Mishnah and Scripture

When we come to the world of Scripture, we enter the world of discourse that Mishnah's own framers wish us to see as theirs. For the authorities of Mishnah's Division of Agriculture approach their chosen topic from the perspective of the Hebrew Bible which, as we shall see, provides all of the basic facts that the text before us uses and interprets. The rabbis want to know exactly what Scripture requires of Israelites who grow food upon the land of Israel. Therefore they explore in depth the meaning of each of the Hebrew Bible's agricultural laws.

Yet we would err were we to claim that Mishnah's division is primarily an interpretation of Scripture's relevant materials. For the rabbis' work in Mishnah is quite unlike that which we normally refer to by the term exegesis. Rather, while the Mishnaic rabbis take up concerns known only from the Hebrew Bible, the result of their analysis of those topics is to create a code of law quite unexpected within the frame of Biblical thinking about agriculture. This is evident at even the most superficial level of examination of the materials before us. For while Scripture states its agricultural laws episodically, in a smattering of rules scattered through the Pentateuch,[15] Mishnah's framers provide a methodical approach to the agricultural law as a whole. Each of Scripture's topics, that is to say, is fully explored so as to facilitate the implementation of Scripture's tersely stated rules. Mishnah and not Scripture thus sees in the agricultural life of the people of Israel a concern worthy of protracted and exacting attention.[16] This is particularly clear when we recall, as I mentioned above, that no other Jewish work of Mishnah's own period sees in the agricultural law a topic worthy of sustained interest.

Mishnah's Division of Agriculture is further distinguished from its Scriptural antecedents by the set of issues and legal theories that Mishnah's rabbis bring to their deliberations. The rabbis' larger themes, on the one hand, are not surprising. They concern the conditions under which produce must be grown, harvested, prepared and eaten so as to assure its meeting the conditions of holiness understood to have been set down by God. These themes derive directly from the Scriptural legislation that delineates proper use of the land of Israel and that describes the agricultural offerings that Israelites must separate. Yet, on the other hand, in treating these themes Mishnah's authorities both ask specific questions unforseen by Scripture and suggest a larger, encompassing approach to the agricultural law that exceeds the original interest of the writers of Scripture.

What sets Mishnah apart from Scripture is the former's insistence, to be documented in a moment, that the system of agricultural laws provides a means through which Israelites are to control and properly dispose of the holiness that results when Israelites grow food upon the land understood to be the possession of God. Unlike Scripture, that is to say, Mishnah does not view the separation of tithes--a topic which takes up the majority of both Scripture's and Mishnah's discussions about agriculture--as primarily a system of taxation that supports the poor and the Temple authorities and that, to some small extent, engenders the performance on the part of the Israelite of certain, annual, Temple-centered activities, e.g., the eating of second tithe and the ritual that accompanies the presentation of the first fruits.[17] Rather, Mishnah views these laws to have a central importance on a day to day basis within the home and community life of individual Israelites. This is because, for Mishnah, by observing the agricultural regulations, Israelites maintain the order and sanctity of the world established by God at the time of creation. First and foremost, Mishnah understands God to play a central role in the Israelites' production of food. God therefore has a lien upon the ripened produce of the land. This lien upon the crops he helps grow must be paid before Israelites can take the food for their own use. This is accomplished when they set aside from the produce the required agricultural offerings. The separation of heave-offering and tithes thus is viewed by Mishnah not as a way of supporting the cult, but as a way of returning to God what by right is his and what therefore is, by definition, holy.

While Scripture refers to certain agricultural offerings as holy things,[18] it does not focus upon the fact that what the Israelites separate for the priest, for instance, is consecrated. Nor does it dwell upon the implication that Israelites' ability to designate produce to be holy means that the Israelite has responsibilities similar to those of a priest, who, in his ministrations at the altar, works with and controls the holy. In line with the focus of Scripture as a whole, rather, the center of the Biblical agricultural laws is the priest and the Temple, the final recipients of the produce set aside by Israelite householders. Mishnah, however, all but ignores the rules for giving tithes to the priests. In focusing upon individual Israelites instead, Mishnah's rabbis designate their fields and hearths to be central loci of sanctification within the Israelite world.

The way in which Mishnah's authorities build upon the Biblical agricultural laws is apparent in both the Yavnean and Ushan strata of the Division of Agriculture. While the Yavnean materials are undeveloped in terms of a specific legal ideology, they do treat all of the topics that concern the Israelites' production and preparation of food. The divergence of Mishnah from Scripture becomes even clearer, however, as we recognize the point, particular to Mishnah, that emerges from the division as a whole. This point is represented in the insistence of Mishnah's final generation of authorities that compliance with God's law depends not so much upon the physical actions of Israelites as upon the intentions and perceptions with which they perform those actions. Particular to Mishnah thus is the notion that, rather than being confined to a preordained set of laws and definitions, in farming the land and eating its produce, Israelites themselves determine what accords or does not accord with God's will. While the set of facts taken up in this division derives from Scripture, Mishnah's real concern thus is familiar from the rest of Mishnah, which likewise sets out to define how Israelites' intentions and perceptions contribute to the nation's living a life of holiness.[19]

In order to illustrate both the systematic character of Mishnah's treatment of the law of agriculture and to show how the division as a whole makes the point to which I have referred about intention and perception, I survey the topics and main points of each of the pertinent tractates in this division. I list the tractates according to the role their topic plays in the unfolding of the systematic agendum of the division as a whole. This topical arrangement shows the division to be organized in five major headings, covering the continuum of cultic activities necessary when seed is planted, harvested, cooked and eaten. These topics cover 1) the production of crops, 2) the conditions under which those crops become subject to the separation of agricultural offerings, 3) the processes through which those offerings are physically set aside, 4) how the offerings are to be maintained once they have been separated and 5) how common food and agricultural offerings properly are to be eaten.[20]

A.   Producing Crops under Conditions of Holiness

1.   Shebiit

The tractate legislates for the observance of the Sabbatical year (Lev. 25:1-7), during which Israelites must refrain from all agricultural labors normally carried out in the other six years of the Sabbatical cycle. The foundation of the Scriptural idea of the Sabbatical year is the notion that the land of Israel is a special possession of God, given to the people of Israel as a sign of the unique relationship between this people and their Lord.[21] As the special possession of God, the land must be treated in ways commensurate with God's own holiness. One central characteristic of God is that, in creating the world, he ceased working on the seventh day. In keeping with this characteristic of God, the holy land that is God's possession likewise must be made to rest each seventh year.[22] Mishnah's special contribution to this topic is found in its Ushan stratum, which rejects Scripture's notion that all field labor indeed is forbidden in the Sabbatical year. Ushans claim instead that the permissibility of field labor during the Sabbatical year depends not upon the concrete nature of that labor but upon the intentions of the Israelite who carries it out and the perceptions of those who see his activities in the fields. Only what is intended by and appears to Israelites to violate the seventh year is forbidden, regardless of the concrete effects of the particular labor (Newman, pp. 17-19).

2. Kilaim

In planting the fields of the land of Israel, Israelites must maintain the distinctions, established by God at the time of the creation of the universe, between different types of produce. The Israelite thereby maintains the order and concomitant sanctity of the world, just as God created it. The special point of the tractate before us, again found in its latest stratum, is that what is orderly, and therefore permitted, or disorderly, and so forbidden, depends primarily upon the perceptions of common Israelites. Their ability to look at a field and determine whether or not the different crops growing in it comprise an illicit confusion determines the status of those crops (Mandelbaum, pp. 2-4).

B.   Conditions Under which Produce Becomes Subject to Sanctification

1. Maaserot

Scripture is clear that in order to support the priestly and Levitical castes, Israelites must separate from produce grown on the land of Israel certain agricultural gifts. Mishnah develops this notion to hold that this separation constitutes the Israelite's designation of the produce to be holy. The question of Tractate Maaserot, unforeseen by Scripture, concerns the conditions under which produce becomes subject to such sanctification. Only after those conditions are met may an Israelite validly separate an offering from the produce. The tractate's point, developed in its almost exclusively Ushan materials, is that produce becomes subject to sanctification as an offering when Israelites 1) desire it for food and 2) take concrete actions that show their intention to use the food in a meal at their own tables. The tractate thus holds that God cannot claim his share of produce whenever he wants. God's right to a portion of the crop of the land of Israel, rather, is a reflex of Israelites' own desire to use the food of the land (Jaffee, p. 4-5).

2. Hallah

The tractate describes the conditions under which produce becomes subject to dough offering, described at Num. 15:17-21. Comparable to the issue of Tractate Maaserot, the tractate questions the circumstances under which the Israelite's preparation of grain renders the food produced subject to sanctification as dough offering. Suggesting a concept unforeseen by Scripture, it assumes that not all dough is subject to this agricultural gift. Liability, rather, depends upon the specific ingredients used as well as method by which the dough is prepared. By talking about the role of human processing in rendering food subject to tithe, Tractate Hallah complements Tractate Maaserot, which refers to the significance of human desire to use the food still ripening in the field. Unlike the other tractates of this division, however, Hallah contains predominantly Yavnean materials. It therefore does not bring into play the role of human perception in determining whether or not, in a case of doubt, a mixture is subject to dough offering. It holds instead that this depends upon definitions, applied in all cases, of what is bread and what is subsumed under some different category of food.

C.   The Designation of Produce to be an Agricultural Offering
1.   Terumot 1:1-4:6
     This section of Tractate Terumot takes up the metaphysical requirements of the valid designation of agricultural offerings. Its point, unknown in Scripture, is that the Israelite who separates heave-offering must 1) have the consciousness of being involved in a sacred activity and must 2) formulate the intention to separate--and thereby consecrate--a quantity of produce for the priest (Avery-Peck pp. 2-16). What a householder separates but does not intend to consecrate as heave-offering remains unconsecrated and does not serve as the heave-offering required of the individual's produce. In addition to this topic, the tractate's first section discusses the conditions under which produce may be separated from one batch as heave-offering on behalf of a different batch. These materials make the point that even an improperly performed separation of heave-offering is valid if the individual who carried it out did so with the requisite intention.

2.   Peah
     Tractate Peah provides a substantive correlate to Tractate Terumot, asking how produce is set aside as tithes for the poor. Poor offerings differ from heave-offering and other tithes insofar as their designation is not completed by the householder alone. The farmer's produce becomes subject to poor gifts

according to the schema laid out in Tractate Maaserot. However the actual designation of these gifts is not complete until the poor themselves acquire the produce. The central task of this tractate thus is to indicate the conditions under which produce is held to have been transferred as an agricultural gift from the possession of the Israelite farmer to the poor. Tractate Peah deals as well with a wide range of issues concerning the separation and distribution of poor offerings (Brooks, pp. 3-5).

3. Bikkurim

The tractate describes the ritual through which the farmer designates, separates and carries to Jerusalem first fruits, described at Dt. 26:1-11, Lev. 23:9-21 and Num. 28:26. Through discussion of the ritual requirements of the separation of an agricultural offering, it complements Mishnah Terumot's description of the metaphysical requirements of that separation. The tractate's most interesting chapters present a systematic comparison of the restrictions that apply to the several agricultural offerings known to Mishnah. Since this material assumes the completed discussions of all of the offerings, it obviously derives from the end of the development of the division as a whole.

D. The Care and Handling of Holy Produce
1. Terumot 4:7-10:12

The body of Tractate Terumot examines situations, for the most part unforeseen by Scripture, in which an Israelite uses consecrated heave-offering in a manner unbefitting its holy status. The offering, for instance, may be mixed with unconsecrated food, planted as seed, cooked with secular food or actually eaten by the non-priest. The point of these materials is that the adjudication of such situations depends ultimately upon the perceptions and intentions of the Israelite who allows the priestly gift wrongly to be used. A non-priest who intentionally violates the holy produce is culpable for sacrilege and can do nothing to replace the offering or placate God, e.g., through payment of a fine to the priest. If the misuse of the heave-offering is unintentional, by contrast, the Israelite simply replaces that which he accidentally has taken and pays a fine to atone for his unintended use of holy food. But he is not deemed by virtue of his unintended action irrevocably to have violated the sanctity of the priestly gift. While the basic notion of a distinction between intentional and unintentional consumption of holy produce is known to Scripture, Mishnah extends this idea to indicate clearly its belief that in all cases, through their own intentions and actions, common Israelites determine what is and what is not holy.

2. Maaser Sheni

Second tithe, derived from the unnamed offering described at Dt. 14:22-26, is separated by the farmer and brought to Jerusalem, where that individual and his family eat it "before the Lord." What prompts Mishnah's interest in this offering is the fact that the individual may sell it and bring to Jerusalem the money he receives, to be used to buy produce eaten in place of original tithe. This offering thus provides the context for a discussion of the effects of the economic world (e.g., increasing and decreasing market prices) upon holy food. While Scripture provides the law that allows for the redemption of the tithe, Mishnah's interest in and rules for the proper handling of holy produce within the secular marketplace are entirely its own.

E. Eating Food Under Conditions of Holiness
1. Demai

The tractate contributes to the Division of Agriculture the notion that Israelites must tithe any produce that leaves their possession. In this way they avoid becoming accomplices in the actions of individuals who would transgress by eating food without tithing at all. The problem is that, while certain Israelites take it upon themselves scrupulously to tithe all produce, others separate only the consecrated heave-offering. The central issue here thus is how those who wish to be certain that they do not eat untithed food are to cope in a world filled with people who are not trusted to tithe what they eat or sell. In such a society, those who do wish to tithe must assure that all they receive and eat is in fact tithed. They also must take steps to prevent themselves from contributing to the trans- gression of someone else who might eat untithed foods. Work on this tractate begins late in the development of the Division of Agriculture, for its basic notion, that individuals must tithe all food that leaves their possession, derives from the Ushan stratum. This idea, as well as the notion of a specific group of

Israelites who alone are scrupulous about tithing, is unknown to Scripture (see Sarason, Demai, pp. 1-2, 9-18).

2. Orlah

Israelites may not consume the fruit of a tree in its first three bearing years (Lev. 19:23). In order to facilitate observance of this requirement, Tractate Orlah clarifies what are classified as fruit trees, defines what produce of these trees comprises their fruit and indicates whether or not an old tree that is uprooted and replanted is deemed a new growth and therefore subject to this restriction. As in other tractates in this division, the latest stratum of these laws presents the distinctive notion that whether or not the tree's fruit is subject to the restrictions of orlah depends primarily upon whether or not the Israelite understands the tree to be a new growth and believes the fruit in question to be its primary crop.

3.   Terumot 11:1-10

The final section of Tractate Terumot completes this division's deliberations on the consumption of produce by detailing proper modes of preparing, consuming and disposing of consecrated foods.[23] The point parallels that made in other sections of this tractate. Heave-offering must be prepared in a manner that assures that none of the consecrated food will go to waste.   The status of consecration of allowable waste is determined according to the attitude of the priest and Israelite. Whatever is deemed still to be worthy as food retains a consecrated status and may be eaten only by priests. Once food no longer is in a condition in which it normally would be eaten, or if the Israelite's actions indicate that he no longer is concerned with it, by contrast, it loses its status of sanctification and may be used by the non-priest. These materials thus present the logical correlate to the materials in Section C, which hold that produce takes on the status of sanctification in the first place when Israelites deem it worthy of that status and intentionally designate it as holy.

The preceding summary makes clear two important facts about the Division of Agriculture. The first is that the division comprises a sustained essay. It discusses each of the pertinent aspects of its larger theme and, within these subtopics, it presses home a single, identifiable point. In illuminating Scripture's several, diverse rules concerning how Israelites are to treat the holy land and its crops, Mishnah's authorities analyze the proper modes of planting, harvesting, preparing and consuming food. These topical sections describe in full each aspect of the agricultural life of the Israelite nation and show how, within each area of law, Israelites' own perspectives contribute to a determination of what is permitted and forbidden.

The second fact is that, in interpreting Scripture's rules on these topics, Mishnah's own framers have made choices unexpected on the basis of Scripture and therefore clearly indicative of their own beliefs and attitudes. In particular, the Mishnaic rabbis use Scripture's agriculture law as a context in which to talk about the role of individual Israelites in the sanctification of their world. This larger interest in sanctification is seen, on the one hand, in the concentration of Mishnah's authorities upon those aspects of farming and the production of food that entail the handling of holiness, either in the separation of consecrated offerings or in the proper use of the land so as not to violate the holy character in which God created the universe in the first place.

The perspective of Mishnah as a redacted document is clear, on the other hand, from the particular attitude that Mishnah's final generation of framers brings to the law. For each of the topical units just described I have documented the insistence of Ushan authorities that the common Israelite does not confront an already shaped universe. According to this view, rather, through their own actions and intentions, individual Israelites impose order upon the world, themselves determining that it conforms to the holy image originally designed by God and described in Scripture's revelation. A central point of this division thus is that through their actions in preparing food for consumption, Israelites themselves assure that God's sanctity properly is maintained and disposed in the world. By giving common Israelites this responsibility, Mishnah attributes to them the powers over the holy normally assigned only to priests, who minister in the cult. One central accomplishment of the rabbis who created the Division of Agriculture thus is the articulation of a clear program by which the people of Israel are, in concrete ways, made a kingdom of priests. Mishnah assigns to Israelites the power to lend ultimate meaning to the otherwise commonplace

activities of farming the earth, reaping its crop, and preparing
food for human consumption.

IV. The Division of Agriculture in Context
        The first sections of this introduction characterized the
Division of Agriculture as a creation of the first centuries.
One fact we have uncovered is negative, the result of the
comparison of the rabbinic materials with the Greco-Roman
writings on agriculture. For in selecting the topics of this
division, rabbinic authorities ignored those questions and
problems that, in their same day, attracted other writers on
their topic. This fact, pointing to this division's inattention
to historical context, is of course consonant with the character
of the Mishnah as a whole. While living during the period of the
destruction of the Temple in Jerusalem and the failed Bar Kokhba
revolt, the authorities before us do not focus upon those events
and indeed, hardly ever mention them. Nor do they suggest
explicitly how the changed situation of the Jewish people in the
land of Israel might affect the meaning or implementation of the
laws first stated in Scripture. This is particularly striking
for the division before us, in so far as its laws are so closely
bound with the Israelite understanding of God's role as guardian
over the people and land of Israel.
        The first fact with which we deal thus is the inattention of
the Division of Agriculture's authorities to historical setting.
This is seen in the division's relationship to other contemporary
writings on farming and in its general characteristic, with
Mishnah as a whole, of not speaking of those central events that
shaped the world of its framers.
        The second result of the analyses carried out thus far is to
make clear the overall concerns and intellectual goals of
Mishnah's rabbis. The issue of this division is sanctification
and, in particular, the role of the individual Israelite in
maintaining the proper order of the universe God created. In the
view of this division, the Israelite assures the proper
functioning of the world by 1) planting and cultivating crops in
manners commensurate with the way in which God created the world
in the first place, and 2) by paying from the ripened crop the
share owed to God from all produce grown under divine supervision
from a land whose ultimate owner is God.
        These two facts, Mishnah's inattention to history, on the
one hand, and its concern for sanctification, on the other, point

us towards the significance that the rules before us had for those who, in the first centuries, worked on the agricultural law. The actual history that these individuals endured did not conform to that which was promised the people of Israel in their holy Scripture. As a result, in the material before us, Mishnah's framers, on the one hand, turn away from history, ignoring the larger events that shaped their own day.

At the same time, the focus that Mishnah's authors do choose serves to counter the meaning that Israelites in the first centuries might have been expected to derive from the events of their day. The powerlessness of the Israelite nation in the face of the Roman empire is balanced by the claim of the division before us that the Israelite people in fact has powers much greater than those exercised on the stage of political history. These powers assure that the world will continue along those paths established by God at the time of creation. In this way the Israelite nation is made responsible for the eventual perfection of the world and its return to the perfect state of holiness in which it was created. The people of Israel, however subjugated in earthly terms, actually hold the key to all that is powerfull and important in the universe. This power is exercised when Israelites who plant, cultivate and consume the produce of the land of Israel conform to the divine will that stands behind the creation and maintenance of the world.

V. Conclusion

The analyses contained in the first three sections of this chapter represent an initial characterization of the contents and meaning of the Division of Agriculture. This characterization allows us to see the perspective of those rabbis who initiated the analysis of Scripture and who brought Mishnah as a whole into the form in which it stands before us today. While these authorities built upon the foundations laid by Scripture, both the mode of presentation and the ideas found in the Division of Agriculture are their own. To plumb the true meaning of this division, we therefore must examine in detail the system of law before us, taking seriously its origins in rabbinic, and not Biblical, religion. We already have seen in general terms both the character of the division's content and the nature of the development in legal thinking that occurred between the periods of Yavneh and Usha. Our task now is to provide an exacting account of the content and concerns of the division as a whole, beginning with its origins in the period before 70 and continuing through the period of its final formulation. Only with such an account in hand can we claim correctly to evaluate the meaning of this division's rules within the confines of each historical period and then in the larger perspective of the Division of Agriculture as a whole.

The method to be followed at this point already has been described in detail in the Introduction. The point, we recall, is two-fold:

1) By isolating and examining in detail the thematic units of each of the tractates in this division, we come to see clearly the content and focus as well as the specific ideas of the Division of Agriculture as a systematic whole.

2) By organizing the attributed statements of each thematic unit according to the generation of Mishnaic authorities to whom they are assigned, and by testing the authenticity of these attributions, we develop a historical picture of the growth of the law of agriculture. This allows us to identify the particular assumptions, interests and contributions of each generation of authorities.

Addressing these two concerns allows us to depict the development of rabbinic thought in the first centuries. This means, first and foremost, detailing the intellectual growth of the nascent rabbinic movement. It means as well plotting the growth of rabbinic Judaism in light of the political history of the centuries during which the rabbis formulated this law. We judge, that is to say, the specific attitudes and issues relevant in each period of the law's formation on the basis of the larger political and social context in which that generation's rabbis worked.

Analysis of the historical unfolding of the law in each of the tractates of the Division of Agriculture thus serves two purposes. The chronology of Mishnah's law, first, provides a key to the cognitive world of the rabbinic authorities who lived before 70 and later, in the periods of Yavneh and Usha. Second, this information leads to an examination of the perspectives of Mishnah's authorities against the larger historical environment in which they carried out their work. In doing this, this study takes seriously the fact that the parameters of the meaning of the work of each of Mishnah's generations of authorities must be sought in the historical moment in which those rabbis conceived the ideas that their laws express.

PART II

THE DEVELOPMENT OF THE TRACTATES

CHAPTER TWO

PEAH

I. Introduction

Scripture knows six offerings of produce that Israelite
farmers must leave behind for collection by sojourners, orphans
and widows, that is, the needy among the people of Israel. The
tractate before us is organized so as to treat each of these
charity offerings in turn. The corner of the field that is left
unharvested for the poor (Lev. 19:9, 23:22) is discussed in the
tractate's first two units (M. Pe. 1:1-4:9). Gleanings, Lev.
19:9, 23:22, take up unit iii (M. Pe. 4:10-5:6). The forgotten
sheaf (Dt. 24:19) comes next (M. Pe. 5:7-7:2). The laws for the
defective cluster (Dt. 24:21) and grape gleanings (Lev. 19:10)
appear in unit v (M. Pe. 7:3-8). Finally, poorman's tithe (Dt.
14:18-19) is the topic of unit vi (M. Pe. 8:1-9).

The tractate's practical and unembellished organization,
designed to expound in turn each of the unconsecrated offerings
that Scripture assigns to the poor, must not be allowed to mask
the presence of a deeper problematic that underlies the
legislation found here. The generative question of the tractate
concerns how a certain portion of produce grown upon the land of
Israel comes to have the status of an agricultural offering, such
that it may be collected and eaten only by certain individuals,
under specifically prescribed conditions. In asking this
question, Mishnah's authors see a close parallel between these
poor gifts and other, consecrated, agricultural offerings.
Indeed, as we shall see, the laws for the separation of poor
tithes parallel closely the rules that pertain to heave-offering
and second tithe.

The point of the tractate is that produce is subject to poor
gifts--like all other agricultural offerings--only at the point
at which the farmer wishes to make personal use of it. His own
interest in the ripening crop awakens God's interest in the food
and, with it, the obligation to tithe. This fact is stressed in
the tractate's notion that even such produce as is known early in
its growth to be destined for the poor--e.g., defective
clusters--remains the property of the householder until the

35

harvest begins. Until the farmer shows that he wants the produce, the poor have no right to it. In light of its central concern in the process through which produce is designated for the poor, Tractate Peah barely touches upon the social and economic problems associated with the administration of a poor tax. For instance, the question of which poor may collect these offerings and how much they should collect, let alone that of how we assure that these gifts are paid at all, never are satisfactorily answered (see unit vi). Rather, the poor are important in this tractate only in light of the special role that they play in the designation as a poor gift of the produce left by the Israelite farmer. What makes these agricultural gifts particularly interesting to Mishnah's framers[1] is that their achieving the status of an offering depends upon two individuals. I already have explained the role of the farmer, whose own actions in harvesting the produce set into play the requirement to pay the shares of the crop outlined in Scripture. Unlike in the case of other offerings, however, here the tithe's recipient--the poor person--also has a central role. The obligation of the farmer is fulfilled when, during the harvest, he either intentionally or unintentionally leaves certain produce behind in the field. Now the desires and actions of the poor come into play. Only by completing the harvest and thereby showing their own desire for the food of the land do they validly acquire that produce as a poor offering. In this way, Tractate Peah indicates the deep significance for the Division of Agriculture of Israelites' human desires for food, which Mishnah consistently understands to be represented in their actions in harvesting crops. Food becomes subject to poor gifts only after the harvest begins. It actually takes on the status of a poor offering only when the poor, by showing their own hunger for the food, invoke God's requirement that the needy be fed.[2]

This aspect of the meaning of the tractate comes into clear focus when we turn to the actual unfolding of the law of Tractate Peah in the period before 70 and at Yavneh and Usha. In order to make intelligible the specific laws of the tractate, however, we need first to review the Scriptural passages upon which these rules depend.

> (Lev. 19:9-10) When you reap the harvest of your land, you shall not reap your field to its very border, neither shall you gather the gleanings after your harvest. And you shall not strip your vineyards bare (l' t^cwll), neither

shall you gather the fallen grapes of your vineyard (prt);
you shall leave them for the poor and for the sojourner: I
am the Lord your God.

(Lev. 23:22) And when you reap the harvest of your
land, you shall not reap your field to its very border,   nor
shall you gather the gleanings after your harvest: I am the
Lord your God.

(Dt. 24:19-22) When you reap your harvest in your
field, and have forgotten a sheaf in the field, you shall
not go back to get it; it shall be for the sojourner,   the
fatherless, and the widow; that the Lord your God may bless
you in all the work of your hands.   When you beat olive
trees, you shall not go over the boughs again; it shall be
for the sojourner, the fatherless, and the widow.   When you
gather the grapes of your vineyard, you shall not glean (1'
t^cwll) it afterward; it shall be for the sojourner, the
fatherless, and the widow.   You shall remember that you once
were a slave in Egypt; therefore I command you to do this.

(Dt. 14:18-19) At the end of every three years you
shall bring forth all of the tithe of your produce in the
same year, and lay it up within your towns; and the Levite,
because he has no portion or inheiritance with you,   and the
sojourner, the fatherless, and the widow, who are within
your towns, shall come and eat and be filled; that the Lord
your God may bless you in all the work of your hands that
you do.

Both the Holiness Code and D prescribe amounts of produce to
be given to the poor. According to D this is in recognition of
the fact that all Israelites once were in need, as slaves in
Egypt (Dt. 24:22). Alternatively it assures that God will
continue to sustain the people as a whole, by causing the land to
be fertile (Dt. 14:19). Mishnah takes from these passages the
basic description of each of the poor gifts it treats. Peah (the
unharvested corner) and grape gleanings (prt) derive from Lev.
19:9-10. Other gleanings are based upon Lev. 23:22. The
forgotten sheaf is described at Dt. 24:19, poorman's tithe at Dt.
14:18-19. Mishnah derives its notion of the defective grape
cluster, which must be left for the poor, from the use, at Lev.
19:10 and Dt. 24:21, of the root ^cLL, normally, "to do a second
time," hence, "to glean." Authorities who stand behind the
Mishnah, by contrast, wish to differentiate the meaning of that
term from Lev. 19:9's "prt". By claiming that the root ^cLL
refers to defective clusters, they resolve the apparent
redundancy in the Biblical text.

With the Scriptural basis of the tractate clear, we turn now
to the unfolding of Mishnah's law in its major periods of
development.

A. Peah Before 70

Only one discussion can be verified to have taken place in the period before 70. It concerns Dt. 24:19's rule that a sheaf a farmer forgets in the field becomes the property of the poor. The Houses (iv.A.6:1D-6:3, 6:5) dispute the conditions under which this law applies. The Shammaites exempt from this restriction any sheaf that has distinctive features. The farmer might at a later moment recall such a sheaf to mind. This being the case, the Shammaites deem it never to have actually been forgotten. The Hillelites do not deem probative the fact that the farmer might later remember the sheaf. It presently is forgotten and therefore falls under the restriction of the forgotten sheaf. While the issue of how we judge what is "forgotten" is intrinsically interesting, it has no implications for later developments in this tractate's law.

B. Peah in the Time of Yavneh

Yavneans established the agendum of issues that concerns this tractate as a whole. These issues revolve around the crucial question of how produce comes to have the special status of an agricultural offering, in this case, a poor gift. In light of this basic issue, the ideas of this tractate's Yavnean stratum often parallel and depend upon notions found in the Yavnean strata of Tractates Terumot and Maaserot, which deal with this same problem. Yavneans thus are clear (iii.B.4:10) that the rights of the poor to their share begin only at the point at which the farmer desires to take produce for his own personal use. As in the case of heave-offering and tithes, the process through which produce becomes the property of the poor thus is set in motion by the farmer's claiming of food to be his own. Yavneans further note (i.B.1:6) that produce designated to be a poor offering, like produce that is either heave-offering or tithes, is exempt from the separation of other agricultural gifts.

Certain details of these notions, accepted in Ushan times as normative, come under dispute in the names of Yavnean figures. Defective grape clusters are the property of the poor (Dt. 24:21). Yavneans argue the rule for a field all of which is defective clusters. Against Aqiba, Eliezer takes the view that all of the produce of a field cannot take on the status of an agricultural offering, for this would preclude the formal act of designation through which the farmer 1) shows his desire for what is to become his own share and 2) distinguishes that share from the gift being made to the poor person, Levite or priest. While under dispute at Yavneh, Eliezer's view, that validly to set aside an agricultural offering the farmer must keep some produce for himself, is normative at Usha (i.C.1:3C-E, i.D.1:2). Yavneans also argue whether or not the farmer may give poor tithes to any poor person he desires, just as he presents heave-offering and tithes to the priest or Levite of his choice (ii.B.4:9A-C). Ushans resolve that he may not, basing this view upon their notion that these offerings take on their special status only when the poor take them for themselves.

Yavneans develop the Shammaite view that distinctive sheaves do not fall under the law of the forgotten sheaf (iv.B.6:6). They do this by giving specific examples of what constitutes a distinctive sheaf. This discussion is further developed at Usha. Another matter subject to continued attention in the Ushan period concerns what constitutes a field. This is an important issue because of the underlying assumption that peah must be designated in each individual field. Yavneans argue whether a field is defined on geographical terms, as an area distinguished by natural boundaries, or whether the farmer's own attitude, indicated in the way he plants and harvests a plot of land determines what is a field (i.B.2:3-4, 3:2). In Ushan times,[3] the latter view takes precedence, such that, so long as the farmer's own intentions come into play, these override the natural boundaries that separate one plot of land from another (i.D.3:3). Finally, an issue introduced in the Yavnean periods remains moot in Usha. This concerns whether gleanings are comparable to consecrated offerings, such that the specific produce that is a gleaning must go to the poor. Alternatively, because gleanings are unconsecrated, so long as the poor receive the required amount of produce, they need not be given the actual produce that was left behind in the field (iii.B.5:2G-K). Ushans greatly expand the discourse on this question. The basic issue however of the character of produce paid to the poor to satisfy God's lien upon the crops of the land of Israel remains unresolved.

C. Peah in the Time of Usha

Ushans develop the Yavnean discussions and conclude that, in most cases, the rules for the setting aside of poor gifts correspond to those for the designation of heave-offering and tithes. Ushans determine that the farmer may not designate all of his field to be peah (i.C.1:3C-E, i.D.1:2). In doing this, the farmer would fail to make the required distinction between what is his and that which is set aside as the agricultural gift. In refusing to exercise his own right to the produce the farmer does not set into motion the system of restrictions that, in the first place, requires that he set aside produce for the poor, priests and Levites. The same notion, that the obligation to set aside offerings is a reflection of the farmer's own claim to the produce, is revealed in the Ushan idea that no poor gifts belong to the poor until the farmer begins harvesting. This is the point at which he lays claim to his own share. This applies even in the case of defective clusters (v.C.7:5, 8) which, because of their distinctive shape, are known early in their growth and ripening to be destined for the poor. Gentiles may not set aside poor gifts (ii.D.4:9D-E), just as heave-offering they separate is not valid (Terumot, ii.C.3:9). This is in line with the notion that agricultural offerings are paid to release the lien upon the produce held by God, who provides Israelites with the land upon which they grow their food. God did not give the land to gentiles and therefore cannot be held even to sanction their growing of produce upon it. Accordingly, God has no share in the crops that result from gentiles' farm work. Gentiles may, of course, make gifts of produce to whomever they please. But since they have no share in the bounty provided by God, they may not validly designate the agricultural offerings that recognize that bounty.

Finally, repeating the substance of the general discussion concerning all tithes (see Maaserot, i.C.1:1), Ushans restrict the separation of poor gifts to agricultural produce grown upon the land of Israel and subject to harvesting and use as food. Only in the case of such produce have Israelites demanded the help of God in producing crops. Only from these foods, accordingly, is God due a share, in this case, in the form of poor tithes.

Unlike the Yavneans, Ushans are clear that, in one major respect, peah and gleanings differ from heave-offering and tithes. While the latter are given by the householder to whichever priest or Levite he desires, these poor gifts, Ushans state, must be left in the field for the poor themselves to

collect (ii.C.4:1-2, ii.D.4:3). On the one hand, Ushans appear
simply to be stressing what is clear in Scripture, that the poor
are to go through the fields and take for themselves what is left
behind after the harvest. At a deeper level, however, this Ushan
development of an issue moot at Yavneh (ii.B.4:5, 4:9A-C) details
a particularly Ushan metaphysic. As we have seen, Ushans hold
that produce becomes peah or gleanings through the purposeful act
of the farmer who leaves incomplete the harvesting of his field.
By leaving part of his produce unpicked, the farmer gives up his
right to that food. The functional analogue to this conception
is that the poor, for their part, take possession of this same
produce only when they complete that act of harvesting the
produce left incomplete by the farmer.[4] In this way, Ushans
assure that, in the designation and collection of poor gifts,
nothing is left to chance or to intention not made concrete
through specific behaviors. The poor, for instance, cannot gain
possession of peah or gleanings simply through an oral
declaration that they are his. Validly to acquire the produce,
the poor person must actually pick it (ii.D.4:3). The transfer
of the produce from the hands of the farmer to those of the poor
thus is formalized through the actions of the harvest that, in
the system of tithes as a whole, indicate Israelites' purposeful
use of the God-given land. This same Ushan attitude is found in
the Ushan consensus that, should a farmer's notion of what
constitutes a field be indicated in what crops he plants and
harvests as a unit, his attitude, and not geographical
boundaries, determines what constitutes a single field for
purposes of the designation of peah (i.C.3:4, 5, i.D.3:3).

Along with the theoretical issues just described, Ushans
provide practical rules that make possible the implementation of
these tithing laws. They indicate exactly where in each field
peah is to be set aside (i.C.1:3A-B) and detail who is
responsible for designating it (i.C.3:5, i.D.2:7-8). Ushans
define what constitutes a defective cluster (v.C.7:4) and clarify
the conditions under which the law of the forgotten sheaf applies
at all (iv.C.6:10, 7:1, 2). Finally, Ushans indicate the
quantity of poor tithe that the farmer is to distribute to each
poor person (vi.C.8:5, vi.D.8:6, 7).

II. The History of Tractate Peah

i. The Designation of Produce to be Peah

The unit assumes that peah must be designated individually within each of a farmer's distinct fields. This theory engenders the present material's central question, of what defines an autonomous field within which the poor offering must be set aside. The two possible answers both find expression here. The first, stated in anonymous rules attested to Yavneh and Usha (i.B.2:3-4 and 3:2; i.C.2:1-2 and 3:4), holds that a field is defined by geographical considerations, e.g., on the basis of physical boundaries that set off one area of land from the property surrounding it. In this view, even if a farmer harvests in separate batches the produce of his geographically defined field, he still must designate peah only once, for the crop as a whole. The farmer's own actions and attitudes do not affect his obligations regarding the designation of this offering. The alternative view is found in the names of both Yavnean and Ushan authorities, i.B.2:3-4, 3:2 and i.C.3:4. This view holds that the way in which the farmer treats the land determines what is a field for purposes of setting aside peah. By harvesting produce at different times he shows his belief that the two batches of produce are distinct. He therefore must separate peah individually for each batch, even if all of the produce grew in a single geographic area. In the same way, if the farmer had small plots of one kind of produce growing among a different kind, he may designate peah once for all of the plots that he harvests together, for he thereby treats them as a single crop. Both of the conceptions detailed here appear in Yavnean and Ushan materials. At i.D.3:3, the view that the farmer's own use of his land is determinative appears as undisputed law, apparently signaling the ultimate, Ushan, resolution of this issue.

Other minor issues pertinent to the designation of peah occur here. Yavneans determine that produce designated to be peah is exempt from the separation of heave-offering and tithes (i.B.1:6). Yavneans also dispute the minimum area of land which, deemed a field, is subject to peah (i.B.3:6). Ushans argue whether peah must be designated in the back corner of the field, as its name implies, or whether it may be set aside anywhere in the field that the farmer chooses (i.C.1:3A-B). The issue is resolved in favor of the former view, that _peah_ is specific to the rear of the field (i.D.2:7-8).

Rules given here regarding the quantity of _peah_ to be designated depend upon the parallel discussion at Terumot, ii.B.4:5 and ii.A.4:3. Judah notes that, as is the case for heave-offering, a farmer may not designate all of his crop to be _peah_ (i.C.1:3C-E). An anonymous, but probably Ushan, rule notes that the quantity of produce to be designated as _peah_ depends upon external factors, such as the quantity of the field's yield and the number of poor people to be supported (i.D.1:2). The rule is comparable to that of Terumot, ii.A.4:3, which states that the required quantity of heave-offering is determined on the basis of the attitude of the householder from whose produce the offering is taken.

A. Before 70

2:5-6 A field sown with a single type of seed requires a single designation of _peah_, even if the crop is brought to the threshing floor in two lots. If the field contains two types of seed, it requires two separate designations of _peah_, even if the crops are brought to the threshing floor in one lot. In the case of two different types of wheat, the farmer's actions are determinative. If he harvests in one lot, he designates a single portion of _peah_. If he harvests in two lots, he designates two separate portions of _peah_. Precedent involving Simeon of Mispah, Gamaliel the Elder and Nahum the Scribe, which restates this latter rule.

The issue is derivative of a concern argued both at Yavneh, i.B.2:3-4, and Usha, i.C.2:1-2. In particular, this pericope takes up an issue left open by the Ushan materials, of what happens if the farmer does not harvest his field in accordance with the natural divisions that separate it into autonomous areas. Note as well the usually Ushan consideration found here, that the Israelite's own attitude determines whether what he harvests is to be deemed one or two crops. For these reasons, it is unlikely that this material is authentic in the mouths of authorities who lived before 70. It seems rather to be a creation of the Ushan period.[5]

3:1 Plots of grain sown among   The issue of whether or not
olive trees--the House of Shammai   the trees separate the plots
say: He designates peah for each   of grain into distinct
individual plot, unless the plots'   fields is raised in exactly
edges touch. The House of Hillel   these same terms in Ushan
say: In all cases he designates   times, i.C.3:4. It
peah once for all of the plots.   therefore is unlikely to be
                                         authentic in the mouths of
                                         the Houses. See also
                                         i.B.3:2 and i.D.3:3.

B. The Time of Yavneh
1:6 Produce that is designated to   Produce becomes liable for
be peah or that is put to some   tithes when its processing
other use before the grain-pile is   is completed, signified by
smoothed over is exempt from the   the point at which the
separation of heave-offering and   grain-pile is smoothed over.
tithes. So Aqiba.   If, before that point, it is
                                         designated as a particular
                                         agricultural gift, it never
                                         becomes subject to other
                                         tithes. Once it is liable,
                                         however, it cannot again be
                                         rendered exempt, even if it
                                         is put to a use that, before
                                         the completion of processing,
                                         would have removed it from
                                         the system of tithes.
                                         Assumed throughout this
                                         division, considerable
                                         development of the idea
                                         contained here occurs in the
                                         Ushan strata of Tractates
                                         Terumot and Maaserot.

2:3-4 Fences divide areas planted   The assumption is that peah
with trees into separate orchards.   is to be designated
Gamaliel: For olive trees, all of   separately in each field
a single farmer's trees comprise an   the farmer owns. We
orchard. With carob trees, all   therefore must define what
that are in sight of one another   constitutes an autonomous
are a single orchard. Eliezer bar   field. Yavneans begin the

Sadoq in Gamaliel's name: The rule
for carobs is the same as that
for olives.

work for the case of
orchards. The issue is
further discussed at Usha
for the case of fields of
grain, i.C.2:1-2.

3:2 One who reaps the ripe
portions of his field and leaves
the unripe--Aqiba: He designates
peah separately for each area he
harvests. Sages: He designates
peah once for all of these areas.

Sages hold that since all of
the areas the farmer has
harvested are located in a
single field, peah must be
designated only once. Aqiba,
by contrast, notes that,
through his own actions, the
farmer has created
geographically distinct
areas. Therefore peah must
be separated from each
individually. Ushans engage
in this same dispute for
the case in which, in a
single harvest, the farmer
reaps otherwise distinct
fields of grain, i.C.3:4.
Final resolution of the
issues comes at i.D.3:3,
which rules that the farmer's
own attitude and intentions
determine what is deemed a
field.

3:6 Dispute over minimum area
subject to peah--Eliezer, Joshua,
Tarfon and Judah b. Betherah give
specific figures familiar in part
from Kilaim, ii.B.2:10. Aqiba
disagrees and states that all land,
of however small an area, produces
a crop subject to peah (see Shebiit
v.B.10:6).

Four Yavnean authorities
agree that small parcels of
land are inconsequential.
Aqiba, by contrast, holds
that all tracts of land have
lasting value and therefore
are subject to peah and have
the full status of real
estate. Placement at Yavneh
is on the basis of cited

authorities and the parallel
Yavnean rule at Kilaim,
ii.B.2:10.

C. The Time of Usha

1:3A-B Simeon and an anonymous
rule dispute whether peah may be
designated anywhere in the field or
whether, to constitute the required
offering, it must be designated in
the field's rear corner.

The issue is how literally
we are to understand Lev.
19:9's injunction not to
harvest the corner of the
field. Unlike the
anonymous rule, Simeon
wishes to take the word
corner to mean exactly what
it says.

1:3C-E Judah: In order validly to
designate peah the farmer must
retain for himself at least one of
the field's stalks of grain. A
designation of the whole field
to be peah is not valid.

To be valid, the designation
must distinguish what is to
be peah from other produce
that the farmer wants for
himself. Yavneans developed
this idea for the designation
of heave-offering (Terumot,
ii.B.4:5), supplying a firm
basis for assigning this
application of the theory to
the Ushan stratum.

2:1-2 Natural landmarks and
boundaries establish the borders of
a field for purposes of the
designation of peah. Meir and
sages dispute a specific item.
Judah: An irrigation ditch that
prevents a tract of land from being
harvested as one creates two
distinct fields.

This continues the discussion
initiated at Yavneh, i.B.2:3-4,
adding nothing to the theory
presented there.

3:4 Plots of onions sown among
plots of vegetables--Yose: He
designates peah from each
individual plot. Sages: He

The Yavnean materials asked
whether a geographically
unitary field might be
treated in two or more parts

designates peah in one plot for
all of them.

because of the actions or
attitude of the farmer.
Ushans carry this forward to
ask whether the farmer's
actions in harvesting
together separate plots allow
him to treat them as one for
purposes of designating peah.

3:5 Joint owners of a field
designate peah once for the whole
field. If they individually own
separate portions of the field,
they designate peah separately.
A person who owns the trees but
not the ground in which they are
planted must designate peah
individually from each tree.
Judah: If the land's owner still
owns some trees, he must designate
peah for the orchard as a whole.

Ownership determines whether
a field is a single entity,
from which peah is
designated once, or two or
more distinct entities,
from which peah must be
designated several times.
This notion is carried to
its logical conclusion in
the final rule. A person
who owns no land does not
have an orchard in which he
can designate peah once.
A person who owns all the
land and some of the trees,
by contrast, does possess an
orchard and therefore is
responsible for all of the
peah.

3:7-8 Development of theory of
Aqiba, i.B.3:6, that all pieces
of land, however small, are
significant and deemed to be
real estate. Glosses by Yose
and Simeon.

Continued discussion here
at Usha supports the
assignment of i.B.3:6 to the
Yavnean stratum.

D. Unassigned
1:1 The quantity of peah and
first fruits, the value of the
appearance offering, the quantity
of righteous deeds and the amount
of time to be spent in study of

The claim that peah has no
fixed measure is contradicted
by the following entry.

Torah are not subject to a fixed,
required measure.

1:2 Peah must comprise at least
one-sixtieth of a field's produce.
The quantity designated should
accord with the size of the field,
the extent of the yield and the
number of poor people in the
vicinity.

Cf., Terumot, ii.A.4:3, which
states that one-sixtieth is
the minimum acceptable
percentage for a separation
of heave-offering. Like the
present rule, the latter
holds that more may be
separated depending upon
the particular attitude of
the farmer. Since the
particular issue discussed
here for the case of peah
does not appear elsewhere,
I see no way of establishing
whether it is early or late.

1:4-5 Whatever is edible,
cultivated, grown from the land of
Israel, harvested as a crop and
preserved in storage is subject
to designation as peah.

If there is no harvest, a
portion of the field cannot
be left behind. If the food
will spoil quickly, it need
not be left, for it might go
to waste. The other
provisions given here are
familiar from Maaserot,
i.C.1:1, their primary
setting. Like the rule
upon which it is based, this
pericope derives from no
earlier than Ushan times.

2:7-8: Whoever harvests the back
portion of a field is responsible
for designating peah for the field
as a whole. If the back part is
not harvested, e.g., if it is
destroyed or taken by robbers or
gentiles, no peah is designated
for any of the field.

This assumes the position of
Simeon, i.C.1:3A-B, that
peah must be designated in
the rear corner of the
field. The rule therefore
cannot derive from before
the period of Usha.

3:3 One who puts part of the
produce of his field to one use
and harvests part later for a
different use designates peah
individually for each part. If he
harvests at two separate times
but intends to put all that he
harvests to a single use, he
designates peah once for the
whole field.

This develops the rules of
i.B.3:2 and i.C.3:4, to
state firmly that the
farmer's own attitudes and
intentions determine the
number of times he needs to
designate peah from a single
crop. Resolving an issue
moot at Yavneh and Usha, it
derives at earliest from
Ushan times.

ii. The Distribution of Peah to the Poor

Yavneans come to no firm conclusions regarding how peah
should be distributed to the poor. Their larger concern is the
fairness of the method of distribution. They therefore argue
whether the farmer should allow the poor into his field few or
many times during the day (ii.B.4:5). Allowing them in many
times assures equal access but represents an inconvenience by
forcing the poor to wait by the edges of the field all day long.
Allowing the poor in just a few times a day has the opposite
results. The greater issue, however, and the one which is
developed in Ushan times, concerns the right of the landowner
himself to pick and distribute that which he designates as peah.
Eliezer holds that the rich landowner may indeed pick and
distribute this produce to whomever he desires. This is
comparable to his right to distribute heave-offering and tithes
to any priest or Levite he desires. In the interests of equity,
sages hold that he must give it to the first poor person he meets
(ii.B.4:9A-C).

Ushans reject the very notion that the landowner normally
may pick peah (ii.C.4:1-2). Once it has been designated, it no
longer is the farmer's property. He therefore does not have the
right to harvest it at all. At ii.D.4:3, this notion, that peah
must be left unharvested for the poor, is developed to its
logical conclusion. The rule holds that the poor acquire peah
only if they complete the act of harvesting that the farmer left
unfinished. The farmer's leaving of this produce unpicked
signified its designation to be peah. The corrolary is that such
produce enters the poor's possession only when the poor

themselves finish harvesting it. Any attempt to gain possession
of it without picking it is null.

A. Before 70

———

B. The Time of Yavneh

4:5 Three times daily the poor   Aqiba and Gamaliel dispute
may enter the fields to collect   whether the anonymous rule
peah, morning, noon and afternoon.   intends to assure that the
Gamaliel: The farmer may permit   poor have adequate access to
them to enter more times per day,   peah or whether it is meant
but not fewer. Aqiba: He may   to prevent the farmer from
permit them to enter fewer times,   forcing the poor to stand
but not more.   at the edge of the field all
                                      day waiting for each time
                                      that he will allow them to
                                      enter. Placement in the
                                      Yavnean stratum is on the
                                      basis of attributions alone.

4:9A-C If a rich person picks   The issue is whether a rich
peah and declares that it is for a   person may distribute peah
certain poor person, Eliezer deems   in the same way that he
his declaration to be valid. Sages   distributes heave-offering
say that he must give the peah   and tithes, i.e., to whom-
to the first poor person he   ever he pleases. Sages
encounters.   view is taken up in the
                                      development of this law,
                                      ii.C.4:1-2, which holds
                                      that the farmer himself may
                                      not harvest and distribute
                                      peah at all. This
                                      relationship to ii.C.4:1-2
                                      provides sound grounds for
                                      placement of this pericope
                                      in the Yavnean stratum.

C. The Time of Usha

4:1-2 Peah is designated from   The basic rule repeats the
produce that is yet unharvested.   sense of Lev. 19:9-10, which
But if the produce grows high   states that the farmer

on trees or on the householder's trellis, he should cut it down and distribute it. Simeon glosses.

should not reap his fields to their borders. Ushans add that, if the poor who collect the peah might hurt themselves or damage the farmer's property, the farmer may harvest the produce and distribute it. Placement is on the basis of Simeon's gloss and the relationship between this pericope and ii.B.4:9A-C.

4:6 Produce harvested by a gentile before he converts is not subject to gleanings, the forgotten sheaf and peah. Judah: It is subject to the forgotten sheaf, for that restriction applies only after the produce has been bound in sheaves.

At the point at which the produce would have become liable it was not owned by an Israelite. It therefore never becomes liable. This notion, a commonplace in the Division of Agriculture, is attested to Usha by Judah, who disagrees not with the theory but only with its application in a particular case.

D. Unassigned

4:3 If a poor person attempts to acquire peah by spreading his cloak or other produce over it, his actions are null.

The poor person justly acquires peah only by physically reaping it. In this way he completes the harvest, purposely left unfinished by the householder. Discussion occurs at Usha, T. Peah 2:1. Parallel in concern to ii.C.4:1-2 and developing ii.B.4:9A-C, this anonymous rule presumably derives from Ushan times.

4:4 The poor may not use garden tools in order to collect peah. This is so that they will not strike one another.

This presumably derives from Ushan times, along with the larger discussion of which it is a part, ii.C.4:1-2 and ii.D.4:3.

4:7-8 If, at the point at which it normally becomes subject to the agricultural restrictions, produce is owned by the Temple, it never becomes subject. If it is dedicated to the Temple and redeemed before it becomes subject, or if it already is subject when it is dedicated and then, still later, it is redeemed, it is liable.

The theory is the same as at ii.C.4:6, attested to Usha by Judah. In this particular case, since the produce already is in the hands of the Temple, God need receive no further share of it. This exemption from tithes does not however apply if, when the produce becomes subject to agricultural gifts, God, through the agency of the Temple, does not own it.

4:9D-E Forgotten sheaves, gleanings and peah left by a gentile and taken by an Israelite are subject to tithes.

The gentile's designation of these poor offerings is not valid. The poor therefore must tithe the produce, just as they would tithe other ordinary food given to them. The notion that the gentile may not validly designate agricultural offerings occurs at Terumot, ii.C.3:9. The present rule accordingly derives from no earlier than the Ushan period.

iii. Gleanings

Yavneans define gleanings as produce that the farmer cuts with his sickle and momentarily possesses but that he then accidentally drops (iii.B.4:10). As with the other offerings, then, the harvest marks the beginning of the farmer's liability to leave gleanings. Produce he picks but drops prior to the harvest is not subject to this restriction. Like peah, the poor take possession of gleanings by completing the harvesting left incomplete by the farmer. In this case this means their searching for and picking up the dropped food. Yavneans leave two issues of definition unresolved. They argue whether or not gleanings are comparable to consecrated offerings (iii.B.5:2G-K). If they are, the poor must receive the exact produce that the farmer drops as well as any produce about which there is a doubt whether or not it is a gleaning. If gleanings are not comparable to consecrated offering, the poor may be given a quantity of produce equal to that which the farmer drops but need not be given the exact produce or any food the status of which is in doubt. This same issue is moot at Usha. The notion that the poor must receive the exact produce which the farmer drops appears at iii.C.4:11 and iii.D.5:1A-C. The opposite view is found at iii.C.5:1D-F. Yavneans also dispute the definition of the poor person who is allowed to collect and keep poor-offerings. The question is whether that right is determined on the basis of net wealth or, alternatively, by the individual's needs at some specific time and place (iii.B.5:4). This issue too remains moot and is not referred to elsewhere in the tractate.

Along with the issue of the character of gleanings, Ushans discuss minor details concerning the collection of this poor-offering. The farmer may not irrigate his field so as to make it difficult for the poor to collect their share (iii.C.5:3). A more basic point, familiar from the concerns expressed in the preceding unit, is that, in the interests of fairness, a person may not collect gleanings from produce over which he already has rights of ownership (iii.C.5:5F-L, iii.D.5:5D-E, 5:6).

A. Before 70

_____

B. The Time of Yavneh

4:10 Gleanings are produce that the farmer harvests and momentarily takes into his possession but then accidentally drops. Whether or not he has taken final possession before the produce falls is

This initial definition of gleanings is attested to Yavneh by Ishmael and Aqiba.

determined by the place on the
sickle from which the produce
falls. Ishmael and Aqiba dispute
the rule for an ambiguous case.

5:2G-K If a stalk of grain that is
gleanings is lost in a heap of
grain, the householder takes two
stalks, designates one to contain
the tithes required of the other
and then gives the fully tithed
stalk to a poor person in
place of the gleaning that was
lost. Eliezer: The poor
must gain possession of the
actual stalk that was lost.
Therefore the farmer begins
by assigning the poor half
of the heap as a whole.

Eliezer holds that the
original gleaning is
comparable to a consecrated
offering set aside only for
the poor. The poor person
therefore must receive that
particular stalk before he
may exchange it for a
different piece of grain.
This view is disputed by the
anonymous rule, which
requires simply that the
lost gleaning be replaced.
Developed at iii.C.5:1D-F,
this material is firmly
attested to the Yavnean
stratum.

5:4 A householder who is away from
home and has no money may collect
poor-offerings. Eliezer: When he
returns home he must repay to the
poor the amount of produce he took.
Sages: He need not repay.

The issue is how we
determine whether or not
someone is poor. Eliezer
goes by net worth. Since
the householder here really
was not poor, he did not
have the right to collect
the offerings and must make
repayment. Sages by
contrast look at the
individual's present
situation. The householder
was in need and therefore
had the right to collect poor
offerings. He need not make
not make repayment. Placement in the Yavnean stratum
is based on the attribution
to Eliezer. See Terumot,

iv.B.8:1-3, where, in
determining a person's
status, Eliezer again
refuses to take into account
mitigating circumstances.

C. The Time of Usha

4:11 Produce that ants carry off
to ant holes belongs to the farmer.
After the harvest, produce at the
bottom of ant holes belongs to the
farmer and that which is on top
belongs to the poor. Meir: All
this produce belongs to the poor,
for in a case of doubt, produce
is deemed gleanings.

Produce carried away by ants
never was possessed by the
farmer. It therefore does
not have the status of
gleanings (iii.B.4:10).
After the harvest, it is
unclear whether the produce
in the ant holes was dropped
by the harvesters or carried
off by ants. For this
reason its status is subject
to dispute. Carrying forward
the principle outlined at
iii.B.4:10, this unit is
firmly placed in the Ushan
stratum.

5:1D-F If wind scatters sheaves
over an area from which gleanings
have not yet been collected, they
give the poor a quantity of
produce estimated to equal the
gleanings that would have been
found there. Simeon b. Gamaliel:
They give the poor the amount of
grain needed to sow the field.

The assumption is that the
poor person must be given an
amount of produce equal to
the gleanings that were
mixed with common produce.
The poor need not be given
the actual gleanings. A
different view of matters is
found in Meir's position
in the preceding entry, and
at iii.D.5:1A-C.

5:3 Meir: They may not irrigate a
field that has been harvested until
the poor have collected their
produce. Sages permit.

The dispute focuses on
whether or not a farmer may
tend his field in a manner
that makes it difficult
for the poor to collect

their share. Continued
discussion is at Usha,
T. 2:20.

5:5F-L   One who contracts to
harvest a field may not take for
himself poor-offerings.   Judah:
This applies only if the harvester
is paid with a percentage of the
total yield.   But if he receives
a percentage of what he harvests,
he may take gleanings, forgotten
sheaves and peah, for the
individual has no claim of
ownership until a much later time,
when the produce is brought to the
threshing floor.

The principle that a poor
person may not collect poor-
offerings from a field he
owns in whole or in part
assures that such
individuals cannot hoard
these offerings or prevent
others from collecting them.
Judah assures that this
restriction will be applied
only in a case in which
the poor person actually
does own some portion of the
crop as a whole.   Placement
is on the basis of the
attribution.

D.   Unassigned
5:1A-C   If a pile of grain is
placed upon ground from which
gleanings have not yet been
collected, all produce touching
the ground must be given to the
poor.

Any of the produce on the
ground might be the original
gleanings.   This unit
assumes that the poor must
be given that particular
produce and, with it, any
grain the status of which is
in doubt.   The theory is
that gleanings are
comparable to to other
consecrated offerings, which
must go to their designated
recipients and which cannot
be exchanged for other food.
Reflecting the views of
Eliezer, iii.B.5:2G-K and of
Meir, iii.C.4:11, this rule
may derive from Yavnean or
Ushan times.

5:2A-F A stalk that is left
standing next to unharvested stalks
belongs to the householder. If it
is left unharvested when the farmer
finishes with the field as a whole,
it is deemed a gleaning.

This extends the defintion
of a gleaning, iii.B.4:10,
to a further sort of case.
Discussion by Aqiba,
T. 2:21, attests this issue
to Yavneh.

5:5A-C A poor person may trade
poor-offerings for untithed produce
owned by someone else. The poor-
offerings remain exempt from tithes.
That which the poor person receives
remains subject to tithes.

Unlike consecrated,
offerings, poor-tithes may
be used by the poor person
in any manner he wishes.
Even if they are given to a
rich person, they retain
their original status, such
that they remain exempt
from tithes. This rule is
in line with the position
of Simeon b. Gamaliel,
iii.C.5:1D-F. It appears
to derive from Ushan times.

5:5D-E Two men who independently
sharecrop halves of a single field
may give to each other the
poorman's tithe they separate.

This rule assumes the
principle attested to Ushan
times, iii.C.5:5F-L, that
a person may not take
poorman's tithe from his own
field.

5:6 One who sells his field may
thereafter collect poor offerings
from it. The buyer may not.

This is a simple statement
of the principle found at
iii.C.5:5F-L.

iv. The Forgotten Sheaf (Dt. 24:19)

Sheaves of grain that the farmer binds but forgets in the
field become the property of the poor. So Dt. 24:19. Mishnah's
authorities determine the circumstances under which a sheaf is
deemed forgotten and not simply momentarily left behind.
Discussion begins with the Houses, who question the case of
sheaves that have distinctive characteristics. The Shammaites
hold that since the farmer can easily call such sheaves to mind,
he probably will return to collect them. They therefore remain

his property. The Hillelites, by contrast, take into account only the present fact, that the farmer has left the sheaves behind. Therefore, they belong to the poor. The possibility that the farmer might later remember them and return is irrelevant to their status, which is established at the moment at which they are forgotten (iv.A.6:1D-6:3, 6:5).[6]

Yavneans and Ushans accept and carry forward the Shammaite position. Yavneans define as distinctive large sheaves or several sheaves standing side by side (iv.B.6:6). Ushans develop this by discussing what sorts of produce join together to comprise the quantity of produce that Yavneans deem distinctive (iv.C.6:9, 7:1, 7:2).

Ushans dispute a further issue, quite basic to the discussion of the forgotten sheaf. The question is whether this restriction applies only to produce actually bound in sheaves or whether these restrictions apply as well to any produce that is forgotten by the farmer. Judah (iv.C.6:10) and Yose (iv.C.7:1) take the former view. Their opinion apparently is a minority view, for most of the anonymous Ushan material assumes that any produce that the farmer leaves behind is in the status of a forgotten sheaf and therefore belongs to the poor.

An anonymous Ushan rule develops the previous discussion of the conditions under which sheaves are deemed distinctive, bringing into play the consideration of the farmer's intentions for a specific sheaf. iv.D.5:8 states that so long as the farmer has future plans for a sheaf, that sheaf does not become the possession of the poor, even if the farmer momentarily should forget about it. Ushan authorities thus take seriously the powers of intention by which a person can recall to mind an idea or object upon which he has not consciously focused for some period of time.

A. Before 70

6:1A-C House of Shammai: Property declared ownerless for the benefit of the poor validly is declared ownerless. House of Hillel: It is not ownerless unless it is given for the use of the rich as well. Produce that is ownerless is exempt from tithes. The Hillelites say that validly to give up ownership, the householder must release all control over the food. If he controls who may take the food, it is not really ownerless. The Shammaites

hold that it is sufficient
that the farmer has given
up his own right to eat the
produce. Insofar as any
poor person may take the
food and the farmer himself
may not, it is ownerless.
The issue expressed here
appears nowhere else in
this division, such that
there is no way to test the
authenticity of the
attributions to the Houses.[7]

6:1D-6:3 If a sheaf left in a   Since the farmer can easily
field has a distinguishing   distinguish and remember
characteristic such as size or   this particular sheaf, the
location, the Shammaites hold   Shammaites hold that it
that it is not a forgotten sheaf.   cannot be deemed forgotten.
The Hillelites state that it is.   The Hillelites by contrast
                                        take into account only the
                                        present facts. The farmer
                                        has forgotten the sheaf,
                                        such that it goes to the
                                        poor. Whether or not he
                                        might recall it later is
                                        irrelevant. Discussion of
                                        the point of each House's
                                        opinion is found at both
                                        Yavneh and Usha, T. 3:2-3,
                                        supporting the claim that
                                        this issue is authentic in
                                        the mouths of the Houses.

6:5 Two sheaves left next to each   The Hillelites now are made
other in the field are subject to   to agree to the Shammaite
the restrictions of the forgotten   position of the preceding
sheaf, but three sheaves are not.   entry, such that they simply
So the Hillelites. The Shammaties   dispute its application in
say: Three sheaves lying side-by-   a particular case. The
side are not subject to the   Shammites moreover now hold

restriction of the forgotten sheaf, but four are.

the stringent position, an odd state of affairs. While the specific opinions assigned to the Houses here and in the preceding cannot be reconciled, the issue of these pericopae may be authentic to the period before 70. It is attested to Yavneh by Gamaliel, iv.B.6:6.

B. The Time of Yavneh
6:6 A sheaf containing two seahs of grain is not subject to the restrictions of the forgotten sheaf. Gamaliel: Two sheaves of one seah each likewise are not subject. Sages: They are.

This assumes the Shammaite opinion, iv.A.6:1D-6:3, that a distinctive sheaf is not subject to the law of the forgotten sheaf. The issue is what specifically constitutes a distinctive sheaf. Gamaliel and sages debate their positions along lines suggested by iv.A.6:5.[8] Development of the rule to which both sages and Gamaliel agree is at iv.C.6:9, providing grounds for assignment of this dispute to Yavneh.

C. The Time of Usha
6:9 Uprooted and not uprooted produce, picked and unpicked produce do not combine to create the two seahs that are exempt from the law of the forgotten sheaf (iv.B.6:6). Yose: A forgotten sheaf that belongs to the poor prevents sheaves lying around it from joining together to comprise the quantity

This develops the rule of iv.B.6:6. The first rule supplies the common Ushan notion that produce in different stages of processing or of different species does not join into a single batch (see Terumot, i.C.2:4). Yose makes the same point in a slightly

of produce exempt from the law.

different way. Since the farmer does not own all of the produce, it cannot comprise a single grain pile. The different batches of produce therefore must be treated separately, just as above.

6:10 Produce that is not yet bound into sheaves is not subject to the restriction of the forgotten sheaf. Tubers that the farmer stores in the ground--Judah: These are not subject. Sages: They are subject.

Judah and sages dispute what is taken for granted in the anonymous rule. The issue is whether or not what is not bound into sheaves can be subject to the law of the forgotten sheaf. Judah, who apparently stands behind the anonymous rule, takes seriously the term "sheaf." The anonymous authorities by contrast, require simply that produce be forgotten so as to fall under the law (cf., Brooks to M. 6:10). Placement in this stratum is on the basis of the attribution to Judah and the parallel issue at iv.C.7:1.

7:1 As for olive trees that have distinguishing characteristics-- their fruit does not enter the status of forgotten sheaves. Two trees left unharvested are subject to the restriction of the forgotten sheaf; three are not. Yose: The law of the forgotten sheaf does not apply to olive trees at all.

The anonymous rules apply to olive trees the law of iv.A.6:1D-6:3, 6:5. In agreement with Judah, iv.C.6:10, Yose rejects the very notion that unharvested and forgotten olives fall under the restrictions of the forgotten sheaf. They are not "sheaves" and therefore are not subject to this law at all.

Placement depends upon the attribution and the parallel to iv.C.6:10.

7:2 An olive tree the branches of which contain two <u>seahs</u> of produce is not subject to the restrictions of the forgotten sheaf, so long as the farmer has not yet begun to harvest it. Once he begins the harvest, both produce in the tree and that which has fallen to the ground is under the law of the forgotten sheaf. Meir: This is the case only after the worker has gone by with the harvesting rod (see Dt. 24:20).

The initial rule repeats for the case of the olive tree the law of iv.B.6:6. Meir's point is that only once the farmer has passed with the harvesting rod has he conducted a harvest of this produce. Only after that point does the law of the forgotten sheaf apply, as below at iv.D.6:4. Developing rules known at Yavneh and attested by an Ushan authority, this material is firmly placed in the Ushan stratum.

D. Unassigned

5:7 1) If workers or the householder did not forget about a sheaf, 2) or if that sheaf was hidden by the poor, it is not in the status of a forgotten sheaf. It remains the householder's possession.

1) The workers are deemed agents of the householder. A sheaf that they remember is not, therefore, "forgotten." This rule is attested to the periods of Usha and after Usha, T. 3:1, suggesting that it derives from no earlier than Ushan times. 2) As in the case of gleanings, the householder must not be constrained to forget the sheaf (see iii.B.4:10). What the poor cause him to forget does not take on the status of a forgotten sheaf. Its logical relationship to a Yavnean rule

supports assignment of this
law to Yavneh.

5:8 What the farmer does with
sheaves he removes from the field
determines whether or not the
sheaves he leaves behind may be
deemed forgotten. So long as we
may assume that he intends to
leave some sheaves in the field
none of what he leaves behind
has the status of a forgotten
sheaf.

The Israelite's actions and
intentions determine what
produce falls into the
category of forgotten
sheaves. Even if he
accidentally "forgot" a
sheaf in the field, the
sheaf remains his possession
if its location conforms
to his overall plans for it.
Reference to the role of the
Israelite's intentions
provides grounds for placement at Usha. Discussion
is by Judah, T. 3:1.

6:4 Dt. 24:19 states: When you
reap your harvest and forget a
sheaf in the field, you shall not
go back to get it. Only sheaves
that those who complete the
harvest have passed and forgotten
are subject to the restriction of
the forgotten sheaf. If the sheaf
is in an area from which sheaves
have not yet been collected, it
cannot be deemed forgotten.

By definition a worker
cannot have forgotten a
sheaf that he has not yet
passed. This expansion of
Scripture's rule may derive
from any point in the
development of Mishnah's
laws on the forgotten sheaf.
It accords in particular
with the Yavnean idea that
the harvest signifies the
point at which these
restrictions first apply.

6:7-8 Two seahs of standing grain
that are forgotten in the field are
not subject to the law of the
forgotten sheaf. The presence of
this standing grain likewise
prevents a sheaf forgotten near
it from entering the status of a
forgotten sheaf. If the standing
grain presently contains less than

These rules depend upon and
develop iv.B.6:6, meaning
that they derive at earliest
from the Yavnean period.
Ushan discussion, T.3:5-6,
makes it likely that the
material is in fact Ushan.
The rules hold that we must
assume that the farmer will

two seahs but will later reach a
growth of two seahs, it is not
subject.

return to collect grain of
two seahs or more in
quantity. At the same time
he will take any sheaves
that have been left nearby.

6:11 If a farmer harvests or
binds sheaves at night, or if he
is blind, the sheaves he leaves
behind still are deemed forgotten
sheaves. If he purposely collected
only large sheaves, the small ones
he leaves behind are not deemed
forgotten. A stipulation that the
farmer will return and collect all
that he has forgotten is not valid.

1) Since the farmer himself
decided to harvest at night,
darkness is not a constraint
that invalidly caused him to
leave the sheaf behind (see
iii.B.4:10 and iv.D.5:7).
This therefore differs from
a case in which the poor
hide sheaves from the
farmer. 2) The farmer's
stipulation designed to
circumvent the law is not
valid, for the fact remains
that, in the meantime,
certain sheaves have been
forgotten and therefore
belong to the poor.
Developing iii.B.4:10 this
may be Yavnean or Ushan.

v.   Defective Clusters and Grape Gleanings (Lev. 19:10)

I begin with the Ushan material, in which the major work on
this topic is carried out. Ushans define the defective cluster
as one that is improperly shaped (v.C.7:4). In cases of doubt,
the cluster goes to the poor. This parallels the Ushan idea
concerning gleanings, iii.C.4:11. Yet if the cluster is hidden
from view so that the farmer cannot tell if it is defective, his
own actions are determinative. If he takes it, it is his, even
if it turns out to be defective. Thus the farmer's own attitude
towards produce in his field determines its status, just as we
shall see is the case for other agricultural offerings. Ushans
dispute a second question, of when in their growth and ripening
defective clusters become the property of the poor (v.C.7:5, 8).
Meir holds that since no act of designation on the part of the
householder is required to establish which clusters must go to

the poor, the clusters become the property of the poor as soon as they are known to be defective. Disagreeing, Judah and Yose again see the rules for defective clusters as parallel to those for other agricultural offerings. These take on their special status only as a result of specific actions on the part of the householder. They state that the defective clusters do not become the property of the poor until the farmer begins the harvest. Only when the landowner takes final possession of his own fruit does God's right to the food, and with it the poor's claim upon their share, become effective.

Yavneans discuss a case in which a vineyard produces all defective clusters. Examined in its own terms, the operative issue here concerns whether defective clusters are defined by a single standard, applied to all fields, or whether definition is relative to the character of the clusters in each individual field. Eliezer takes the latter view. If all the clusters in the field are the same, none should be deemed defective. Aqiba, by contrast, applies an objective criterion (such as is suggested in specific terms in the Ushan period, iv.C.7:4). In this view all clusters that lack, for instance, shoulders and pendant must be left for the poor, even if all the clusters in the field look that way.

Seen in the perspective of the Ushan material of this unit, which clearly refers to the requirement of a designation of produce to be defective clusters, this Yavnean dispute appears to concern a different issue. In refusing to allow all of the produce of a field to become an offering, Eliezer is in line with the view of Judah and Yose (iv.C.7:5, 8), that a farmer who has not kept produce for himself cannot validly designate an agricultural offering (see also Judah at i.C.1:3C-E and the Yavnean opinion at Terumot, ii.B.4:5). Aqiba, on the other hand, is in agreement with Meir, that in the case of defective clusters, no formal act of differentiation is required.[9] In this case we thus see clearly how a question of definition--common in the Yavnean stratum--took on new and different meaning as it was developed in Ushan times.

v.D.7:3 defines separated grapes, which also go to the poor, in the same terms that iii.B.4:10 defined other gleanings. They are produce that accidentally falls during the harvest. The rule, a singleton, may therefore be as early as Yavnean. In another singleton, the Houses (v.A.7:6) dispute whether or not produce of the fourth year of a vineyard's growth (Lev. 19:23-25)

is in all respects comparable to produce in the status of second
tithe. It is impossible to verify this issue to the period
before 70.

A. Before 70

7:6 Shammaites: Produce of a
vine in its fourth year of growth
is not comparable to second tithe.
It therefore is not subject to
the added-fifth (M. M.S. 4:3) or
removal (M. M.S. 5:6) but is
subject to the restrictions of
the separated grape and defective
cluster. Hillelites: This
produce is in all respects
comparable to second tithe. It
therefore is not subject to the
law of the separated grape or
the defective cluster.

The Hillelites hold that
produce from the fourth year
of a vineyard's growth
is comparable to produce in
the status of second tithe.
The Shammaites disagree.
Each of the restrictions
referred to here is
Scriptural (see Maaser Sheni,
vi.A.5:3), and the only
other reference to this
issue is at T. M.S. 5:17,
where Rabbi and Simeon b.
Gamaliel dispute the
meaning of the position of
the House of Shammai. While
the dispute was known and
discussed in Ushan times,
it is unclear whether or
not it goes back to the
historical Houses. See the
parallel at Maaser Sheni,
vi.A.5:3.

B. The Time of Yavneh

7:7 As for a vineyard that is
entirely defective clusters--
Eliezer: The fruit belongs to
the farmer. Aqiba: It all goes
to the poor. + Debate based upon
Scripture.

Aqiba holds that defective
clusters are defined by an
objective standard. The
alternative, suggested by
Eliezer, is that the
definition is relative to
the norm in each field.
Placement is on the basis
of the attributions and the
general Yavnean interest in
poor offerings (e.g., at
iii.B.4:10 and the

apparently Yavnean
iv.D.5:7). See also the
parallel concern at Terumot,
ii.B.4:5.

C. The Time of Usha

7:4 A defective cluster, which
belongs to the poor, does not have
a wide upper part and cone-shaped
lower part. A case of doubt goes
to the poor. If it is lying on
the ground so that one cannot
tell--if it is harvested by the
farmer, it belongs to him. If it
is left behind, it goes to the
poor. Judah: Single grapes,
which do not grow in a cluster at
all, are deemed a normal cluster.
Sages: They are a defective
cluster.

These definitions are
attested to Usha by Judah.
In a case of ambiguity, such
as when the farmer cannot
distinguish the shape of the
cluster, his own actions
determine whether or not
that cluster takes on the
status of a poor offering.
This is a typically Ushan
idea.

7:5 Judah: One who thins his
grape vines may thin both his own
produce and defective clusters.
Meir: He may not thin defective
clusters, for they belong to the
poor.

The issue is the point at
which the clusters become
subject to the law that
assigns them to the poor.
Judah takes the view
operative for the case of
gleanings, peah and the
forgotten sheaf. The rights
of the poor begin only when
the farmer begins to harvest
the field. Meir, by
contrast, notes that, in
this case, what belongs to
the poor is determined by
the natural process of
growth. As soon as the
clusters are known to be
defective, they belong to
the poor, such that the
farmer may not harm them.

7:8 If one dedicated his field to the Temple before the defective clusters appeared, they belong to the Temple. If the dedication was after they appeared, they belong to the poor. Yose states that, if so, the farmer must give the Temple the value of the clusters that grew after the point of the dedication but that were given to the poor.

The anonymous rule follows the position of Meir in the preceding entry. As soon as the clusters are known to be defective they belong to the poor, such that the farmer may not dedicate them to the Temple. Yose is in the position of Judah. The clusters do not enter the status of poor offerings until the farmer begins the harvest. The farmer's dedication of these clusters to the Temple therefore was valid. If they anyway are to go to the poor, as the anonymous rule demands, then the farmer must give to the Temple their value in their stead.

D. Unassigned

7:3 Separated grapes that belong to the poor are those that fall to the ground during the harvest. If the cluster fell and broke because it became entangled in the vine, it belongs to the householder. One who places a basket under the vine to catch separated grapes steals from the poor.

This definition of what goes to the poor is familiar from iii.B.4:10 and iv.D.5:7. Note also v.B.7:7. This may therefore be as early as Yavnean. The point again is that what the harvester is constrained to drop does not enter the status of a poor offering.

vi. Poorman's Tithe and General Rules

These Ushan rules make the point that, in the distribution of poorman's tithe, each poor person should be given sufficient food to last a day (vi.C.8:5, vi.D.8:7). If the farmer has too little tithe to allow this, he lets the poor themselves distribute the offering (vi.D.8:6). Three other, unrelated, points occur in the Ushan stratum:

1) Once the poor have had ample opportunity to collect gleanings and other produce left for them in the field, the remaining food is deemed ownerless and may be taken by anyone (vi.C.8:1).

2) The notion that people who are not poor may eat poor-offerings is developed with the rule that poor people may sell their share and that, when they do so, it remains exempt from tithes (vi.D.8:2-4).

3) Poverty is determined by an individual's ability to support himself, not simply on the basis of lack of assets. One who supports himself from a small amount of capital is not deemed poor (vi.D.8:8, 9).

A. Before 70

_____

B. The Time of Yavneh

_____

C. The Time of Usha

8:1 After the aged-poor have gone through the field, anyone may enter the field and collect gleanings. After the poor have twice gone through the vineyard to collect separated grapes, anyone may collect such produce. After the second rainfall anyone may take forgotten produce in olive trees. Judah: Some farmers do not even harvest olives until this time. All may collect after the point at which a poor person who went to the orchard could not collect four issars-worth of olives.

Produce left for the poor but not taken by them has an ambiguous status. On the one hand it certainly is not the farmer's to take. On the other, the poor seem to have forsaken their right to it. The problem is resolved by treating the produce as though it were ownerless and available for anyone to take. The issue is at what point we deem the poors' exclusive right to the produce to be exhausted. The rules for each type of poor-offering seeks to assure that the poor will have ample opportunity to gather that which was left for them. Judah's dispute is a quibble over the facts of the harvest. It serves

to attest this construction
to the time of Usha.

8:5   In dispensing poorman's tithe
the householder may not give each
poor person less than certain set
quantities of each type of produce.
The quantities are disputed by
anonymous authorities, Meir and
Aqiba. For the case of produce
other than wheat, barley, wine and
oil, Abba Shaul holds that each
poor person must be given enough
produce to sell and use the
revenue to purchase two meals.

While discussion may begin
in Yavnean times, its
conclusion and the
redactional imposition of a
consideration intended to
control exegesis of the
whole occurs only in Ushan
times, with the statement of
Abba Saul. In light of his
position, the concern here
seems to be that each poor
person receive enough food
to support himself for a
day. The other authorities
simply argue how much
of specific commodities
comprises this amount.

D.   Unassigned
8:2-4 Poor people who sell
produce are believed when they
state that it is in the status
of poor-offerings and exempt from
tithes if 1) it is the proper
time of year for the particular
poor-offering and 2) the produce
is of a sort normally left for
the poor, e.g., if it is
unprocessed.

Poor-offerings sold by the
poor have a high market
value, since they are not
subject to tithes. Under
the theory that the poor
might deceive buyers so as
to command a high price for
what they sell, these rules
detail the conditions under
which the poors' claims may
be believed. Discussion is
at Usha, T. 4:1. There is
no evidence that this rule
was known before Ushan times.

8:6   A farmer may give only half
of his poorman's tithe to his own
relatives. If he has less than
the quantities indicated at
vi.C.8:5, he places that which he

The initial rule prevents
farmers from depriving each
poor person of a proper
share. The second rule
develops vi.C.8:5 and

has before the poor and they
distribute it themselves.

attests this construction to
Ushan times.

8:7 Poor people who are travelling
must be given sufficient food to
last their day's journey, to spend
the night, or the Sabbath. Other
rules define who may take from a
soup kitchen or communal fund.

The line of questioning is
familiar from vi.C.8:5 and
vi.D.8:6, indicating that
this belongs in the Ushan
stratum.

8:8 A person who has less than two
hundred zuz in liquid assets may
collect poor-offerings. One who
has more than this may not.

As in the preceding entry,
the issue is familiar from
Ushan times.

8:9 He who has less than two
hundred zuz but conducts business
with them so as to earn an income
may not collect poor-offerings.
Those who wrongly collect poor-
offerings are subject to
punishments at the hands of Heaven.

This too presumbly derives
from the time of Usha.

III. Conclusion

The distinctive agendum of issues of this tractate, like
that of Tractate Terumot to which it is parallel, was set in
Yavnean times. In that period each of the major questions that
would, by the end of Mishnah's formulation, be asked about this
topic was in fact posed. Only in the Ushan period, however, do
the questions first posed at Yavneh receive answers that reveal
an overriding theory of law. This theory holds that the
Israelite farmer's desire for the produce of his land triggers
his responsibility to pay the agricultural gifts demanded by God.
The poor people's acquisition of their share likewise is bound up
in the act of harvest, in the needy individual's completing the
actions purposely left incomplete by the farmer. Mishnah's great
contribution to Scriptural law thus is to look at Scripture's
poor tax--paid according to Scripture in recognition of the fact
that all Israel once was, and again might be, in need--as a tithe
comparable to all other agricultural offerings and therefore
susceptible to designation according to the same rules that apply
in those other cases.

CHAPTER THREE

DEMAI

I. Introduction

Tractate Demai describes how individuals who themselves properly separate all required agricultural offerings are to assure as well that all of the food they eat outside of their homes or purchase to bring home has properly been tithed. Mishnah Demai thus indicates how foods are to be eaten in accordance with the same set of divine laws that controls their growth and processing. To accomplish this, the tractate indicates how one may determine whether or not someone else is trustworthy regarding tithing, legislates responsibility for tithing produce that leaves one's possession, and details the procedure for tithing produce about which there is a doubt whether or not it already was tithed.

The problem of the tractate arises when one group living within a society determines to impose upon the act of eating mythic dimensions ignored by other members of their society. Tractate Demai, however, does not describe a self-contained sect living apart from, or even at the fringes of, the larger society. Mishnah Demai, that is, knows of no group comparable to the sect that existed at Qumran. Indeed, the very problem of this tractate--of how to deal with cases of doubt whether or not food is prepared properly for consumption--can arise only in the context of continuing interaction among people with different food preparation habits. While concerned with intra-group relations, Mishnah Demai thus does not describe a self-contained sect. This is not entirely surprising, given the character of the rabbinic program and its clear intention to create of the people of Israel as a whole a nation living in holiness.

The specific problem of the tractate arises not with Pharisees, as we might expect, but late in the formation of the law, when Ushans determine that the responsibility to tithe extends not only to what one prepares to eat in his own home, but also to all produce that the individual sells in the market, gives away as a gift, or even finds in the street and then discards (Sarason, Demai, p. 4). If, instead, each individual were deemed responsible to tithe only that which he prepares to

73

eat in his own meal (as the majority of the materials in Tractate
Maaserot would have it), no problem of doubtfully tithed produce
could arise at all. Each individual would know exactly what
offerings had been separated from his own food. In light of this
fact, it will be quite clear in my description of the unfolding
of the law that this tractate as a conceptual whole comes into
being only in Ushan times. While early authorities, including
the Houses, know that certain Israelites fully tithe their
produce and others do not, the Ushans alone legislate that one
must tithe all produce that leaves his possession. In this
(late) concept lies the foundations of Tractate Demai, for only
in light of it need each Israelite wonder whether or not a
different Israelite has properly, or improperly, tithed produce.

In light of their particular perspective, Ushans define a
group of individuals who are trusted to tithe and with whom one
therefore may do business and share hospitality. While
continuing to live within the larger society, this group's
interaction with outsiders is defined and limited by the basic
premise that one cannot trust an outsider to observe one's own
food laws, even if on a particular occasion that individual
claims to have done so. In this regard too the Ushan materials
in this tractate are striking. The general weight of the Yavnean
legislation is to rule leniently, so as to allow those who tithe
and those who do not to eat at the same table or otherwise to
exchange produce. Ushan law, by contrast, strictly limits
interaction between the haber and neeman and non-group members.
In this way, Ushans define a society not envisioned by earlier
rabbinic authorities and certainly not foreseen by Scripture's
agriculture law. In this society, strict lines demarcate one
group, which tithes, from another group which does not (or, which
does so imperfectly). Those who tithe are set above the rest of
the people of Israel. Indeed, in light of the Ushan insistence
that they do all in their power to prevent others from eating
improperly tithed foods, they are made responsible for the
salvation of the nation as a whole.[1]

A. Demai Before 70

One idea goes back to the period before 70. Basic to the
tractate as a whole is the Shammaite notion, ii.A.3:1C-H, that an
individual is responsible to prevent others from transgressing,
for instance, by giving untithed produce as charity only to
individuals known to tithe. While disputed by anonymous

authorities, by Ushan times this idea leads to the pervasive notion that, to prevent others from transgressing, one must tithe all produce that leaves his possession. In this Ushan claim lies the foundation of the tractate as a whole. For, if it had been decided instead that each individual should tithe only that which he brings into his own home to eat, there would be no issue of doubtfully tithed produce at all (see Sarason, Demai, p. 2). While the Shammaite position does not itself constitute the generative problematic of the tractate (indeed, it assumes that people may give away untithed food), it thus presents the tractate's underlying legal proposition that one individual is responsible to prevent another from transgressing. Without this idea, Tractate Demai could never have been created.

B.   Demai in the Time of Yavneh
     Yavneans provide only a smattering of comments. These indicate their period's low level of inquiry into the topic of demai and reveal their general lack of interest in the problems created by membership in a clique that follows dietary restrictions considerably more stringent than those of the larger community in which the group exists. Indeed, regarding produce that might not have been tithed, Yavneans legislate a laxity totally uncharacteristic of the overall, Ushan, intent of the tractate's legislation. They allow a householder to distribute doubtfully tithed produce to poor people who eat at this table (ii.B.3:1A-B). This differs considerably from Ushan proscriptions, which prevent the giving of untithed produce to others and which indeed require the designation of all agricultural offerings that might not already have been separated from produce (iv.D.5:1). While certain problems considered in the Ushan stratum thus do arise in Yavnean times, it is clear that the focus and point of the tractate as a whole is determined by the later authorities.

     The Yavnean willingness to treat leniently cases of doubt is highlighted in their discussion of how one treats individuals who claim to have tithed but who are not known to be trustworthy. They rule that testimony of these people may be accepted in any circumstance in which the questioner has no alternative but to believe--for instance, if he otherwise will not be able to eat at all (iii.B.4:1). The topic is taken up by the Ushans, who reject the notion that, because of extenuating circumstances, one may believe someone who normally is not trusted. Instead, Ushans

develop a theory of evidence that judges the likelihood that the
testimony is true. Unlike Yavneans, Ushans would rather go
hungry than eat possibly untithed food.

One minor point receives mention in the Yavnean stratum.
The owner of a tract of land may take from a sharecropper
offerings that are appropriate to him (v.B.6:3, 4). If the owner
is a priest or Levite, that is, he may take heave-offering or
tithes that derive from the field. If the sharecropper is a
priest or Levite he may take the same percentage of the field's
offerings as he takes of the crop as a whole.

C. Demai in the Time of Usha

Ushan legislation defines membership in a group distinguished by observance of tithing and purity laws.[2] Ushans
delineate how the group member is to follow these laws while
living in a society comprised primarily of individuals who cannot
be trusted properly to tithe or even to respect the group
member's needs. The basic requirements for group membership are
found at ii.C.2:2, 3, 4, 3:3E-G, 4, 5, and 6. These pericopae
describe the neeman, an individual who undertakes to tithe any
food that he eats or that, having come into his possession, he
gives away. The Ushan stratum also describes a more stringent
group member, the haber, who makes certain only to eat foods in a
high level of cultic cleanness, as though they were being
consumed in the Temple. This individual may not purchase
possibly unclean foods from those not trusted to follow group
laws. Group membership thus severely limits social and economic
interaction with those outside of the group.[3] Descriptions of
the means and extent of the permitted contact takes up the
majority of the Ushan material before us. As might be expected
in light of the nature of the issue, these rules are primarily
practical in nature. Their single theoretical underpinning,
deriving as we have seen from the period before 70, is that one
must do whatever is possible to prevent someone else from
transgressing, for instance, by eating improperly tithed produce.
Let us examine the concrete cases in which Ushans view this as an
issue.

The responsibility to tithe all produce that leaves one's
possession creates a problem for a haber who sharecrops land
owned by an individual who does not normally tithe. Need the one
who tithes separate agricultural offerings from all of the
field's crop, so as to prevent the landowner from transgressing

by eating untithed food? The Ushan answer eases the potentially strained relationship between the two individuals by noting that the haber is obligated to tithe only produce that he has actually possessed and later determines to sell or give away. In the case at hand, the landowner's share contractually belonged to that landowner all along. The sharecropper need not tithe it because it never was his (v.C.6:1, v.D.6:7, 8-9, 10, 12). The case of a gentile land owner is special. Since gentiles are not deemed validly to own property within the land of Israel, the Israelite sharecropper of a gentile must tithe all of the harvest, as though it were from his own field (v.C.6:2).

Group members must determine who is trustworthy to state that produce in the marketplace already has been fully tithed. Yavneans hold that most testimony that food has been tithed may be accepted. Ushans, by contrast, provide a theory of evidence that tests the probability that the testimony is reliable. If testimony may be checked through inquiry to a trusted source, it is accepted as true (iii.D.4:5). All agree, further, that if the individual receives no personal gain by claiming that produce has been tithed, his word may be accepted (iii.C.4:7, iii.D.4:6). A related problem occurs when a haber gives an untrusted person food to prepare for the haber's own meal. The haber must tithe the food that he hands over for preparation, lest the individual take it and eat it himself. This means of course that the haber must tithe a second time, when the prepared dish is served, in case it contains food other than that which the haber originally tithed and handed over for preparation (ii.C.3:3E-G, 3:4, 5, 6).

Ushans develop a complete system for tithing produce about which there is a doubt whether or not it already is fully tithed. The assumption is that even those who do not tithe according to the rabbinic system do separate the Biblical priestly gift. The other offerings are designated in a manner described at iv.D.5:1. Ushans define the circumstances in which this tithing practice must be used. For instance, if the doubtfully tithed produce is subject to a further doubt whether or not it need be tithed at all (e.g., if it might have been grown as fodder), no additional tithing is required (i.C.1:1, i.D.1:3C-D). Another problem concerns a case of doubt in which tithes are to be designated in one batch on behalf of a different batch. If tithes already had been fully removed from one of the batches, this operation is invalid (Terumot, i.A.1:5). Ushans therefore detail cases in which one may assume that all of the produce involved derives from the same source, such that it is equally tithed or untithed (iv.C.5:3-5, 5:9, iv.D.5:6, 7G-K, 7L-P, 8).

II. The History of Tractate Demai

i. Produce that is not Tithed as Demai

The basic point of this tractate is that food about which there is a doubt whether or not it was completely tithed must undergo a secondary tithing process. This is to assure that all of the required agricultural gifts are in fact designated. The opening unit delineates the range of cases in which the secondary tithing procedure must be carried out. It holds that, if the doubtfully tithed produce does not clearly fit into the category of foods which must be tithed in the first place, we may dispense with the secondary tithing process. So long as there are two matters of doubt as to whether the food requires tithing, we rule leniently and do not require the separation of agricultural gifts. The question of whether or not food is subject to tithing at all pertains in particular to produce that might not be consumable by humans but which is, rather, intended as animal feed. The larger point thus is that the agricultural restrictions do not apply equally and automatically to all produce grown upon the land of Israel. These restrictions pertain only to produce that Israelites normally deem useful as food. If that usefulness is in doubt, and the produce might have been tithed already, then that produce may be eaten without the further separation of agricultural offerings. This qualification of the basic theorum of the tractate derives from the Ushan period, from which all of the rules of this unit derive.

A. Before 70
1:3G-I See i.D.1:3G-I.

B. The Time of Yavneh
_____

C. The Time of Usha

| 1:1 Ten types of produce are subject to a leniency: If they are _demai_ they are exempt from | The things listed here are inferior types of produce, not generally valued or |

being tithed. Judah qualifies three of the list's entries.

cultivated, and not commonly eaten. There is a question whether or not they meet the criteria of Maaserot, i.C.1:1 for being liable to tithes at all. If there is a possibility that they already have been tithed, we therefore do not bother to tithe them as demai. The attribution here to Judah as well as the dependence upon a principle in Maaserot attested only in Ushan times gives us sound grounds for placing this construction in the Ushan stratum.

1:2 Second tithe separated from demai-produce is not subject to the restrictions that normally apply to produce in the status of second tithe, listed at Maaser Sheni, v.D.4:3, iv.C.3:5, viii.D.5:12, iii.A.2:7 (with its developments at Yavneh and Usha). Meir and sages dispute the application to second tithe separated from demai of the rule at Maaser Sheni, i.D.1:5D-E, an apparently Ushan rule.

The point is the same as in the preceding entry. Since the second tithe separated from demai-produce might not have the sanctified status of true second tithe, it is not subject to the stringencies that normally apply to second tithe. Involving Meir and dependent upon rules found in the Ushan stratum of Maaser Sheni, this formulation is firmly placed in the Ushan stratum.

D. Unassigned
1:3A-B Fodder, flour for dressing hides and oil to be used in a lamp or for greasing utensils that is purchased from an am haares is not tithed as demai-produce.

The point is the same as a i.C.1:1. While normally edible, the items listed here are not going to be used as foods. Therefore we do not bother to tithe them as demai. We need be

certain only that produce
that we eat has been tithed.
There is no evidence that
this illustration of
M. 1:1's principle derives
from before the time of
Usha, to which that
principle is assigned.

1:3C-D Produce grown in Kezib
and northward is exempt from being
tithed as demai.

Kezib marks the northern
border of the land of
Israel. While it falls
within the Biblical borders
of the land, it is not in
practice like the rest of
the land, since few Jews
live there. We therefore
rule leniently and do not
require the tithing of
produce purchased in that
area if we do not know
whether or not it already
was tithed. This rule
depends upon the Yavnean
discussion of Kezib at
Hallah, iv.B.4:8, and it
clearly advances the larger
theory of the preceding
entry and i.C.1:1. The
rule therefore appears to
derive from Ushan times.

1:3E-F An am haares's dough
offering, mixtures of heave-
offering and unconsecrated
produce, produce purchased with
second tithe-coins and residue
of meal offerings are exempt from
tithing as demai.

Three of the four items are
eaten only by priests
anyway. Therefore there is
no need to separate heave-
offering for the priest.
The case of second tithe is
different, for this produce
is eaten by the householder
himself, in Jerusalem.

Presumably in a case of
doubt, heave-offering is not
separated from this produce
since, in all events, the
produce itself will be eaten
in the holy city, under the
restrictions that apply to
all holy food. The theory
of this rule is different
from that of the preceding
entries, such that there
are no grounds for inter-
preting its role within the
logical unfolding of the
law.

1:3G-I Spiced oil--The House of
Shammai declare it liable to
tithing as demai. The House of
Hillel deem it exempt.

The spiced oil will be
"consumed" by being used as
an unguent. The issue is
whether this mode of
consumption is comparable to
"eating," such that the oil
must be tithed as demai (=
Shammaites), or whether it
is comparable to the non-
food uses of produce listed
at i.D.1:3A-B, which do not
obligate tithing as demai
(= Hillelites). This is a
subtle clarification of an
issue that appears to derive
from Usha times (i.C.1:1
and i.D.1:3E-F). Indeed,
further discussion and
refinement of the Houses'
position takes place at
Usha (Simeon b. Eleazar, T.
1:24, and Nathan, T. 1:27).
This dispute therefore
appears to date from Ushan
times.

1:4A-G Demai-produce that has not
yet been tithed may be used in an
erub; they may recite a benediction
for it and invite others to recite
the communal grace after eating it;
they may separate tithes from it
naked and at twilight on the eve
of the Sabbath; and they may
separate second tithe from it
before first tithe.

There are two points. 1)
Untithed produce, demai is
is not strictly forbidden
for consumption. It therefore may be treated as other
edibles and used in an erub.
2) Since this produce may
already have been tithed,
the restrictions that apply
to the tithing of certainly
untithed produce do not
apply to it, e.g., the order
in which tithes are to be
separated (Terumot,
ii.D.3:6-7), or the
requirement of a blessing
(Terumot, i.D.1:6). In
light of these two points,
the larger theory of the
pericope is that demai
produce is treated more like
already-tithed food than it
is like untithed produce.
This theory is congruent
with ii.B.3:1A-B, ii.B.4:3
and iii.B.4:1, indicating
that the present rule may
derive from Yavnean times.

1:4H-I Oil with which the weaver
lubricates his fingers is liable
to tithing as demai. Oil that
the wool-comber puts on wool is
not liable.

The point is that of
i.D.1:3A-B and 1:3G-I. The
oil put in the wool is not
used as food and therefore
need not be tithed as demai.
What the weaver puts on his
fingers, by contrast, is
consumed as an ointment.
It therefore must be tithed
(= Shammaites, M. 1:3G-I).
Like the pericopae the issue
of which it parallels, this

anonymous rule presumably
derives from Ushan times.

2:1 Certain foods known to   This qualifies 1.D.1:3C-D.
derive from the land of Israel   Since these items surely
and commonly exported are subject   derive from the land of
to tithing as demai in every   Israel, they are clearly
place.   subject to tithes and, if in
                                     the status of demai, must be
                                     tithed as such. Like
                                     M. 1:3C-D, this rule must
                                     derive from Ushan times.
                                     This conclusion is supported
                                     by the post-Ushan gloss of
                                     this pericope at T. 2:1, in
                                     the name of Eleazar b. Yose.

ii. Tithing Produce that Leaves One's Possession

The unit introduces one of the central ideas of this
tractate, that an individual must take actions to prevent someone
else from transgressing the law. The Shammaites, ii.A.3:1C-H,
hold that a charity collector should give untithed food to those
who will tithe and tithed food to those known not to tithe. In
this way he assures that all individuals will eat tithed produce.
While the reliability of the attribution of this specific case to
the Shammaites is questionable, the idea the law expresses is
assumed and carried forward in Yavnean times. Yavneans hold that
one should not give untithed produce to any individual. This is
the case unless that produce might already have been tithed
(i.e., if it is in the status of demai), and unless it is certain
that the recipient will complete the required tithing process
(ii.B.3:1A-B). In Ushan times, strict adherence to these norms
defines an individual as "trustworthy regarding tithing," such as
to regulate and limit his interaction with all other Israelites.
Now the scrupulous individual must tithe everything he buys,
sells, eats or even picks up in the road and then drops. He
takes full responsibility for his own adherence to the law, as
well as for the adherence of others, insofar as he is able to
tithe food that they will, or might, eat. Only in the case of
well defined business relationships may the individual refrain
from tithing, e.g., if he is a wholesaler, since, by law, the

retailer will tithe (ii.C.2:4, 5). In these cases as well as in
day-to-day social contact with the people around him (see
ii.C.3:4-6), the individual's actions are limited by his desire
to follow the law and are controlled by his concomitant
responsibility not to be party to a situation in which others
might transgress.

This unit thus charts the development of a corpus of laws
that only in Ushan times is made to define membership in a sect
devoted to tithing and cultic cleanness (ii.C.2:3). This fact is
of central importance when we consider that, in the period
between two and three hundred years before Ushan times, the
Pharisees, later seen as the founders of the rabbinic movement,
likewise distinguished themselves within the rest of the people
of Israel on the basis of their observance of tithing
restrictions and rules of purity. It appears clear that,
whatever the character of the Pharisaic table fellowship, its
rules of conduct and modes of self-definition were not taken over
by the authorities cited in Mishnah. The materials before us
have only a very general legal foundation in the period before
70. Yavneans, and primarily Ushans, by contrast, are busy
defining proper adherence to the laws of tithing and purity.
Their definition, not one inherited from pre-rabbinic times,
ultimately defines membership, as a haber, in the rabbinic sect
composed of individuals who are trusted to tithe all produce and
to eat their own secular food in a state of cultic cleanness.

A.   Before 70

3:1C-H The House of Shammai: The issue does not involve
Charity-collectors give what is demai-produce, but rather
tithed to those who do not tithe, food that the charity-
and give what is not tithed to collector knows is or is
those known to tithe. Sages: not tithed. The question
Distribution of charity is done is whether one takes action
indiscriminately. to avoid a violation of the
law (= the Shammaites), or
simply does nothing
(= sages). Since the
specific question discussed
here still is moot at Usha
(see Meir, T. 3:17), it is
unlikely that it is
authentic in the mouth of

the Shammaites. Still, the underlying belief of the Shammaites, that one should prevent others from transgressing, is a basic datum of this tractate (see e.g., ii.B.3:1A-B, ii.C.2:2-5 and ii.D.3:2). It must derive from early in the development of this tractate. Cf., Maaser Sheni, vi.C.5:1.[4]

B. The Time of Yavneh

3:1A-B Demai-produce may be fed to the poor or transient guests. Gamaliel would feed his workers demai-produce.

The theory here is very different from that found in the Ushan stratum, which requires the individual to tithe all produce that leaves his possession.

C. The Time of Usha

2:2 One who undertakes to be trust-worthy tithes what he eats, sells or purchases and does not accept the hospitality of an am haares. Judah: He may accept hospitality.

One who is "trustworthy" scruplously observes all of the rules of tithing. Produce purchased from such a person therefore is not considered demai. This definition is assigned to the Ushan stratum on the basis of Judah's disputing gloss.

2:3 One who undertakes to be a haber does not sell any produce to an am haares, does not buy from him wet produce (which is susceptible to uncleanness), does not accept the hospitality of an am haares or offer hospitality to an am haares who is wearing his own, unclean, clothes. Judah:

The haber differs from one who is "trustworthy" in that, in addition to following the tithing laws, he is careful to consume unconsecrated food in a state of cleanness, as though he were a priest eating heave-offering. He

Also--he should not raise small cattle, make many vows, defile himself through contact with the dead or minister in the house of study (alt.: banquet hall).

further does not aid others who transgress. Judah suggests four more requirements, only one of which--the rule regarding corpse uncleanness--has to do with the purity laws. As at M. 2:2, his attestation serves to place this unit in Ushan times. T. provides further evidence of the late provenance of this discussion. See T. 2:2 and 3 (Meir), T. 2:5 (Yose b. Judah), T. 2:7 (Simeon), T. 2:9 (Meir, Judah, Simeon and Joshua b. Qorha), T. 2:10 (Simeon), T. 2:13 (Abba Saul), T. 2:14 (Simeon b. Gamaliel) and T. 2:17 (Simeon b. Eleazar). Cf., the Houses at T. 2:12, apparently pseudepigraphically speaking speaking on a secondary issue of the type prevalent in Ushan times.

2:4   Bakers must separate from demai that they sell only heave-offering of the tithe and dough offering. They need not separate second tithe. Retailers must separate all three offerings. Wholesalers need not remove any of them. They may sell demai-produce.

In accordance with M. 2:2, the individual should assure that what he sells is completely tithed. If the produce is demai that means separating heave-offering of the tithe, dough offering and second tithe. (The am haares from whom the produce originally was purchased is assumed to have separated heave-offering.) The baker need not separate second tithe, however, since

it would be extremely
burdensome for him to have
to take large quantities of
second tithe-dough, or
coins, to Jerusalem to eat
there. Wholesalers sell to
retailers, who will
themselves tithe the
produce. The wholesaler
himself therefore is exempt.
This unit is assigned to
Usha because of the
continuation of the issue,
in the following entry,
which clearly attests the
whole to Ushan times.

2:5 Meir: Whatever usually is
sold in bulk always is subject to
the rule for bulk sales (M. 2:4),
even if it should be sold in a
small quantity. The same applies
to what normally is sold in small
quantity that is sold in bulk.
Yose: Baskets of figs, grapes
and vegetables are sold without
tithing.

This is secondary to the
material in the preceding
entry. Meir wants to avoid
confusion that could result
in produce's being tithed
twice or not at all. Yose's
point is the same as that
made before. T. indicates
further discussion of the
issues of these pericopae to
have taken place in Ushan
times. See T. 3:10-11
(Meir, Nehemiah), T. 3:12
(Ishmael b. Yohanan b.
Beroqah and Simeon b.
Gamaliel) and T. 3:13
(Meir).

3:3E-G Anything that a man is not
permitted to sell as demai he is
not permitted to send to his friend
as demai. Yose permits if the

Sending is equivalent to
selling, such that the rules
of ii.C.2:4 and 5 apply.
Yose's comment, which serves

produce is certainly untithed and he informs him.

as a second reason for assigning this rule to Usha, is self evident. If the receiver of the produce is informed that it is untithed, he will not be mislead and transgress by not himself tithing. Secondary discussion, at T. 3:14, likewise is in the name of an Ushan, Simeon b. Gamaliel.

3:4 One who brings tithed produce to a Samaritan or am haares--when he reclaims the produce it is deemed still to be certainly tithed. If he leaves produce with a gentile, when he reclaims it it is deemed either to have been exchanged with produce of an am haares, such that it is demai, or with the gentile's own produce, such that it is certainly untithed. Simeon: It always is treated as demai.

The am haares and Samaritan are assumed to respect the other person's scruples and to treat his tithed produce with care, so as not to mix it with other, untithed or or doubtfully tithed, produce. The gentile is not assumed to be careful in this way. The continuation of this discussion, in the following entries, likewise is assigned to Ushan authorities.

3:5 One who gives produce to an innkeeper to prepare for him tithes what he gives and that which he receives back. Yose: He tithes only what he receives.

The innkeeper is suspected of exchanging the guest's produce for food of inferior quality. Therefore the guest must tithe before eating. The anonymous notion, that he also must tithe what he gives over, is based upon ii.C.2:2. Yose disagrees in this case and holds that we need not take responsibility for tithing if the other person will acquire the untithed produce

through deceit. Dependence
upon M. 2:2 and the
attribution to Yose provide
firm grounds for placing
this rule at Usha.

3:6 One who gives his tithed
produce to his mother-in-law, an
am haares, to prepare for him
tithes what he gives her and what
he receives in return. Judah
explains why.

As Judah explains, the
mother-in-law is suspected
of substituting her own,
better, produce if that of
the owner is spoiled or
ruined while she is
preparing it. The point is
the same as at M. 3:5, and
we thus have good reason for
placing this rule in Ushan
stratum.

D. Unassigned

3:2 He who trims away vegetable-
leaves to lighten his load should
tithe them before throwing them
away. If he purchased vegetables
and wishes to return them, he
should first tithe them.

The individual must tithe
produce that he owns and
that leaves his possession,
lest someone else take it
and eat without tithing.
Reflecting the concerns of
ii.C.2:2, these rules
persumably date to the
Ushan period. The first is
attested to that period by.
Yose, T. 4:2.

3:3A-D One who finds produce on
the road and takes it to eat but
then decides to put it down must
tithe. If he took it but did
not intend to eat it, he need not
tithe.

The concern is the same as
in the preceding entry.
What this rule adds is that
intention is efficacious in
determining whether or not
produce is deemed food, such
that it is subject to the
tithing laws at all. Like
M. 3:2, this item presumably
derives from Ushan times.

iii.   Believing Those Who Are Not Normally Trusted

An individual who is scrupulous about eating properly tithed foods must be able to determine who he may trust to prepare food for his consumption.   His relationship with other haberim presents no problem.   They follow the same rules that he does. But Mishnah is clear that the haber lives primarily among individuals who are not trusted to tithe.   The question is under what circumstances the haber may accept the claim of one of these people to have tithed or to know individuals who do properly tithe.   The problem receives minimal attention in Yavnean times. Yavnean authorities state that, in a case of necessity, the word of one who normally is not trusted may be accepted.   On the Sabbath, for instance, the haber may accept testimony that food he purchased before the holy-day was tithed.   Since he may not tithe on the Sabbath, the alternative would be not to eat.   After the Sabbath, however, the haber must tithe.   It no longer is necessary to trust the am haares's word, and therefore the haber may not do so (iii.B.4:1).

This Yavnean approach is logically weak, for it declares that the acceptability of testimony depends upon extenuating circumstances, not upon whether or not the testimony is likely to be true.   Ushan legislation corrects this problem by giving criteria for judging the intrinsic reliability of testimony.   We trust an individual who will not gain from his words (iii.C.4:7, iii.D.4:6) or whose testimony can be verified (iii.D.4:5).   In this way Ushans develop clear and logical standards for relationships between those who always properly tithe and those who do not.

A.   Before 70

_____

B.   The Time of Yavneh

4:1 He who purchases produce from one who is not trustworthy to tithe inquires of him on the Sabbath and may eat the produce if the vendor states that it indeed has been tithed.   But after the Sabbath the man must tithe before eating the produce.   Simeon of

The two cases make the same point.   In an emergency situation--i.e, if the individual cannot eat because tithing is forbidden on the Sabbath, or if all of his produce will be deemed to take on the status of

Shezur: If heave-offering of the tithe separated from demai-produce falls back into the batch, one may ask the vendor whether or not the produce already had been tithed and may accept his word.

heave-offering because it has been mixed with heave-offering of the tithe-- we rely on the word of one who normally is not trusted regarding the tithing laws. The concept is assigned to Yavneh on the basis of the attribution of this theory to Simeon of Shezur along with the Ushan development of these concerns at T. 5:2 (Rabbi and Simeon b. Gamaliel) at iii.C.4:7.

C. The Time of Usha
4:3 Eliezer: One need not designate poorman's tithe from demai-produce. Sages: He must designate it but need not separate it.

Eliezer holds that since the tithe will not be distributed anyway, we may dispense as well with the designation. Sages require the designation, so that the tithing procedure for demai-produce will formally parallel that for certainly untithed produce. Since this Eliezer is attentive to the extenuating circumstance, that the tithe will not be distributed anyway, I assume I assume that it is an Ushan Eliezer, not the Yavnean Eliezer b. Hyrcanus, who consistently refuses to take into account extenuating facts. See e.g., Terumot, iv.B.8:1-3.

4:7 Ass-drivers who entered a city and made mutually beneficial claims are not believed. Judah: They are believed.

The anonymous view holds that the individuals are in collusion, each recommending the other's produce. This

is parallel to the view of
Rabbi, T. 4:30. Judah holds
that, while we may not
accept an individual's
testimony concerning
himself, we in all events
rely upon his statements
concerning someone else.
Judah presumably assumes
that, if the individual
wished to lie, he would have
made up something to benefit
himself directly. This
same opinion occurs in the
mouth of Simeon b. Gamaliel,
T. 4:40. It develops the
Yavnean concern of
iii.B.4:1. Both substance
and authority cited therefore provide grounds for
placing this at Usha.

D. Unassigned

4:2 By means of a vow, someone
not deemed trustworthy in the
matter of tithing compels his
friend, who observes the laws
of tithes, to eat with him on
the Sabbath. During the first
Sabbath the friend may eat with
him, so long as the host states
that the food has been properly
tithed. In subsequent weeks,
the friend may not rely upon the
host's word, but must himself
tithe.

The case is parallel in
principle to iii.B.4:1. The
individual who tithes is in
a position in which he has
little choice but to rely on
the other person's word. He
is allowed to do so. We
assume that in subsequent
weeks the guest will have
the opportunity to see to
the tithing of the food
before the onset of the
Sabbath. Since there is no
real need to do so, he no
longer may, trust the other
individual's claim.

4:4 One who designates heave-
offering of the tithe or poorman's
tithe during the week should not
actually separate and distribute
them on the Sabbath. But he may
feed them to a priest or poor
person who regularly eats with
him on the Sabbath, provided that
he informs them that they are
eating tithe.

The separation and
distribution of agricultural
offerings is an act distinct
from the designation of
these things. The
separation and distribution
therefore may not be carried
out on the Sabbath. If the
recipients of these
offerings eat at the
individual's house, there is
no physical separation.
This procedure therefore is
allowed on the Sabbath.
There is no way of placing
this unattested material
within the unfolding of the
tractate's law.

4:5 If one says to someone who
is not deemed trustworthy to
separate tithes, "Purchase produce
for me from someone who is
trustworthy"--the agent is not
later believed. If he told him,
"Purchase for me from so-and-so"
--the agent is believed.

To begin with we do not
trust the agent regarding
matters of tithing.
Therefore we cannot rely on
him to have carried out
general instructions to buy
from someone who tithes.
But whether or not he
purchased from a specific
individual can be verified,
such that in the second case
we have every reason to
trust him. The Ushan, Yose,
attests this principle to
Ushan times, T. 5:3.

4:6 He who enters a city and asks,
"Who here is trustworthy"--someone
who says, "I am," is not believed.
But if he names someone else, he
is believed. If the person who is
named then sends the buyer back to

The principle operative here
is stated explicitly by
Simeon b. Gamaliel, T. 4:30.
We do not believe a man's
testimony concerning himself
with regard to a matter in

the original individual, he too
is believed.

which he is suspect. We do
however rely upon his
testimony concerning
someone else. Like the
preceding entry, this one
presumably derives from
Ushan times. It is parallel
to the view assigned to
Judah, iii.C.4:7.

iv. Separating Tithes from Distinct Batches of Produce

Even individuals who do not separate all of the required
agricultural gifts might separate certain of the offerings. The
problem is how the haber goes about removing the rest of the
required tithes. He must be careful not to separate offerings
that already were removed (see Terumot, i.B.1:5). Yet he also
may not risk leaving any of the required offerings in the
produce. A solution to this problem is developed in the Ushan
stratum, where we also find a complete strategy for tithing
demai-produce. Important for our historical evaluation of the
Division of Agriculture is the fact that, as in unit i of this
tractate, definition of and legislation for a category of produce
called demai occurs very late in the formation of the law.

A. Before 70

_____

B. The Time of Yavneh

_____

C. The Time of Usha
5:3 Meir: One who buys bread
from a baker who is not trusted
concerning tithes may separate
tithes from warm bread on behalf
of cold and from diverse molds.
Judah forbids, lest the wheat
derives from different sources
and some already has been
tithed. Simeon forbids with
regard to heave-offering of the

This rule depends upon
Terumot, i.B.1:5. Tithes
may not be separated from
produce that is liable
on behalf of produce that is
not liable, and vice versa.
Meir simply holds that all
of the baker's produce will
have derived from the same
source, such that we need

tithe but permits with regard to dough-offering.

not worry about this prohibition. Judah's view is as given. Simeon agrees with Meir, but notes that, since the produce did not become suspectible to dough offering until it was made into dough, all of this baker's dough will be equally liable to that offering.

5:4 Meir: If he purchased bread from a bread store, he must separate tithes from each mold individually. Judah: From one mold for all, except in the case of a monopolist.

In the case of the bread store, the wheat certainly derives from different sources, such that Meir wishes tithes to be separated from each individual loaf. Judah's rule for the bread store inexplicably contradicts his view of M. 5:3.

5:5 He who purchases from a poor man, or a poor man to whom they gave slices of bread, separates tithes from each item individually. If it is dates or dried figs, he takes tithes from the whole mass. Judah: This applies only if each individual gift of produce was large.

The first rule makes the same point as the preceding two entries. In the case of the figs, the mixture of the produce from the different sources is uniform, such that each part of it is equally susceptible to or exempt from the separation of tithes. Judah requires large quantities, so that we can be certain that there is an even mixture. Dependent upon the preceding rules and again citing Judah, this pericope is firmly placed in the Ushan stratum.

5:9 They separate tithes from gentiles the produce of Israelites on behalf of the produce of gentiles or Samaritans or <u>vice versa</u>. They separate tithes from the produce of one Samaritan on behalf of the produce of a different Samaritan. Eleazer (alt.: Eliezer) prohibits.

Gentiles do not tithe at all and Samaritans do not tithe that which they sell in the market. Since all of this produce surely is subject to tithes,[5] tithes may be taken from the Israelite-batch on behalf of the gentile- or Samaritan-owned produce. The issue that concerns Eleazar is whether or not Samaritans indeed do not tithe what they bring to the market. If some do, we must be careful not to take tithes from one Samaritan's produce for another's. While the attribution here is not unambiguous, the commonality of this unit's issue with that of the other, Ushan, materials of this unit provides solid grounds for assignment to Usha. See also T. 5:21-23.

D. Unassigned

5:1 He who purchases a loaf of bread from a baker who is not trusted concerning tithes, how does he tithe it? + Formula for the tithing of <u>demai</u>-produce.

We assume that even one who is not trustworthy has separated heave-offering. The purchaser therefore must now separate produce sufficient for first tithe, heave-offering of the tithe and dough offering. Second tithe is designated and redeemed with coins. While the notion that <u>demai</u> is produce from which we can be certain only that heave-offering was separated is a fundamental datum of the

tractate, there is no
evidence that this
description of how such
produce is to be tithed
derives from an early
period. Other specifics of
how demai-produce is tithed
are moot at Usha, iv.C.5:3,
4 and 5, indicating that the
present description
probably is late.

5:2 He who wishes to separate
from fully untithed produce
heave-offering and heave-
offering of the tithe together,
in a single act of separation,
does as follows...

The problem is the same as
in the preceding entry.

5:6 One who purchases from a
wholesale dealer and returns
and purchases more must separate
tithes individually for each
batch. The wholesaler is
believed that the food derives
from the same supply, such that
tithes may be separated once
for all of the produce.

The point is the same made
at iv.C.5:4-5, placing this
rule in the Ushan period.
The second rule that,
since he receives no
benefit, the wholesaler is
believed, likewise appears
to be Ushan. See iii.C.4:7
and iii.D.4:5 and 6.

5:7G-K One who purchases from a
householder and returns and
purchases more may take tithes
at once for all of the produce.

Since the householder sells
only his own produce, there
is no issue of some of the
produce's already being
tithed and other not. Like
the preceding entry, this
presumably derives from
Usha.

5:7L-P If a householder in the
market-place is selling his own
produce, they separate tithes from
one item for all. If he is selling

The points of M. 5:6 and
M. 5:7G-K are correlated as
a single rule. Dependent
upon those Ushan laws, this

produce from the gardens of others,
each item must be tithed
individually.

construction can derive from
no earlier than Ushan times.

5:8 If he purchases fully
untithed produce from two different
vendors, he may take tithes from
one portion on behalf of the other.

The rule is rather obvious
on the basis of what has
preceded.

5:10 They may separate heave-
offering from produce grown in a
perforated pot on behalf of
produce grown in the ground and
vice versa. If the pot was not
perforated, his separation is
valid, but he must separate
heave-offering again.

A perforated pot is like the
earth, such that produce
which grows in it is subject
to tithes. What grows in
an unperforated pot is not
subject. A subtle continuation of the issues
discussed at iv.C.5:3-5 and
9, these rules are Ushan or
later.

5:11 If one separated heave-
offering from demai-produce for
other demai-produce, or from
demai for what is certainly
untithed, it is valid, but he
must separate heave-offering
again.

Since demai-produce is
assumed throughout this
tractate not to be subject
to the separation of heave-
offering at all, the point
of this pericope is unclear.
See Sarason, Demai, pp. 198-
200.

v. Tithing Commonly Owned Produce

The present materials qualify the principle of unit ii, that
one should tithe whatever leaves his possession. We now learn
that this responsibility extends only to produce that the
individual actually owns. A sharecropper, for instance, need not
tithe the portion of the crop that belongs to the landowner. He
incurs responsibility to tithe only if he pays the field-owner's
share out of his own personal produce, for example, using food
that was grown in a different field. Since that produce belongs
to the sharecropper himself, he must tithe before giving it away
(v.C.6:1). The sharecropper also must tithe all the produce if
the landowner is a gentile. The non-Jew's ownership of property

in the land of Israel is not recognized, such that the share-cropper himself is deemed the land's true owner (v.C.6:2).

These rules, which constitute the central focus of this unit, derive from Ushan times. Placement there is on the basis of attributions and the material's clear relationship to the Ushan principle of unit ii. The Yavnean material in unit v addresses a different issue. Yavneans dispute whether an owner or sharecropper has preemptive rights to agricultural gifts that derive from the common produce and that are appropriate to him. For example, may a landowner who is a priest take for himself all of the heave-offering that derives from produce grown in the field (v.B.6:4)? Unlike in the Ushan materials just described, Yavneans do not recognize a sharp distinction between what is owned by the landowner and what belongs to the sharecropper. The weight of the law therefore is that the field's owner may take whatever tithes are appropriate to him. The particular issue, however, remains moot in the Ushan period (v.C.6:5), such that the relationship between it and the other materials in the Ushan stratum is not clear.

The impression that work on the specific topic of demai-produce is confined to the period of Usha is reenforced by the final materials of this tractate, v.D.7:1-5. Apparently deriving from Ushan times, these rules provide further central details of the tithing procedure for produce about which there is a doubt whether or not it previously was tithed.

A. Before 70

6:6 The Shammaites say: One may sell olives only to a haber, who is trusted to maintain them in a state of cleanness. The Hillelites say: Also to one who separates tithes, even if he is not trustworthy regarding matters of cleanness.	There is no evidence that this issue arises before Ushan times, when the definition of the haber first is discussed. The Hillelite position is out of phase with the law of this tractate as a whole. It assumes that the individual will sell the olives before separating tithes from them, a flagrant violation of ii.C.2:2, with which the Shammaites, by contrast, accord.[6]

B. The Time of Yavneh

6:3 A priest or Levite who sharecropped a field of an Israelite--they divide between them the heave-offering and tithes just as they divide the other produce. Eliezer: No. The heave-offering or tithes belong to the priest or Levite.

The question of the division of produce grown in a share-cropped field is initiated here and, at Usha, will be developed for the issue of the tithing of the produce, v.C.6:1 and 2.

6:4 An Israelite who sharecropped in the field of a priest or Levite--the heave-offering and tithes belong to the field's owner. Ishmael: If a provincial share-cropped a field for a Jerusalemite, the second tithe belongs to the latter individual. Sages: The sharecropper himself may bring it to Jerusalem and eat it.

The field's owner has preemptive rights which allow him to take produce that is specifically appropriate to him. Sages disagree concerning the the case of the second tithe, for the reason given. Furthering the issue introduced above, and attested by Ishmael, this pericope clearly belongs in the Yavnean stratum. It receives further development at v.C.6:5.

C. The Time of Usha

6:1 One who sharecrops a field may give the landowner his share out of untithed produce. If he leases the field, he pays the rental out of produce from which heave-offering already has been separated, at the threshing floor, but he need not remove tithes. Judah: If he gave him produce of a different kind or from a different field, he must separate heave-offering and tithes.

The theory of ii.C.2:2, 4, 3:3E-G, 5 and 6, that one must take actions to assure that another individual does not eat untithed produce, does not apply in these cases. In the case of the sharecropper, the landowner's share is deemed his possession all along. The sharecropper therefore need not tithe it. The rent paid by the leasee, likewise, is a set amount of produce that belongs to the leasor

all along. Heave-offering
must be separated at the
usual time, at the threshing
floor, but the leasee is not
responsible for paying the
tithes. Judah clarifies
the point. Produce paid
from a different kind or
from some other field is
fully the possession of
the sharecropper. If that
individual is a haber he
must tithe it before turning
it over. Qualifying an
Ushan principle and attested
by Judah, this rule is firmly
placed in the Ushan stratum.

6:2 If land is leased from a
gentile, heave-offering and tithes
must be separated from the produce
paid as rent. Judah: He who
sharecrops a field once owned by
his father but now possessed by a
gentile pays the gentile's share
with fully tithed produce.

The gentile's ownership of
property in the land of
Israel is not recognized.
It is as though the land
were owned by the Israelite
tennant farmer himself.
Therefore all produce which
is paid out from the field
must be tithed, in
accordance with the rules
of section ii. For the same
reasons given in the
preceding entry, these rules
are firmly placed in the
Ushan stratum. Discussion
of these issues in T. also
is in the names of Ushans:
Simeon b. Gamaliel (T. 6:1),
Simeon (b. Yohai, T. 6:2)
and Meir (T. 6:3). Cf.,
T. 6:7, which has Yose b.
Meshullam and Nathan in
the name of Eleazar Hisma,
on a parallel issue.

6:5 He who sharecrops olive trees for oil--they divide between them the tithes as well as the unconsecrated produce. Judah: If the owner is a priest or Levite, the tithes belong to the owner.

This is a secondary development of v.B.6:4. Once the crop has been processed for oil, the field-owner no longer has a preemptive right to take that which he wants. Now he and the sharecropper equally divide the tithes. Judah disagrees with this reasoning and follows the rule given at v.B.6:4.

D. Unassigned

6:7 Two men who gathered their grapes into a single winepress-- the one of them who separates tithes removes the required offerings from his own share of the wine as well as for his grapes, wherever they might be in the mixture.

The individual who tithes is responsible only to tithe that which belongs to him. Therefore he tithes the wine that he takes from the press. But he also must be certain that his grapes, which he brought to the press, have been tithed. Otherwise it is as though he gave untithed produce to the other person. This, we know, is forbidden (section ii). Since this issue is derivative of a theory propounded at Usha (ii.C), and found here as well in the Ushan stratum (v.C.6:1, 2, 5), it must derive from Ushan times.

6:8-9 Joint owners of a field-- the one who tithes may say to the other, "You take the produce in such-and-such a place and I will take the produce elsewhere." But

Each of the men has an equal share in all of the crops. So as to prevent the one who tithes   from   needing   to separate the offerings

they may not divide by type of
produce.

required for all of the
produce, he designates a
specific share of the crop
as his own. He need tithe
it alone. Since they have
equal ownership of each kind
of produce, however, they
cannot divide the produce
by kind. Taking barley, for
instance, would not exhaust
the ownership of wheat of
the one who tithes. Like
the preceding entry, this
derivative problem derives
from Ushan times.

6:10   Same case as M. 6:8-9
for a proselyte and his gentile
brother.

The theory is the same as in
the preceding: The
individual may designate
certain property to be his
sole possession and leave
the rest as the property of
the joint owner.

6:11   One who sells produce in
Syria and says, "It is from the
land of Israel," is believed.
If he subsequently said, "It is
tithed," he is believed, for the
mouth that forbade is the mouth
that permitted.

The pericope is substantively
unrelated to the present
context. It fits topically
in section iv, on conditions
under which we believe those
who normally are not trusted.
It does not however depend
upon or carry forward the
specific theory of any of
the material in that section,
such that placing it in the
logical unfolding of the
law is impossible.

6:12   A haber who makes a purchase
part of which is for an am haares
may give the am haares his share
without tithing it. But if,

The theory is the same as at
M. 6:8-9. The haber has
ownership of, and need
tithe, only that which he

once he determined what portion
was for the am haares, the
produce became mixed up, the haber
must tithe all of the items.

designates for himself.
But once he makes the
designation, it is binding
and cannot be changed.
Like M. 6:8-9 this belongs
in the Ushan stratum.

7:1-5 Description of the tithing
procedure for individuals who do
not trust those who have invited
them for a meal, for laborers, and
for those who purchase from
Samaritans. The point is that
the oral designation valdidly
can be made the day before the
actual separation of the required
offerings.

This differs from the
description at iv.D.5:1-2
only in that here the
individual is unable to
measure out and separate the
required tithes at the same
time that he recites the
designation-formula. The
material at M. 5:1-2 appears
to be Ushan, and there
likewise is no evidence
that M. 7:1-5 was known
before Ushan times.
Discussion in T. is in the
name of Ushans, Judah
(T. 8:5), Yose, Meir, Judah
and Simeon (T. 8:6-7) and
Yose (T. 8:12).

7:6 A designation of the tithes
required of one batch to be in a
different batch is valid. If he
said, "The tithes of this one are
in that one and vice versa,"
only the first batch is tithed.
If he said, "The tithes of each
are designated in the other,"
tithes validly have been designated
for both.

This development of the
preceding discussion of the
proper formula for
designating tithes
presumably derives from the
Ushan stratum. Each
aspect of the individual's
oral designation is effective immediately upon its
being uttered. Thus in the
middle case, as soon as he
states that the tithes
required of the first batch
are in the second, the first
batch is fully tithed. It
no longer can be used as a

source of the tithes
required of the second
batch. This problem does
not arise in the other two
cases described.

7:7 Produce from which heave-   The problem is of the same
offering has been separated and   sort introduced in the
produce from which heave-offering   preceding entries.
has not yet been separated that
became mixed together--how does
one separate heave-offering and
tithes from the mixture? Same
problem for case in which fully
tithed produced is mixed with
first tithe and the individual
needs to separate heave-offering
of the tithe.

7:8 He who had ten rows   While thematically different
containing ten jugs of wine each,   from what has preceded, the
and said, "One outside row is   issue--taking tithes only
made first tithe," and it is not   from produce that is subject
known which row it is, takes two   to the specific offerings--
jugs at diagonal corners, etc.   remains the same. I assume
                                        that, along with the
                                        preceding entries, this
                                        derives from Ushan times.

III. Conclusion
       Distinguished for their adherence to the laws of tithing and
cultic purity, the Pharisees from the period before 70 generally
are regarded as the forbears of Mishnah's rabbis. It therefore
is surprising that, in Tractate Demai, materials from the period
before 70 are particularly scarce. For this tractate 1) defines
a group of individuals who tithe and 2) regulates the relations
between those people and others who do not follow the
agricultural restrictions. These are exactly those matters that
we believe concerned the Pharisees most. Yet only a single,
very general, comment of any importance may be traced back to the
House of Shammai. They state that each individual is responsible
to prevent another person from transgressing. As we have seen,

this one rule hardly can be said to account for the large corpus of law that, in the Ushan stratum of this tractate, sets out the requirements for living a life dedicated to those ideals assumed to have been upheld, in the period before 70, by the Pharisees.

The absence of rules from the period before 70 has important implications for our understanding of rabbinic intellectual history. It implies that, whatever the claims of later rabbinic authorities, the early rabbinic movement did not inherit and make use of a substantial corpus of law and tradition deriving from the Pharisees. So far as the important evidence of Tractate Demai, and, in fact, the Division of Agriculture as a whole, indicates, early rabbinic legislation does not take up and develop in concrete ways principles developed while the Temple stood. The interests and concerns of the Pharisees and later rabbis may well have been similar. As for specific laws, however, the rabbinic movement began afresh. Later rabbinic masters presumably claimed Pharisaic lineage so as to substantiate their claim to be authoritative teachers within the people of Israel. In doing this they adopted as their ancestors the group that non-rabbinic and rabbinic sources after 70 agree had had the greatest power and esteem among the people. The later rabbinic movement's description of its origins thus is designed to lend authority to a movement that, as this tractate's description of general Israelite tithing practices shows, had little power on its own to impose its will upon the nation as a whole.[7]

CHAPTER FOUR

KILAIM

I. Introduction

The tractate concerns the Scriptural prohibitions against commingling different kinds of plants, animals and fibers. Based upon Lev. 19:19 and Dt. 22:9-11's demand that different species be kept separate, the tractate questions what constitutes a species and asks how different classes of things are to be kept separate from one another. The point is that God created the world in an orderly manner. These rules assure that, in using the resources of that world, humans will maintain it in a proper state of orderliness. Notably, in the priestly conception that stands behind Lev. 19:19, order is a precondition for holiness. In Tractate Kilaim, Mishnah's authorities thus describe in concrete terms how Israelite farmers are to raise their crops in conformity with the world's original order. By doing this, Israelites prepare the world for a sanctification by God comparable to the act of consecration that completed the earth's original creation (Mandelbaum, p. 3).

The most basic question left open by Scripture concerns how different species are to be kept separate. This issue attracts the attention of the Houses and continues to constitute the focus of concern through the conclusion of the formation of the tractate's law. This is not to say, however, that the tractate is the creation of the early period. For while its issue is known by the time of the Houses, the proposed answer shifts dramatically in the period of Usha. Ushans begin anew to probe the issue addressed by previous generations of authorities. As a result, the tractate presents two strikingly different answers to the question of how the Israelite is to grow crops in conditions of holiness. These two answers correspond to divergent notions of what ultimately constitutes the source of holiness in the world.

The Houses and Yavnean authorities define a species in light of botanical characteristics. They therefore hold that Scripture's law has been transgressed whenever these different classes have been sown together within a single, geographically defined, field. The early authorities are concerned solely with the

107

physical character of the mixture of different classes. This means that they understand orderliness to be a preordained condition of the world. By abiding by <u>natural</u> barriers among different kinds of plants, animals and fibers, and through attentiveness to the <u>geographical</u> boundaries that separate one plot of land from another, the Israelite maintains the orderly-- and therefore holy--state in which God originally created the world.

Pervasive before 70 and at Yavneh, the notion that the world contains within itself a preestablished order is abandoned at Usha. Ushans instead hold that, through intentions and perceptions, Israelites themselves impose order upon the world. Their attitude towards different types of plants determines whether they are to be called Diverse Kinds. Their perceptions of different crops growing together in a single field establishes whether those foods have been planted as a confused, and there-therefore forbidden, mixture, or in an orderly, and hence permitted, pattern. According to Ushans, that is, the Israelite himself, "both defines what constitutes a class and determines how to keep the different classes distinct from one another. Man thus imposes upon an otherwise disorderly world limits and boundaries which accord with human perception of order and regularity... [W]hat appears to man as orderly becomes identified with the objective order of the world" (Mandelbaum, p. 1). In this view, then, Israelites themselves bring the potential for sanctification into an otherwise disordered world.

Before examining the specific rules through which each period's authorities make their point, let us quickly review the Scriptural foundations of the tractate.

> (Lev. 19:19) "You shall keep my statutes. You shall not let your cattle breed with a different kind; you shall not sow your field with two kinds of seed; nor shall there come upon you a garment of cloth made of two kinds of stuff."
> (Dt. 22:9-11) "You shall not sow your vineyard with two kinds of seed, lest the whole yield be forfeited to the sanctuary, the crop which you have sown and the yield of the vineyard. You shall not plow with an ox and an ass together. You shall not wear a mingled stuff, wool and linen together."

Both sources agree that it is forbidden to plant together two different kinds of crops (units i-iii in the following), to place together two different kinds of animals (unit iv) or to wear a garment made of different kinds of fibers (unit v). Mishnah's authorities ignore the discrepancy in the specific acts of commingling referred to by the separate sources. Instead they view the two passages together, so as to prohibit all of the acts of commingling referred to by Leviticus and Deuteronomy. With the focus of the tractate and its Scriptural origins clear, we now review in detail the formation of its law.

A. Kilaim Before 70

Dt. 22:9 states that one may not plant a vineyard with two kinds of seed. In the only material of this tractate going back to the period before 70, the Houses dispute the definition of a vineyard that is subject to Scripture's law (iii.A.4:1-3, 5, 6:1). Their argument concerns the number and configuration of vines that comprise a vineyard and the area of tillage deemed integral to that vineyard such that it may not be planted with a different kind.

B. Kilaim in the Time of Yavneh

The approach of the Houses is taken up by Yavneans, who do little to develop the basic issue established before 70. Like the Houses, Yavneans are concerned primarily with the definition of the specific areas of land that, because of their size, may be deemed autonomous of adjacent ground. Yavneans thus define the smallest area that may be called a separate field (ii.B.2:10) and suggest several configurations in which rows planted with different kinds of seeds are held to comprise distinct, and therefore permitted, areas (ii.B.3.3, 4, 6). The point is that, like the Houses, Yavneans are not concerned with the overall appearance of the area, but with its conformity to unvarying space requirements. The character of this formalistic approach is made clear at iii.B.4:8, where the Yavnean Hananiah b. Hakinai notes that the original layout of a vineyard, and not the way it appears at the present time, determines whether or not seed may be planted between the rows of vines.

The same formalistic attitude towards the defintion of a field informs the Yavnean approach to a case in which produce actually is planted as Diverse Kinds. Unlike Ushans, who, as we shall see, are careful to take into account the intentions of the farmer, Yavneans rule that even if Diverse Kinds are accidentally planted in a field, the second kind immediately must be destroyed (iii.B.5:7). If it is not, all of the produce will be rendered forbidden. Unlike later law, Yavneans countenance no delay on the part of the farmer.

Yavneans touch briefly on two other matters. They dispute whether or not plants that do not produce food are subject to the restrictions of Diverse Kinds (iii.B.5:8). The opinion of Eliezer, that they do not, appears to be normative within the Yavnean period itself. Yavneans rule that a vine growing upon part of a tree renders that part alone in the status of a trellis. Seed may not be planted under that part, which has the status of an area of tillage, but may be planted under the rest of the tree (iii.B.6:4). Ushans develop this rule to take into account the difference between a barren tree and a fruit tree. Their rule, as we shall see, takes into account the intentions of the farmer who trains a vine upon his tree.

Yavneans offer a small comment upon an area of law greatly developed in the Ushan period. They make explicit that the restriction of Lev. 19:19 and Dt. 22:11, that one should not wear a garment made of wool and linen together, indeed applies only to clothing. Mingled fabrics may however be used for other purposes, so long as they do not serve as a garment (v.B.9:3, v.D.9:4).

C. Kilaim in the Time of Usha

Ushans offer a new theory regarding the determination of what is forbidden under the restrictions of Diverse Kinds. They state that what matters is whether individuals who look at an area planted with several kinds of seed will perceive that area to be a confused mixture of different types of plants or whether they will view it as a logically mapped out grid of several distinct crops. What concerns Ushans, that is, is not the specifics of the size of any area of planting, but the perceptions of the Israelites who will look at it and who, on the basis of appearances, will determine whether or not the farmer has properly planted his fields.

This underlying attitude is found in each of the areas of law upon which Ushans touch. The tone of their work is set by their definition of what constitutes a Diverse Kind, i.C.1:1-3. Ushans claim that Diverse Kinds of seeds are defined on the basis of appearance, not botanical divisions. Different kinds of plants that look alike may therefore be planted together, for they will not give the appearance of being Diverse Kinds. This same approach is played out in Ushan materials concerning forbidden and permitted layouts of different kinds of crops. So long as the onlooker will be able to perceive a logical order in

the way the farmer planted his field, Ushans deem that planting
to be permitted. Moreover, they are unconcerned with the
specific amount of space each individual crop takes up (ii.C.2:7,
9, 3:1). Certain Ushans are even disposed to allowing Diverse
Kinds of seeds to be mixed together and planted. Their only
concern is that the secondary seed will be of a sufficiently
minimal quantity as not to give the field the outward appearance
of a confused mixture of different types of crops (ii.C.2:1-2).[1]
Finally, along these same lines, Ushans define a vineyard as any
group of vines that people in general call a vineyard
(iii.C.5:1). This is quite different from the approach of the
Houses, who gave specific requirements of number of vines and
their configuration.

The Ushan concern for appearances is brought to bear as well
in a case in which a farmer plants crops that are not Diverse
Kinds but that appear to comprise a forbidden combination. Since
onlookers will perceive the farmer to have transgressed, he
should not plant in such a manner (iii.C.7:2D-F). While the
farmer who does so anyway has not objectively transgressed and
therefore cannot be held culpable, Ushans insist that he should
in the first place not cause even the appearance of a sin.
Carried over and applied to the law of the seventh year of the
Sabbatical cycle, this Ushan idea accounts for the majority of
the materials in Tractate Shebiit.

According to Ushans, the perceptions and intentions of
Israelites are important as well in determining whether a field's
being planted with Diverse Kinds has caused all of the crop of
the field to become sanctified and forbidden for consumption.
Ushans hold that this occurs only if the farmer intends the
Diverse Kinds to grow in his field. If he does not, then even if
he maintains the illegal mixture for some time, for instance,
while waiting for the opportunity to rectify the matter, the
produce remains permitted (iii.D.5:6). This is quite different
from the Yavnean approach (iii.B.5:7), which requires the farmer
immediately to destroy the offending crop. The Ushan view leads
to the logical conclusion that an individual who plants a Diverse
Kind in his neighbor's field does not render forbidden all of the
produce of that field (iii.C.7:4-5, iii.D.7:6). So long as the
person who owns the field has not sanctioned the growth of the
secondary crop, the presence of that crop has no effect. Upon
discovering the offending plants, the field's owner need simply

destroy them, indicating that he does not desire the food they produce.

This same Ushan perspective is brought into play in a case in which the farmer trains vines upon a tree (iii.C.6:3, 5). If the tree is barren, the farmer clearly wishes to use it as a trellis. The whole area under the tree therefore is deemed an area of tillage and may not be sown. If, by contrast, a vine is planted under part of a fruit bearing tree, only the affected branches are deemed a trellis. The rest of the tree, clearly desired by the farmer for its fruit, retains the status of a tree, such that no area of tillage need be left under it. Grains may be planted there, and if they should be grown over by the vine, the vine needs simply to be cut back. It does not render the properly planted seed forbidden.

Ushans take up the Biblical prohibition against weaving a fabric of wool and linen. While the topic received only minor Yavnean attention, Ushans go ahead to define forbidden cloth (v.C.9:8, 9, 10) and, as before, make clear that, although the restriction applies only to wool and linen, one should be careful not to wear other mixtures that appear to be forbidden (v.D.9:2). The prominence for Ushans of appearances is indicated by their allowing the use of cloth that actually contains both wool and linen. This is permitted so long as the ratio of one to the other is such that the presence of a mixture is not apparent (v.D.9:1).[2] On this topic Ushans rule, finally, that in cases of ambiguity, the user's attitude determines whether or not a cloth object is deemed a garment (v.D.9:5-6).

A topic ignored in the earlier periods receives some attention at Usha. This concerns the mating or harnessing together of different kinds of animals (Lev. 19:19, Dt. 22:10). Again, Ushans concentrate upon appearances. They therefore rule that different kinds of animals may not be tied together in any way that looks as though they are harnessed to work as a team (iv.C.8:3, 4). This is the case even if, in actuality the animals are not working together. In a minor note, Ushans state that mixed breeds, such as mules, are deemed a kind unto themselves and may be harnessed together (iv.C.8:5).

II. The History of Tractate Kilaim

i. Mixtures that are Diverse Kinds

This unit concerns the definition of different types of produce or animals that are deemed heterogeneous, such that they may not be yoked, planted or grafted together. Two different theories are presented. The first theory is attributed to Ushan authorities. It holds that the criteria for determining Diverse Kinds is whether or not the types of produce look alike. According to this view, even if two kinds of produce are of distinct genuses, if they look alike, they may be planted together in a field. So long as people in general will not view the field as being planted with heterogeneous seeds, the field is not subject to the restrictions of Diverse Kinds. The second theory, occuring in anonymous material, shares the formalistic approach attributed elsewhere in this tractate only to Yavneans. It holds that appearances do not count, but that what matters, rather, is whether the plants are of the same, or distinct, species. If they are of distinct species, then no matter how alike they look, they may not be planted together.

A. Before 70

_____

B. The Time of Yavneh

_____

C. The Time of Usha
1:1-3 List of twenty pairs of types of produce that are not Diverse Kinds. Judah glosses 1:2; Aqiba glosses 1:3.

These items are not deemed Diverse Kinds because, even though they are of different genuses, each pair's grains or fruits look alike. The larger point thus is that, to comply with the rules for Diverse Kinds, a field simply must not appear to be sown with different kinds of seeds, even if it actually is. Placement at Usha is on the basis of Judah's attestation. While discussion of specific items may have come earlier, as Aqiba's gloss indicates, the construction as a whole comes no earlier than Judah's day, along with the larger theory expressed here and in the following.

1:7-8 They may not graft together different kinds of trees or vegetables. Nor do they graft a tree onto a vegetable or a vegetable onto a tree. Judah permits the latter.

The only noteworthy claim here is Judah's, the point of which, unfortunately, is not clear. See Mandelbaum, pp. 51-52. The basic, anonymous, point seems obvious: One may not perform a graft which creates a hybrid of Diverse Kinds. Placement of the whole unit is on the basis of Judah's gloss.

D. Unassigned
1:4 Grafting is permitted in the case of fruits of a single genus. It is forbidden in the case of fruits which are not of the same genus, even if they are similar in appearance.

Unlike i.C.1:1-3 this rule takes seriously the criterion of genus in determining what are Diverse Kinds. Since there is no attribution, I see no sound method of placing this in historical relationship with that other pericope. Note however that, according to T. 1:4, the issue of permitted and prohibited grafting did arise in Yavnean times.

1:5 List of items which, even though they are similar in appearance, are deemed Diverse

The theory of the preceding entry is carried forward.

Kinds, for they are of separate
genuses.

1:6 Same rule as in the preceding   The theory of the preceding
for seven pairs of types of   is exemplified again.
animals.

1:9A-D Burying a vegetable under   The vegetable is neither
a vine does not constitute a case   grafted nor actually
of forbidden grafting or planting.   planted, such that the rules
                                            of Diverse Kinds do not
                                            apply.

        ii. Sowing Together Different Kinds of Crops

        Yavneans initiate discussion of the conditions under which
different kinds of crops may be sown alongside each other without
constituting forbidden Diverse Kinds in a field. Such planting,
they rule, is permitted if each kind takes up a sufficient area
of land as to be deemed sown in a field of its own. While all
authorities agree to this basic theory, they dispute the specific
size of the area which, under several different circumstances,
constitutes an autonomous field (ii.B.2:10, 3:3, 4, 6).

        The discussion continues at Usha, where the Yavnean theory
is expanded within the common frame of Ushan thinking. Ushans
make clear that at issue is the overall appearance of the area
planted with several kinds, not the specific acreage that any
single kind covers. For Ushans, that is, crops do not comprise
Diverse Kinds so long as humans can perceive lines of demarcation
that separate one area of planting from another. Ushans thus 1)
permit the corner of one field to extend across the boundary of a
different field, 2) allow a field to be flanked with a single
furrow of a different kind (ii.C.2:7) and also 3) permit a single
field to be sown with many patches of different kinds of seed
(ii.C.2:9). Some Ushans even allow a second kind of seed to be
mixed with the primary seed sown in a field. This is the case so
long as that second kind is of so minimal a quantity as not to be
readily visible within the field (ii.C.1:9E-H, 2:1-2). Ushans
thus carry to a striking conclusion the line of thinking
initiated in Yavnean times. Since the one pericope of this unit
attributed to the period before 70 does not appear to be
authentic, there is no evidence that this discussion as a whole

derives from earlier than the period of Yavneh. The majority of
the work, as we shall now see, is done at Usha.

A. Before 70

2:6 A plot of land so wide as
three furrows is deemed a distinct
field--so the House of Shammai.
The House of Hillel say: It must
be so wide as the width of a
Sharon yoke.

Beds of minimum sizes given
by the Houses are deemed
separate fields, which may
be planted with different
kinds. While the idea given
here is not striking (see
iii.A.4:1-3, 5, 6:1),
attribution of this specific
issue is not on solid
grounds. T. 2:1 states
these Houses' opinions
anonymously, in a pericope
attested to Usha by Eleazar
b. Simeon and Abba Yose b.
Hanan.

B. The Time of Yavneh

2:10 An area of secondary
planting must be of requisite size
so as not to constitute Diverse
Kinds with the primary crop of
that field. Eliezer (alt.:
Eleazar) disputes specific area
required.

The specific figure given
here for an autonomous area
of planting, six by six
handbreadths, is assumed by
Aqiba in the following
entry as well as at Usha,
ii.C.3:1. See also Peah,
i.B.3:6.

3:3 If his field is planted with
one kind of vegetable and he
wishes to plant it with a
different kind--Ishmael: He must
plant a furrow the length of the
whole field. Aqiba: He must
plant the area of a garden bed.
Judah refines Aqiba's position
to refer to the size of a furrow.

The concerns are the same as
at M. 2:10, which Aqiba's
opinion indeed reflects.
Judah's alteration of
Aqiba's view adds credence
to the supposition that the
issue originally derives
from Yavnean times.

3:4 One may plant two rows each of several kinds of plants, but not one row each. If the two rows of the same kind are not adjacent, Eliezer permits, but sages prohibit.

Eliezer holds that the two rows define an individual field, even though they are not adjacent to each other. Sages hold that the rows must be alongside each other, so as to create a single area containing one kind. This carries forward the issue of the preceding entries.

3:6 One who wishes to plant rows of gourds among onions--Ishmael: He uproots two rows of onions and replaces them with one row of gourds. Aqiba: He replaces them with two rows of gourds.

The two rows that have been cleared comprise an independent field, as we know from the preceding entry. Aqiba therefore allows the individual to replant these rows with gourds. Ishmael is concerned that the gourds will spread and begin to cover the onions that remain on either side. To prevent this mixing of Diverse Kinds, he allows the farmer to plant only one row of gourds in the two rows he has cleared.

C. The Time of Usha
1:9E-H Sowing wheat and barley together constitutes sowing of Diverse Kinds. Judah: This is the case only if there are two grains of wheat and one of barley or vice versa.

The issue appears to be the question of what constitutes a field planted with Diverse Kinds (Mandelbaum, p. 64). Judah simply states that the heterogeneous kinds of crop are not deemed planted "in a field" (Lev. 19:19), unless there are at least three plantings. Placement in

this stratum is on the basis
of attribution alone.

2:1-2 One may not sow a _seah_ of
one kind of seed if it contains a
quarter-qab of a different kind of
seed. They may plant it if they
lessen the quantity of seed of the
second kind to less than a
quarter-qab. Yose: They must
entirely remove the second kind.
Simeon glosses.

The anonymous rule states
that we need only take
actions to avoid the
appearance of sowing
together Diverse Kinds, even
if, in fact, two or more
different types of seeds
will be sowed together in a
field. Yose, by contrast,
takes literally the notion
that only one kind of seed
may be sown in the field.

2:3 If a field is sown with wheat
and he wishes to sow it with
barley, he must first plow over the
wheat and only then may plant the
barley. Dispute involving Abba
Saul concerning mode of plowing.

The initially sown grain
must be killed before a
subsequent crop may be
planted.

2:7 It is permitted for the corner
of a field planted with one kind to
extend into a field planted with a
different kind. A farmer may plant
the edge of his field with the kind
planted in his neighbor's adjacent
field. Simeon: A field may be
flanked with a furrow of any kind
of seeds. Yose: One may plant
one furrow of a different kind in
the middle of a field.

The planting must not
produce the appearance of
Diverse Kinds. Therefore
the distinct type must be
readily defined as a border-
area, or must look like part
of a neighbor's field. Yose
and Simeon allow the single
furrow for purposes of
testing the soil. Since the
one furrow clearly is not
intended to produce a crop,
all who see it will realize
that the farmer has
demarcated a distinct area
in his field and is not
guilty of planting Diverse
Kinds.

2:9 One may plant his field with
patches of different kinds of
produce so long as there are not
more than twenty-four patches per
bet seah. Meir: Only three patches
of mustard are permitted in a field
of grain. Sages: Nine. Eliezer
b. Jacob: No matter how large the
field, only one patch of a
different kind may be sown in it.

The issue and theory is the
same as in the preceding
pericope. Mustard creates a
special problem. It looks
like grain and therefore is
likely to appear to create a
haphazard mixture. Meir
therefore wishes to prevent
much mustard from being
planted in a field of grain.
Eliezer b. Jacob shows this
same general concern
whenever more than one kind
is to be planted in a field.
So as to prevent the
haphazard appearance of a
field planted with Diverse
Kinds, he allows only one
secondary planting in each
field.

2:11 If one kind of produce
growing in one field leans over
a different kind of produce,
growing in some other field, all
the produce remains permitted.
Meir: The chate melon and the
cowpea may not be allowed to lean
over any other plant.

Since the plants do not
become intertwined and are
not actually growing in the
same field, they are not
deemed Diverse Kinds. Meir
forbids in the case of a
climbing plant that could
overgrow the other field,
creating a situation in
which more than one kind was
growing in a single field.
Developing the notions of
this stratum and attested by
Meir, this is firmly placed
at Usha.

3:1 Five kinds may be sown in a
garden bed measuring six by six
handbreadths, one kind in the
middle and a different kind at
each side. Judah: Six kinds may

The notion that an area of
six by six handbreadths
constitutes a distinct field
derives from Yavneh,
ii.B.2:10.[3] We now have

be sown in the middle. If the
garden has a border, thirteen
different kinds may be planted
in it.

further consideration of
how that field may be broken
up into clearly discernable
areas, each planted with a
different kind. Placement
is on the basis of this
development and the
attribution to Judah.

3:7 Gourds planted among
vegetables are deemed a secondary
planting, which requires a space
of six handbreadths square
(ii.C.2:10). If the gourds are
to be planted in a field of grain,
Yose disputes the required area.
Meir and Yose b. HaHotef report
that Ishmael did not allow other
types of seed to be planted in an
area that contained three gourds.

This cites and makes use of
materials that derive from
Yavneh. Since gourds
spread, we must be careful
to allow them sufficient
room for growth.

D. Unassigned
2:4 If his field was sown with
vegetables or grain and he decided
to plant vines, or vice versa, he
must overturn or uproot the
original crop before he plants the
new one.

The point is the same as at
ii.C.2:3, such that this
rule as well appears to
belong to the Ushan
stratum.

2:5 One may not sow a second crop
on top of a type of seed that
remains in the ground for three
years and only then sprouts.
Grains that grow wild among
cultivated grains are not deemed
Diverse Kinds. But if one should
weed out any of these wild grains,
he must weed out all of them.

In the first case, there
will be no appearance of
Diverse Kinds, since the
second type of seed remains
in the ground. Even so,
an actual circumstance of
two types of seeds growing
in a single field must be
avoided. As for the second
case, since the wild grains
are not cultivated, they do
not come under the restrictions of Diverse Kinds. If

one weeds out only some of
the wild grain, however, he
indicates that he wishes the
rest of it to grow. Coming
under the farmer's will,
this too is now subject to
the restrictions of Diverse
Kinds. This is all a rather
subtle development of
ii.C.2:3 and ii.D.2:4, such
that it presumably belongs
in the Ushan stratum.

2:8 They may flank a field of
vegetables with mustard or
safflower, but may not flank a
field of grain with these things.

Mustard and safflower are
close in appearance to
grain, such that growing
next to each other, these
things would look like
Diverse Kinds. Since the
mustard and safflower look
entirely different from
vegetables, these may be
planted next to each other.
The farmer will appear
simply to have planted two
separate areas. Carrying
forward the issue of
ii.C.2:7, 9, this belongs
in the Ushan stratum.
Further discussion occurs in
the names of Rabbi, Judah,
Simeon, Simeon b. Gamaliel
and Meir, T. 2:4-5.

3:2 A garden bed planted with
various kinds around its edges
must, in its center, be planted
with vegetables, not seeds.
If the bed's border (ii.C.3:1)
diminished in height, thirteen
kinds still may be planted in it.

This develops the Yavnean
notion (ii.B.2:10) that an
area of six by six
handbreadths is deemed a
separate field only if
vegetables are grown in it,
but not as regards other
seeds. It further depends

upon the Ushan material at
ii.C.3:1, which it carries
forward. These rules
therefore derive from the
Ushan period.

3:5 Different kinds of melons
may be planted in a single hollow
so long as they lean in different
directions.

The concern is to prevent
the different kinds from
appearing as though they are
growing together.
Comparable to ii.B.3:4, this
may derive from as early as
Yavneh.

iii. Sowing Crops Among Vines

According to Dt. 22:9, if seed is planted in a vineyard,
both that seed and the vines are rendered forbidden under the
laws of Diverse Kinds. The present unit addresses primary
questions left open by this rule of Scripture. The first issue
is to determine what constitutes a vineyard, such that it must
have its own autonomous area of growth free from other types of
crops. If a farmer's vines do not meet this definition--that is,
if they are not considered a vineyard--the normal rules of this
unit will not apply at all. If however the farmer's vines do
compromise a vineyard, a second question must be answered,
comparable to that addressed in unit ii for the case of the field
planted with seed. This question concerns the specific area of
land surrounding the vineyard that must remain free of any other
type of produce.

Work on these questions appears to have begun in the period
before 70. The Houses define the minimum size of a vineyard in
terms of specific measures of acreage and number of vines
(iii.A.4:1-3, 5). Yavneans carry matters forward along the lines
set out by the Houses. They refer in particular to cases of
ambiguity. They also ask other basic questions, specifically,
whether or not the restrictions of Diverse Kinds apply to
agricultural products that are not edible, e.g., hemp (ii.B.5:8),
and whether grain may be planted under a tree upon which a vine
has been trained (ii.B.6:4). The Yavnean answer, that only the
area under the vine itself need be treated as an area of tillage,
is greatly expanded by Ushans, who take into account the attitude

of the farmer who in the first place trained the vine upon the tree (iii.C.6:3, 5).

Ushans qualify the earlier, formalistic, approach, which focuses upon the physical dimensions of the vineyard. They prefer to take into account the intentions of the farmer who plants the vines and the attitude of onlookers who will see and judge what the farmer has done. Ushans therefore define a vineyard as that which people generally consider a vineyard (iii.C.5:1, 5:2). In the same theory, they treat as forbidden under the restrictions of Diverse Kinds only what appears to be Diverse Kinds in a field, whether or not it actually is (iii.C.7:2D-F, 7:8). The approach, which takes into account extenuating circumstances and not only the concrete facts of the case, has its logical conclusion in the Ushan rule at iii.D.5:6. Produce grown as Diverse Kinds in a vineyard is forbidden only if the farmer desires the second type to grow upon his land. If he does not want that second crop and intends to uproot it, then even if he leaves it to grow for a short time, his produce is not rendered forbidden. This same approach accounts for the application, at iii.C.7:4-5, of the Yavnean concept than an individual cannot sanctify what he does not own. Here this is taken to mean that he cannot render forbidden under the law of Diverse Kinds produce growing in his neighbor's field. So long as the neighbor did not intend to grow Diverse Kinds, his produce remains permitted.

A. Before 70

4:1-3 The Houses dispute the minimum size an area in a vineyard must be in order to be sown with a different kind. Judah glosses, defining the location of the specific areas referred to. He also gives the requisite measures for concrete boundaries that divide the vineyard into separate areas.	The Houses' statements are explained and developed by Yavneans and Ushans, here, at iii.B.4:8 and at iii.D.4:4. It therefore is likely that the attributions to the Houses are authentic.
4:5 The House of Shammai: One row of five vines constitutes a vineyard. House of Hillel: Two	While the Houses' views are subject to definition and expansion only by Ushans

rows containing a total of five vines.

(iii.C.4:7, iii.D.4:6), the relationship between this and the other Houses' materials in this unit suggests that the dispute is authentic to the period before 70.

6:1 Vines trained on a fence or ditch--House of Shammai: The vines' area of tillage is measured from the base of the vines to the field. House of Hillel: It is measured from the fence to the field. Yohanan b. Nuri: The area of tillage is measured between the vines and the fence. If there is sufficient room, he may sow the rest. Aqiba: A single vine requires six square handbreadths of tillage.

The topic of the vine trained along a fence (espalier) is attested to Yavneh both in the present pericope and at iii.B.6:2. Further development appears to have occurred at Usha, T. 4:5 and 4:7. The basic positions assigned to the Houses therefore appear to derive from the period before 70.[4]

B. The Time of Yavneh

4:8 To plant seed between rows of vines, the farmer must have sufficient area to allow the seed to grow in an area of its own. The size of the area depends upon the number of rows of vines. If a row is laid waste: Eliezer b. Jacob in the name of Hananiah b. Hakinai says that we treat the case as though the row were still there.

Hananiah's point is that the original layout of the vineyard, not the appearance it has at any given moment, determines whether or not a second kind may be planted in it. Hananiah thus follows the common Yavnean perspective that appearances have no legal weight. Attested to Usha by Eliezer b. Jacob and further developed at iii.C.4:9, we have good reason to assign this to Yavneh.

5:7 If seed accidentally is sown in a vineyard: Aqiba: If it sprouts blades, it must be

What happens if grain is sown in a vineyard that does not contain sufficient area

overturned; if it begins to ripen, the ears of grain must be broken off; if it is ripe, the ripe grain must be burned.

to constitute a separate field? Aqiba's response details methods required to destroy the grain at each stage of growth (see Mandelbaum, pp. 191-92). Unlike in the Ushan development of this issue, Aqiba shows no concern for the attitude of the farmer who allows the seed to grow into ripened ears of grain.

5:8 He who allows thorns to grow in a vineyard--Eliezer: He has sanctified the field. Sages: He has not. As for hemp--Tarfon: It is not considered Diverse Kinds in the vineyard. Sages: It is.

Eliezer holds that useless plants, which produce no food, do not constitute Diverse Kinds. Sages disagree, holding that the issue does not concern edibility, but only homogeneity of kind. The second dispute assumes that Eliezer's view is normative and questions whether hemp is a food, since its seeds may be used to make oil, or an inedible, inasmuch as its main use is in the manufacture of rope or fabric. This rather basic issue of the range of applicability of the laws of Diverse Kinds is assigned to Yavneh on the basis of the attributions here and the further discussion in the names of Yavneans at T. 3:16.

6:4 Ishmael permits Joshua to sow under part of a fig tree not covered by a vine. He prohibits sowing under a sycamore branch

The vine affects only that part of the tree upon which it is growing. By turning turning that part into a

upon which a vine is trained, but permits sowing under other parts of the same tree.

trellis, the vine prevents the farmer from sowing seeds under it. Ushan authorities, iii.C.6:3, 5, develop this rule to take into account the type of tree involved and, presumably, the individual's intention in training a vine on it. This provides firm substantive grounds for assigning this basic consideration to Yavneh.

C. The Time of Usha

4:7 Description of the ways in which the two separate rows of vines may come together so as to meet the minimum requirements of a vineyard, iii.A.4:5. Judah glosses and attests to Usha.

This depends upon and carries forward the view assigned to the Hillelites, that to be deemed a vineyard, the vines must be located in two rows. The specific issue is what obstacles may separate the individual rows and yet allow them to be deemed a single vineyard.

4:9 Description of application of iii.B.4:8--Judah supports anonymous view against that of Meir and Simeon.

This development of a Yavnean rule is attested to Usha by Judah, Meir and Simeon.

5:1 A vineyard which lay waste-- if it still contains ten vines planted in the form required by M. 4:7, it is deemed a vineyard. An irregularly planted vineyard is deemed a vineyard if one can discern two rows. Meir: In all events it is deemed a vineyard.

The application of iii.A.4:5 in ambiguous cases is determined. Meir holds that all that really matters is whether people in general would call the area a "vineyard."

5:2   If the rows are planted   This continues the issue of
closer than usual--Simeon: It   the preceding. Contrary to
is not deemed a vineyard. Sages: Meir, Simeon wants to be
It is as though the intermediate   able to distinguish the
rows were not there.   requisite number and
                                     configuration of rows. Like
                                     Meir, sages are concerned
                                     only with the overall
                                     appearance of the area.

5:3   Eliezer b. Jacob: A ditch   The area in question looks
that extends all the way through   like an autonomous domain
a vineyard forms its own autonomous and therefore may be treated
domain, which may be sown. If the   as such, regardless of its
ditch does not extend all the way   actual size. Discussion of
through the field, it is like a   this issue continues along
wine press. Eliezer: If it is of   these same lines in the
sufficient size, it may be sown.   following entry, providing
A watchman's mound of this same   further grounds for placing
requisite size may be sown.   these materials, the
                                     attributions of which are
                                     ambiguous, in the Ushan
                                     stratum.

5:4   If a vine is planted in a   A winepress or hollow may
wine-press or hollow, they allow it be sown with a different
its area of tillage and sow the   kind (M. 5:3). What if
rest with a different kind. Yose: there already is a single
There must remain four square   vine growing there? So long
amot, or he may not sow the rest.   as there is sufficient space
                                     to allow each kind its own
                                     clearly distinct area of
                                     growth, the second kind may
                                     be planted. Yose simply
                                     repeats what we already know
                                     to be a vine's area of
                                     tillage.

6:2   Eliezer b. Jacob: An   If the farmer cannot stand
espalier on a terrace prohibits   on the ground and harvest
for the planting of a different   it, the vine on the espalier

kind the four <u>amot</u> around it only
if the grapes growing on it can
be harvested from the ground.
Eliezer (alt.: Eleazar): The
vines growing on an espalier
combine with those growing on
the ground only if they are
not higher than ten handbreadths
above them.

6:3, 5 If a vine is trained on
part of a latticework or a barren
tree, one should not sow seed
under the other part. If he did
so and the vine grew over the seed,
it has been sanctified. If the
vine is trained over part of a
fruit tree, one may put seed under
the rest of the tree. If the vine
extends over the seed, he cuts it
back. Meir: All trees are deemed
barren except for the olive and
fig. Yose: Any tree that
one would not plant as a whole
grove is called barren. Anonymous
rule: A barren tree is one that
does not produce fruit.

6:7 If an espalier extends between
two parallel walls, they allow it
its area of tillage and sow the
rest. Yose: This is the case

is deemed to grow in its own
autonomous area. Both
Eliezer b. Jacob and
Eliezer/Eleazar make the
same point in slightly
different terms. Note the
parallel point made by Yose
at iii.C.6:7.

This develops the Yavnean
discussion of iii.B.6:4.[5]
An inanimate object or non-
fruit producing tree is
deemed to have the status of
the vine growing on it.
Since the farmer clearly
intends it only as a
trellis, seed should not be
planted in its area of
tillage, even under that
part upon which no vine is
trained. The fruit bearing
tree, by contrast, is not
intended as a trellis and
therefore retains its own
status. Seed may be sown
under any part of it that
does not actually support a
vine. Along with its clear
relationship to the Yavnean
rule at iii.B.6:4, this rule
is attested to Usha by Meir
and Yose, who define the
barren tree upon economic,
not botanical, considerations.

The espalier and walls form
a small alcove. Yose wants
to be certain that this
area is large enough that,

only if there are four <u>amot</u> available for planting the second kind.

planted with vines and seeds, it will not appear like a field of Diverse Kinds. Developing concerns prominent at Usha (iii.C.6:2), this is firmly assigned to the Ushan period.

7:2A-C Sunken vine-shoots that are visible combine with their parent vines to create a vineyard if there are from four to eight <u>amot</u> between the parent-vines and the shoots. So Eleazar b. Zadoq.

Even though the shoots and the parent vines might still be attached to each other, they are deemed distinct plantings. If they are growing at a sufficent distance from one another to create the appearance of two separate rows of vines they form a vineyard (see iii.A. 4:5).

7:2D-F One should not sow seed near a withered vine, but if one does so anyway, the seed is not sanctified. Meir: One should not sow seed near a cotton tree, but if one does so, the produce remains permitted. Eleazar b. Zadoq in his name: One should not sow above a vine shoot, but if one does, the produce is not sanctified.

In each case the sowing of the seed creates the appearance of Diverse Kinds. But since in none of these cases will two distinct kinds actually be growing from the same soil, there is no infringement of the law such that the produce is not rendered forbidden. Placement here is on the basis of the attributions and congruence to the larger concept of this stratum, that one must avoid creating the appearance of Diverse Kinds. See iii.D.7:1, upon which Eleazar b. Zadoq's ruling depends, and iii.D.7:3, which carries forward the larger idea (and

literary form) of the
present pericope.

7:4-5 One who trellises his   Ushans, Yose and Simeon,
vine over a neighbor's grain-   make use of a notion known
field has sanctified that   already in the time of
neighbor's grain. Yose and   Aqiba, that one may not
Simeon: A man cannot sanctify   impart a status of
that which is not his own. Yose   sanctification to that which
provides a legal precedent   he does not own (see also
involving Aqiba and the laws of   Terumot, i.C.1:1). This
the Seventh Year.   means that the restrictions
                                     of Diverse Kinds can have
                                     effect only in an individ-
                                     ual's own field but cannot
                                     apply in the case of
                                     distinct kinds growing
                                     together but owned by
                                     different people.

7:8 Regarding the rules of   The point is the same as at
Diverse Kinds, what grows in a   M. 7:2D-F, providing firm
perforated pot is comparable to   grounds for placement at
that which grows in the ground.   Usha. In Simeon's view,
Simeon: Whether it is in a   what grows in a pot is not
perforated pot or unperforated   comparable to what grows in
pot, it should not be left to   the ground. It therefore
grow under a vine, but if it   does not really constitute
does grow there, it does not   a second kind growing in a
sanctify all the produce.   vineyard. Since that which
                                     grows in the pot does however
                                     create the appearance of
                                     Diverse Kinds, the farmer
                                     should not leave such a pot
                                     in his vineyard.

D. Unassigned
4:4 Measures for permissible   This depends upon and
breaches in fences that divide a   carries forward the rules
vineyard into distinct areas.   assigned to Judah (see
                                     iii.A.4:1-3), such that it

can derive from no earlier
than the Ushan period.

4:6 Descriptions of configurations
of five vines that meet the
definition of a vineyard given by
the Hillelites, iii.A.4:5.

This is an aspect of the
same work of definition
attested to Usha by Judah,
iii.C.4:7. It presumably
belongs to that same period
in the unfolding of the law.

5:5 One who plants vegetables in
a vineyard that does not contain
requisite area to allow sowing of
a different kind has sanctified
(i.e., rendered forbidden for
consumption) both the vegetables
and the fruit of a certain number
of vines.

The rule derives directly
from Dt. 22:9, with M.
adding only the specific
number of vines rendered
forbidden. The specifics
of this pericope are
attested to the period after
Usha by Simeon b. Eleazar,
T. 3:11, such that this
particular expression
appears to be late.

5:6 If one sees vegetables growing
in his vineyard and says that he
will uproot them when, in the
course of his work, he gets to
them, the field is not rendered
forbidden. But if he left them
until he would return, and in the
meantime they increased in size,
the field is rendered forbidden.

This develops M. 5:5,
describing the circumstance
under which a field planted
with two kinds is rendered
forbidden. The point is
that unless the farmer
clearly sanctions the growth
of the second kind, that
crop is of no consequence.
In light of its relationship
to the preceding entry and
its concern for the
intentions of the farmer,
we have good reason for
assigning this to the Ushan
stratum. This notion is
very different from that
current at Yavneh,
iii.B.5:7, where the field's
status of sanctification is

held to depend solely upon
the stage of growth the
second kind of seed has
reached.

6:6 A gap in an espalier which
measures a little more than
eight amot may be sown with a
different kind.

Discussion of sowing a
different kind next to a
vine-planted espalier begins
before 70 and is current in
the Yavnean period. It
therefore is possible that
this rule, which establishes
the measure for an auto-
nomous area within an
espalier, derives from
Yavneh. Indeed, it is
rather less complicated than
the Ushan case on essen-
tially the same issue,
iii.C.6:7.

6:8 If reeds extend beyond the
end of an espalier and he refrains
from trimming them, it is permitted
to sow a different kind under them.
If he prepares them for use in the
espalier, it is prohibited to sow
a different kind under them.

This is a more sophisticated
development of iii.B.6:4 and
iii.C.6:3, 5. What grows
next to an espalier is
considered part of that
espalier only if the farmer
shows clear intention to use
it for his vines. Depending
upon and developing an Ushan
rule, and bringing into
consideration the intentions
of the farmer as determinative of the status of a
structure, this clearly
belongs in the Ushan
stratum.

6:9 A vine shoot that extends
beyond the end of the espalier or
that is suspended from tree to

Developing the discussion of
ambiguities arising from
vines planted upon espaliers

tree renders prohibited for the
planting of a different kind the
area directly below it.

or trees (iii.C.6:3, 5),
this derives from the Ushan
period.

7:1 One may plant seed above a
vine-shoot sunk at least three
handbreadths into the ground. If
the soil is stony, sowing on top
of the shoot is permitted even if
the shoot is not deeply sunk.

Layering of the two kinds
will not produce Diverse
Kinds, so long as the roots
of the seeds cannot reach
the sunken vine-shoot. The
rule is attested to Usha by
Meir, Yosah and Simeon b.
Gamaliel (pseudepi-
graphically citing the
Houses; see Mandelbaum in
Neusner, Mishnah, p. 289),
T. 4:11, and by Eleazar b.
Zadoq II, iii.C.7:2A-C.

7:3 One should not sow areas of
a vineyard that are not of
sufficient size to compromise an
autonomous field. But if one
does, the produce is not
sanctified. If one sows in the
area of tillage of the vine, or
right under the vine, the produce
is sanctified.

The point is the same as at
iii.C.7:2D-F. One should
not sow near vines, for this
creates the appearance of
Diverse Kinds. So long as
the seed will not actually
derive nourishment from the
same soil as the vine,
however, the planting does
not create Diverse Kinds,
such that the produce
is not rendered forbidden.
Repeating iii.C.7:2D-F's
conception, this clearly
derives from Ushan times.

7:6 If a usurper sowed a
vineyard, when the rightful owner
recovers possession he must cut
down the second kind.

The point is the same as is
made at iii.C.7:4-5,
indicating the Ushan
origins of this rule. The
usurper's planting of a
second kind in another's
vineyard does not cause all
of the produce to be

sanctified. The rightful
owner therefore need not
burn the food. But he must
prevent the different kinds
from continuing to grow,
lest he be culpable for
maintaining a field planted
with Diverse Kinds.

7:7 If different kinds growing
separately are blown together by
the wind, the farmer must return
them to their original positions.

This develops the point of
the preceding entry.
Different kinds that turn
out to grow together are
not sanctified unless their
owner approves of their
growing as Diverse Kinds.
At T. 4:10 the Ushan Abba
Saul reports the issue of
this pericope to be under
dispute by the Yavneans,
Aqiba and Ben Azzai. While
the issue may have been
first discussed in Yavnean
times, it apparently
remained moot until the
Ushan period.

iv. Diverse Kinds of Animals

Ushans work out the meaning of Dt. 22:10: <u>You shall not
plow with an ox and an ass together</u>. Ignoring what is explicit
in Scripture, they provide their own definition of forbidden
harnessing of different kinds of animals. This definition is
expected on the basis of the Ushan approach to the law in the
preceding units. Ushans forbid the individual to tie together
different kinds of animals in any fashion that causes them to
appear as though they are harnessed together in order to work as
a team. One may not even tie a second kind of animal to the side
of a wagon, for this gives the appearance that Diverse Kinds are
working together. In a minor note, Ushans (iv.C.8:3) dispute the
question left open by Scripture of the consequences of forbidden
harnessing of Diverse Kinds.

The second major point of this unit likewise rejects what Scripture makes clear, that the prohibition applies only to oxen and asses. Instead, it determines that Diverse Kinds are defined not only on the basis of species, but also in light of other characteristics, e.g., whether an animal is domesticated or wild, clean or unclean (iv.D.8:2). In all, this unit gives us no reason to believe that the issues it addresses were raised from the time of Scripture up to the Ushan period itself.

A.   Before 70

B.   The Time of Yavneh

C.   The Time of Usha

8:3 One who leads a yoke of Diverse Kinds receives forty lashes, as does one who sits in a wagon drawn by Diverse Kinds. Meir exempts the latter. A third animal tied to the harness of a wagon pulled by a team of animals of a different kind is forbidden.

The interesting point is Meir's. He exempts the passenger from liability, because that individual does not overtly act to lead the forbidden pair of animals. In the final rule, the third animal does not actually pull the wagon. Since it creates the appearance of a forbidden pairing, it may not, however, be tied together with the other beasts. Placement in the Ushan stratum is on the basis of the attribution to Meir.

8:4 They do not tie an animal of one kind to the side or rear of a wagon drawn by an animal of a different kind. Judah: Mules of similar parentage may be yoked and mated together. But the offspring of a female horse and

The initial rule is the same as that given in the preceding entry and is attested to Usha by Meir and Judah, T. 5:4-5. Judah makes a different point. Animals bred of Diverse

male ass may not be yoked with
the offspring of a male horse and
female ass.

Kinds themselves form a
species, so long as they
have the same parentage.

8:5 Mules of unknown parentage
may not be yoked or mated together.
A "wild man" is considered a kind
of wild animal. Yose: When dead,
he conveys uncleanness in a tent.
The weasel--Yose says: The House
of Shammai say that, when dead,
it conveys uncleanness like a wild
animal.

The first, anonymous, rule
develops the preceding entry
and so belongs in the Ushan
stratum. Classification of
other creatures as wild or
domesticated is called for
by iv.D.8:1. It is a
subject of Ushan concern
here and in the following'.

8:6 A wild ox is a kind of
domesticated animal and a dog is
a kind of wild animal. Meir
disagrees in both cases.
Classifications of other animals.

Assignment to Usha is on the
basis of the attribution to
Meir.

D. Unassigned
8:1 Seeds may not be sown in a
vineyard, and if they are, the
produce that results is forbidden
for any use. Different kinds of
seeds should not be planted
together, but if they are, the
produce may be eaten. Garments
of wool and linen may be
produced but may not be worn.
Different kinds of animals may be
reared and maintained together,
but they may not be cross-bred
or yoked together.

This large formal
construction summarizes the
restrictions described in
the first two sections of
the tractate and serves to
introduce this third
section, on Diverse Kinds
of animals. Since it
assumes and works to
correlate the basic facts
described throughout the
tractate, it presumably
derives from late in the
formation of the law.

8:2 All possible pairings of
domesticated, wild, clean and
unclean animals are prohibited
from being yoked together to plow,
pull a wagon, or be led.

A "kind" of animal is
defined not only by species
but also by other
classifications, e.g., wild
or domestic, clean or
unclean. This rewriting of

the rule of Dt. 22:10
('You shall not plow with an
ox and an ass together') is
a basic datum of the solely
Ushan discussion that
comprises this unit of the
tractate.

v. Fabrics from Diverse Kinds of Fibers

Dt. 22:11 prohibits the wearing of fabrics containing both
wool and linen (shaatnez). Yavneans state that this restriction
indeed applies only to clothing, but that fabrics of wool and
linen may be used for other purposes (v.B.9:3). The rest of the
unit is Ushan. Ushans define the forbidden mingling of wool and
linen as spinning, weaving or hackling these fibers into a single
fabric (v.C.9:8-9) or as connecting by means of a full stitch
individual fabrics made of wool and linen (v.C.9:10). Ushans
indicate which imported fabrics must be examined in order to
determine whether or not they contain mixed fibers (v.C.9:7).
Finally, in line with other Ushan rules in this tractate, we
learn that so long as a fabric does not contain so much of a
secondary fiber as to appear to contain a forbidden mixture, that
fabric may in fact be worn (v.D.9:2).

A. Before 70

B. The Time of Yavneh

9:3 Hand-towels, bath-towels and scroll-wrappers are not subject to the restrictions of Diverse Kinds. Eliezer holds that they are. Barbers' towels are prohibited.

Both parties agree that the law only applies to garments. The anonymous rule simply notes that the listed items are not worn and so should not be subject. Eliezer's view takes account of the fact that they can be used to warm one's hand or might be wrapped around one's body. Barber's towels are unambiguous, for they are used to protect a person

while his hair is being cut.
Meir and Judah, T. 5:17,
attest this dispute, with
Judah insisting that the
positions of Eliezer and
sages have been reversed.
Since there are no other
Yavnean rules on this topic,
we have no further grounds
dating.

C. The Time of Usha

9:7 A birrus, bardaicus, dalmatic
or shoes of coarse wool--one must
examine them for Diverse Kinds
before wearing them. Yose: If
they come from the seacoast or
from distant lands, they need
not be examined.

These heavy woolen garments
may contain flax below the
surface and therefore
require examination. Yose
seems to hold that, in the
areas he mentions, cheaper
hemp will have been used
instead of linen.
Therefore there is no
possibility of Diverse
Kinds, such that examination
is not required. Placement
here is on the basis of
the attribution to Yose.

9:8 Wool and linen create a
forbidden fabric only if they are
spun or woven together + Dt. 22:11
as prooftext. Simeon b. Eleazar
suggests an alternative
interpretation.

The issue of what
constitutes a forbidden
fabric is developed in the
name of Ushans, Yose and
Judah, in the following.
Simeon b. Eleazar's
interpretation of the word
shaatnez ("It turns his
Father in Heaven away from
him") is independent and
does not serve to attest
this rule to Usha.

9:9 Hackled fabrics of wool and
linen are prohibited. A fringe of

Yose's view of what
constitutes a forbidden

wool on a garment of linen is
forbidden. Yose: This is because
one bastes the cord to the garment.

fabric is much more
stringent than the initial
rule here or than the rule
of M. 9:8. His partici-
pation in the issue serves
to attest it to Ushan times.

9:10 Wool and linen fabrics
connected by a half stitch are not
subject to the prohibition of
Diverse Kinds. The stitch does
not comprise a connector for
uncleanness, and one who undoes
it on the Sabbath is not culpable.
But a full stitch is a connector
for purposes of Diverse Kinds and
uncleanness, and one who undoes
it on the Sabath is culpable.
Judah: This applies only in the
case of three stitches.

Judah requires clear
evidence that the individual
intends to connect the
different kinds of fabric
in a permanent fashion.
This theory, that an
individual's actions must
serve to indicate his
intentions, is attributed
to Judah elsewhere in this
division and serves to
attest the present rule to
the Ushan period.

D. Unassigned
9:1 The restrictions that pertain
to Diverse Kinds in garments apply
only to mixtures of wool and linen.
If a mixture of camel's hair and
wool is mostly camel's hair, it
may be combined with linen. If a
mixture of linen and hemp is
mostly hemp, it may be mixed with
wool.

Dt. 22:11 is explicit that
only mixtures of wool and
linen are prohibited.[6] M.
adds that in a mixture of
permitted materials, the
status of the fabric is that
of the majority of the
fibers. The point
presumably is that people
generally consider a fabric
to be whatever fiber is in
the majority, ignoring the
secondary fiber it
contains.[7] Insofar as it
takes into account the
perceptions of the
Israelite and does not
simply judge matters by the
objective character of the
fabric, this rule is

parallel to the Ushan
materials of this tractate,
particularly at ii.C.2:1-2,
and at iii.C in general.

9:2   Silk and bast-silk are not
subject to the law, but are
prohibited for appearance's sake.
Matresses are not subject to the
law so long as one's flesh will
not touch them.   One may not wear
a garment of Diverse Kinds even on
top of ten other garments.

Two types of silk resemble
wool and linen such that,
for appearance's sake, they
should not be woven in a
single garment.   As just
noted, the consideration of
appearance's sake is Ushan
(contrast iii.B.4:8), such
that the initial rule
appears to derive from no
earlier than the Ushan
period.   The rest of the
pericope's discussion is
familiar from Yavneh,
v.B.9:3.

9:4   Shrouds and a pack-saddle of
an ass are not subject to the
restrictions of Diverse Kinds.
But one should not place the pack-
saddle on his shoulder.

Definition of a garment,
familiar from the preceding
entry and v.B.9:3, continues.
As before, the Yavnean point
is that the rules of Diverse
Kinds apply only to that
which is worn by a human
being.   This excludes
shrouds, worn by the dead,
to whom the restrictions
of the law do not apply.

9:5-6   Clothes-dealers and tailors
may hold garments of Diverse Kinds
on their lap or back, so long as
they do not intend them to protect
them from the sun or rain.   The
scrupulous ones carry such garments
on a stick or leave them on the
ground.

The notion that the
individual's intention in
wearing the article
determines whether or not it
is subject to the law
provides grounds for placing
this rule in the Ushan
period.

III. Conclusion

   Tractate Kilaim principally describes how Israelites are to
grow crops in conditions of holiness. They do this by maintaining the distinctions, established by God at the time of creation,
between different classes of plants, animals and fibers. The
tractate thus serves as a prolegomenon to the Division of
Agriculture as a whole, with its larger emphasis upon the
processes of sanctification through which Israelites actually set
aside produce to become the holy offerings ordained by Scripture.

   The overall point of the tractate emerges from its Ushan
stratum. This material comprises the majority of the tractate's
laws[8] and, moreover, introduces a concept that appears throughout
the tractates of this division. Ushans hold that the character
of a field--ordered or disordered--or the culpability of an
action--permitted or forbidden--is determined in light of the
perceptions and intentions of the Israelites involved. These
perceptions, that is, determine whether different plants growing
together in a field have been planted in a logically ordered, and
so permitted, manner. Ushans further hold that only in light of
the intentions of the farmer may we judge whether or not his
actions in planting together different kinds of plants are
culpable in the first place.

   According to Ushans, then, order, and with it holiness, is
not dependent upon a pre-ordained, transcendent, model. It is,
rather, a function of each Israelites' own desire to order, and
thereby sanctify, the world. This notion of the role of common
Israelites in establishing conditions of holiness is further
developed in Tractate Shebiit, which follows. That tractate
comprises Mishnah's second essay on how Israelites are to grow
produce under conditions of holiness.

CHAPTER FIVE

SHEBIIT

I. Introduction

Lev. 25:1-7 insists that, just as God ceased working on the seventh day and therefore designated it perpetually as a day of rest, so too God established the seventh year as a Sabbath for the land of Israel.[1] Each seventh year the land accordingly must be left untilled. Israelites may not sow their fields or in any way prepare them for planting. Nor may the farmers work the orchards or vineyards so as to enhance the crop they will produce. The people must, rather, survive upon whatever produce grows on its own. This food is shared equally by all of the people, without regard to who owns the land upon which it is found.[2] In a separate, though perhaps related, idea, Dt. 15:1-3 states that, in the seventh year, even monetary demands of one Israelite upon another are cancelled.[3]

Tractate Shebiit's concern, dictated by Scripture, is that Israelites use their land in accordance with God's plan of the time of creation. In light of this, the tractate's function within the Division of Agriculture parallels that of Tractate Kilaim and, we shall see, Orlah. These tractates describe how Israelites are to grow food in conditions of sanctity.[4] The parallel in function, moreover, corresponds to a commonality of the basic points made by Tractates Shebiit and Kilaim. The Ushan authorities of Tractate Shebiit, like those in Mishnah Kilaim, rule that what is permitted and forbidden depends largely upon the intentions of the Israelite who carries out an action and upon the perceptions of those people who see and judge the character of what he has done. While describing a return to the perfect state in which God created the world, the compilers of both tractates thus judge the success of that return only in light of the desires and perceptions of Israelites. What Israelites characterize as right and good is identified with the objective order and sanctity of the world.

This point, found in the Ushan stratum of this tractate, comprises the one aspect of the laws before us absent from Scripture and distinctive to Mishnah.[5] As the idea that generates the majority of the materials in the tractate, it must

143

be deemed the central focus of Tractate Shebiit's own
formulators. Yavnean rabbis by contrast simply detail that which
Scripture itself makes relatively clear. The Yavneans forbid all
field work that has a concrete effect upon the growth of seventh
year produce. In this Yavnean view, the appearance that the
farmer is doing right or wrong has no role in determining the
culpability of his actions. Like the Yavnean authorities in
Tractate Kilaim, those in the materials before us thus see an
established and unvarying set of norms as defining proper
conduct. These norms are applied without regard to extenuating
circumstances or concern for the meaning an action has to those
who carry it out or see it being done. This approach leads not
to the tractate before us but to a simple listing, predictable on
the basis of Scripture, of those field labors deemed to promote
the growth of produce and those held to have no effect upon the
land. During the Sabbatical year the latter may be performed.
The former may not.

Before turning to the specific rules through which these
points of the tractate are made, let us review the Scriptural
basis of these materials.

(Ex. 23:10-11)[6] "For six years you shall sow your land
and gather its yield; but in the seventh year you shall let
it lie fallow, that the poor of your people may eat; and
what they leave the wild beasts may eat. You shall do
likewise with your vineyard and with your olive orchard."
(Lev. 25:1-7) The Lord said to Moses on Mount Sinai,
"Say to the people of Israel, When you come into the land
which I give you, the land shall keep a sabbath to the Lord.
Six years you shall sow your field, and six years you shall
prune your vineyard and gather in its fruits; but in the
seventh year there shall be a sabbath of solemn rest for the
land, a sabbath to the Lord; you shall not sow your field or
prune your vineyard. What grows of itself in your harvest
you shall not reap, and the grapes of your undressed vine
you shall not gather; it shall be a year of solemn rest for
the land. The sabbath of the land shall provide food for
you, for yourself and for your male and female slaves and
for your hired servant and the sojourner who lives with you;
for your cattle also and for the beasts that are in your
land all its yield shall be for food."
(Dt. 15:1-3) "At the end of every seven years you
shall grant a release. And this is the manner of the
release: every creditor shall release what he has lent to
his neighbor, his brother, because the Lord's release has
been proclaimed. Of a foreigner you may exact it; but
whatever of yours is with your brother your hand shall
release."

A. Shebiit Before 70

As at Demai, ii.A.3:1C-H, the Houses dispute whether or not a person is responsible to prevent another from transgressing (ii.A.4:2A-H, I-K, 5:8). The Shammaites again state that one is. He therefore may not sell tools that could be used to transgress the prohibitions of the Sabbatical year.   The Hillelites disagree, holding that so long as no sure proof exists that the buyer will transgress, the seller need not scruple.   The Shammaites' position is repeated as normative, ii.D.5:6, 7. We recall that this same view is a basic datum of the Yavnean and Ushan strata of Tractate Demai.

Hillel instituted a legal fiction designed to circumvent the Scriptural   remission   of   debts   in   the   Sabbatical   year (v.A.10:3-4). A document called a prozbul assigns a private debt to a court for collection. The public institution, a court, can collect the debt even after the advent of the seventh year. The subject of a little essay evolving over the periods of Yavneh and Usha, the basic notion of the prozbul appears to originate in the period before 70.

B. Shebiit in the Time of Yavneh

The central ideas which, in the Ushan period, become the focus and point of this tractate appear under dispute in Yavnean times. The most basic issue argued by Yavneans concerns whether or not the restrictions of the Sabbatical year are to be extended back to the end of the sixth year of the Sabbatical cycle (i.B.1:4I-K). Anonymous authorities argue that they are, so as to prevent farmers from doing field work in the sixth year that will aid the growth of the crop in the seventh.   This notion, under dispute by Ishmael, is the foundation of the tractate's first two, otherwise wholly Ushan, chapters.   It thus is noteworthy that this idea was rejected by Yavnean Ishmael, who claimed that the Sabbatical restrictions apply only in the seventh year itself, and that the farmer is permitted to do any field work he desires through the whole of the sixth year, as the plain sense of Scripture indicates.

Yavneans argue whether or not a farmer may, during the seventh year, perform permitted field labors that appear to onlookers to be forbidden. A farmer gathering rocks for building might, for instance, appear to others to be clearing his field for prohibited planting. Aqiba, ii.B.4:6, and the weight of the Yavnean material (see e.g., ii.B.3:10) are clear that neither the

intentions of the farmer who carries out the work nor the
perceptions of those who watch him are to be taken into account
in determining whether or not that labor is forbidden. This view
refuses to take into account extenuating circumstances or
appearances, looking rather only at the concrete facts of whether
or not the farmer's actions promote the growth of a seventh-year
crop. The dominance of this view would have precluded the Ushan
discussions found in this tractate's fifth, sixth and eighth
chapters. Behind that large quantity of Ushan material stands
the Yavnean minority opinion of Yose (the Galilean), iii.B.4:6.
He holds that a farmer may do nothing that appears to be
forbidden, even if it is in fact a permitted activity.

C. Shebiit in the Time of Usha

Unlike the Yavneans, who dispute the tractate's central
issues, Ushans agree upon a pointed ideology through which the
tractate as a whole presents an identifiable message. They
insist upon the primacy of the intentions and perceptions of
Israelites in determining what is forbidden and permitted in the
Sabbatical year. To understand how Ushans make this statement,
we must first describe their larger theory of the restrictions of
the Sabbatical year.

Ushans are concerned that the farmer not do field work that
promotes the growth of produce in the seventh year. This means,
on the one hand, that the farmer must be careful to avoid labors
that prepare his field or trees for the crop of the Sabbatical
year. Certain activities therefore must be curtailed in the
sixth year. On the other hand, since the Ushans are concerned
only that the farmer not promote the growth of the seventh year's
crop, they do not prohibit all field activities that the farmer
may wish to perform during the Sabbatical year. They allow him
to carry out all work that, while necessary for the maintenance
of the land, does not directly promote the growth of the
Sabbatical year's crop.

In light of their central concerns, the majority of the
Ushan materials addresses a narrow range of issues. The first is
to define those field labors that, because they prepare the land
for the following year's crop, are prohibited in the sixth year
itself (i.C). The second, most prominent, element of the
tractate as a whole concerns those activities that are not
intended to promote the growth of the Sabbatical year's crop and
which therefore are permitted in the seventh year itself. The

problem is that, in carrying out these permitted activities, the farmer will appear to transgress. Presumably building upon the Shammaite notion that each individual is responsible to prevent others from breaking the law, Ushans are concerned that, by appearing to transgress, the farmer will lead others actually to sin. They therefore insist that even permitted actions be carried out in a manner that assures that all who look on will recognize that the individual is not engaged in a transgression. What matters for Ushans thus is not the concrete character and purpose of an action, but the way in which Israelite onlookers perceive that action. Ushans therefore detail how the individual is to alter his method of working so as not to appear to transgress. This takes up all of the Ushan materials in unit ii, as well as iv.C.8:6 and large sections of the unassigned pericopae. These too presumably derive from the Ushan period.

Other materials in the Yavnean and Ushan strata detail matters of law that stand outside of the identifiable ideational structure now described. Yavnens and Ushans are clear that any growth of produce during the Sabbatical year is subject to the restrictions that pertain to that year (iii.B.5:3, 6:3, iii.C.5:1, 2, 6:4). This is the case even if the produce began to grow and ripen before the onset of the Sabbatical year or if it will not actually mature and be eaten until the seventh year has ended. Yavneans introduce the notion that produce of the Sabbatical year must be used as food (iv.B.8:9-10), so as to assure that all of the people of Israel are properly fed during the seventh year. Ushans develop this idea to state that what grows in the seventh year may not be used in any business transactions (iv.C.7:3-4, see iv.A.8:3). While Yavneans thus are concerned primarily with the logistics of feeding the people in a year in which agricultural work is prohibited, the Ushans move ahead to treat that which does grow in the seventh year as though it were an agricultural offering such as second tithe or heave-offering. The law of removal, which holds that, in the seventh year, food no longer found in the fields may not be stored in people's homes, receives attention in both periods. Yavneans legislate for a case in which different kinds of produce have been mixed together (iv.B.9:5A-E). The problem is that the different vegetables in the mixture will be subject to removal at different times. Ushans define specific conditions under which produce is subject to removal (iv.C.9:2-3, 4, 5F-G, 8). The prozbul is the subject of its own essay, located primarily in the

unassigned material (v.B.10:6, 7, v.C.10:1, v.D.10:2, 5, 8, 9).
The several Yavnean and Ushan items listed here round out
Mishnah's discussion of the laws of the Sabbatical year and allow
implementation of the Scriptural ordinances upon which they are
based. Unlike the Ushan materials concerning the role of
perception in determining what is forbidden and permitted, these
ideas do not present an identifiable ideology.

II. The History of Tractate Shebiit

i. Regulation of Labor in the Sixth Year

The point of this unit emerges in the Ushan stratum. In the
final months of the sixth year, the farmer may not perform field
labor that will benefit the growth of produce in the Sabbatical
year. Such field labor is deemed comparable to actually
cultivating produce in the seventh year. That, of course, is
forbidden. In line with their larger concern, Ushans indicate
until when in the sixth year one may plow a field of grain
(i.C.2:1), define an orchard in which plowing is not permitted in
the sixth year (i.C.1:5, 6-7) and list other types of
agricultural labor that are permitted, since they benefit the
crop of the sixth year itself, or are forbidden, since they
enhance growth of crops in the Sabbatical year (i.C.2:2-5, 6).
In certain cases the farmer's own intentions determine whether a
certain field labor is permitted or forbidden (i.C.2:9).

In agreeing that certain field work is forbidden in the
sixth year, Ushans move a step beyond the discussion found in the
single Yavnean pericope in this unit. There Ishmael rejects the
notion that any field labor is forbidden before or after the
Sabbatical year. Scripture's prohibition, he holds, applies only
to the seventh year itself (i.B.1:4I-K). Since this issue is
moot in Yavnean times, it appears that a Houses' dispute in which
both Houses agree to the Ushan principle just described is not
authentic to the period before 70 (i.A.1:1). If it were
authentic it would be hard to explain the Yavnean dispute and the
hiatus of some 75 years in discussion of the specifics of the
issue it describes.

A. Before 70
1:1 The House of Shammai: The pericope assumes that,
During the sixth year they may   even in the sixth year, the

plow in an orchard only so long
as the plowing benefits that
year's crop. The House of Hillel:
They may plow until Pentecost.

farmer must not do field
work that will improve the
crop of the Sabbatical year.
The Houses simply dispute at
what point in the sixth year
plowing must cease. The
theory underlying this
dispute is under debate in
Yavnean times (i.B.1:4I-K).
The specific question under
dispute still is moot at
Usha, i.C.2:1, where Simeon
proclaims the Hillelite
position as law. This lends
considerable doubt to the
authenticity of the
attributions to the Houses.
See Gordon, in Neusner,
Judaism, pp. 289-90.

B. The Time of Yavneh
1:4I-K Ex. 34:21 proves that
certain agricultural labors are
prohibited in the sixth year and
eighth (= first) years of the
Sabbatical cycle. Ishmael rejects
this exegesis and, with it, the
notion that certain types of
field work are prohibited before
or after the Sabbatical Year.

Yavneans here dispute what
in Ushan times will be taken
for granted, that certain
agricultural labors are
prohibited in the sixth and
eighth years.

1:8A-D Eleazar b. Azariah, Joshua
and Aqiba dispute definition of a
sapling.

This dispute is ancillary to
i.C.1:6-7 and independent of
the larger issue of this
unit. Its concerns are
developed at i.C.1:8E-G.

C. The Time of Usha
1:5 Three trees belonging to
three different individuals join
together to comprise an orchard.
Simeon b. Gamaliel: To comprise

This develops i.A.1:1 by
defining the orchard to
which that rule refers. The
attribution here to Simeon

an orchard, the three trees must
be separated by sufficient space
for an ox with its yoke to pass
through.

b. Gamaliel provides further
evidence that i.A.1:1 is a
late construction.

1:6-7 If saplings are spread out
evenly through a _seah_-space, in
the sixth year they may plow the
whole space. If the saplings are
in a line, they plow only the
vicinity of each sapling. A
mixture of saplings and gourds is
comparable to all saplings.
Simeon b. Gamaliel: If there are
all gourds, they plow the entire
seah-space on their behalf.

The considerations are the
same as in the preceding
entry. Continued discussion
in the name of Simeon b.
Gamaliel is at T. 1:3.

1:8E-G Simeon: If a tree is
chopped down and the stump
produces shoots, under certain
circumstances these may be
deemed saplings.

This develops the issue of
i.B.1:8A-D.

2:1 In the sixth year they may
plow in a field of grain until
the ground-moisture is gone.
Simeon: This puts the law in
the hands of each individual.[7]
Rather, they plow in a field of
grain until Passover, and in an
orchard until Pentecost.

The issue is familiar from
i.A.1:1 and i.B.1:4I-K.
Simeon states that the
opinion assigned at i.A.1:1
to the Hillelites is law.

2:2-5 List of field labors
permitted until New Year of the
Sabbatical Year. Glosses by
Simeon, Joshua, Eleazar b. Zadoq
and Judah attest the construction
to the Ushan stratum.

These activities provide an
immediate benefit to the
produce of the sixth year.
Even though there will be a
residual benefit to the crop
of the Sabbatical year, the
procedures therefore are
permitted. Some activities,
which prevent irreparable
damage to the trees, are

permitted in the seventh year itself. While discussion seems to have begun at Yavneh, the majority of the materials here are assigned to Ushan authorities. Further discussion is attested to Usha at T. 1:5, 6, 8, 9 and 11.

2:6 Within thirty days of the start of the Sabbatical year they do not plant a tree, sink a vine-shoot or make a graft. Judah: Rooting takes place within three days. Yose and Simeon: Two weeks.

If the new plant takes root after New Year, this would violate the injunction against cultivating the land during the Sabbatical Year. The dispute is over a matter of detail, how much time must be allowed for the plant to root. Futher discussion is attributed to Rabbi, T. 1:12, supporting placement of this unit in the Ushan stratum.

2:7-8 Produce that grows over two calender years is tithed in accordance with the year in which it takes root. If it takes root in the sixth year, it is not subject to the restrictions of the seventh. Simeon Shezuri, Simeon and Eleazar supply specific types of produce.

This is a continuation the issue of the preceding entry, supplying a firm basis for placement in the Ushan stratum.

2:9 If a plant might be used as seed or as a vegetable, the farmer's treatment of it indicates its status. If he withholds water thirty days before the New Year, it is treated as a seed and subject to the law as is the

The basic problem is the same as in the preceding entry, except that here the farmer's own intentions for the plants come into play. Placement is on the basis of Meir's attestation and

produce referred to at M. 2:7-8.   the relationship to
Meir and sages dispute rule for   M. 2:7-8. Further Ushan
naturally-watered field.   discussion is at T. 2:5,
                                      6 (where Simeon b. Gamaliel
                                      provides a Houses' dispute),
                                      9 and 13.

2:10H-K Simeon permits irrigation   The issue is whether or not
during the Sabbatical year.   irrigation is required to
Eliezer b. Jacob prohibits.   prevent irreparable damage
                                      to the field (i.C.2:2-5).
                                      Parallel in concern to
                                      another Ushan pericope and
                                      assigned to Ushan
                                      authorities, this is firmly
                                      placed in the Ushan stratum.

D. Unassigned
1:2-4H Definition of an orchard.   The issue is the same as at
If the trees do not comprise an   i.C.1:5. This material is
orchard, in the sixth year the   Ushan or later.
farmer may only plow the area
surrounding each tree. The
remainder of the field is subject
to the rules for fields of grain,
i.C.2:1.

2:10A-G Gourds that have been   The underlying theory is no
left out and become inedible when   different from that of
it is yet the sixth year may be   i.C.2:7-8 and 9. This
tended for their seeds in the   provides firm grounds for
seventh year. But if they still   assigning this unit to Usha.
are edible when the seventh year
begins, they are subject to the
rules of the Sabbatical Year and
must be used as food.

ii. Field Work During the Sabbatical Year

In the Sabbatical year it is forbidden to do field labor
that benefits the growth of that year's crop. It is, however,
permitted to do work that does not benefit the seventh year-

produce. The farmer may, for instance, trim trees in order to obtain wood or material for weaving. He even may prepare his fields for cultivation in the year following the Sabbatical. The problem is that, in carrying out these permitted activities, the farmer will appear to others as though he is transgressing. Yavneans are clear, on the one hand, that the farmer must prevent any actual infringement, even if it occurs as a result of permitted labor (ii.B.3:10). They are not, on the other hand, certain that one should be prevented from doing what is in fact permitted simply because it appears to be a transgression. This question is disputed by Aqiba, who holds that all that counts is the actual status of the labor, permitted or forbidden, and Yose, who wishes to be certain that the individual does not even appear to transgress (ii.B.4:6).[8]

In the Ushan period, Yose's view is accepted as normative and forms the basis for a long series of examples. Each of these describes the way in which a person who does a type of permitted field work should alter his mode of working so as to avoid the appearance of doing what is forbidden. These examples take up all of the pericopae in the Ushan statum as well as those listed as unassigned. One Houses' dispute, ii.A.4:4, assumes this same, Ushan, principle, such that it too presumably derives from Ushan times.

The Houses dispute a second issue that may genuinely reflect issues current in the period before 70. The question is the responsibility of one individual not to benefit from the transgression of another person. The Shammaites (ii.A.4:2A-H, 4:2I-K) consistently hold that once someone has done forbidden field work or otherwise transgressed the rules of the Sabbatical year, even a different person may not eat the affected produce. In a related point they state that a person may take no risk of aiding another who might transgress, e.g., by selling the tools required for the transgression (ii.A.5:8). This same position is stated anonymously at ii.D.5:6, 7 and 9 and is, as we have seen, a basic datum of Tractate Demai. The Hillelites take the opposite view. They hold that the improper field labor does not affect the produce that benefitted from it, and that one person is not responsible to prevent another from transgressing, unless he is absolutely certain that that individual intends to sin. Notably, in this case, in which the Hillelites' view stands against the pervasive trend of the law, Judah, ii.A.4:2I-K, claims that the positions of the Houses have been reversed.

A. Before 70

4:2A-H A field that was cleared of thorns in the seventh year (a permitted activity) may be sown in the following year. But a field that was improved in a forbidden way during the seventh year may not be sown in the following year. A field that was improved in the seventh year--Shammaites: They do not eat produce which grows in it in the seventh year. Hillelites: They may.

Both Houses can agree to the anonymous rule, which holds that the farmer may not benefit from his forbidden labor. The issue between them is the status of the fruit of the seventh year itself. The Shammaites hold that since it benefits from forbidden field-work, it too is forbidden. The Hillelites are attentive to the fact that its growth is not solely a function of forbidden work. They therefore deem it permitted. This issue appears in the Yavnean stratum, iv.B.9:9, lending weight to its placement before 70.

4:2I-K Shammaites: One may not eat produce of the seventh year given as a favor by the field's owner. Hillelites: They may. Judah: The positions are reversed.

Produce of the Sabbatical Year belongs to whomever gathers it. The field's owner therefore does not have the right to take it as his own to give away. As in the preceding entry, the Shammaites prohibit consumption of produce that is tainted by some forbidden activity. The Hillelites likewise are consistent. The produce is not affected by what is done with it and therefore may be eaten.[9]

4:4 One who thins out olive trees--Shammaites: He should cut them at ground level. Hillelites:

Thinning is necessary for the continued growth of all of the trees. It therefore

He may uproot them, so long as he is not removing many trees.

is permitted in the Sabbatical year (i.C.2:2-5). The Shammaites want the man to remove the trees in a way which makes it clear that he does not intend to perform forbidden tilling of the soil. The Hillelites agree in theory and simply hold that this is not a problem so long as the man removes only a few trees. Dependent upon the Ushan notion of i.C.2:2-5 and accepting an underlying assumption which, while moot at Yavneh (ii.B.4:6), is taken for granted in Ushan times, this material cannot derive from the historical Houses. Note also the parallel discussion at ii.C.4:5.

5:8 Shammaites: During the seventh year a person may not sell to another a heifer suited for plowing. House of Hillel: He may, since the buyer might slaughter it. + Three examples of the Hillelite view.

The Shammaites want the seller to take no risk that he will aid the buyer in transgressing. The Hillelites hold that so long as he cannot prove that the sale will lead to a violation of the law, he is not culpable. The Shammaite opinion is parallel to their view at Demai, ii.A.3:1C-H, and this issue, moot here, is resolved and developed in this tractate at ii.D.5:6 and 7. It may indeed derive from the period before 70.

B. The Time of Yavneh

3:10 During the Sabbatical Year
one who builds a fence between his
property and the public domain may
dig down to rock level. Joshua:
He should use the dirt he digs up
to fix the road. Aqiba: He may
not do that.

Since the area on the fringe
of the individual's land is
not normally suitable for
cultivation, there is no
problem with the individ-
ual's digging there to build
a fence. The problem is
what he should do with the
dirt, for placing it on his
own land prepares his field
for cultivation. Aqiba
does not even allow the
person to place the dirt
in the road, lest this
creates an arable area. The
fact that the individual
does not intend to cultivate
the field is not taken into
account.

4:6 One who snips vines or reeds
during the Sabbatical year in
order to obtain material for
weaving or use as wood--Yose the
Galilean: He should snip a
handbreadth from the place at
which one normally would trim
for cultivation. Aqiba: He may
cut in his usual manner.

The issue is whether or not
one who performs permitted
labor in the seventh year
must avoid the appearance of
doing what is prohibited.
Yose holds that he must,
Aqiba that he need not.
Moot at Yavneah, this issue
is resolved in Ushan times
in favor of Yose's view.
Exposition of that view
takes up the majority of the
Ushan and unassigned
materials in the unit. See
T. 3:19.

C. The Time of Usha

3:1-2 At what point in the
Sabbatical Year may they begin to
bring manure out to the fields as
fertilizer for the eighth year?

The farmer may engage in
field labor designed to
prepare for the planting of
the crop of the eighth

Meir: From the time at which
fertilizing for the present year
normally would cease. Judah:
When the ground moisture has
dried up. Yose: When the ground
forms clumps. They may make up
to three dung-heaps of ten baskets
each per seah-space. Simeon:
They may create more dung heaps.

(=first) year, so long as
this does not indirectly
benefit the crop of the
Sabbatical year. Ushan
authorities dispute the
point in the seventh year
after which fertilizing does
not aid the growth of that
same year's crop. Parallel
in issue and theory to
i.C.2:1, this clearly
derives from Ushan times.
The development of this
issue at M. 3:2 concerns the
manner in which the dung
may be brought into the
field so as to avoid the
appearance of fertilizing in
the Sabbatical Year. This
too is Ushan.

3:3 Simeon, Meir and Eleazar b.
Azariah dispute the issue of
M. 3:2, that is, of how the
farmer may bring dung into his
field without appearing to
transgress the restrictions of
the Sabbatical Year.

By piling his dung in heaps
or by placing it in areas
slightly higher or lower
than ground level the farmer
makes clear that the dung is
intended as fertilizer for
the following year. Eleazar
b. Azariah is made to repeat
the position assigned to
Meir. His name is out of
place in discussion of this
clearly Ushan concern.

3:4 One who, in the Sabbatical
Year, uses his field as a fold
must build pens to prevent the
animals from dropping dung
throughout the field and thereby
fertilizing it. As each enclosure
is filled with dung he may move
it to a new area, up to a total

The problem is derivative of
that discussed in the
preceding entries. Along
with the attribution to
Simeon b. Gamaliel this
provides firm grounds for
placement of these rules in
the Ushan stratum. Further

size of eight <u>seah</u>-spaces. So
Simeon b. Gamaliel. Ultimately
he must remove the dung from the
enclosures and pile it as required
by M. 3:1-3.

Ushan discussion is at
T. 2:15-18.

3:9 To build terraces (see
ii.D.3:8) the farmer may bring
large stones from anywhere, even
his own fields. Contractors
may bring small stones from
anywhere. Yose and Meir dispute
definition of large stones.

The problem is that the
individual who removes
stones from his field might
appear to prepare the field
for cultivation in the
seventh year, which is
forbidden. If the stones
are very large, he obviously
wants them for construction
and so avoids this
appearance. Professional
builders are not subject to
this suspicion at all.
Attested to Usha by Meir and
Yose and continuing the
clearly Ushan theme of
ii.D.3:5-8, this is firmly
placed in the Ushan stratum.
See also T. 3:4.

4:5 In the Sabbatical Year one
who cuts branches for lumber may
not seal the stump in the way
normally used to cultivate the
growth of new branches. Judah:
One does the cutting in an
unusual manner, so as to indicate
clearly that he does not intend
to cultivate new branches.

The issue again is how the
farmer performs permitted
labor in a manner that makes
it clear to observers that
what he is doing indeed is
allowed. Judah and the
anonymous rule simply
disagree concerning the type
of deviation that is
required. Continued Ushan
discussion is at T. 3:14-15.

D. Unassigned
3:5 During the Sabbatical year
one may not open a stone quarry in
his field, unless the field

In removing stones from the
field the individual may
appear to be preparing the

contains enough stones to build three piles of hewn blocks.

field for cultivation, forbidden in the seventh year. If the field contains substantial amounts of rock, it is clear that this is not the man's intent. The rule is attested to Usha by Judah and Simeon b. Gamaliel, T. 3:1-2. Since its basic conception is parallel to that of ii.C.3:1-2, 3 and 4, we have good reason to assign it to Ushan times.

3:6 Same theory as at M. 3:5. An individual may tear down a stone wall, provided that he does not appear to be clearing the field for cultivation. To prevent this appearance it must be clear that the individual requires the stones from the wall for construction.

Grounds for placement of this rule in the Ushan stratum are the same as in the preceding entry, to which it is parallel in content and theory. Note also the attestation to Usha by Yose and Meir, ii.C.3:9.

3:7 Partially uncovered stones in a field may be removed only if doing so requires the efforts of two men.

The large stones clearly are useful in construction. Like the preceding material, this is Ushan.

3:8 Building terraces late in the year prepares the land for cultivation in the following year. The farmer therefore may not do this in the sixth year but may do so during the seventh. He may not build a dirt retaining wall, for this looks like an act of cultivation.

This develops the preceding entries and follows their same theory. In the Sabbatical year the individual may prepare the land for planting in the following year, so long as in doing so he does not appear to transgress. Like what has preceded, this is Ushan. See ii.C.3:9.

4:1 At first people were allowed to collect large stones from their own fields (see ii.C.3:9). When people began to transgress, each person was permitted only to gather stones from his neighbor's field, and his neighbor from his, so long as they did not engage in a mutual favor.

This depends upon an Ushan law and presents a further development beyond that stage in legal thinking. An individual who takes stones from his neighbor's field clearly requires them for building and does not intend to prepare the land for cultivation.

4:3 They may lease from gentiles fields plowed in the seventh year, but not from Israelites. They may verbally encourage[10] gentiles who perform agricultural labors during the seventh year, but not Israelites.

The point is the same as in the anonymous rule at ii.A.4:2A-H. Gentiles are not bound by the restrictions of the law. In the eighth year, Israelites therefore may make use of fields they plowed in the seventh (cf., the Shammites, ii.A.4:2A-H). Greeting and encouraging the gentile does not implicate the Israelite in the work, which he himself is forbidden to perform.

5:6 In the Sabbatical Year an artisan may not sell tools used only to perform forbidden field-work. But he may sell tools used to carry out permitted activities.

The artisan may not become an accessory to the other individual's transgression. This notion, that one should prevent others from transgressing, is found in the earliest stratum of this tractate, ii.A.5:8 (the Shammaites' view), as well as in Demai, ii.A.3:1C-H, ii.B.3:1A-B, ii.C.2:2-5 and ii.D.3:2.

5:7 During the Sabbatical Year a potter may sell each individual

The theory is the same as in the preceding entry. Since

no more than five oil containers and fifteen wine containers.	the individual is not permitted to carry out a regular harvest and to store what he produces, he should not need many containers. The potter is not allowed to sell him the vessels that would allow him to break the law.
5:9 A woman may lend tools to a neighbor suspected of violating the law, but she may not help her when it is apparent that she is actually committing a transgression.	This develops the foregoing by drawing a fine distinction between lending tools that might be used illegally and actually participating in a transgression.

iii. Produce Subject to the Sabbatical Restrictions

Produce that grows in the Sabbatical year is subject to certain restrictions, described in detail in the following unit. These restrictions apply to produce which grows and ripens before the seventh year, but which is stored in the ground and continues to grow in the Sabbatical year itself (iii.B.5:3, 6:3). They apply as well to produce that sprouts in the seventh year but which takes several years to ripen and become edible. Such produce is subject to the restrictions of the Sabbatical year whenever it actually is eaten, in the first or second year of the cycle (iii.C.5:1). As Ushans make clear, this means that even after the Sabbatical year, buyers must be careful not to purchase food that grew in the seventh year and that therefore is subject to the Sabbatical restrictions (iii.C.5:5, 6:4).

A second principle assumed by Yavneans and Ushans derives from the Houses (iii.A.4:10A-C). All produce of the Sabbatical year must be allowed to ripen and be used to feed the needy of the people of Israel. This means that, once trees have borne fruit, farmers may not prevent that fruit from developing and becoming edible. Cutting down a tree, for instance, constitutes misuse of food that belongs to all of the people of Israel.

A final issue is first debated in Yavnean times (iii.B.6:2) and is fully developed in the period of Usha (iii.D.6:1). This concerns the extent to which the prohibitions of the Sabbatical

year apply in Syria and within the various areas of the land of
Israel itself. The larger point, iii.D.6:1, is that the level of
restrictions that apply in each area depends upon the duration of
time during which Israelites have lived in that area. The longer
the Israelites have lived in an area, the greater the level of
sanctity of that place and, concomitantly, the more stringent the
restrictions that apply. Later authorities thus equate the
holiness of the land of Israel with the actual presence there of
Israelites.

A. Before 70

4:10A-C The House of Shammai: In the Sabbatical Year, once trees have produced fruit, the farmer may not cut them down. The House of Hillel: For certain trees, one may not cut them down right after blossoms or berries appear.

The Houses agree on the basic principle that one may not destroy fruit that is growing in the seventh year. This fruit is the property of all Israelites, to be gathered and used as their food. The issue is one of fact, that is, when do we deem the tree to have borne fruit. The theory agreed upon by the Houses is assumed throughout this unit. The dispute may therefore be authentic.

5:4 Arum and other produce of the sixth year that is stored underground in the Sabbatical Year-- Shammaites: They dig them up with wooden rakes. Hillelites: They may use metal spades, the usual tool.

The issue is familiar from unit ii. The Shammaites want to assure that the individual does not appear to be performing forbidden field work. Since what he is doing is in fact permitted, the Hillelites, by contrast, allow him to do it in the usual manner. This same issue is moot at Yavneh, ii.B.4:6, and is resolved in Ushan times. It thus is possible that this

dispute is authentic to the
period before 70.

B. The Time of Yavneh

5:3 If a farmer stored arum
underground and, in the seventh
year, it sprouted leaves, these
leaves belong to the poor. If
the poor did not collect them,
the farmer must give them a
portion of the arum tuber when
he unburies it. So Eliezer.
Joshua: In such a case, he
owes them nothing.

All agree that the leaves
are produce of the
Sabbatical Year and go to
the poor. Eliezer deems the
tuber and leaves a single
entity. If the poor did not
take the leaves, they
therefore have a share in
the tuber itself. Joshua
deems the two parts of the
plant to be autonomous,
such that the poor have a
claim only upon the leaves
and not the tuber.
Developed at iii.C.5:2 and
5, this is firmly attested
to Yavneh.

6:2 In Syria they may not
cultivate and harvest produce,
but produce that grew on its own
and was picked may be processed
in the normal manner. Aqiba:
Syria is just like the land of
Israel itself.

The anonymous rule holds
that since Syria is not part
of the land of Israel
proper, it is not subject to
all of the restrictions of
the Sabbatical Year. Aqiba
disagrees, holding that
since Syria is inhabited by
many Israelites, it is to
be treated just like the
land. The unstated theory
of the anonymous rule is
given explicitly at
iii.D.6:1. Aqiba's theory
is taken up by Simeon,
iii.C.6:5-6.

6:3 Onions which grew in the
sixth year, were left in the
ground in the seventh, and

The agreed-upon principle is
that if the onions grow anew
in the seventh year, they

sprouted--if the leaves are dark in color, the onions are subject to the restrictions of the Sabbatical Year. Hanina b. Antigonos: The onions are subject if they can be uprooted by the leaves.

are subject to the restrictions of that year. The dispute concerns the secondary problem of how we determine whether or not the onions are growing in the Sabbatical Year. Parallel in principle to iii.B.5:3 and attested by a Yavnean authority, this clearly belongs in the Yavnean stratum. Development occurs at iii.C.5:1 and 2.

C. The Time of Usha

4:10F-H In all years of the Sabbatical cycle, how much fruit need there be on an olive tree for it to come under the restriction found at Dt. 20:10-20? Simeon b. Gamaliel disputes.

Israelites are forbidden to cut down trees during a siege. The issue is the minimum amount of produce that may not be destroyed. The problem is autonomous of this tractate and is placed in the Ushan stratum on the basis of the attribution to Simeon.

5:1 White figs which appear in the Sabbatical Year but which take three years to ripen are subject to the restrictions of the Sabbatical Year in the second year of the cycle, when they are eaten. Judah: The same applies to Persian figs, which take two years to ripen.

Produce that appears in the seventh year is subject to all the pertinent restrictions. The fact that the particular type of produce will not be eaten until after the Sabbatical Year does not change that fact. Placement is on the basis of the attribution to Judah.

5:2 One who stores arum for preservation during the Sabbatical Year must prevent it from

Storing food grown before the Sabbatical Year is permitted so long as in

sprouting. Meir and sages
discuss how this is done.

doing so the farmer does not
wind up having planted the
produce that he buries. The
question of how the farmer
prevents this from happening
is secondary to the issue
presented at iii.B.5:3.
Along with the attribution
to Meir, this provides firm
grounds for placing this at
Usha.

5:5 At the end of the Sabbatical
Year one may purchase arum
immediately. So Judah. Sages:
One must wait until the new
produce reaches the marketplace.

Judah's point is familiar
from iii.C.5:1. Since the
arum in question sprouted in
the year before the
Sabbatical, it is not
subject to the restrictions
of the seventh year at all.
Sages disagree and hold
that, because the majority
of the growth of the arum
occurred in the seventh
year, it is subject to the
restrictions of that year.
Continued Ushan discussion
is at T. 4:4.

6:4 After the Sabbatical Year
they may purchase produce in the
market when the new produce of
its same type has become ripe.
Once the early ripening produce
in one location is available,
produce of its type may be
purchased in other locations.
Rabbi permitted the purchase of
vegetables immediately at the
end of the Sabbatical Year.

The anonymous rule wants the
buyer to be certain that the
produce he purchases did not
grow in the seventh year.
Rabbi takes the radical
position that once the
Sabbatical Year has ended,
the restrictions that
applied in that year no
longer pertain. This
perspective has no parallel
in the late stratum of the
law.

6:5-6 During the Sabbatical Year they may export produce from the land of Israel to countries outside of the land. Simeon: I have heard that they may export the produce to Syria. They may not import heave-offering from outside of the land to the land. Simeon: They may import it from Syria.

Simeon qualifies the anonymous rule, taking the position elsewhere given by Aqiba (iii.B.6:2), that Syria has the same status of the land of Israel itself. These are solid grounds for placement of this rule in the Ushan stratum. Other Ushan discussion is found at T. 5:1-2.

D. Unassigned

4:7-9 After what time during the Sabbatical Year may they eat the fruit of trees? They may snack of it when it becomes edible; they may gather it into their homes for use in a regular meal once it has fully ripened and become subject to tithes.

Produce of the seventh year must be put to its normal use, as a food. It therefore is important that individuals not be allowed to gather and eat this produce until it would be deemed ready for such consumption in other years of the Sabbatical cycle. Concern for the general issue referred to here is found in both the Yavnean and Ushan strata of this unit. I see no basis for specific placement of this pericope.

4:10D-E Once the fruit on a tree is subject to tithes, it is permitted to cut that tree down.

This develops the principle articulated at iii.A.4:10A-C in light of the facts given in the preceding entry. When the fruit is subject to tithes, it is autonomous of the tree, for it is deemed a fruit in its own right. Specific placement is impossible.

6:1 Land occupied in the time of Joshua and again after the Babylonian exile may not be cultivated during the seventh year. If it is, the produce may be eaten. Land occupied in the time of Joshua but not after the exile may not be cultivated. But if it is, the produce may be eaten. Land in which Israelites never settled may be cultivated during the Sabbatical Year, and the produce may be eaten.

The sanctity of the land, and concomitantly the level of restriction of the Sabbatical year, depends upon the duration of time during which Israelites have lived there. Stating as law what is moot at Yavneh, iii.B.6:2, and attentive to the power of Israelites themselves within the processes of sanctification this appears to derive from Ushan times.

iv. Restrictions Upon Produce of the Sabbatical Year

The theory of the unit is in place by the Yavnean period, in which we find the principle that oil of the Sabbatical year must be used as a food and not as a lubricant (iv.B.8:9-10). This basic notion--that produce of the seventh year must be put to its usual purpose--is developed by Ushans. They make the following points:

1) Since produce of the Sabbatical year is intended for use as food (iv.B.8:9-10; see iv.D.8:1 and 2), it may not be used in any sort of business transaction, e.g., sold as a regular market commodity or used to discharge a debt (iv.C.7:3-4, iv.D.8:4, 5 and 8; and the apparently Ushan iv.A.8:3).

2) The produce may not be processed as a market commodity, in large quantities intended for sale. It may be processed only in small amounts, and the individual who does so must make clear to others that he is not engaged in a business activity (iv.C.8:6).

3) One must not cook produce of the seventh year with heave-offering, for if the mixture becomes unclean, the food of the Sabbatical year would have to be burned (iv.C.8:7, under dispute by Simeon).

4) Like other agricultural restrictions, those that pertain to the Sabbatical year apply only to cultivated produce and not to that which grows wild (iv.C.9:1). As we shall see in detail in Tractate Maaserot, the system of agricultural tithes and

restrictions is set in motion by Israelites, who exploit the land of Israel by cultivating food for their sustenance.

The second major discussion of this unit concerns the rule that, once produce of a certain type no longer is found in the fields, individuals who have collected that type of food in their homes must remove it so as to make it available to those who are in need. Yavneans refer to the question of autonomous types of produce that have their own distinct times for removal (iv.B.9:6-7). In the same vein they question how one carries out the removal of several different types of produce that have been cooked together into a single dish (iv.B.9:5A-E).

Ushans have their own interests, which take up a quite basic set of questions concerning the removal. They establish divisions of the land of Israel, so that the removal can be carried out according to the particular agricultural conditions in different parts of the country (iv.C.9:2-3). They define the conditions under which a type of produce is deemed no longer to be available, such that the law of removal applies to it (iv.C.9:4). Finally they question who may take produce that has been removed, whether anyone or only the poor (iv.C.9:8). I see no consistent theory which ties together these several ideas.

A.   Before 70

8:3 During the Sabbatical Year they do not sell produce in standard measures of volume, weight or quantity. Shammaites: They also may not sell in bunches. Hillelites: What is not customarily sold in bunches may, during the seventh year, be sold in bunches.

Produce of the seventh year may not be used in a business transaction, (iv.C.7:3-4.) This extends that principle by preventing the use of standard measures, which allow the seller to get fair market value. If the produce is not measured out, the individuals involved in the sale are not culpable of engaging in a regular business transaction. The Shammaites simply add that a bunch is a standard measure. The Hillelites by contrast allow the sale of a bunch, so long as that is not the measure

in which the produce is sold
in other years of the cycle.
Their concern is appearances
and not the actual use of
the produce in a business
deal. Based upon iv.C.7:3-4
and reminiscent of the
clearly Ushan rule at
Terumot, i.C.1:7, this
attribution to the Houses
appears pseudepigraphic.

B. The Time of Yavneh

8:9-10 A hide rubbed with oil of
the Sabbatical Year should be
burned. So Eliezer. Sages say:
The one who smeared it with oil
must replace the oil. Aqiba
glosses.

This attests to Yavneh the
notion fully developed at
Usha that produce of the
Sabbatical year must be used
in its usual manner as a
food. Developed at iv.C.8:6
and iv.D.8:1 and 2, this is
firmly placed in the Yavnean
stratum.

9:6-7 Fresh herbs, reeds or
leaves are removed early in the
seventh year, when the ground
moisture dries up or when leaves
in the field fall off of their
stems. Dried herbs, reeds or
leaves are removed much later,
at the time of the second
rainfall.

The anonymous rule holds
that dried and fresh
varieties of the same
produce are deemed different
kinds with respect to the
law of removal. Fresh
produce therefore is removed
as soon as no more fresh
produce is left in the
field. That which is dried,
by contrast, may be kept in
one's home much later, until
all such produce is gone
from the fields. Aqiba
disagrees, for he is
attentive only to the
botanical species of the
produce. Placement in the
Yavnean stratum depends upon

Aqiba's attestation and the fact that this unit is parallel in issue to the preceding entry.

9:9 One who receives as an inheritance or gift produce of the Sabbatical Year after the time of removal may keep and eat the produce. So Eliezer. Sages: The sinner may not benefit from the transgression. The one who receives the produce must distribute its value among everyone.

Eliezer takes up the Hillelite view, ii.A.4:2A-H. Since the recipient of the produce is not responsible for the transgression, he may accept and use that which he is given.[11] Sages have the Shammaite view. The produce is tainted by not having been removed. Its new owner must assure that its value is distributed, just as the produce itself should have been. Attributed to a Yavnean authority and standing in close relationship to an idea assigned to the Houses, this is firmly placed in the Yavnean stratum.

C. The Time of Usha
7:1-2 1) All produce which is edible or used for dyeing is subject to the restrictions of the Sabbatical Year. 2) Annuals also are subject to removal. Perennials are not. Meir: Money gained through the sale of perennials is subject to removal, just as it is subject to the restrictions of the seventh year. Sages disagree.

The law of the Sabbatical Year applies not only to foods (Maaserot, i.C.1:1) but also to common market commodities, such as dyes. In the seventh year the earth thus is allowed to rest from production of all market commodities. 2) The law of removal applies only to produce that actually disappears from the field. Placement is on the basis of the attestation to Meir.

7:3-4 During the Sabbatical Year   One may not do business with
a dyer may dye for himself but   produce of the Sabbatical
not for a fee. They may not gather   Year or with other forbidden
produce to sell, but if they   things. Judah and sages
gathered and had too much, what   dispute what constitutes
is left over may be sold. Judah: doing business. While sages
One who has an opportunity to   have regard for the
buy an unclean animal may purchase   individual transaction,
it and then sell it at a profit,   Judah is concerned only with
so long as he does not do this for   what the person does day-to-
a livelihood. Sages prohibit.   day as his living. Place-
                                       ment depends upon the
                                       attribution to Judah, who
                                       applies the common Ushan
                                       perspective that defines a
                                       category, in this case,
                                       business, in terms of the
                                       perspective of the
                                       individual involved. Rabbi
                                       and Simeon join in the
                                       discussion, T. 5:10.

7:6 Aromatic plants are classified   Supplying specific examples
as dyeing matter. Simeon exempts   of the rules found in the
basalm from the restrictions of   preceding entry, this is
the Sabbatical Year, for it is   firmly placed in Ushan
neither a plant nor a fruit.   times. See T. 5:12.

8:6 Produce of the Sabbatical   The principle is familiar
Year must be processed in an   from unit ii, that one must
unusual manner. Simeon glosses.   avoid the appearance of
                                       forbidden labor. This idea
                                       is debated at Yavneh,
                                       ii.B.3:10, and greatly
                                       expanded at Usha, e.g.,
                                       ii.C.3:1-2, 3. Placement of
                                       the present rule accordingly
                                       is on firm grounds.
                                       Continued Ushan discussion
                                       is at T. 6:27, 28 and 29.

8:7 They may not cook produce of the seventh year in heave-offering oil, lest the oil become unclean and the produce be made inedible. Simeon permits.

The anonymous rule wants to prevent any potential waste of produce of the Sabbatical Year (see iv.D.8:1). Simeon, by contrast, is concerned only with the circumstances of the moment. The cooking itself does not render the produce forbidden and therefore is allowed. Dependent upon an apparently Ushan rule and attested by an Ushan authority, this is firmly placed in this stratum.

9:1 Produce that grows wild and never is cultivated is exempt from tithes and may be purchased from anyone during the Sabbatical Year. Judah: Produce which might have been cultivated, but which grows wild in abundance, may be purchased from anyone in the Sabbatical year. Simeon: All aftergrowths are permitted, on the assumption that they were not cultivated. Sages: All aftergrowths are forbidden, since they might have been cultivated.

Produce that grows uncultivated stands outside of Mishnah's system of agricultural restrictions (see also Maaserot, i.C.1:1). Aftergrowths, disputed by Judah, Simeon and sages, present a different problem. These might have grown on their own. Alternatively, they may have been cultivated in violation of the laws of the Sabbatical Year. Judah says we use logic to determine whether or not it is likely that the produce was cultivated. Simeon's point is no different. Only sages disagree, holding that a case of doubt is adjudicated stringently. If there is any chance that the produce was cultivated, it may not be purchased in the Sabbatical year.

9:2-3 For purposes of the application of the law of removal, the land of Israel is divided into three regions, and each region is divided into three areas. Simeon: There are three separate areas only within Judea. Sages: All the regions are considered one for purposes of the removal of olives and dates.

Produce becomes ripe, is harvested and finally disappears from the field at different times in different places within the land of Israel. For this reason the land is divided into areas, within each of which the removal can be carried out as appropriate to that specific place. Placement is on the basis of the attestation by Simeon. Continued Ushan discussion is at T. 7:11 and 15.

9:4 They may retain in their homes produce of the Sabbatical year if produce of the same type is growing in the fields, accessible to all. Yose: They may retain it even if produce of its type is growing only in privately-owned courtyards. They may retain in their homes choice grain of the Sabbatical year if late-ripening grain still is found in the fields. Judah: They may retain it even if only winter grain is found in the field, so long as that winter grain began to ripen before the end of the summer.

When produce of a certain type is not available in the fields, Israelites who have collected and stored that kind of produce in their homes must release it for use by all who are in need. The issue here is what constitutes availability of a particular kind of produce. In each case the anonymous rule holds that the law of removal takes effect as soon as the produce is not readily available for anyone to collect and eat. Judah and Yose, by contrast, hold that the law of removal does not take effect until the type of produce has entirely disappeared from the land. Placement is on the basis of the attributions to Judah and Yose.

9:5F-G Simeon: All vegetables
are regarded as a single species
with regard to the laws of
removal + example.

Simeon holds that all
vegetables are subject to
removal at the same time.
So long as any vegetables
are growing in the field,
the householder need not
remove that which he has
stored in his house.
Rejecting the basic
supposition that underlies
iv.B.9:5A-E, this is firmly
placed in the Ushan stratum.

9:8 When the time of removal
comes, the individual sets aside
sufficient produce for three
meals for each member of his
household and then removes the
rest. Judah: Only the poor may
eat the produce that has been
removed. Yose: Poor and rich
alike may eat it.

Judah holds that what is
removed is comparable to a
poor-offering, and may be
eaten only by those who are
in special need. Yose by
contrast states that removal
is intended simply to assure
that all Israelites have
equal access to the produce
of the Sabbatical Year.
Rich and poor therefore may
take what has been removed.
Placement is on the basis of
attribution to Ushan
authorities. Continued
Ushan discussion is at
T. 8:1.

D. Unassigned
7:5 Examples of produce that
falls under the rules of
iv.C.7:1-2.

This can derive from no
earler than Ushan times. It
is discussed by Ushan
authorities, T. 5:11.

7:7 If produce of the seventh
year is inextricably mixed with
produce of a different year, all
of the produce becomes subject to
the laws of the Sabbatical Year.

This rule depends upon
clearly Ushan notions. See
Terumot, vii.C.10:1, 3, 8,
and 11A-D. Rejecting ideas
current at Yavneh (Terumot,

If, however, the seventh-year produce can be removed from the mixture, the other produce is unaffected.

8:1 That which grows in the Sabbatical Year must be used for its normal purpose, either as a food, emollient or as cattle feed. If it has a secondary use as a wood-fuel, and the individual gathered it for that purpose, he may burn it.

8:2 Produce of the Sabbatical Year must be used for its usual purpose, eating, drinking or anointing. This same law applies to heave-offering and second tithe, except that clean oil of the Sabbatical Year may be kindled in a lamp.

8:4 An individual may say to a worker, "Here is an _issar_ as a gift. Gather vegetables of the Sabbatical Year for me." He may not say, "In return for this _issar_ gather vegetables for me."

vii.B.10:11E-H), it cannot derive from earlier than the Ushan period.

Produce of the seventh year must be used in its ordinary fashion, as a food or lotion. This assures that the land's yield will be available to meet the basic needs of Israelites during the seventh year. This principle, that consecrated produce must be put to its usual purpose, is known from Yavnean times, Terumot, viii.B.11:3. Attested to Yavneh and Usha, T. 5:15, this particular application of that principle may be as early as Yavnean.

The point is the same as in the preceding entry. This construction appears to be Ushan, as the parallels at Terumot, viii.C.11:1 and Maaser Sheni, i.C.2:1A-H show.

Produce of the Sabbatical year may be given as a gift, but it may not be purchased (iv.A.8:3). This rule thus establishes a legal fiction by which the individual may acquire produce of the Sabbatical year without actually purchasing it.

Dependent upon an apparently
Ushan rule (iv.A.8:3), there
is no evidence that this law
is known before Ushan times.

8:5 Produce of the Sabbatical
Year may not be used to pay the
wages of hired laborers. It may
however be exchanged for food or
water.

The point is familiar from
before. The seventh year-
produce may not be used in a
financial transaction, e.g.,
to discharge a debt. It
may, however, be given as a
gift or traded for other
food.

8:8 They may not use money gained
from the sale of seventh year-
produce to purchase non-edibles
or to discharge debts. If they
do, they must purchase and eat
other produce of equal value,
following the restrictions of the
seventh year. If one used seventh
year-oil to treat leather, that
oil must be replaced.

Money gained from the sale
of produce of the Sabbatical
Year has the same
consecrated status as that
produce. It therefore may
not be used in a financial
transaction. If it is, it
must be replaced with other
money, to be treated as
though it were derived from
seventh year-produce. The
notion of the replacement of
misused consecrated things
is detailed at length in
unit iv of Tractate Terumot.
The present construction may
be as early as Yavnean. See
Shebiit iv.B.8:9-10.

8:11 One may bathe in a bath
heated with straw and stubble of
the Sabbatical Year. But a highly
regarded person should not do so.

Since the straw is available
for use as animal fodder, it
should not be used as a fuel
(iv.D.8:1). The bather
presumably is not respon-
sible for the transgression
and may therefore enjoy the
bath. Rejecting the position assigned to Eliezer,

iv.B.8:9-10, this may be
Yavnean or later.

v. The Release of Debts in the Sabbatical Year

In the seventh year all loans made between Israelites are
cancelled. The creditor may exact no payment from the borrower
(Dt. 15:1-2). In the period before 70 (v.A.10:3-4, v.D.10:2H-I),
a legal fiction is designed which prevents this cancellation of
debts. The lender writes a document, called a prozbul, that
turns the debt over for collection by a court. Since private,
but not public, loans are released in the seventh year (see
v.D.10:2F-G), the prozbul allows the collection of the debt
despite the advent of the Sabbatical year. The theory of the
prozbul is developed by Yavneans. They hold that only secured
loans may be turned over to a court (v.B.10:6, 7). This is
because, having the security, the creditor can claim already to
have been repaid, even before the seventh year. The court simply
presides over the exchange of the security for cash payment.
Yavneans further detail the correct procedure for the case of a
borrower who has no property to which to secure the loan.

Ushans do not carry forward the preceding discussion in
specific ways. Instead, they provide a systematic account of
quite basic matters of definition. Specifically, they detail the
sorts of debts that are cancelled in the Sabbatical year
(v.C.10:1). Their point is that loans, but not accounts
receivable, are released. Ushans therefore go ahead to describe
the conditions under which a sum of money owed, for instance, as
wages is deemed a loan.

The unassigned material contains several points of general
interest, which cannot be placed within the unfolding of the law.
A prozbul or other document may not be ante- or post-dated, so as
to give the creditor an undue right to collection (v.D.10:5). A
creditor must tell a borrower that a loan has been released by
the seventh year (v.D.10:5). If the borrower should anyway
desire to repay the loan, this is allowed and, indeed, is
praiseworthy (v.D.10:9).

A. Before 70
10:3-4 Hillel the Elder saw that   The prozbul is a legal
before the Sabbatical Year people   fiction which prevents the
refrained from lending money. He   cancellation of debts in the

instituted the prozbul, a document which authorizes a court to collect a loan on the lender's behalf. Such a loan, owed to a court, is not cancelled by the Sabbatical Year.

Sabbatical Year by placing them in the hands of the court. Discussion continues in Yavnean times, v.B.10:6 and 7. It therefore seems likely that the notion of the prozbul derives from the period before 70.

B. The Time of Yavneh

10:6 They may write a prozbul only if the borrower owns land. If he does not, the lender transfers to him some miniscule amount of property. Huspit: In writing a prozbul they may rely upon the borrower's wife's property or, if the borrowers are orphans, upon their guardian's property.

The property is used to secure the loan (see v.D.10:2H-I). Since even the smallest piece of land has lasting, indeterminate, value (so Aqiba, Peah, i.B.3:6), it serves this purpose. If the borrower does not himself own land, property owned by others and transferred to him will serve. Since v.A.10:3-4 does not mention the need to tie the loan to property, this rule, attested by Huspit, clearly develops the earlier notion. Along with the Aqiban parallel, this provides good grounds for placing this entry at Yavneh.

10:7 A bee-hive that sits on the ground but is not attached to it-- Eliezer: It is real estate, and therefore they write a prozbul against it. Sages: It is not real estate, and they do not write a prozbul against it.

This is a secondary development of the preceding. While the attribution to Eliezer is ambiguous, I assume this belongs at Yavneh, with the other discussion of this particular aspect of the prozbul.

C. The Time of Usha

10:1 In the Sabbatical Year, all loans are cancelled. Other debts, such as wages or accounts payable, are not cancelled. Judah: When a buyer incurs a new debt, his former debt with the same shopkeeper becomes a loan and is cancelled in the Sabbatical Year. Yose: Wages for work completed during the seventh year are deemed a loan made by the worker to the employer and therefore are cancelled. If the work continues after the Sabbatical Year, the wages are simply a debt and are not cancelled.

Dt. 15:1-2 is clear that in the seventh year loans, but not other debts, are cancelled. The problem is how to determine when a commercial debt becomes a loan, such that it should be cancelled. Judah and Yose offer distinct criteria. Judah notes that as a shopkeeper continues to sell on credit, previous balances--which he does not expect to collect immediately--become loans. Yose adds that if a worker has ceased working and not collected his wage, he must understand that wage as a loan to the employer. This too is cancelled. Further Ushan discussion is at T. 8:3.

D. Unassigned

10:2A-E As for a debt incurred on New Year of the year following the Sabbatical--if the month is intercalated, the debt is cancelled. If the month is not intercalated, the debt is not cancelled.

In an intercalated month, the first day of the new month is also the last day of the preceding month. The point here therefore is straight forward: A debt incurred on the last day of the seventh year is cancelled. The specific case cited here contradicts the basic rule of v.C.10:1. I see no way of placing this entry within the unfolding of the law.

10:2F-G Fines and penalties owed by felons are not cancelled by the Sabbatical Year.

These are not loans. Under the rule of v.C.10:1 they therefore are not cancelled. Dependent upon an Ushan principle, this too must derive from no earlier than Ushan times.

10:2H-I Secured loans and loans handed over to a court are not cancelled by the Sabbatical year.

The security is a temporary repayment of the loan. Since the secured loan is never actually outstanding, it is not cancelled in the seventh year. This same point was made at v.B.10:6.

10:5 An ante-dated prozbul is valid; a post-dated one is invalid. Ante-dated bonds are invalid; post-dated ones are valid. The lender drafts a separate prozbul for each of his outstanding loans.

The creditor may not date a prozbul or bond so as to allow him to collect money to which he is not entitled. But he may give away the right to collect the funds, e.g., by ante-dating a prozbul, which turns over to the court the right to collect, or by post-dating a bond, which prevents him from collecting on the bond until the future date. This singleton cannot be placed within the unfolding of this tractate's law.

10:8 In the seventh year a lender must refuse to accept repayment of a loan and must inform the borrower that the loan is cancelled. If the borrower states that he wishes anyway to pay the loan, the lender then may accept the payment.

This truth-in-lending statute assures that the borrower knows that he need not repay the loan and that his doing so is completely voluntary. There is no basis for placing this in the unfolding of the law.

10:9 Sages are pleased with one   This continues the thought
who voluntarily repays debts in   of the preceding entry. It
the Sabbatical Year. + Two other   offers no grounds for
cases in which sages are pleased   placement within the history
with one who keeps an agreement   of the law.
even though by law it is invalid.

III. Conclusion
     Certain ideas in this tractate derive from the period before
70. These include the concept of the prozbul, on the one hand,
and, on the other, the idea of general importance, that each
individual is responsible to prevent others from transgressing.
The generative issue that stands behind the tractate as a whole
and accounts for the majority of its material, however, still is
under dispute in Yavnean times and is accepted as normative only
in Usha. This idea, that the concrete effects of field labor are
not the sole basis for determining its permissibility in the
Sabbatical year, parallels the generative idea of Tractate
Kilaim. For both tractates, Israelites' perceptions and
intentions serve as the standard by which conformity to God's law
is determined. This distinctively Mishnaic point of view
represents an important step beyond the Yavnean materials
contained in each tractate, which judge actions solely in light
of their material consequences.
     This shift in attitudes within Mishnah is particularly
important when we consider the view of Scripture's priestly
source, from which the basic ideas of both of these tractates
derive. In that view, order is a precondition of holiness. This
idea is developed in the priestly account of creation, found at
Gen. 1:1-2:4a. God establishes an ordered and hierarchial world,
with living things created in sequence of ascending importance:
plants, animals and then human beings. Each is created according
to its kind. For the priestly source creation thus is "an act of
ordering, the purpose of which is to make the world perfect and
thus prepare it to be made holy" (Mandelbaum, p. 3). The actual
sanctity of the land of Israel depends upon God's designating it
as holy. The Sabbath and, like it, the Sabbatical year are made
holy by God's proclamation of the day of rest, which marks the
completion of creation.
     Compiled during and after the exile that followed the
destruction of the first Temple, the priestly rules regarding

Israelites' yearly planting of their fields and special use of the land during the seventh year thus demand that these Israelites "restore the world from its present condition of chaos to its original orderly state...so to make the world ready once again for sanctification" (Mandelbaum, ibid.). This priestly view, which claims the existence of a transcedent and unchanging order, is reflected in the Yavnean materials before us. Yavneans too look for concrete indicators of what is right and wrong, holy and profane. In the Ushan period, by contrast, we see an important step beyond this earlier picture. While Yavneans had Israelites reconstruct a preordained order of creation, these later authorities regard Israelites as imposing order upon their world and so actually participating in the processes of creation and sanctification.

For the specific case of Tractate Shebiit, this means that, in the Ushan view, the sanctification of the Sabbatical year depends upon the Israelites themselves. They determine when in the sixth year the restrictions of the seventh begin to apply. Through their intentions and perceptions Israelites further establish exactly what is permitted and forbidden during the holy time. In perhaps the tractate's most striking statement, an apparently Ushan rule claims that the very sanctity of the land of Israel is in direct relation to the amount of time Israelites have dwelled upon it. In the view of Leviticus, the land is sanctified by God alone. In Tractate Shebiit, Israelites add to the holiness of the ground upon which they dwell.

Viewed as a whole, the message of Tractate Shebiit thus is that the sanctity of the land of Israel and of the seventh year is activated and regulated by the intentions and actions of common Israelites. This same notion, we shall now see, is foremost in Tractate Terumot, which ascribes powers of sanctification to Israelites who set aside some of the produce of the land as the consecrated agricultural offerings ordained by Scripture.

CHAPTER SIX

TERUMOT

I. Introduction

A single fact about heave-offering interests Mishnah's authorities and generates all of their discussion in this tractate. This fact is that heave-offering is holy. As Num. 18:8--from which the concept of heave-offering is derived-- indicates, it is a sanctified Holy Thing, comparable to any animal sacrifice placed upon the altar of the Temple in Jerusalem. Heave-offering is the property of priests and may be eaten only by them and their families (Lev. 22:10-14). To eat heave-offering these individuals must be in a high state of cultic purity, just as is the case for eating other holy offerings. The central point for the authorities of Tractate Terumot, then, is that this agricultural gift, paid by Israelites to God's representatives, has a high level of consecration.

With this much established, Mishnah Terumot takes up a very specific line of questioning. It wants to know, units i-ii, how and why this gift to the priest, comprised of produce grown upon the land of Israel, comes to be holy. Most of the produce of the land may be eaten or otherwise used by anyone, without restriction. How does heave-offering come to be different? The second, closely related, issue is the effect this holy produce has upon other, secular, food with which it is mixed (unit iii). Does the heave-offering impart its own consecrated status to that other food, such that all must now be deemed holy? This second issue is expanded to talk about other situations in which heave-offering is used as though it were secular, for instance, cases in which it is eaten by a non-priest (units iv-vii). Finally, to conclude their essay, the authorities of Tractate Terumot discuss the conditions under which heave-offering ceases to be holy, the end point of the process that began with its initial sanctification (unit viii).

In all, Tractate Terumot covers the rabbinic notion of sanctification that underlies this division as a whole. In discussing how things become holy, it parallels the topic of Tractates Peah and Bikkurim. Concerning the care and protection of consecrated produce, its topic is like that of Tractate Maaser

Sheni. Together these tractates present a rabbinic theory of
sanctification. They detail, that is to say, the locus and means
of sanctification that Mishnah's authorities understood to be
operative in their own day.

The questions through which Mishnah's rabbis approach this
topic are in place in Yavnean times. Yavnean legislation forms
the backbone of each of the topical divisions of Tractate
Terumot. As we saw clearly in the cases of Tractate Kilaim and
Shebiit, however, in continuing along thematic lines established
by Yavneans, Ushans incorporate their own, distinctive, attitude.
Indeed, the divergent legal perspectives held by Yavneans and
Ushans, with which we have become familiar in those other
tractates, inform as well the two major strata in the formation
of Tractate Terumot.

Yavneans, again, depict a pre-ordained, transcendent order
in the world. Through their actions, Israelites manipulate
holiness in ways predictable on the model of a physical
substance.[1] In this view, Israelites' own perspectives and
intentions play no role in determining what is or is not holy.
Israelites' power, rather, is limited to their ability physically
to manipulate the location of that which represents God's share
of the crop of the land of Israel.

For Ushans, like Yavneans, Israelites who pay agricultural
offerings transfer to their proper recipients shares of produce
that, because they are owed to God, are understood to have a
status of consecration. Yet in depicting what Israelites can do
with holiness, Ushans see as central the people's own desires and
perceptions. These internal aspects of the Israelite's
consciousness are envisioned to control holiness in ways that
Yavneans' attention to physical transfer precludes. In the Ushan
understanding, that is, the will of the Israelite to consecrate
food brings a status of sanctity upon that food. Physical
actions are secondary, such that, according to Ushans, a wrongly
executed physical separation of heave-offering still yields a
consecrated priestly gift. This is the case as long as, in
performing the separation, the individual forumulated proper
intention. The attitude of the common Israelite further
determines the effect the consecrated offering has upon other
produce with which it is mixed or cooked. This attitude, that
is, and not the physical character of the dish, takes precedence.
Finally, the Israelite's own perception that food no longer is

worthy of a status of consecration establishes the point at which
what was holy again is deemed secular. For Ushans, holiness thus
is not transferred and maintained according to physical laws of
exchange. Israelites rather manipulate it--bringing a status of
holiness to bear upon certain produce and later removing that
status again--according to their own will, without regard for
concrete acts of transfer such as are deemed central to the
preceding generation.[2]

Before turning to the specific rules through which each
generation of authorities presents its point, we need to review
those Scriptural passages upon which the tractate depends. This
will allow us as well to discuss the Scriptural derivation of
Mishnah's heave-offering.

> (Num. 18:8-13) Then the Lord said to Aaron, "And
> behold, I have given you whatever is kept of the offerings
> made to me, all the consecrated things of the people of
> Israel; I have given them to you as a portion, and to your
> sons as a perpetual due. This shall be yours from the most
> holy things, reserved from the fire; every offering of
> theirs, every cereal offering of theirs and every guilt
> offering of theirs, which they render to me, shall be most
> holy to you and to your sons. In a most holy place shall
> you eat of it; every male may eat of it; it is holy to you.
> This also is yours, the offering of their gift (terumat
> matanam), all the wave offerings of the people of Israel; I
> have given them to you, and to your sons and daughters with
> you, as a perpetual due; every one who is clean in your
> house may eat of it. All the best of the oil, and all the
> best of the wine and of the grain, the first fruits of what
> they give to the Lord, I give to you."
> (Lev. 22:10-14) "An outsider shall not eat of a holy
> thing. A sojourner of the priest's or a hired servant shall
> not eat of a holy thing; but if a priest buys a slave as his
> property for money, the slave may eat of it; and those that
> are born in his house may eat of his food. If a priest's
> daughter is married to an outsider she shall not eat of the
> offering of the holy things. But if a priest's daughter is
> a widow or divorced, and has no child, and returns to her
> father's house, as in her youth, she may eat of her father's
> food; yet no outsider shall eat of it. And if a man eats of
> a holy thing unwittingly, he shall add the fifth of its
> value to it, and give the holy thing to the priest."

Num. 18:8-13 delineates those offerings that the people of
Israel contribute to the support of the Aaronide priesthood.
After discussing Temple-offerings, parts of which belong to the
priests, the passage turns to agricultural dues. It is difficult
to determine the number and nature of the offerings listed in
vss. 11-13. "The offering of their gift," vs. 11, appears to be
a general term, referring to all agricultural gifts that are
eaten by the priests and including wave offerings (vs. 11), the
best of the oil, wine and grain (vs. 12) and first fruits (vs.

13). People who stand behind Mishnah, however, have read "the offering of their gift" in conjunction with vs. 12's "best of the oil, wine and grain, the first of them." In this manner they identify a single agricultural gift, distinct from the "first fruits" of vs. 13. In Mishnaic parlance this gift is called "heave-offering" (terumah), although it is also known by the term "first," suggested by vs. 12 (ii.D.3:6-7).[3]

A. Terumot Before 70

The Houses, ii.A.4:3, dispute the quantity of heave-offering to be separated from each batch of produce. Their underlying assumption is that this quantity depends upon the temperment of the individual who owns the produce. That is to say that, as in the case of any charitable contribution, certain people are expected to be more generous than others. While the issue discussed by the Houses is basic to any consideration of the separation of agricultural gifts, it plays little role in the development of the law. Later authorities assume that the individual will separate the quantity indicated by the Hillelites to be average, one fiftieth of the crop. At the same time, however, these later rabbis legislate that the actual separation must be carrried out through an estimation, not an exact measurement, of the quantity of produce being taken as heave-offering. The Houses' discussion therefore has little actual weight in later deliberation.

B. Terumot in the Time of Yavneh

The basic Yavnean datum of the tractate, drawn from Scripture, is that heave-offering comprises a consecrated offering, comparable to animal sacrifices offered and eaten in the Temple. Yavneans want to know how and why produce that an Israelite sets aside becomes holy, and they further question what happens when holy produce comes into contact with objects and foods within the secular world. Yavneans thereby develop a complete picture of the processes of sanctification and desanctification.

The Yavnean understanding of how produce comes to be holy is common to all of the law of this division. Since God provides the land upon which Israelites grow food, a share of their crops must be paid to God's representatives. For Yavneans, the physical act of separating heave-offering represents a determination on the part of the householder that what he has separated

is to comprise this share. Like all that belongs to God, it
henceforth is deemed holy and, accordingly, may be eaten--in the
case of heave-offering--only by a priest. Since the lien held by
God upon the remainder of the batch has now been paid, that
produce, by contrast, may be eaten by anybody.[4]

Particular to the Yavnean perspective, as distinct from
Ushan law, is the notion that God's share of produce is removed
from the crop and maintained solely through physical actions.
Yavneans, for instance, view each separate batch of produce as a
distinct entity from which God's share must be paid
independently. Since the householder's actions in separating
heave-offering from one batch have no physical effect upon the
other batch, they leave the produce in that distinct batch in an
untithed state (i.B.1:5). This is the case even if the
householder takes from one batch sufficient produce to pay the
heave-offering required of all of the produce. If, by contrast,
all of the produce is the same as regards state of cleanness,
year of growth, species and certain other characteristics, the
Israelite may place the several batches together, so as to create
a single entity. Now the physical action of separating heave-
heave-offering clearly pertains to all of the produce, such that
it is effective in preparing that produce for common consumption.

The same notion presumably underlies the Yavnean determination of the maximum percentage of a batch that has the
potential, upon the designation of the householder, of taking on
the consecrated status of heave-offering (ii.B.4:5). All
authorities agree that not all of a batch can be designated holy.
Such a designation would not physically distinguish God's share
from what the Israelite takes as his own. It leaves the batch
physically unchanged and therefore is invalid.

If heave-offering is mixed with unconsecrated produce, the
whole mixture may need to be treated as heave-offering (iii.B).
This is the case if a large quantity of heave-offering is mixed
with the unconsecrated food, such that the batch as a whole is
deemed to take on a sanctified status. If, by contrast, a small
amount of heave-offering is mixed with much unconsecrated food,
the holy produce is understood to be so thinly distributed as to
take on the character of the unconsecrated food with which it is
mixed. All of this produce therefore may be eaten by a
non-priest.[5] In accordance with their general perspective,
Yavneans apply this rule only if there is a physical mixing of
the priestly gift and other produce. Ushans, by contrast, will

apply the law of neutralization in a much wider range of cases, including those in which heave-offering is not physically mixed with common food.

Heave-offering planted as seed yields a crop in the status of heave-offering (vi.B.9:4), since the crop is deemed a physical extension of the original seed. Yavneans however are not concerned that heave-offering be cooked or otherwise prepared with secular food (vii.B.10:11E-H). So long as the heave-offering remains distinct and can be removed from the dish, so as not to be eaten by the non-priest, it has no effect upon the produce with which it was cooked.[6]

Active in each of the tractate's topical sections, Yavneans establish basic ideas regarding the mechanics of separating heave-offering and outline the punishments for those who, in one way or another, transgress the pertinent restrictions. While this constitutes the fundamental data with which Ushans will work, the Ushan materials do not develop the specifics of the Yavnean ideas. This is the case except for one quite central instance. The Yavneans Joshua and Eliezer dispute an issue of basic importance within Mishnah's legal system as a whole. The view of Joshua sets the stage for the analysis of the topic of heave-offering carried out in the Ushan period. Before turning to the Ushan materials, let us therefore review the details of Eliezer and Joshua's argument.

Eliezer and Joshua dispute the role played by the perceptions and intentions of common Israelites in determining culpability for wrong actions, on the one hand, and the validity of right actions, on the other. Eliezer, for his part, is clear that the privileges and restrictions of the agricultural laws operate mechanically. Extenuating circumstances, such as an individual's intention in performing a deed, are of no weight. In Eliezer's view it therefore is of no consequence that an individual who turns out not to be a priest ate heave-offering under the conception that he is a priest. Nor is it important to Eliezer that a non-priest who eats heave-offering has no way of knowing that what he is eating is a priestly gift (iv.B.8:1-3). Eliezer holds that since, objectively, the individual did what is prohibited, he is culpable. Joshua, by contrast, claims that an individual may be held culpable only if he could have known that his actions are prohibited. If he eats heave-offering under the life-long assumption that he is a priest, and only afterwards it turns out that he is not a priest, he is not held liable. The

individual's perception of an act thus determines whether or not
it constitutes a transgression. This notion, that the privileges
and restrictions of the agricultural system are activated by the
intentions and perceptions of Israelites, forms the central
ideology of the Ushan stratum in this tractate and, as we have
seen, in Tractates Kilaim and Shebiit. As our review of the
Yavnean materials showed, however, that attitude is quite foreign
to Joshua's own generations of masters. Agreeing with the view
of Eliezer, these authorities generally do not see intention or
perception as determining the character of an act.

C. Terumot in the Time of Usha

The Ushan contribution to this tractate is to read together
the Yavnean picture of the processes of sanctification with
Joshua's view concerning the primacy of the intentions and
perceptions of Israelites. Ushans, that is to say, no longer
view holiness in physical terms, claiming that it is manipulated
only through physical acts of transfer. They understand
holiness, rather, to be a function of the desires and perceptions
of the Israelite householder who separates the priestly gift,
protects it in his secular domain and ultimately turns it over to
a priest. Through these intentions and perceptions, Ushans hold,
the Israelite controls what will be holy, determines the proper
conditions under which that sanctified produce must be maintained
and, finally, establishes the circumstances under which the
produce ceases to be holy. For Yavneans, Israelites' physical
actions alone determine what will be holy. These physical
actions are efficacious only if they conform in all respects to
Yavneans' conceptions of present norms and unvarying rules.
Ushans, by contrast, claim that physical actions are secondary to
the Israelite's purposeful will. Holiness for Ushans thus
functions as a reflex of the desires and attitudes of common
Israelites, not as a result of the simple physical processes and
established procedures through which food is set aside for a
priest.

The Ushans' ideology is first expressed in their notion of
how produce comes to have the status of heave-offering. Ushans
state that this depends upon more than the whim of an Israelite
who happens to set some produce apart from the rest of the batch
(i.C.1:1). Validly to separate heave-offering the Israelite must
be capable of formulating the intention to render that which he

separates holy. Individuals not deemed to have powers of intention therefore are excluded from separating heave-offering. In a common Ushan idea, these authorities further require that, having formulated the intention to separate heave-offering, the individual make an oral declaration through which he expresses his plan (ii.C.3:5, ii.D.3:8). Through this oral declaration intention is rendered efficacious. The net result of the Ushan picture is that, through thought, word and, only at the end, deed, the Israelite determines which produce and how much of it is to be holy.

This primacy of intention is apparent in the Ushan laws concerning the conditions under which a wrong separation is deemed valid. We know from the Yavnean stratum that produce in one batch may not be separated as heave-offering for produce in a different batch. This is because the physically distinct batches cannot both be affected by a separation of heave-offering from only one of them. Ushans disregard this physical problem. They state that so long as the householder who designated and separated heave-offering did so with proper intention, even if the specifics of his actions were incorrect, that which he has separated is a consecrated priestly offering (i.C.2:1, 2, 4, 3:3-4).

The same idea appears in the Ushan discussion of the laws for a non-priest who eats produce that might be heave-offering (iv.C.7:5-7). If one of two batches contains heave-offering, but it is known which, an individual who eats one of them is not culpable. He may simply declare that the other batch, which he did not eat, contains the priestly gift. Someone else who subsequently eats the other batch may make the same claim, and he too is not culpable. The issue for Ushans is not the indisputable fact that someone certainly has eaten heave-offering. Rather, the perception of each individual that he did not eat the holy produce is primary and determines his culpability--or lack of culpability--for what he has done.

Yavneans are clear that, whenever a farmer sows heave-offering as seed, the crop that results has the status of heave-offering. The farmer must cultivate this crop and, when it ripens, sell it to a priest at the low price of heave-offering. Ushans, again, are concerned with the intentions of the Israelite who planted the seed. If he did so purposely, then, as the Yavneans claim, he is culpable and must suffer for his misdeed.

What if he planted the seed without knowing that it was heave-offering and later discovered his error? Now Ushans refuse to deem him culpable. He may plow up the field so as to avoid growing the sanctified crop of heave-offering seed. On the one hand, he may not make personal use of what he now knows is heave-offering seed. On the other, he is not deemed a transgressor and is not made to suffer additional financial loss by being forced to continue cultivating the sanctified crop.

Unlike Yavneans, Ushans are clear that heave-offering imparts its own status to unconsecrated food with which it is cooked. This is the case whenever heave-offering flavors the secular food. For if this happens, even if the Israelite is able to remove the consecrated produce from the dish, he still will perceive himself as having benefitted from the flavor which it gave his own common food (vii.C.10:1, 3, 8, 11A-D). Judah carries this idea to its logical conclusion. If the householder does not desire the flavor that the heave-offering imparts, his unconsecrated food remains uneffected. The effect that holiness has within the secular world thus is mitigated by the perceptions--the likes and dislikes--of common Israelites.

Anonymous materials that express this same theory presumably derive from Ushan times (viii.D.11:4-8). These hold that produce in the status of heave-offering loses its consecrated status at the time at which a priest or Israelite no longer deems it useful as food. Then it may be consumed by anyone, just like ordinary produce. In light of this idea, the anonymous materials list a variety of manners in which one may determine whether or not an individual still considers the produce edible or worthy of his continued concern.

The Yavnean picture of sanctification's being manipulated only through physical separation and exchange gives way in the Ushan period to a highly metaphysical understanding of holiness. In this understanding, sanctification revolves around Israelites. Their intentions determine what is to become heave-offering; their perceptions assure that the heave-offering is not misplaced and destroyed through sacrilege; and, according to Ushans, common Israelites' own attitudes towards heave-offering determine when the holy has become secular, such that it may be consumed by anyone. Through these ideas Ushans broadly reinterpret the Yavnean material and present a theory of sanctification that comprises the focus of this tractate as a whole.

II. The History of Tractate Terumot

i. The Designation and Separation of Heave-Offering

The unit focuses upon two issues. First, it delineates the manner in which heave-offering validly is designated and separated. This is a problem in particular if an individual owns two different batches of produce and desires to separate from one of them the heave-offering required of both. Second, it details what sorts of individuals are permitted to separate heave-offering in the first place. The point here, made in the Ushan stratum, is that, to do this, the individual must be able to formulate and express the intention to consecrate produce as a priestly gift.

Yavneans legislate concerning the former topic. They state that the produce from which heave-offering is to be separated must constitute a single, homogeneous batch (i.B.1:5). This means that the produce must all be in the same status as regards tithing and share other characteristics as well. While Ushans make explicit that the produce should be of the same species[7] and status of cleanness (i.C.2:1, 2, 4), they are clear that even if the individual fails to meet these criteria, if he separates heave-offering with proper intention, his separation is valid (see also i.C.3:3-4).

The distinctive Ushan perspective is apparent again in the rule for who may separate heave-offering. Ushans rule that validly to do this, the individual must be conscious of the character of the act in which he is involved. He is not simply setting aside an amount of food as a tax, but rather, in designating food as God's share, actually is consecrating it as a holy offering. He therefore must formulate the intention to impose upon that which he separates a status of sanctification (i.C.1:1). The importance of intention also is stressed in the Ushan notion that in general, an individual is culpable only for what he does intentionally (i.C.2:3). This same idea will arise many times in the continuation of this tractate.

A. Before 70

| 1:4 They may not separate olives as heave-offering for oil or grapes as heave-offering for wine. If they do so, the House of Shammai | The issue is the homogeneity of different forms of produce for purposes of separating heave-offering. |

say: It is valid for the olives
themselves. The House of Hillel
say: It is not valid at all.

Attribution of this issue to
the Houses appears
pseudepigraphic in light of
the broad Ushan interest in
this same question,
i.C.2:4-6. See also T.
4:1b-4. At T. 3:14, 16 and
25, Ushans cite other
Houses' disputes which
parallel their own deliberations on this issue.

B. The Time of Yavneh
1:5 They do not separate heave-
offering from produce that is not
subject to that offering. They
may not use exempt produce as a
source of the heave-offering
required of produce that is
subject. To separate heave-
offering from two different
batches at once, all of the
produce must have the same status.

Only produce upon which God
has a claim can yield a
holy offering, which, by
definition, is produce owed
to God. Further, the
separation of heave-offering
is efficacious only for the
single batch from which
produce is taken. In the
case of two batches, all of
produce must be the same,
such that it can be deemed a
single entity. While stated
anonymously, this rule
stands behind materials
found both at Yavneh (see
Aqiba, i.C.3:3-4) and at
Usha (i.C.2:4, 3:3-4 and
ii.C.4:1-2). I assume it
derives from Yavneh, the
earliest period to which it
is attested.

C. The Time of Usha
1:1 Deaf-mutes, imbeciles, minors
and those who do not own the
produce may not separate heave-
offering. If they do, the
separation is not valid.

The rule makes two points:
1) The validity of a
separation of heave-offering
depends upon the ability of
the individual who performs

it to understand the
character of that separa-
tion. This idea is Ushan,
as the discussion of it by
Judah and Yose, i.C.1:3,
indicates. 2) One may not
consecrate that which he
does not own. This idea is
a commonplace in Yavnean
times, as the attestation of
it by Aqiba, Kilaim,
iii.C.7:4-5, shows.

1:2 Definition of the term
"deaf-mute," which appears at
M. 1:1.

This continuation of the
preceding entry is further
attested to Usha by Judah,
Isaac and Simeon b.
Gamaliel, T. 1:1.

1:3 Judah: A minor who has not
produced two pubic hairs validly
separates heave-offering (contrary
to M. 1:1). Yose: We rule on
the basis of whether or not he
has reached the age of vows.

Ushans carry forward the
discussion of one of
i.C.1:1's items, with which
Judah here disagrees. Yose
is consistent with the
theory of M. 1:1. Once the
youth has reached the age of
vows, he is subject to
religious obligations he
takes upon himself. At the
same age, Yose says, he will
understand the character of
the separation of heave-
offering and therefore
validly may carry out that
rite.

2:1 One may not separate clean
produce as heave-offering for
unclean, unless both are part
of a single batch. Eliezer:
They may separate clean produce
as heave-offering for unclean.

A separation of heave-
offering normally should
physically affect the
produce for which the
offering is taken. This is
possible only if all of the

produce comprises a single
batch. So the anonymous
rule. Eliezer ignores this
restriction in the present
case. For here the house-
holder intentionally
separates heave-offering
from clean produce, so as to
give the priest a share
that he can in fact eat.
Eliezer's theory regarding
intention occurs again at
i.C.2:2, 3, 4, 5 and 6.[8]

2:2 They may not separate unclean
produce as heave-offering for
clean. If one purposely did so,
the separation is invalid. But
if he did so accidentally, it
is valid. Judah: If he knew
that the produce was unclean,
but then forgot, it is as though
he acted purposely.

The point is the same as in
the preceding. If the
individual purposely takes
unclean produce, which the
priest cannot eat, he
obviously does not have
proper intention to separate
the priest's share. If he
does not know that what he
separates is unclean, then
the separation is valid,
since the individual did
carry it out with the
intention to give the priest
his portion. Judah agrees
with the theory, but refuses
to take into account
forgetfulness.

2:3 One who intentionally
transgresses various rules of the
Sabbath may not benefit from his
actions. If he did so
unintentionally, he may benefit.

Again the individual is held
culpable only for what he
intentionally does. Sharing
the theory of M. 2:2, these
rules are assigned to the
Ushan stratum.

2:4 They may not separate heave-
offering from produce of one

In separating heave-
offering, the taxonomic

species for produce of a different
species. One may separate heave-
offering from one kind within a
species for a different kind within
that same species. Judah: In
doing this he always should
separate heave-offering from the
choicest produce.

categories established by
God at the time of creation
must be preserved. The
basic rule appears to have
been known in Yavnean times,
iv.B.6:6. Judah, applying
the consideration of the
individual's attitude
towards the produce, attests
this construction to Usha.

2:5 The rule of M. 2:4 is applied
to the specific case of a large
and a small onion in the status
of heave-offering. Judah: They
designate as heave-offering the
onion of the best quality.

Nothing has changed from
M. 2:4.

2:6 Specific examples of Judah's
view of M. 2:4-5. + General
principal detailing that opinion.
Judah disputes an anonymous rule
concerning whether or not two
types of grain are distinct
species.

Judah's participation again
indicates the Ushan origins
of this pericope.

3:3-4 Partners who separated
heave-offering one after the other
from the same produce--Sages:
Only that separated by the first
is valid. Aqiba: That separated
by both is valid. Yose: If the
first separated sufficient
heave-offering, that which the
second separates is not valid.
Anonymous rule: Aqiba's view
applies only if they made an
arrangement that both would
separate heave-offering.

Sages reflect i.B.1:5, which
states that heave-offering
may be separated only from
produce from which that
offering never before has
been taken. Aqiba seems to
agree, but suggests that,
since each individual has a
share in the produce, each
validly separates heave-
offering from his own share.
Yose and the final anonymous
statement provide the
typical Ushan perspective.
Both separations are

valid only if we have good
reason to assume that the
partners intended to have
the offering separated
twice.

D. Unassigned

1:6 Mutes, drunkards, naked
people, blind people and those
who have had a nocturnal emission
may not separate heave-offering.
Since they have proper intention,
if they do separate heave-
offering, their separation is
valid.

These individuals are not
permitted to recite the
blessing that accompanies
the separation of heave-
offering. Therefore they
should not separate the
offering. Since they have
proper intention, however,
their separation is valid
post facto. Making the same
point as i.C.1:1, 2:1 and
2:2, this rule must be
Ushan.

1:7 Heave-offering may not be
separated by a measure of volume,
weight or number of pieces of
produce.

Produce to be sanctified as
heave-offering is chosen
randomly. This idea is
Ushan, as Judah's parallel
statement, ii.A.4:3,
indicates. The present rule
contradicts the Houses'
theory, ii.A.4:3, that a set
amount is to be taken as
heave-offering.

1:8 They may not separate olives
or grapes the processing of which
is not completed as heave-offering
on behalf of olives or grapes the
processing of which is completed.
If they do so anyway, the
separation is valid, but heave-
offering must be separated a
second time, to assure that the

The issue of the separation
of heave-offering from
different sorts of the same
type of produce is familiar
primarily from Usha,
i.C.2:4, 5, 6. The present
rule assumes Judah's
statement, i.C.2:4, 5, that
the priest must receive the

priest receives his proper share
of fully processed produce.

choicest produce. It
therefore appears to derive
from Ushan times.

1:9 They may separate heave-
offering from grapes or olives that
are completely processed in one
manner on behalf of grapes or
olives that are completely
processed in some different manner.

This develops the preceding
entry and is attested to
Usha by Simeon b. Gamaliel,
T. 3:15.

1:10 They may not separate heave-
offering from fully processed
produce on behalf of produce the
processing of which is not
complete or vice versa. Nor may
they separate heave-offering from
that which is not fully processed.

This is the general
principle which stands
behind the preceding items.
This statement derives from
Usha or later, along with
consideration of the spe-
cific rules just discussed.

3:1 If a chate-melon separated as
heave-offering is found to be
bitter, heave-offering must be
separated a second time. In the
case of wine--if it went sour
before the original separation,
it is not valid heave-offering.
If it turned sour after it was
separated as heave-offering,
the separation is valid, and
heave-offering need not be
separated a second time. If it
is in doubt--the separation is
valid, but heave-offering must
be separated a second time.

The unit takes up and
develops the theory familiar
from i.B.1:5, that to be
separated as heave-offering,
the produce must be useful
as food. The problem is
what we do if we do not know
whether or not, at the time
of the separation, the
produce was edible. This
development of M. 1:5 is
probably Ushan, to which
stratum it is attested by
Yose and Ishmael b. Yose,
who speaks in Yose's name
T. 4:5, 6.

3:2 Of the two quantities
separated as heave-offering at
M. 3:1, only one is true heave-
offering, but it is not known
which. How do we deal with this
uncertainty in a case in which

This too depends upon
i.B.1:5's notion that heave-
offering may not be
separated from produce that
is not subject to that
offering. Along with the

some or all of this doubtful
heave-offering is mixed with
unconsecrated produce?

preceding item, which it
develops, this pericope
presumably belongs in the
Ushan stratum. It assumes
that the Israelite's own
perceptions determine which
of the two quantities of
produce is the true heave-
offering.

ii.   The Rite of Separating Heave-offering

The unit indicates how much heave-offering an individual must separate from his produce and details the specific procedure through which the separation is carried out. The Houses initiate discussion of the former topic, providing specific percentages of a batch to be separated by individuals who are miserly, average or generous. The particular claim of the Houses, that specific types of people separate different quantities of heave-offering, is largely ignored by later authorities. But both Yavneans and Ushans do carry forward this topic in general. Yavneans dispute the largest percentage of a batch that may be designated as heave-offering. Ushans bring the central ideas of unit I to bear upon the question of what happens if an individual separates less than the required amount. In line with i.B.1:5, they rule that additional produce may not be separated from the partially exempt batch as heave-offering on behalf of a different batch. Ushans further make clear that, unlike what the view of the Houses implies, a fixed quantity of produce is not to be measured out as heave-offering. The actual separation is performed in a random manner (see Judah, ii.A.4:3 and the anonymous rule of i.D.1:7).

Ushans discuss how the individual indicates that he has formulated the intention required validly to separate heave-offering (see i.C.1:1). This is done through an oral declaration (ii.C.3:5, ii.D.3:8), in which the person announces what he intends to do. Other central questions remain moot in the Ushan period, in particular, the question of the right of Samaritans and gentiles to separate heave-offering.

A.   Before 70

4:3 The Houses of Hillel and
Shammai dispute the correct

This is one of the most
basic issues regarding the

quantity of produce to be separated as heave-offering by individuals of various dispositions, generous, average, miserly. Judah, an Ushan, glosses on how to handle situations in which the individual mis-estimates and separates the wrong amount.

separation of heave-offering and might well go back to the historical Houses. The percentages given here are deemed normative by Yavneans (Eliezer, Tarfon, Ishmael, Aqiba) at ii.B.4:5, Ushans (Judah here, Simeon b. Gamaliel at T. 5:6a and Yose and Ishmael b. R. Yose at T. 5:8a) and after Usha (Rabbi at T. 5:6a). Judah's opinion actually is separate. It assumes that heave-offering is not separated in an exact amount, contrary to what the Houses say. See the apparently Ushan i.D.1:7.

B. The Time of Yavneh
4:5 Eliezer, Ishmael, Tarfon and Aqiba dispute how much of a batch of produce has the potential of taking on the status of heave-offering.

This carries forward the discussion, begun before 70, of how much heave-offering is contained in a batch of produce. The Yavnean authorities all assume that the formal act of disting- uishing heave-offering from the rest of the produce prevents the whhole batch from becoming a priestly gift. See Peah, i.C.1:3C-E.

C. The Time of Usha
3:5 The exact wording of the oral designation of heave- offering and heave-offering of the tithe is under dispute by Simeon, Eliezer b. Jacob and Eleazar Hisma.

An oral designation proves that the individual has the proper intention required for a valid separation of heave-offering (i.C.1:1). Such a designation is first known here in the Ushan

period, where its specific
character still is under
dispute. The issue is
carried forward by Simeon
b. Gamaliel and Rabbi,
T. 4:9.

3:9 Gentiles and Samaritans may
designate heave-offering, tithes
and may dedicate produce to the
Temple. Judah and sages dispute
whether or not their fields are
subject to the restrictions of
the fourth year (Lev. 19:24).
Simeon and sages dispute whether
or not produce separated by a
gentile indeed is true heave-
offering.

The question of the status
of the gentile as regards
the agricultural laws still
is under dispute at Usha.[9]
(i.C.1:1 states simply that
a gentile may not act as the
agent of an Israelite to
separate heave-offering for
him.) In T., Judah, Simeon
b. Gamaliel, Rabbi and
Simeon b. Eleazar discuss
this further.

4:1-2 If one separates some of
the heave-offering required from
a batch of produce, he may not
later separate produce from that
same batch to be heave-offering
on behalf of a different batch.
Meir: He may.

The underlying supposition
is Yavnean, that heave-
offering only may be
separated from produce that
is subject to that offering.
Sages here hold that once
some of the heave-offering
is separated, the batch as
a whole is partially exempt
from the further separation
of that offering. Partially
exempt produce may not later
be separated as heave-
offering for fully liable
produce. According to Meir,
the partial separation
leaves some of the produce
fully exempt and the rest
fully liable. The fully
liable produce still may be
designated heave-offering

for a different batch.
Meir's view evidences the
typically Ushan assumption
that, in his later
separation, the Israelite
will determine that the
produce he separates is in
fact that which still is
subject to the priestly
gift.

D. Unassigned

3:6-7 The correct order for the
separation of agricultural gifts
is first fruits, heave-offering,
first tithe, second tithe. +
Scriptural prooftext.

This anonymous rule is a
singleton, independent of
all other legal statements
and ideas in the tractate.
It is impossible to place
it in the chronological
unfolding of M. Ter.'s law.

3:8 One who, in making an oral
designation, says heave-offering
instead of first tithe, or burnt-
offering instead of peace-offering,
etc., has said nothing.

To be valid, one's intention
must be correctly expressed.
This rule concerning the
validity of oral
designations can come no
earlier than Ushan times,
where the oral designation
of heave-offering is first
discussed (ii.C.3:5).

4:4 An agent separates the
quantity of heave-offering
normally separated by the
produce's owner. If he does not
know that amount, he separates
the average quantity, one-
fiftieth.

The law assumes the position
of the House of Hillel
(ii.A.4:3) and the Ushan
rule that an agent may
separate heave-offering on
behalf of a householder,
i.C.1:1.

4:6 Heave-offering is separated
at three set times during the
year, through an estimation of

This reads together the idea
that a specific quantity of
heave-offering is to be

the required quantity of the   separated (ii.A.4:3) and the
offering, based upon a calculation   notion that the actual
of the amount of produce from   separation is done in a
which the offering is due.   random manner (i.D.1:7).
                                      Like the latter idea, this
                                      presumably is Ushan.

iii. Neutralization

When a small quantity of heave-offering is mixed with a large amount of unconsecrated food, the heave-offering loses its status of consecration. Then it may be treated as unconsecrated produce and may be consumed by the non-priest along with the rest of the food with which it is mixed. The non-priest simply removes from the mixture a quantity of produce equal to the heave-offering that was lost. This goes to the priest as his share. This theory of neutralization develops in Yavnean times, in which period the exact characteristics of the process of neutralization are under dispute. Yavneans dispute the ratio of heave-offering to unconsecrated food in which the priestly gift is neutralized (iii.B.4:7). They further argue the circumstances under which heave-offering is neutralized and, in particular, dispute whether neutralization occurs in a case in which the priestly gift could be recovered from the produce with which it is mixed (iii.B.4:8-11, 5:5-6).

The questions under dispute at Yavneh are largely resolved at Usha. Ushans are clear that heave-offering is neutralized only if it actually is lost within a batch of unconsecrated produce, such that it is not clear whether any single piece of produce is heave-offering or unconsecrated (iii.C.4:12, 13). Neutralization thus is not a mechanical process but rather a function of the householder's own recognition that heave-offering has been lost. Ushans further assert that, once heave-offering is neutralized and a replacement offering is separated from the mixture, that mixture is in all respects comparable to unconsecrated produce (iii.C.5:7). More heave-offering that falls into it is neutralized, just as was the first heave-offering. An anonymous rule, which states that a house-holder's intentional actions designed to cause heave-offering to be neutralized are void (iii.D.5:9), appears to be Ushan, for it reflects the theory of iii.C.4:12-13.

A. Before 70

5:4 A _seah_ of unclean heave-
offering falls into a hundred
seahs of clean heave-offering.
The House of Shammai declare it
permitted. They are willing to
ignore the small quantity of
unclean produce it contains.
+ Debate which rephrases this
dispute in terms of
neutralization. Eliezer and
sages argue the same issue, as
phrased in the debate.

The issue, whether or not we
may ignore a small quantity
of unclean heave-offering
that has been mixed with a
large quantity of clean
heave-offering, is parallel
to that of neutralization.
The Houses however do not
dispute the issue in terms
of neutralization, such that
they do not appear to have
an awareness of that
concept. Their use of the
language permitted
forbidden, instead of
neutralized/not neutralized
is clear on this. It
appears that Yavneans or
Ushans have made use of the
earlier Houses' material and
have themselves created the
Houses' debate. The
appearance here of Eliezer
makes the attributions in
the debate extremely
suspect.

B. The Time of Yavneh

4:7 Heave-offering is neutralized
in a total of one hundred and one
parts of produce, so Eliezer.
Joshua: Slightly more than that.
Yose b. Meshullam: One sixth more.

This discussion of the exact
ratio of heave-offering to
unconsecrated produce in
which the heave-offering is
neutralized is carried
forward at Usha, by Simeon
(T. 5:10), as well as after
Usha, by Simeon b. Judah
(T. 5:10). Ushan
attestations give us solid
grounds for the placement
of this initial discussion

at Yavneh. Throughout
Yavnean and Ushan times, the
figure given here by Eliezer
is normative.

4:8-9 Joshua: Black figs serve   Unlike Ushans, Yavneans
to neutralize white ones and   disagree concerning whether
vice versa. Large figs neutralize   or not heave-offering is
small ones and vice versa. Round   neutralized if the
ones neutralize square ones and   householder can identify it
vice versa. Eliezer: They do   and remove it from the
not. Aqiba: It depends upon   unconsecrated produce.
whether or not the householder   Aqiba introduces the
knows which produce is the   consideration that is
heave-offering.   central in the later period.

4:10 If one stuffed a litra of   The issue is the same as at
heave-offering figs in the mouth   M. 4:8-9, although the
of a stone jar containing   positions of Eliezer and
unconsecrated figs--Eliezer: Joshua are reversed.
These figs are all deemed mixed   Eliezer now holds that even
together such that the heave-   though the heave-offering is
offering may be neutralized.   discernable, it is
Joshua: They are not mixed   neutralized; Joshua takes
together.   the opposite view. Since
                                     the theoretical problem is
                                     the same as in the previous
                                     Yavnean materials, we must
                                     assign the issue to the
                                     Yavnean stratum. The
                                     positions of the authorities
                                     involved apparently have
                                     become garbled.

4:11 If one skimmed the seah out   The problem and positions
of the mouth of the store jar,   are the same as at M. 4:10,
and in the portion skimmed off   such that again we are on
there is one hundred seahs of   firm grounds in assigning
produce--Eliezer. The heave-   this to Yavneh. Simeon b.
offering is neutralized.   Yohai attests this material
Joshua: It is not neutralized,   at Usha, T. 5:12.
for it could have been recovered.

5:2 A <u>seah</u> of unclean heave-offering that fell into more than a hundred <u>seahs</u> of clean unconsecrated produce--let a <u>seah</u> be lifted up and burned, as though it were certainly unclean; so Eliezer. Sages: Let the <u>seah</u> that is removed be eaten in small bits, so that it does not impart uncleanness to the priest who consumes it.

As in the preceding Yavnean pericopae, the issue is the character of the process of neutralization. The priest must be given produce to replace the <u>seah</u> of heave-offering that was neutralized. Eliezer holds that the replacement <u>seah</u> is the same produce that originally was mixed in the unconsecrated produce.[10] It is unclean. Sages hold that in the process of neutralization, the heave-offering is diffused throughout the unconsecrated produce. The replacement offering therefore contains both clean and unclean produce.

5:3 A <u>seah</u> of clean heave-offering that fell into a hundred <u>seahs</u> of unclean unconsecrated produce should be lifted up and eaten in small bits.

This is the view of sages, M. 5:2, that heave-offering is fully mixed with the unconsecrated produce in which it is neutralized. The case presumably is Yavnean, like the larger ideational structure of which it is a part.

5:5 A <u>seah</u> of heave-offering is neutralized in unconsecrated produce. The replacement offering falls into other unconsecrated produce. Eliezer: It imparts the status of heave-offering as would true heave-offering. Sages: The replacement offering contains only a proportion of true heave-offering.

Eliezer is consistent with his view at M. 5:2. What fell into the unconsecrated produce is that which later is taken out of it. Sages too maintain their previous view, that when heave-offering is neutralized it is diffused evenly throughout the batch.

5:6 Heave-offering falls into
less than a hundred <u>seahs</u> of
unconsecrated produce and imparts
its status to the batch. Some
of the mixture falls out and is
mixed with other unconsecrated
produce--Eliezer: What falls
out is treated as true heave-
offering. Sages: That which
falls out of the mixture contains
only a proportion of true heave-
offering.

The issue and positions are
the same as in the preceding
unit.

C. The Time of Usha
4:12 If two bins together contain
one hundred seahs of unconsecrated
produce, and heave-offering falls
into one of them, but it is not
known into which, that heave-
offering is neutralized. Simeon:
This applies even if the bins are
in different cities.

Each of the hundred seahs
has been rendered suspect
regarding whether or not it
contains the heave-offering.
The ruling, that the heave-
offering is neutralized,
develops the principle
agreed upon by Eliezer and
Joshua at Yavneh
(iii.B.4:8-11). So long as
the heave-offering cannot be
recovered from the
unconsecrated produce, it is
neutralized. This adds the
common Ushan perspective,
which has no regard for the
physical boundaries of a
batch of produce.

4:13 A case came before Aqiba
concerning fifty bundles of
unconsecrated vegetables, and
one bundle half of unconsecrated
and half of heave-offering-
vegetables. Yose rules that
the heave-offering is neutralized.

The Ushan point is the same
as at M. 4:12. The status
of all of the produce is in
doubt such that, even though
it is divided into separate
bundles, it joins together
to neutralize the heave-
offering. For the reasons
given at M. 4:12, this

pericope too is firmly
assigned to Usha.

5:7 A seah of heave-offering fell
into more than a hundred of unconsecrated produce, and one lifted
it out and more heave-offering fell
into the same unconsecrated
produce--the unconsecrated produce
remains permitted to a non-priest.

Once the process of
neutralization is complete
and the replacement offering
is taken, the original one
hundred seahs of produce
are deemed fully
unconsecrated. This
develops the basic Yavnean
ideas presented at
iii.B.5:2, 3, 5 and 6. See
the following entry.

5:8 A seah of heave-offering
fell into a hundred of
unconsecrated produce and was not
lifted out before more heave-
offering fell into the same
batch--that batch now has the
status of heave-offering. Simeon:
The second seah is neutralized
just as was the first one.

Eliezer and sages,
iii.B.5:5-6, would agree
with the anonymous rule.
Since the mixture contains
two seahs of heave-offering
and only one hundred seahs
of unconsecrated produce,
the heave-offering imposes
its own status upon the batch.
That is, even though the
heave-offering is
neutralized, it retains the
essential qualities of a
priestly gift. In his
disagreement, Simeon
presents the more developed
Ushan theory of
neutralization found as well
at M. 5:7. Once heave-
offering is neutralized, it
is in all respects like
unconsecrated produce. This
notion is further developed
after Ushan times, by
Simeon's son, Eliezer, T.

6:5, who brings into the
play the role of human
intention.

D. Unassigned

5:1 A seah of unclean heave-
offering that fell into less than
a hundred seahs of unconsecrated
produce--let all the produce rot.
If the heave-offering was clean--
sell the mixture to a priest.
If the unconsecrated produce was
unclean, the priest eats the
mixture in small bits, which do
not convey uncleanness.

Normally a mixture of heave-
offering and less than one
hundred times its quantity
in unconsecrated produce
should be eaten by a priest.
If some of the produce in
the mixture is unclean we
follow the status of the
heave-offering. If it was
clean, then whether the
unconsecrated produce was
clean or unclean, the
mixture must be consumed by
the priest. The issue and
its adjudication are
substantively the same as
what is found in the dispute
between Eliezer and Joshua
at Yavneh, iii.B.5:2.

5:9 A mixture of heave-offering
and unconsecrated produce that is
ground up and the quantity of
which increases or diminishes--
the proportion of heave-offering
to unconsecrated food remains the
same. This is the case unless
it is known for certain that the
proportion changed. Actions
taken by the householder with
the express purpose of causing
heave-offering to be neutralized
are void.

This material concerns a
secondary level of
investigation, dependent
upon and carrying forward
the inquiry of Yavneh into
the conditions under which
heave-offering is
neutralized. Reference to
the role of human
intention, an issue settled
only in Ushan times, is
sound grounds for placing
this anonymous pericope in
the Ushan stratum.

iv. Heave-offering Eaten by a Non-Priest

A non-priest who unintentionally eats a holy thing must replace that holy thing and pay, as a fine, an additional fifth of its value (Lev. 22:14). Eliezer and Joshua dispute whether or not an individual who believes that he has the right to eat heave-offering is culpable when, after the fact, it turns out that he did not have that right (iv.B.8:1-3). Eliezer takes into account only the objective facts. The individual should not have eaten the heave-offering and therefore must pay the principal and added fifth. Joshua, by contrast, holds that self-perception matters. Since the individual truly believed that he was permitted to eat heave-offering, he may not be held culpable. Yavnean authorities thus dispute the idea, so common in Usha, that the intention with which an individual performs a deed determines the significance of that action.

Both Yavneans and Ushans discuss the regulations that pertain to the payment of the principal and added fifth. The issue is whether or not this payment is subject to the same restrictions that apply to the individual's initial separation of heave-offering. The issue is moot at Yavneh, iv.B.6:6, where Eliezer and Aqiba argue whether the individual may pay restitution with a type of produce different from that which was eaten, and at iv.C.6:5, where Meir and sages dispute whether produce already in the status of an agricultural offering may be used as restitution.

Ushans resolve the Yavnean question of whether or not self-perception determines culpability (iv.C.7:5-7). They ask how to adjudicate a case in which it is not certain whether a non-priest ate heave-offering. They state that so long as the individual may assume that he actually ate common produce, he is not culpable. In determining guilt, self-understanding thus counts. This is the expected Ushan resolution of the Yavnean dispute between Eliezer and Joshua.

An anonymous rule that appears to derive from Ushan times defines as culpable any unintentional act of eating, drinking or anointing with heave-offering (iv.D.6:1). Inclusion of the prohibition against anointing prevents the non-priest from deriving any benefit from the priestly offering.

A. Before 70

B. The Time of Yavneh

6:6 Eliezer: They pay restitution with produce of one kind even for produce of a different kind. Aqiba: They pay restitution from produce of one kind only for produce of its same kind.

The issue is whether the rules that apply to the householder's original separation of heave-offering apply as well to the payment of the principal and added fifth. The issue is carried forward at Usha, iv.C.6:5.

8:1-3 The wife of a priest was eating heave-offering and was told, "Your husband has died," such that she no longer had the right to eat the priestly ration-- Eliezer: She is culpable. Joshua: She is not culpable (+ five substantively parallel cases.)

Eliezer holds that the wife's belief that she had the right to eat heave-offering is irrelevant. Objectively she did not have that right. Joshua holds that self-perception counts. The woman acted rationally, under the assumption that she could eat heave-offering. Even when it turns out that this was not permitted, she is not held to have transgressed. While the specific issue here is not taken up at Usha, a comparable question of the role of individual's self-perception is resolved at iv.C.7:5-7.

C. The Time of Usha

6:3 One who gave his workers heave-offering to eat--he pays the principal and they pay the added fifth: so Meir. Sages: The workers pay both the principal and the added fifth, and he gives them the value of their meal.

The issue is whether the principal, like the added fifth, is paid only by those who eat heave-offering, or whether it also is paid by people, such as the employer, who in other ways benefit from heave-offering,

e.g. by using it in place of
their own food. See
iv.D.6:1.

6:5 They do not pay the principal
and added fifth out of produce in
the status of an agricultural
offering; so Meir. Sages: They
do.

The question is whether the
restrictions that apply to
the householder's original
designation of heave-
offering apply as well to
payment of the added fifth.

7:2 The daughter of a priest
marries an Israelite and then
unintentionally eats heave-
offering--Meir: She pays the
principal but not the added
fifth; if the husband was
ineligible for marriage to
priestly stock, she pays both
the principal and the added fifth.
Sages: In both cases she pays
the principal but not the added
fifth.

The issue is whether the
woman is treated like a
person of priestly lineage
or as an Israelite. Meir
says that this depends upon
whether or not, upon divorce
or widowhood, she may return
to her priestly father's
house. Sages say that in
all cases she is treated as
having priestly status.
Since she ate heave-offering
that did not belong to her,
she must return the heave-
offering to its rightful
owner (= the principal), but
she pays no fine (= the
added fifth). The larger
issue, that of the character
of the priestly caste, has
no antecedents in this
tractate. Placement in this
stratum is on the basis of
the attribution to Meir.

7:5-7 Two bins, one filled with
heave-offering and one filled with
unconsecrated produce--if heave-
offering fell into one of them but
it is not known which, we hold that

So long as we are not
certain of the contrary, we
assume that heave-offering
was not misused by any
particular non-priest. We

it fell into the heave-offering.
If it is not known which is filled
with heave-offering--the one which
someone should eat or otherwise
misuse is deemed unconsecrated and
the other thereafter is treated as
heave-offering. But someone who
eats from the other bin is still
not culpable. Meir: The second
bin is subject to dough offering.
Yose exempts.

maintain the assumption of
innocence for all parties
even if it is an
indisputable fact that one
of them did indeed
misappropriate the priestly
gift. What counts is each
individual's perception not
to have tampered with
consecrated produce. Meir
holds that we still must
take seriously a condition
of doubt. Dough offering is
to be separated from any
dough that might be
unconsecrated. This entry
develops along typically
Ushan lines the basic rules
for neutralization and
payment of restitution
already in place in the
period of Yavneh.

D.   Unassigned

6:1 A non-priest who
unintentionally eats, drinks or
anoints with clean or unclean
heave-offering pays the priest
the principal and added fifth.
He pays it with unconsecrated
produce, which takes on the
status of heave-offering.

This concept is developed
from Lev. 22:14, which
simply states that a non-
priest who eats a holy thing
pays back the principal plus
an added fifth. This
clarifies iv.C.6:3 and 6:5,
such that it can come no
earlier than Ushan times.
See also the contributions
of Yose and Simeon, T.5:8b,
Simeon, T. 7:1, Abba Saul,
T. 7:2, and Simchos, T. 7:7.

6:2 The daughter of an Israelite
who unintentionally ate heave-
offering and afterwards married

Once married to a priest,
the Israelite woman has the
right to eat heave-offering.

a priest--if the heave-offering
she ate did not belong to any
particular priest, she pays to
herself the principal and added
fifth. If the heave-offering
she ate belonged to a priest,
that priest must receive the
principal, but she may keep the
added fifth.

If she does not owe the
principal to someone in
particular, she therefore
may keep it for herself, to
be eaten as heave-offering.
In any case, she may keep
the added fifth, for this
is a fine that has no set
recipient. Developing the
line of questioning begun
at iv.C.7:2, this pericope
appears to be Ushan.

6:4 One who steals heave-offering
pays twice its monetary equivalent
(= Ex. 22:7). If he unintentionally ate it, he pays two
principals and one added fifth.
If it was heave-offering that
had been dedicated to the Temple,
he pays two added fifths and
one principal.

The rules for theft and for
restitution paid for produce
dedicated to the Temple are
brought to bear upon a
single case. I see no way
of placing this Scriptural
exegesis in the unfolding of
the law.

7:1 A non-priest who intentionally
eats heave-offering pays back the
principal but does not pay the
added fifth. That which is paid
as restitution does not take on
the status of heave-offering.
The priest therefore may refuse
to accept it.

An individual who
intentionally eats heave-
offering is subject to
execution. He therefore is
not required to pay the
fine of the added fifth.
This phrasing is parallel to
iv.D.6:1, such that this
particular rule appears to
be Ushan. Since the rule is
not referred to elsewhere in
the tractate, however, there
is no way to verify this
assignment.

7:3 One who feeds heave-offering
to a person who is not culpable
for his actions (a minor or

Culpability is not incurred
since 1) the individual is
not responsible for his

slave), one who eats heave-
offering separated from produce
grown outside of the land of
Israel, or one who eats only a
little heave-offering pays the
principal but not the added fifth.

actions, 2) the heave-
offering is not a true
priestly ration, or 3) the
amount eaten is insignif-
icant. Therefore, while the
priest's share must be
returned through payment of
the principal, no fine is
paid. In removing culpability because of extenuating
circumstances, this rule is
in line with the Ushan
materials in this unit.

7:4 Statement of general principle
that repeats and correlates
iv.D.6:1 and 7:1.

The rule depends upon M. 6:1
and 7:1, to which it adds
nothing.

v.   The Cultic Contamination of Heave-Offering

Yavneans explore the householder's responsibility to care
for heave-offering that might have been rendered unclean and
which therefore may not be eaten by a priest (v.B.8:8-11).
Eliezer holds that the individual still must protect the
heave-offering in cleanness. It may, after all, actually be
clean. Joshua, by contrast, states that since the doubtfully
clean heave-offering in no event will be eaten by a priest, the
householder himself may render it certainly unclean. Gamaliel
takes a middle position, that the householder may do nothing.
This Yavnean dispute gives way, in the Ushan period, to the
theory that, in cases of doubt, Israelites themselves determine
the status of produce, for instance, by deeming the doubtful
produce actually to be clean.

Ushans also address a quite separate issue, placed here
because of its slight topical relevance to cases of cultic
contamination of heave-offering. They state that if produce,
including heave-offering, appears to have been nibbled upon or
sipped at by a snake, it must be destroyed, lest it contain snake
venom (v.C.8:4, 5, 7, v.D.8:6).

A.   Before 70

B. The Time of Yavnah

8:8 A jug of wine in the status   While the suspect heave-
of heave-offering concerning which   offering may not be eaten,
there arose a suspicion of   lest it be unclean, Eliezer
uncleanness--Eliezer: One must   holds that the individual
still protect it in cleanness.   retains the responsibility
Joshua: He should render it   to take proper care of it.
certainly unclean. Gamaliel: Joshua is attentive to the
He should leave it alone.   mitigating circumstances.
                                          Since the priest may not eat
                                          this heave-offering anyway,
                                          the householder may render
                                          it certainly unclean, so
                                          that it may be destroyed.
                                          The same perspectives of
                                          Eliezer and Joshua appeared
                                          at iv.B.8:1-3 and are
                                          elaborated again at v.B.8:9,
                                          10 and 11. We thus have
                                          firm grounds in assigning
                                          this to the Yavnean period.

8:9 A jug of wine in the status   Eliezer's position is the
of heave-offering that broke in   same as at M. 8:8.
the upper vat and the lower vat is
unclean--Eliezer and Joshua agree
that if he can save the heave-
offering in cleanness, he should
do so. If not, Eliezer says
that he may not render the heave-
offering unclean with his own
hands.

8:10 Same position as at   This is the same as M. 8:9.
M. 8:9, for a case in which oil
in the status of heave-offering
is spilled and is about to be
soaked up into the ground.

8:11 In the cases given at   Joshua's view is the same as
M. 8:9-10, Joshua says: The man   is assigned to him at
himself may render the heave-   M. 8:8.

offering unclean, for it is about
to be rendered unclean anyway.

C. The Time of Usha

8:4 Water, wine and milk that are
left uncovered must be poured out,
lest a snake drank from them and
deposited venom.

The general rule for
uncovered liquids, stated
here anonymously, is assumed
in the following discussions
attributed to Ushans (see
also the Ushan materials at
T. 7:12-14). There is no
evidence that this rule
developed before the Ushan
period.

8:5 If there is sufficient liquid
to dilute venom, it is permitted.
Yose: Uncovered liquid in a
vessel never becomes permitted.
In pools in the ground, more than
forty seahs are permitted.

This Ushan discussion
develops M. 8:4.

8:7 A wine strainer used as a lid
does not prevent a snake from
depositing venom in a jug.
Nehemia: It does.

As at M. 8:5, placement is
on the basis of attribution.

D. Unassigned

8:6 Produce or meat that might
have been bitten by a snake may
not be consumed, lest it contains
snake venom.

The topic and point is close
to that of v.C.8:4, 5, 7.
After Ushan times, Simeon b.
Menasia further develops its
concerns, T. 7:16.

8:12 Women to whom gentiles said,
"Give us one of your number that
we may rape her, or we will rape
each of you," let them all be
raped.

This follows the view of
Eliezer, M. 8:8-10. Judah
and Simeon, T. 7:20, suggest
a parallel case, in which
they apply Joshua's
perspective, that Israelites
may save the many at the

cost of the few. It is
unclear whether this example
derives from Yavneh, with
Eliezer, or Usha, when
discussion of its larger
issue occurs.

vi. Heave-offering Planted as Seed

Yavneans state flatly that what grows from seed in the
status of heave-offering always has the status of a priestly gift
(vi.B.9:2-4). They thus have regard for the objective fact that
holy seed produced a crop and that the farmer who allowed that to
happen has usurped the priest's exclusive right to heave-
offering. As a result, the farmer loses all rights to the
produce of his field. It may be eaten only by a priest. Ushans,
by contrast, take seriously the character of the specific seed
that was planted, on the one hand, and the intentions of the
farmer who planted it, on the other (vi.C.9:5-7). They hold that
a crop has the status of the seed from which it grew only if that
seed is an intrinsic part of the crop. If the seed disintegrates
in the ground, Ushans hold that its status does not pass on to
the crop. That crop is an autonomous entity and therefore is
unconsecrated. Ushans further pay attention to the attitude of
the farmer who planted the seed (vi.D.9:1). He bears the
financial burden of cultivating a field planted with
heave-offering only if he intentionally sowed heave-offering-
seed. But if he planted the seed unintentionally, e.g., not
knowing that it was heave-offering, he may plow it up. While the
farmer may not derive personal benefit from the priestly gift, he
has not committed sacrilege and is not made to suffer the
continued financial burden of cultivating a crop with the low
market value of heave-offering.

A. Before 70

B. The Time of Yavneh

9:4 What grows from heave-offering
has the status of heave-offering.
A second generation of crops from
the original seed is however

What grows from sanctified
seed, such as that of heave-
offering, is sanctified.
This anonymous rule must be

unconsecrated. What grows from the seed of produce subject to other restrictions is not subject to those same restrictions.

placed in Yavnean times, for it stands behind the dispute that follows, between Tarfon and Aqiba, M. 9:2.

9:2 A field that is planted with seed in the status of heave-offering is subject to offerings left for the poor. Tarfon: Only poor priests may glean in such a field. Aqiba disagrees.

Since what grows from heave-offering seed is consecrated, M. 9:4, Tarfon wishes to prevent a poor Israelite from gleaning in the field, lest he eat some of the holy produce. Aqiba trusts the poor person to sell what he gleans to a priest.

9:3 Continuation of M. 9:2. The crop grown from heave-offering is subject to tithes and poorman's tithe. One should thresh this produce by hand. If he uses cattle, the animals must wear a feed bag filled with produce of the same kind, so that they cannot eat the holy produce they are threshing.

The point is the same as at M. 9:2. Like all produce grown by an Israelite, that which grows from heave-offering is subject to tithes. M. 9:2's dispute about who may claim these tithes would apply equally here. The rule concerning the threshing of produce is known in Ushan times, T. 8:3.

C. The Time of Usha
9:5 In the case of heave-offering planted as seed--if that seed is of a type which is not an integral part of the crop, the crop is consecrated.

This principle is unknown to, and disagrees with, the law for heave-offering planted as seed assigned to the Yavnean stratum, v.B.9:4. There is no evidence that the present ruling was known before Ushan times, to which it is attested by Judah, in the following, and by Simeon (alt.: Judah), T. 8:4.

9:6-7A-J The rule of M. 9:5
applies in the case of produce
subject to tithes that is planted
as seed. Arum, garlic and onions
are kinds of produce the seed of
which does not disintegrate.
Judah: In the case of garlic,
the seed disintegrates. An
Israelite may make a chance meal,
without tithing, of a gentile's
produce, even though it was grown
from untithed seed.

The theory is the same as at
M. 9:5 and is attested to
Usha by Judah. Discussion
continues after Ushan times,
with Simeon b. Eleazar,
T. 8:7. The final rule,
concerning a gentile's
produce, presumably refers
to a type of produce the
seed of which disintegrates.

9:7K-N The first crop of a sapling
grown from seed in the status of
heave-offering has the status of a
priestly gift. The second is
unconsecrated. Judah: The second
as well has the status of heave-
offering.

This develops the theory of
M. 9:5-6, applying it in a
new sort of case.
Discussion of this question
continues after Ushan times
with Nathan b. Joseph,
T. 8:8.

D. Unassigned
9:1 If a householder intentionally
sows as seed produce in the status
of heave-offering he may not plow
it up. Unintentionally, he may.
Once it is a viable crop, either
way, he may not plow it up.

The crop grown from heave-
offering has the status of
heave-offering, such that
the householder may not
himself eat it. If he
intentionally planted the
seed, he is culpable for
sacrilege. He must
cultivate the crop and later
sell it to a priest, at the
low value of heave-offering.
If he planted the seed
unintentionally, he is not
culpable. He rectifies his
mistake by plowing up the
heave-offering seed. This
is permitted unless the crop
already is edible. Then it
is deemed heave-offering and

may not be destroyed. This
rule thus brings into play
the usual Ushan concern for
intention. Parallel to
i.C.2:3 and 3, the present
pericope belongs in the
Ushan stratum.

vii.   Heave-offering Cooked with Unconsecrated Produce

The Yavnean theory, that forbidden produce does not impart
its own, forbidden, status to permitted produce with which it is
cooked (vii.B.10:11E-H; vii.D.10:10), is rejected in the Ushan
period. Ushans hold that whenever forbidden produce, including
heave-offering, imparts its flavor to, or is inextricably mixed
with, permitted produce, then the permitted produce too is
rendered forbidden (vii.C.10:1, 3, 8, 11A-D; vii.D.10:2, 4, 5-6,
7, 12). In either case the Israelite will perceive himself as
benefitting from consecrated produce. Judah further develops
the theory that the householder's perceptions determine the
status of food. He holds that the forbidden produce imparts its
own status to that which it flavors only if the householder
desires that flavor to enter his food (vii.C.10:1, 3).

A.   Before 70

B.   The Time of Yavneh

10:9 Zadoq testified that the
brine of unclean locusts does not
impart susceptibility to
uncleanness.

This rule is found in M.
Ter. because of its
relevance to an Ushan
pericope, vii.C.10:8. It
receives no development at
Usha and is not cognate to
other Yavnean material.
Placement is on the basis
of attribution alone.

10:11E-H Aqiba says: All
permitted food which is cooked with
prohibited food remains permitted,
except for what is cooked with
forbidden meat. Yohanan b. Nuri:

This Yavnean rule states the
opposite of the point made
in this topic at Usha, that
when prohibited food (heave-
offering) is cooked with

Forbidden liver renders forbidden that with which it is cooked.

permitted food it <u>does</u> impart to that food its forbidden status. Since the specfic notion of M.10:11E-H occurs only in this one pericope, placement in the Yavnean stratum is on the basis of attribution alone.

C. The Time of Usha

10:1 That which is inextricably mixed with or flavored by heave-offering takes on the status of heave-offering. Judah: An unconsecrated pickled fish cooked with an onion in the status of heave-offering remains permitted, for the purpose of the onion is to absorb the stench, not to flavor the fish.

M. 10:1 gives the principle that stands behind the Ushan and unassigned rules on this topic. A non-priest may not eat what has been flavored or mixed with heave-offering, since, by doing so, he would derive benefit from the priestly ration. Judah develops the basic principle to take into account the purpose for which the heave-offering was cooked with the unconsecrated food.

10:3 If hot bread is placed on a jug of wine in the status of heave-offering--Meir: It takes on the status of heave-offering. Judah: it remains unconsecrated. Yose: It depends on the type of bread.

Yose and Meir agree that so long as the bread absorbs the wine vapor, it takes on the status of heave-offering. Judah appears to follow the same view he expressed at M. 10:1. If the person wanted wine in the bread, he would have acted in a direct fashion, dipping the bread in the wine. Since he did not do that, we assume that he does not want the heave-offering-wine to flavor his bread, and therefore we deem

the actual effects of the
wine upon the bread to be
null.

10:8 Unclean fish pickled in clean
brine--if there is sufficient
unclean fish to impart flavor to
the brine, the brine is rendered
unclean. Judah and Yose dispute
the requisite quantity.

The theory is the same as at
M. 10:1, applied in a case
concerning clean and unclean
produce. This particular
pericope is further
developed after Ushan times
by Simeon b. Menasia and
Yose b. Judah, T. 9:1.

10:11A-D Yose says: Unconsecrated
produce boiled with beets in the
status of heave-offering is
rendered forbidden, since beets
impart flavor. Simeon: Cabbage
grown in an irrigated field imparts
flavor to cabbage grown in a rain
watered field.

The basic theory is that of
M. 10:1. Ushan authorities
apply that principle to the
case of specific types of
produce.

D. Unassigned
10:2 Dough leavened by an apple in
the status of heave-offering takes
on the status of heave-offering.
Water flavored by barley in the
status of heave-offering remains
permitted to a non-priest.

The dough, which has been
improved by the heave-
offering, takes on that
heave-offering's consecrated
status. The barley ruins
the flavor of the water and
therefore does not impart to
it the status of heave-
offering. These rules derive
from no earlier than Ushan
times, when the theory that
governs them was developed,
vii.C.10:1. Discussion is
at Usha and later: Yose and
Simeon, T. 8:9b-10 and
Eleazar b. Simeon, T. 8:13.

10:4 Bread baked in an oven fired
with cumin in the status of heave-

The differentiation between
"smell" and "flavor" is a

offering remains unconsecrated, for
the burning cumin imparts its
smell, but not its flavor.

development of the principle
at vii.C.10:1.

10:5-6 In the case of fenugreek
that is heave-offering or second
tithe, the seed is deemed
consecrated but the stalks are not.
If the fenugreek is produce of the
seventh year or of a vineyard in
which were sown diverse kinds, or
if it was dedicated to the Temple,
the seed and stalk together are
subject to the particular
restrictions. (10:6) One need
not separate tithes for the stalks
of fenugreek. But if one does so
the designation is valid and the
required amount of both stalks
and seed must go to the priest or
Levite.

The stalks of fenugreek are
not normally eaten and
therefore do not have the
status of an agricultural
offering. This is the case
unless the householder
intentionally designates
them to be such, for in
doing so he indicates his
desire to use the stalks
as a food. The stalks
however automatically are
subject to restrictions,
such as those of diverse
kinds, that apply to all
that is growing in a field.
The householder may in no
way benefit from such
produce. Since this unit
depends upon vii.C.10:1 and
develops it for an ambiguous
case, it cannot derive from
before Ushan times. The
attention here to the role
of the householder's
intention is further
evidence that this material
belongs at Usha, as is the
continued discussion of
these issues, at Usha, by
Meir and Judah, T. 8:9a.
See Orlah, ii.C.3:6-8.

10:7 Unconsecrated olives that are
pickled with olives in the status
of heave-offering--if the
consecrated olives are capable of

The principle is the same as
at vii.C.10:1, supporting
placement of this rule in
the Ushan stratum.

flavoring the unconsecrated ones,
the unconsecrated ones take on the
status of heave-offering.

10:10 Unconsecrated produce that   This contradicts what is
is pickled with heave-offering does   explicit at M. 10:7, that
not take on a consecrated status,   heave-offering generally
unless it is pickled with leeks in   flavors and therefore
the status of heave-offering.   imparts its own status to
                                       that with which it is
                                       pickled. Perhaps this rule
                                       belongs in the Yavnean
                                       stratum. See Aqiba,
                                       vii.B.10:11E-H.

10:12 An egg spiced with forbidden   The theory is that of
spices is itself rendered   vii.C.10:1.
forbidden, since even the yolk
absorbs the flavor. Liquid in which
heave-offering is boiled or pickled
is forbidden to non-priests.

viii.   The Processing and Consumption of Heave-offering

Yavneans provide the basic rule for this unit. Produce in
the status of heave-offering must be processed in the manner
usual for food of its type (viii.B.11:2-3). In this way we
assure that no part of the fruit that normally is eaten will go
to waste. This would occur, for instance, if fruits usually
eaten whole were squeezed for juice. Ushans apply this Yavnean
principle in the case of specific types of produce (viii.C.11:1,
10). In anonymous materials, the Yavnean theme is developed
along typically Ushan lines. Refuse from produce in the status
of heave-offering is deemed unconsecrated as soon as the priest
or Israelite deems it unworthy of use as food (viii.D.11:4-8).
Then it may be eaten even by a non-priest. So long as food is
deemed worthy for consumption, however, it retains its status of
consecration and may be eaten only by a priest. The clear point
of these rules is that the attitude of the Iraelite or priest
determines whether or not produce retains the consecrated status
of a priestly gift.

A.   Before 70

_____

B.   The Time of Yavneh

11:3 They may not make produce in the status of heave-offering into fruit juice or otherwise process it, unless it is olives or grapes. The forty stripes for consumption of orlah do not apply to liquids, except for wine and oil. First fruits may not be brought in the form of liquids, except for wine and oil. Fruit juices do not impart susceptibility to uncleanness, except for wine and oil. Liquids other than wine and oil may not be offered at the altar.

While stated anonymously, this pericope contains the principle of the Yavnean rule that follows. There is no evidence that it is known before Yavnean times. Produce in the status of heave-offering must be consumed in its normal fashion, as a food, and may not be allowed, since this causes the loss of much of the produce, e.g., the pulp. This does not apply to grapes and olives, which almost always are prepared as liquids.

11:2 Fruit juices made from produce in the status of heave-offering--Eliezer obligates a non-priest who drinks them to the principal and added fifth. Joshua exempts.

Both parties agree that heave-offering should not be made into fruit juice (= M. 11:3). The dispute concerns what happens if this anyway is done. Eliezer and Joshua's positions are familiar from units iv-v. Eliezer looks only at the objective facts. Joshua by contrast takes into account extenuating circumstances. The non-priest could not have known that the fruit juice was from heave-offering, and therefore he is not culpable.

C. The Time of Usha

11:1 They may not put heave-offering-figs in fish-brine, since this ruins the figs. They may, however, put wine in the status of heave-offering in brine, for it will be eaten with the brine. They may not perfume oil in the status of heave-offering, since then it will not be eaten. They may, however, honey wine in the status of heave-offering, for this is a drink. They may not boil wine that is heave-offering, for this diminishes its quantity. Judah: They may, for this improves its flavor.

On the basis of Judah's gloss, I assume that these several rules belong to the Ushan stratum. They all develop the Yavnean principle, viii.B.11:3, that heave-offering must be prepared in a way in which it can be eaten. The issue of the preparation of wine in the status of heave-offering is carried forward after Ushan times, by Eliezer b. Simeon, T. 9:6b.

11:10 Unclean oil in the status of heave-offering may be kindled in lamps in places in which priests will benefit from the light. Judah: They may kindle such oil at a wedding feast, but not in a house of mourning. Yose: They do so in a house of mourning but not at a wedding feast. Meir prohibits in either case. Simeon permits in both cases.

This is a development of the theory first proposed at Yavneh, viii.B.11:3, that heave-offering must be used to benefit the priest. The point here is that, so long as the priest benefits, it is irrelevant that non-priests enjoy the heave-offering as well. The four-party Ushan dispute that concludes this pericope eludes interpretation, since no indication is given why the rule for a wedding feast should be different from that for a house of mourning. It is placed here on the basis of attributions.

D. Unassigned

11:4 Refuse from produce in the status of heave-offering that has

This rule depends upon and develops the Yavnean and

food value retains the consecrated status of a priestly gift and may not be eaten by a non-priest.

Ushan principle that produce in the status of heave-offering should not be allowed to go to waste.

11:5 Refuse from heave-offering or holy-things that the priest saves retains its consecrated status. If the priest throws the refuse out, it is deemed permitted for consumption by a non-priest. The priest is not required to consume produce in the status of heave-offering which, were it unconsecrated, he would not eat.

The attitude of the priest determines whether or not the refuse is deemed a food and retains the status of heave-offering. This concern for the attitude of an individual is typically Ushan and supports placement of this pericope in the Ushan stratum.

11:6 When one empties a storage bin of wheat in the status of heave-offering, he need not pick up every last kernal before placing unconsecrated wheat in that bin.

As at M. 11:5, the status of produce depends upon whether people normally consider it worthy as food. The few kernals at the bottom of the bin are deemed refuse and therefore need not be eaten by the priest. Like M. 11:5 this rule belongs in the Ushan stratum.

11:7 If oil in the status of heave-offering spills, one may wipe it up with a rag, just as he would do with unconsecrated oil.

The point is the same as in the two preceding items.

11:8 When one empties a jug of wine or oil in the status of heave-offering, he need not entirely clean it of consecrated liquid but may forewith place unconsecrated liquid in it. However, if after emptying the jar he should collect the heave-offering-wine or oil that remains, that liquid retains its sanctified status.

The considerations of M. 11:5-7 apply here as well. The unit emphasizes the role of human intention: If the householder collects and saves what otherwise would be deemed refuse, that which he saves is deemed a food and retains its consecrated status.

11:9 Cattle owned by a priest may be fed with vetches in the status of heave-offering. A priest may not feed such vetches to a cow he has hired from an Israelite, unless he owns a share in the cow.

Vetches are an ambiguous type of food since, while they are edible by humans, more often they are given to cattle as feed. This rule is in line with the Yavnean principle that heave-offering must be used to the benefit of the priest. It is attested to Usha by Simeon b. Gamaliel, T. 10:17.

III. Conclusion

The topics and organization of the tractate reveal the point that its framers wish to make through their discussion of heave-offering. These topics are, first, the role of the Israelite in the designation and separation of heave-offering; second, his responsibility to maintain the priestly gift in conditions of sanctity; and, third, the part he plays in the determination of the point at which heave-offering loses its status of consecration, such that it again may be consumed by non-priests. The tractate as a whole thus focuses upon common Israelites and their role in the processes of sanctification. While this concern was established by Yavnens, who set the agendum of issues discussed in the tractate as a whole, only in the Ushan period does the perspective distinctive to Mishnaic legislation emerge. Based upon the Yavnean minority opinion of Joshua, Ushans rule that in all aspects of the processes of sanctification, the intentions and desires of common Israelites are central. At each point these determine the status of sanctification of produce that the Israelite sets aside as the priest's share. Through the Israelite's powers of intention, produce first comes to be holy. Later, the holiness of the priest's gift is maintained through the Israelite's desire not to commit sacrilege. Finally, the offering again is considered secular when the Israelite himself holds it no longer to be worthy of holiness. Through these claims the tractate as a whole comes to argue that common Israelites exercise powers of sanctification previously believed to be found solely in the

hands of the priests.   In the Division of Agriculture, common
Israelites are described as a central locus of sanctification,
bringing God's holiness into the world and assuring that it
properly is maintained and, ultimately, disposed of.

CHAPTER SEVEN

MAASEROT

I. Introduction

Tractate Maaserot defines the class of produce that is subject to the separation of agricultural offerings and indicates when payment of those offerings must be made. It asks, that is to say, 1) when, in the course of a crop's growth and ripening, may tithes validly be separated from it and 2) when, in the subsequent harvesting and preparation of the produce, must heave-offering and tithes actually be paid (see Jaffee, p. 1)?[1]

Mishnah's answer to these questions depends upon the understanding--derived in part from Scripture--that Israelites owe agricultural offerings to God in return for the use, granted them by God, of the land of Israel for the growing of crops. In light of this idea, the tractate points out that God is owed a share only once the produce actually has ripened and become useful as food. When the crop ripens, that is, God's role in its production is complete, such that he now may be paid the share he is owed.

Even at this point, however, Israelites still may refrain from tithing. They may refrain until they physically appropriate the food for their own personal use, either to sell in the market or to prepare as a meal. In the tractate's view, God's absolute claim for a share of the crops of the land of Israel becomes due only at the point at which Israelites exercise their own final, personal claim to use the produce as their own.

This notion, that the requirement to tithe is a reflex of the Israelites' desire for food, is found primarily in the tractate's Ushan stratum, which, indeed, comprises all but four of the rules before us. Specifically, Ushans rule that the obligation to tithe depends upon the individual's intention regarding the produce. If an individual does not clearly intend food that he eats to constitute a meal, then no matter how much he actually consumes, he need not tithe. By contrast, any time that the individual does take food for a meal, he must tithe, even if the food has not reached a state in its processing at which it normally is eaten.

231

While Yavneans too know that food must be tithed before it is used in a meal, they take no account of unusual or extenuating circumstances. Yavneans instead state simply that produce must be tithed when the individual brings it home, since it is there that he normally eats his meals. This leads only to a minor ambiguity in the law, concerning whether or not courtyards are comparable to a person's home so as to render produce brought into them subject to tithes.

The distinctive attitude that underlies the Ushan approach to the law is familiar from the Ushan strata of the tractates already discussed. For the case of Tractate Maaserot, this attitude is described by Jaffee (pp. 4-5):

> What is striking in all of this is that the entire mechanism of restrictions and privileges, from the field to home or market, is set in motion solely by the intentions of the common farmer. Priests cannot claim their dues whenever they choose, and God himself plays no active role in establishing when the produce must be tithed. Indeed, the framers of Maaserot assume a profound passivity on the part of God. For them, it is human actions and intentions which move God to affect the world. God's claims against the Land's produce, that is to say, are only reflexes of those very claims on the part of Israelite farmers. God's interest in his share of the harvest, as I said, is first provoked by the desire of the farmer for the ripened fruit of his labor. His claim to that fruit, furthermore, becomes binding only when the farmer makes ready to claim his own rights to its use, whether in the field or at home or market.

Describing the classes of produce subject to heave-offering and tithes and outlining the conditions under which these agricultural gifts must be separated, Tractate Maaserot is independent of any particular passage in Scripture,[2] which, for its part, simply assumes that Israelites will tithe the produce of the land.[3] We may therefore turn directly to the specifics of the unfolding of the tractate's law.

A. Maaserot Before 70

The tractate's one dispute attributed to the period before 70 appears to be pseudepigraphic. v.C.4:2 has the Houses dispute whether or not a householder who sets aside figs for consumption on the Sabbath must tithe those figs if he chooses instead to eat them either before or after the holy day. The notion that once produce is designated for a meal it must be tithed itself is Ushan (v.C.4:3). The specific problem addressed by the Houses is a subtle development of that idea. It asks whether the intention to use produce in a meal has a generalized effect upon the produce or whether it applies to the specified meal alone. The dispute's dependence upon an Ushan idea and the appearance in it of Judah, who restates the view attributed to the Hillelites, provide strong evidence that an Ushan concern has here been placed in the mouths of the Houses. This means that the tractate contains no evidence of the discussion of its topic before the period of Yavneh.[4]

B. Maaserot in the Time of Yavneh

While comprised of only four pericopae, the Yavnean material does contain the underlying fact of this tractate. Produce must be tithed when the individual is prepared to use it in a normal meal. Before that point, the food may be eaten as a snack, without being tithed. Since the Israelite has not yet appropriated the food for his own exclusive use, God's claim upon it likewise does not become active.

Yavneans develop this fact in only a minor way. They assume that produce normally will be tithed when it is brought into the individual's home, since it is there that he has his meals. They ask whether or not a courtyard is comparable to a home, such that it too renders food brought into it subject to tithes (iv.B.3:5A-D, 3:9). Yavneans hold that this depends upon the physical fact of whether or not the courtyard offers protection and privacy such as a home provides. In typically Ushan fashion, the following generation of authorities will develop this issue to state that all depends upon the householder's own feelings about the courtyard.

The two other Yavnean pericopae make relatively minor points. A seed-crop is not subject to tithes at all, since it will not be eaten, vi.B.4:5E-H. Yavneans dispute how foods, which must be tithed, are to be defined, vi.B.4:6. One side holds that we take into account only the botanical fact of the item's edibility, such that anything that can be eaten must be tithed. The opposing view follows normal communal behavior, stating that only things that people normally eat are to be tithed. Ushans, i.C.1:1, accept the latter view as normative (see also Terumot, viii.D and Hallah, i.D.1:8). Rather than botanical characteristics, the Israelite's own attitude determines what is or is not food.

C. Maaserot in the Time of Usha

Ushans hold that the requirement to tithe is activated through the desires and perceptions of the Israelite who readies produce for use in a meal. This is expressed in the Ushan rule that, to be subject to tithes at all, produce must not only be edible but, second, must be cultivated purposely by Israelites for use as food and, third, must be privately owned (i.C.1:1, 2-3, 4). Only food that in these ways is subject to the desires of Israelites enters the system of tithes.

With this much established, Ushans, like Yavneans, want to know when produce that is subject to tithes must in fact be tithed. They agree with the general Yavnean notion that tithes must be separated when the householder takes the food for personal use (ii.C.1:5-8). God's claim to the produce, that is to say, is activated at the same point at which Israelites exercise their claim to the food. In light of this notion, the majority of the materials before us consider the question of when the individual is held to have acquired the food for personal use.

In the Yavnean stratum, the single consideration for determining liability to tithes is that the individual has brought the produce into his home. Ushans greatly expand the Yavnean discussion, considering other cases in which it is clear from the individual's actions that he considers the food ready for use in a meal. Meir, for instance, holds that any sale renders the produce subject to tithes, for the new owner has, in a formal way, acquired the produce as his own (iii.C.2:5). The weight of the law, however, holds that such formal acts of transfer and acquisition alone do not affect the status of the produce as regards tithing. Rather, only the purchaser's or recipient's desire to make use of the produce in a meal renders that produce subject to tithes (iii.C.2:2, 8D-J, iii.D.2:1). As in the case of the designation of agricultural gifts, in which physical actions serve to indicate the individual's intentions, so here, further, we judge what the Israelite is thinking by the particular way in which he handles the produce. When he snacks on unprocessed produce--which normally is not subject to tithes--in a way that prevents him from returning the surplus to the processing vat, for instance, we can be certain that he views what he has taken as a little meal unto itself. Accordingly, he must tithe (iii.C.2:4A-C, D-E).

Two other rules highlight the centrality of the Israelite's attitude in activating the system of agricultural restrictions. The home of a traveler, first, is that place at which he feels at ease, as he would in his own house. This is known, for instance, by the fact that he prepares to spend the Sabbath in that place (iii.C.2:3). In like manner, Ushans carry forward the Yavnean discussion of the status of a courtyard (iv.C.3:5E-I, 3:7). Yavneans define a courtyard that renders produce in it liable to tithes on the basis of function. Ushans, by contrast, are concerned with the individual's own attitude towards the courtyard. It is considered comparable to a home only if the individual feels as comfortable and unselfconscious in it as he does in his own house.

II. The History of Tractate Maaserot

i. How Produce Becomes Subject to Tithes

Ushans limit the removal of tithes to agricultural produce alone (i.C.1:1). Tithes need not be separated from what grows wild, without the intervention of Israelites who till the soil. This reflects Scripture's own notion that what Israelites purposefully grow upon the Land of Israel comes to them with the help of God, to whom a share of the food therefore is due (Lev. 27:30, Dt. 26:14-15). An obvious corollary to Scripture's notion is that only what is edible is subject to tithes. The majority of the rules in the unit before us therefore delineate the point in their growth and subsequent processing at which specific types of produce are deemed edible (i.C.1:2-4). God's claim upon the produce, that is to say, becomes effective at the point at which the produce becomes of value to the Israelite who will use it as a food. This theory, which holds that the obligation to tithe revolves around the actions and desires of Israelites, is central in the Ushan stratum of this tractate as a whole. It therefore is important to note the emphasis it receives in this opening, Ushan, unit of the tractate.

A. Before 70

B. The Time of Yavneh

C. The Time of Usha

1:1 All produce that is edible, privately-owned and that grows from the earth must be tithed. It is subject to tithes as soon as it becomes edible.

While stated anonymously, this rule provides the theory that underlies the long Ushan lists of specific types of produce, which follow at M. 1:2-4. The main point here is that produce is subject to tithes when it becomes edible. The task of the next pericopae accordingly will be to establish the exact point in growth at which specific sorts of produce are edible. Since discussion and exemplification of this general rule comes only in Ushan times, it is likely that the general principal itself derives from that period. There is no evidence that it was known earlier, at Yavneh or before 70.

1:2-3 At what point in their growth are various kinds of produce edible, such that they are subject to the removal of tithes? Ten items + dispute by Judah of one item. M. 1:3 provides ten further items, a total of twenty entries in a formally and substantively unitary list.

Attested to Usha by Judah, this list exemplifies the general principle established at M. 1:1. Further discussion of this theory by Simeon b. Gamaliel (T. 1:5, who creates a Houses' dispute on the topic) and reference to an ambiguity involving one of the list's items after Ushan times (Ishmael b. Yose, T. 1:1c) provide grounds for the placement of this material in the Ushan stratum.

1:4 Continuation of preceding.   The anonymous rule follows
Rule for green vegetables. Apples   M. 1:2I-J, which claims that
and citrons are subject large and   produce is subject to tithes
small. Simeon: Citrons are   when the edible portion
subject only when ripe. Rule for   takes shape. Simeon agrees
sweet and bitter almonds.   with M. 1:1 and the dominant
                                       theory at M. 1:2-3. He
                                       holds that the produce must
                                       actually be edible.
                                       Simeon's view is attested
                                       after Usha by Nahorai b.
                                       Shinayya, T. 1:1d. On the
                                       basis of substance and cited
                                       authority we thus are on
                                       firm grounds in assigning
                                       M. 1:4 to Ushan times.

D. Unassigned

    _____

    ii. When Must Produce be Tithed: Processing and Storage

    In unit i Ushans indicate the earliest point at which
produce may be tithed. Now they determine when the produce must
be tithed. This is the point at which the food's owner takes the
produce for his own personal use, either as a meal or, for
instance, to sell in the market.   Having chosen to use the produce for his own benefit, the individual must first separate
heave-offering and tithes, so as to release the lien on the
produce held by God. Before this point the individual may eat of
the produce as a small snack, which does not indicate his final
appropriation of the food for his own use. After this point the
individual may do nothing with the produce unless he tithes.

A. Before 70

    _____

B. The Time of Yavneh

    _____

C. The Time of Usha
1:5-8 At what point in its   1) The owner must tithe his

processing is produce rendered liable to the removal of tithes, such that tithes must be separated before any of that produce may be eaten? A catalog of twelve heavily glossed rulings is attested to Usha by disputes involving Judah and Yose.

produce if he stores it for his own later use; 2) he must tithe when he appropriates the produce for profit or present use. So long as the produce is not subject to either of these criteria, the owner may make a random snack of it, without tithing. This material is placed in this stratum on the basis of its substantive relationship to the Ushan materials in section i and the participation in its discussion by Ushan authorities. See v.C.4:4.

D. Unassigned

---

iii. When Must Produce Be Tithed: Acquisition

This entirely Ushan unit defines the specific conditions under which an individual is deemed to have appropriated food. We deal primarily with two types of cases. In one, the Israelite either is told by someone in the market to take figs for himself (iii.C.2:1, 2) or goes ahead and buys figs (iii.C.2:5). In the other, the individual is engaged in transporting his untithed figs to the market-place (iii.C.2:3). These several cases make a single point. The transfer of produce from one person to another does not in and of itself render it subject to the separation of tithes. It remains exempt unless the person who receives the produce indicates in some concrete way his intention to use the food in a meal. This means gathering all that he purchases into a single bunch and not, for instance, picking out and eating one at a time the figs that he purchases. The further point is that produce always becomes liable when it is brought into the individual's home, for it is there that the person normally uses the produce in a meal.[5] One important issue of this unit therefore is to define what constitutes a person's home.

iii.C.2:4 concerns whether, by prematurely separating heave-offering, the householder shows his intention to use the food as his own, such that tithes must now be separated as well (cf., Jaffee, pp. 71-73). Eliezer, on the one side, deems the separation of the one offering to be an act of acquisition that renders the produce subject to all of the agricultural tithes. Simeon disagrees, presumably holding that the separation of heave-offering is not comparable to other manners in which the individual acquires the food for use in a meal.

A. Before 70

B. The Time of Yavneh

C. The Time of Usha

2:2 If men were in a shop and a passer-by said, "Take figs"--they may snack without tithing. But the shopkeeper must tithe before eating, since the shop is like his home. Judah exempts the owner from tithing unless he turns his face from the public or moves to a private part of the shop.

The men need not tithe, since they have not acquired the produce by "bringing it home." The shopkeeper's store, by contrast, is like his home. Judah shows concern for the individual's intentions and perceptions. The store is analogous to a home only if the owner purposely establishes in it a private area for himself.

2:3 One who transports produce may make an untithed snack of that food until he reaches his destination. Then he must tithe before eating. Meir: He must tithe as soon as he reaches a place in which he intends to spend the Sabbath. A peddler who goes from town to town must tithe as soon as he reaches his night's lodging. Judah: The first house he enters is considered his house, and he must tithe.

This unit again develops ii.C.1:5-8, for it assumes that the individual may make a random meal of untithed produce until he has acquired that produce by bringing it home. The question is what is to be deemed a traveler's home. The anonymous rules and Meir assume that this is any place in which the

individual feels at ease, as
he would in his own house.
Judah disagrees, holding
that what is a home for one
person must be considered
a home for any other person
who enters it as well. He
thus disputes the
application, but not the
theory, of M. 1:5-8.

2:4A-C Produce from which one
separated heave-offering before its
processing was completed, such
that it is not yet liable to
heave-offering and tithes--Eliezer:
In order to eat this produce, he
must tithe as well. Sages: He
need not.

The issue is whether the
premature separation of one
agricultural offering
renders the produce liable
to the separation of other
offerings as well. The same
issue is disputed by Simeon
and sages in the following
entry and occurs at v.C.4:2
and 4:3. I must therefore
assume that reference here
is to an Ushan Eliezer. The
set of rules concerning the
separation of heave-offering
from produce the processing
of which is not yet
completed likewise appears
to be Ushan. See Terumot,
i.D.1:8, 9 and 10.

2:4D-E A basket of unprocessed
figs from which one separated
heave-offering--R. Simeon permits
making a random snack of it.
Sages hold that he must tithe.

The issue is explained in
the preceding entry. Simeon
here has the position of
sages in that pericope;
sages have the view of
Eliezer. Participation in
this discussion of Meir,
T. 2:3, strengthens the
impression that this is an
exclusively Ushan issue.[6]

2:5 One who purchases five figs
for an _issar_ may not eat them
without tithing; so Meir. Judah:
He may eat them one by one without
tithing, but must tithe if he
gathers the purchase together as a
batch.

Meir recognizes that
purchase is an act of
appropriation by which the
purchaser makes his own the
produce that formerly
belonged to another. Like
all acts of acquisition,
purchase renders the produce
subject to tithes. Judah
disagrees and holds that
only what the buyer does
with the produce counts.
The act of purchasing the
produce has no affect,
unless the buyer actually
gathers together what he
bought, for use in a meal.
Developing Ushan principles
and involving Ushan
authorities, these materials
are firmly placed in the
Ushan stratum. Secondary
development of this unit is
found at iii.D.2:6.

2:8D-J If two people exchange
produce, they must tithe before
they eat. Judah: One who
exchanges eating figs for figs
to be dried need not tithe until
the figs he receives actually are
dried.

The exchange of produce is
comparable to a sale which,
we know from iii.C.2:5, may
render the produce liable
to tithes. As at M. 2:5,
Judah holds that the simple
fact of a sale does not
render the produce liable.
It need be tithed only when
its owner desires it as
food. Additional discussion
of this Ushan ruling occurs
at Usha and later, in the
names of Rabbi and Simeon b.
Gamaliel, T. 2:5, and
Eleazar b. Zadoq (alt.:
Simeon b. Yohai), T. 2:7.

D. Unassigned

2:1 One who says, "Take figs for yourself"--the recipient makes a snack of them without tithing until he arrives home. If he said, "Take figs and bring them home"--the recipient shall not make a random snack of them even before he reaches home.

This pericope applies the Ushan principle of ii.C.1:5 in a manner attested to Usha by Judah, iii.C.2:2. According to M. 1:5, produce is permitted as a snack until it is appropriated for the personal use of its owner. Under discussion now is the point at which the produce is deemed to have a new owner, whose own actions and intentions will determine whether or not it must be tithed.

2:6 One who says, "Here is an issar for ten figs, a cluster of grapes, a pomegrante or a melon which I shall choose"--eats the produce a bit at a time without tithing. If he purchased as yet unpicked produce, even if he specified which pieces of fruit he wanted, he is exempt from tithing and may eat the produce however he wishes, until it is picked and processed, when he must tithe.

This is a secondary development of the position of Judah, iii.C.2:5. So long as the buyer does not gather the stipulated quantity into his possession, he may eat without tithing. This rule adds that this applies even to so subtle a case as one in which the buyer cuts off and eats one piece of melon at a time. The final rule is separate, noting that a sale is not determinative in the case of produce which, because it is as yet unpicked, cannot become subject to the separation of tithes. Dependent upon iii.C.2:5, these rules can derive from no earlier than Ushan times.

2:7 One who hires a harvester-- while working the harvester eats

Dt. 23:24-25 gives workers the right to eat produce

without tithing, because the Torah
gives him the right to the produce.
If his dependents eat, they must
tithe.

upon which they are working.
The Ushan principle, that a
sale of produce renders that
produce liable to tithes, is
not invoked, since the
worker is not deemed to
purchase this food with his
labor. This is not the case
if he takes food and gives
it to a relative. Since
this rule assumes the
principle given in the
Ushan iii.C.2:5, it can
derive from no earlier than
Ushan times.

2:8A-C A worker may eat without
tithing only that particular
produce upon which he is working.
He may however refrain from eating
entirely until he reaches the
better produce.

This clarifies the preceding
entry.

3:1 One who brings unprocessed
produce into his courtyard--his
dependents may eat without tithing,
but his workers must tithe if they
have a claim upon him for their
board.

The unprocessed produce is
not yet subject to tithes,
such that the owner and his
family may eat of it without
tithing. Workers who have
contracted for their board,
by contrast, purchase the
produce with their labor.
In accordance with
iii.C.2:5, they must
therefore tithe before they
eat. Like iii.D.2:7-8A-C
this rule derives from no
earlier than Ushan times.

3:2 One who brings his workers to
the field--If they have no claim
upon him for board, they may eat

The point is that of M. 3:1.
Those workers with no
contract for board have not

without tithing. If they do have a claim upon him for board, they may only pick produce from the tree one piece at a time and eat it without tithing.

"purchased" the produce they eat and therefore may make a random snack without tithing. The rule for workers who do receive board is familiar from iii.C.2:5 and iii.D.2:6: If one does not gather together all of the produce he wishes to eat, that produce remains exempt from tithes, even if it was purchased. Dependent upon rules assigned to the Ushan stratum, this pericope can derive from no earlier than Ushan times.

3:3 One who hired gardeners who receive their food as part of their pay--They may eat one by one from the tree without tithing. If they gather produce together, they must tithe.

The principle is the same as at M. 3:2, such that we are on firm grounds in placing this pericope in the Ushan stratum or later.

3:4 If he found harvested figs in the road he may eat them without tithing. But if they had been processed, he must tithe, since they obviously derive from a batch that already is liable to tithes.

The theory is that of M. B.Q. 10:2 and M. B.M. 2:1-2: what is irretrievably lost is deemed abandoned and therefore is exempt from the separation of tithes. This is the case unless the produce had already been processed and become subject to tithes before it was lost. Since the rule that certain forms of processing render produce subject to tithes, ii.C.1:5-8, is Ushan, this too can derive from no earlier than the Ushan period.

iv. When Must Produce Be Tithed: The Courtyard and Home

Basic notions concerning when produce becomes liable to the separation of tithes derive from Yavnean times. We know from the preceding unit that an individual who brings produce into his home will use that produce as part of a meal and therefore must tithe. If his courtyard serves as part of his home, he likewise must tithe produce he brings into it. Yavneans initiate the discussion of which courtyards are comparable to homes (iv.B.3:5A-D). They determine the character of the courtyard on the basis of its design, e.g., by whether or not it affords protection as does a home. Ushans carry forward the Yavnean thinking, using as a criterion the householder's own attitude towards the courtyard (iv.C.3:5E-I). What counts for Ushans is whether or not the householder himself deems his courtyard comparable to his home. Ushans apply this same reasoning to other structures that might or might not be deemed homes (iv.C.3:7).

Yavneans also discuss a case in which produce grows within the courtyard itself. This produce's presence in the courtyard does not reveal the householder's intention to use it in a meal. It therefore is subject to tithes only when the individual actually prepares to eat it, e.g., by gathering the produce together (iv.B.3:9). Ushans carry forward this idea by defining what constitutes gathering the produce (iv.C.3:8).

A. Before 70

B. The Time of Yavneh

3:5A-D What kind of courtyard renders liable to tithes produce which is brought into it? Ishmael: A Tyrian courtyard, for housewares are safely stored in it. Aqiba: A courtyard to which more than one individual has a key does not render produce liable to tithes.

Aqiba and Tarfon dispute what sorts of courtyards afford privacy and protection, such that they are comparable to a home and render liable to tithes produce brought into them. The issue is developed by Ushan authorities, iv.C.3:5E-H and at iii.D.3:1. We thus are on

firm grounds in assigning
inception of this principle
to Yavnean times.

3:9 Grapes, pomegranates or melons
growing in a courtyard--Tarfon:
The individual may pick one cluster
of grapes, one pomegrante or one
melon and eat it without tithing.
Aqiba: To eat without tithing,
he must pick only one grape at a
time, or break off only a small
piece of pomegranate or melon.

If the produce is picked
within the courtyard, it
becomes liable to tithes
only if it is gathered
together as part of a normal
meal. Attributed to Yavnean
authorities and developing
a topic initiated in Yavnean
times, this dispute is
firmly placed in this
stratum. Its principle
receives futher deliberation
at Usha, iv.C.3:8.

C. The Time of Usha
3:5E-I What type of courtyard
renders liable to tithes produce
bought within it? Nehemiah: Any
courtyard in which a man eats
unself-consciously. Yose: Any
courtyard into which one enters
and no one inquires, "What do you
want," does not render produce
liable. Judah: If there are two
courtyards, the inner one renders
produce liable, but the outer
one does not.

The issue first raised in
Yavnean times (iv.B.3:5A-D)
is further developed. While
the underlying theory
remains the same as at
Yavneh, viz., that a courtyard which provides privacy
renders produce liable, the
expression of that theory
takes typically Ushan form.
Ushan authorities are
concerned not with physical
traits (e.g., the shape of
the courtyard or how many
individuals have keys), but
with the attitude of the
individuals who use it.
Judah defines matters in
terms of design. Creation
of an inner courtyard
indicates the home-owner's
intention to have a private

area. This are renders
produce liable to tithes.
An outer courtyard, which is
relatively public, does not.

3:7 Produce that is brought into
storage huts, etc., is not rendered
liable to the separation of tithes.
A potter's hut--the inside renders
produce liable, the outer part
does not. Yose: Only a structure
which serves as a dwelling winter
and summer renders produce liable.
As for a festive hut--Judah:
During Tabernacles it renders
produce liable. Sages: It does
not.

The theme of iv.B.3:5A-D and
iv.C.3:5E-I is carried
forward, with the important
principle under dispute by
Ushans, Judah and Yose.
They agree that the function
of the structure determines
whether or not it is deemed
a home, such that it renders
produce brought into it
liable for tithes. Yose's
point is that only areas
used as permanent dwellings
are deemed homes. Judah
disagrees and holds that the
structure's function at any
particular moment is
determinative. Note that
the anonymous rule, for the
potter's hut, parallels the
opinion attributed to Judah
in the preceding entry.

3:8 A fig tree growing in a court-
yard--the householder eats one by
one without tithing. Simeon: He
may have a fig in each hand and
one in his mouth and still not
tithe.

The underlying principle is
that of iv.B.3:9, that
produce which is picked
within a courtyard but is
not gathered together does
not become liable for
tithes. Simeon develops
that principle, offering his
own theory of the number of
figs a person may have in
his possession and still not
need to tithe.

D. Unassigned

3:6 Produce brought onto a roof is not rendered liable to tithes. Gate-houses, porticos and balconies share the status of the courtyard in which they are found.

This material shares the topic and theory of iv.B.3:5A-D, iv.C.3:5E-I and iv.C.3:7. Interest in the particular question of whether or not specific types of buildings are deemed "houses" that render produce liable for tithes is confined to the Ushan stratum. These rules apparently belong to that level in the development of the law.

3:10 A tree standing in a court-yard with its bough extending into the garden--one may eat from the bough as he pleases, without tithing. If the tree grows in the garden and the bough is in the courtyard, one may eat without tithing only if he picks the produce one piece at a time. In other matters of law the status of the tree is determined by where the roots are growing.

The status of the produce as regards tithing is determined on the basis of where it is picked, not where the tree on which it grows is planted. Carrying forward the interests of iv.B.3:5A-D, iv.C.3:5E-I, 3:7 and 3:8 for a more complicated case, these anonymous rules cannot derive from earlier than Ushan times. Indeed they are discussed by Ushan authorities, Nehemiah, T. 2:20e and Simeon B. Gamaliel, T. 2:22.

v. When Must Produce Be Tithed: Preparing the Meal

Produce normally is not subject to tithes until it is fully processed and designated for use in a meal. The Ushan point here is that whatever an Israelite intends for use in a meal must be tithed, even if its processing is not yet complete or if it has not yet been brought into the home (v.C.4:3, 4:4). Judah (v.C.4:2) carries forward this notion, stating that the individual's intention to use produce in a meal is not reversible. The produce must be tithed even if he changes his mind and decides to eat it before or after the time originally set for the meal.

A.   Before 70
4:2   See v.C.4:2

B.   The Time of Yavneh

C.   The Time of Usha

4:2   Figs hidden away for the
Sabbath which one did not tithe--
even after the Sabbath he shall
not eat of them without tithing.
Produce set aside for the
Sabbath--The House of Hillel say:
He must tithe before eating some
of it before the Sabbath.
The House of Shammai: Before the
Sabbath he may eat without tithing.
Judah: The Hillelite position
applies if he sends produce to a
friend.

Once produce is designated
for use in a meal, it must
be tithed (v.C.4:3). The
issue here is a subtle
development of this. We ask
whether or not the
individual must tithe the
produce if he decides to
consume it as a snack prior
to or after the time
appointed for the meal. The
Hillelite view appears as
well in the initial
anonymous rule and in the
statement of Judah. The
intention to use the produce
in a meal is operative from
from the moment it is
formulated. It is not
reversible. The Shammaites,
by contrast, hold that the
person's intention applies
to the specified meal alone.
The Houses here develop in a
sophisticated way a
principle stated simply in
Ushan times (v.C.4:3-4).
These substantive grounds
and the close link between
the Hillelite position and
that of Judah (see also

T. 3:2b-4) provide strong evidence that an Ushan issue has been placed in the mouths of the Houses. See Jaffee in Neusner, _Judaism_, pp. 293-296.

4:3 Untithed olives that are being softened for pressing--he eats one by one from the bin without tithing. But if he salts a small batch, he must tithe. Eliezer: If the olives in the bin were clean, he must tithe. But if they were unclean, he need not tithe, since he can return the surplus from his small batch to the bin.

Olives being softened normally are not subject to tithes, since their processing is not complete. If the householder takes a batch of them for his own consumption as a small meal, however, they must be tithed. His use of them in a meal is determinative. Eliezer is concerned with the individual's intention. If he only takes olives that he may return to the softening vat he clearly does not intend those olives as a "meal." He therefore may contine to eat of the olives he has gathered without tithing. The principle stated here is in line with the Ushan materials at v.C.4:2 and 4:4. I therefore assume that reference is to an Ushan Eliezer, just as at iii.C.2:4A-C.[7]

4:4 One who drinks wine at the press is exempt from removing tithes, so Meir. Eleazar bar Zadoq declares him liable. Sages: If he mixed it with hot water, he must tithe. If he

Meir holds that the wine is not yet subject to tithes, for its processing is not yet completed. In line with ii.C.1:7, Eleazar bar Zadoq holds that once the

mixed it with cold water, he is
exempt from tithing.

wine is skimmed in the vat,
it is in all events subject
to tithes. Sages frame the
issue in terms familiar
from Eliezer's opinion,
v.C.4:3.

D. Unassigned

4:1 One who pickles, boils or
salts produce in the field is
required to tithe + five sorts
of processing that render produce
in the field subject to tithes.

Produce still located in the
field normally is permitted
as an untithed snack, for
the farmer has not yet
acquired it for use in a
meal. The point here is
that, even in the field,
if the farmer prepares the
produce as he normally
would fix a meal, that
produce is subject to
tithes. This is the same
point made at v.C.4:3 and
4:4. Participation in
the present discussion of
Simeon b. Judah, T. 3:1,
supports the placement of
this rule at Usha.

4:5A-D He may husk and eat one
kernel of barley at a time
without tithing. But if he gathers
a few husked kernels in his hand,
he must tithe.

The point is the same as in
the preceding entry, v.C.4:3
and 4:4. Note also the
participation in this
discussion of Rabbi (alt.:
Meir) and Yose b. Judah,
T. 3:5b.

vi. Ambiguities in the Law of Tithes

The unit is a compilation of various rulings that address
ambiguities in the application of the principles discussed
earlier in the tractate. These primarily concern the question of
what produce is deemed a food, such that it is subject to the
separation of tithes. Yavneans, first, dispute whether or not

parts of a plant that, while edible, normally are not eaten become subject to tithes (vi.B.4:5E-H, 4:6). Eliezer, as usual, along with Gamaliel will not take into account the fact that people normally do not eat something. If they can eat it, they say, it must be tithed. Aqiba disagrees, foreshadowing the view held, as we shall see, by Judah.

Ushans look at a more developed case, in which an individual makes a drink by straining water through grape lees, which themselves are not edible at all (vi.C.5:6). Contrary to the anonymous rule, Judah holds that the householder's intention to create a drink renders the resultant liquid subject to tithes, even though it derives from what itself would not be tithed.

In an anonymous rule, Ushans correlate the rules of unit i with those of units ii-v. They note that, no matter what manner of sale, transfer or other form of acquisition the produce undergoes, it cannot become subject to the separation of tithes until it is fully ripened and ready for use as a food (vi.D.5:1A-D).

A.   Before 70

_____

B.   The Time of Yavneh

4:5E-H If coriander is sown for seed, the leaves are exempt from tithes. If it is sown for the leaves, both the seeds and leaves are subject to tithes. Eliezer: Seeds, leaves and pods of dill are subject to tithes. Sages: That is the case only for cress and fieldrocket.	The farmer's intended use of his crop determines whether or not it will be subject to tithes when it is harvested. It will be subject to tithes only if he originally sowed it for use as a food. Eliezer and sages dispute the application of this theory. Eliezer holds that all parts of the plant which potentially are eaten are under the law of tithes. Sages state that the law extends only to such parts as carry the plant's flavor.
4:6 Gamaliel: Stalks of fenugreek, etc., are subject to tithes. Eliezer: Stalks, berries	Gamaliel and Eliezer are consistent with the principle of M. 4:5E-H. Any

and blossoms of the capor bush are subject to tithes. Aqiba: Only the berries are subject, for they are the fruit.

part of the plant that might be eaten is subject to tithes. Aqiba disagrees with this prevailing theory. He claims that the potential use of seed and stalks as food does not bring them under the law of tithes. Only what normally serves as food need be tithed, regardless of the individual farmer's plan for the particular item.

5:1E-G If he picked produce to send to his fellow before the harvest, it is exempt from tithes until the recipient processes it. Eleazar b. Azariah: If such produce is available in the market, it is subject to tithes before it is sent to the friend.

Normally the sender must tithe the gift, for fear that, thinking tithes already have been removed, the recipient himself will not do so. If the whole crop is not yet harvested, such a precaution need not be taken, since the recipient cannot assume that what he receives has been tithed. This is not the case if such produce is already in the market. This pericope's theory is quite different from the Ushan idea found at Demai, ii.C.3:3E-G, which assumes that all gifts of produce must be sent already tithed.

C. The Time of Usha
5:5 One who purchases a field of greens in Syria--if he bought it before the crop ripened, he need tithe the crop once it ripens. If he bought it after it had ripened,

In Syria, only produce that ripens under Israelite ownership need be tithed. If the crop is ripe when the Israelite purchases the

he need not tithe even the late
ripening produce. Judah: He may
hire workers to pick for him.
Simeon b. Gamaliel: The anonymous
rule applies only if he bought the
land. If he only bought the crop,
under no circumstances is it liable
for tithes. Rabbi: If he owns
the land, he must tithe late
ripening fruit.

field, it remains exempt.
Rabbi takes into account the
point of ripening of each
piece of produce and not of
the field as a whole (see
vi.D.5:3). This material is
placed in the Ushan stratum
because of its citation of
Ushan authorities as well as
its dependence upon the
Ushan principle (i.C.1:1-4),
that produce becomes subject
to tithes when it ripens.[8]

5:6 One who soaks grape-lees for
their liquid--if he extracted the
same amount of water that he added,
the water need not be tithed as
wine. Judah: He must tithe.

Judah takes seriously the
individual's intention to
produce a drink. Even
though it derives from what
normally is not tithed at
all, the drink is subject to
agricultural offerings.
Judah thus follows the
theory often found in his
name, that intention is
central in determining the
status of foods. This
provides firm grounds for
placing this rule in the
Ushan stratum. See
vi.D.5:4.

5:8 Produce that is not grown in
the land of Israel or that is not
food is not subject to tithes.
Meir and Yose suggest specific
sorts of produce which, for these
reasons, are not subject.

These rules depend upon the
Ushan principle (i.C.1:1)
that inedible produce is not
subject to tithes. In T.
other Ushan authorities
participate in this same
discussion: Simeon b.
Gamaliel, T. 3:15, and
Judah, T. 3:16.

D. Unassigned

5:1A-D One who uproots shoots for transplanting need not tithe. If he purchased produce still attached to the ground the produce remains exempt from tithes until it is harvested.

Picking produce for transplanting is not deemed a "harvest" which renders the produce subject to tithes. A purchase of unharvested produce likewise does not constitute a "sale" which renders the produce subject to tithes. These qualifications of Ushan conceptions regarding the effect of a harvest or sale (i.C.1:1-4, ii.C.1:5-8 and iii.C.2:5) cannot derive from earlier than Ushan times.

5:2 One who uproots turnips and radishes as a seed crop must tithe, for this is their harvest. Onions that have rerooted in an attic and are exposed to the sky are subject to the law of tithes.

The first rule is a correlary to M.5:1A-D. The point at which the turnips and radishes are uprooted is that point at which they are edible and available for use as food. Even though they are to be used as seed, they therefore must be tithed. This is the view of Eliezer and Gamaliel, vi.B.4:5E-H and 4:6, which takes no account of the intentions of the farmer. The second rule here develops i.C.1:1, defining what constitutes agricultural produce that will be subject to tithes.

5:3 A man shall not sell his produce, once it has ripened, to one who is untrustworthy to remove tithes. He may however take the ripe fruit for his own use and sell

A person may not give liable produce to one who probably will not tithe it. He must tithe it himself first. The notion that the whole field

the unripened remainder to whomever
he pleases.

does not share the status of
the early ripening produce
is attested by Rabbi,
vi.C.5:5. The present rule
therefore must be late.

5:4 A man shall not sell his
straw, olive-peat or grape-lees to
one who is untrustworthy to remove
tithes. He may, however, remove
what is edible and sell the rest
to whomever he wishes.

The principle, and basis for
assigning this material to
the Ushan stratum or later,
is the same as in the
preceding entry. In holding
that the potable liquid in
grape-lees remains subject
to tithes, this rule also
parallels the Ushan law at
vi.C.5:6.[9]

5:7 Grain found in ant-holes
beside a stack of fully processed
grain is subject to the removal
of tithes. We assume that it
came from that very stack, which
itself is liable.

The notion that grain
becomes liable to the
separation of tithes when it
is smoothed over in the pile
on the threshing floor is
Ushan (ii.C.1:5-8). This
too presumably is from the
Ushan period.

III. Conclusion

The tractate has its origin in Yavnean times, when Mishnah's
authorities determine that, contrary to what Scripture would lead
us to believe, produce is not invariably subject to the separation of agricultural offerings. The systematic exposition of
this idea comes only in the Ushan period, however, when a full
list of the classes of produce subject to tithes and the
conditions under which agricultural taxes must be separated is
developed. The point ultimately made by the tractate as a whole
is Ushan, that God's claim for portions of the produce of the
land of Israel is effective only upon that food that Israelites
purposely cultivate and then take for their own use in the meals
that provide their sustenance. The Israelites' own exploitation
of the land for the production of food, that is to say, brings
with it the obligation to set aside agricultural dues. These

dues recognize God's role in providing the land, the sun and rain which allow the growing of crops in the first place. Food that grows without the intervention of Israelites or that Israelites do not desire for use in a meal, by contrast, is exempt from God's claim. In the case of these things the individual has not appropriated for himself God's blessings. The Lord, therefore, is owed no share.

When we recall Mishnah Terumot's understanding of the Israelite as a locus of sanctification, we see that that tractate along with the present one suggest a unitary picture of the processes of sanctification operative in the Israelite world. We know from Tractate Terumot that, through their will, Israelites impart a status of consecration to a specific quantity of produce; through their desires and perceptions they maintain that food in sanctity; and, finally, Israelites themselves determine the point at which the food no longer is deemed holy. Tractate Maaserot enhances the picture drawn by Tractate Terumot by stating firmly that, just as Israelites control specifically what will and will not be holy, so their own desires for produce and their intentions in growing and processing crops determine what food is in the first place subject to sanctification. Food's being subject to the Israelite's will is a precondition of holiness, Tractate Maaserot tells us. The logical counterpart to that idea is Tractate Terumot's claim that application of the Israelite's intentions actually designates as holy some specific quantity of produce. Israelites' intentions and desires thus account for all aspects of the system of sanctification embodied in the Division of Agriculture. God, to be sure, is the ultimate source of all holiness. Only what is owed or dedicated to him can, in the first place, take on a status of sanctification. The fundamental theological datum of this division, however, is that, in actually establishing what is consecrated and what is secular, God acts and wills only in response to the intentions of common Israelites, who grow food upon the land of Israel and separate the offerings mandated by Scripture.

CHAPTER EIGHT

MAASER SHENI

I. Introduction

The topic of this tractate is second tithe, an amount of produce that Israelites must separate from their crops and carry to Jerusalem, where they eat it "before the Lord." Scripture states that this is so that the Israelites will "learn to fear the Lord your God always" (Dt. 14:23). Mishnah, for its part, has an interest in this offering that parallels the long middle section of Tractate Terumot. It explores the responsibility of Israelites to maintain the consecrated produce in their secular domain, before it is actually eaten in Jerusalem under conditions of sanctity. Indeed the topic of second tithe allows analysis of the question of the handling of holy food from an angle unforeseen by Tractate Terumot. Dt. 14:24-25 states that a person who lives far from Jerusalem may sell his second tithe. The money he receives takes on the consecrated status of the original produce. It must be carried to Jerusalem and used there to purchase food, which is eaten in place of the original tithe. Exposition of this topic gives Mishnah's authorities the opportunity to stipulate the powers of the Israelite who transfers the status of holiness from one object to another, desanctifying the first and sanctifying the second in its place.

As we have come to expect, Mishnah Maaser Sheni's distinctive point is found in its Ushan materials. These comprise almost the whole of the tractate's long shank. Repeating ideas known from Tractate Terumot, the Ushan law states that the designation of produce or other objects to be holy depends upon the Israelite's intentional declaration that he deems them henceforth to be sanctified. In the case of this tractate, of course, such an act of will allows the householder to deem one commodity holy in place of something that previously held that status. In the Ushan view, the validity of this transfer does not depend upon the physical act of sale or exchange in which the householder sells second tithe-produce or uses second tithe-funds to buy food in Jerusalem. The transfer of status depends, rather, upon the simple designation of the Israelite, who indicates what object, food or money he intends to be holy.

259

This is not to say that the Israelite's ability to impose a
status of sanctity has no limits. As we know from Tractate
Maaserot, only produce that grows as a result of the partnership
between God and the Israelites is subject to sanctification in
the first place. Yet just as in Tractate Maaserot the conditions
that allow for sanctification depend upon the Israelite's own
actions and desires, so in Tractate Maaser Sheni, the limits of
the individual's ability to impose a status of sanctification
revolve around his own perceptions and hopes. Israelites
determine[1] exactly what can and should be holy and, in the case
of second tithe, establish the monetary value of those holy
items. For one central point of this tractate is that, in
transferring a status of sanctification from one subject to
another, Israelites determine how much or how little food may
become holy. Tractate Maaser Sheni thus deepens the points made
by Tractates Terumot and Maaserot. It teaches that 1) nothing in
God's creation is intrinsically holy and that, 2) even objects
already holy have no intrinsic value, just because they are
sanctified. Their worth, rather, is a reflex of the Israelite
marketplace, changing with the whims of common Israelite
merchants and shoppers. The result of this perspective is that,
according to Mishnah, Israelites, and not God, have full control
over the process of sanctification. The possibility of
sanctification is contingent, of course, upon the existence of
God. Holiness, however, does not simply exist as a transcedent
and ongoing quality in the world. Its presence, rather, is a
function of the actions and desires of common Israelites and the
everyday workings of their economy.

Along with this main discussion concerning second tithe, the
tractate refers to several cognate topics. These include the
restrictions upon produce of an orchard in its fourth year of
growth. Like second tithe, this fruit must be brought to and
consumed in Jerusalem. This similarity to second tithe accounts
for the placement of these materials in this tractate, instead of
in Tractate Orlah, which deals with the restrictions that pertain
to the first three years of the orchard's growth. This tractate
also covers the law of removal, which states that in every third
year the householder must remove from his home all tithes that he
has collected but not yet distributed. The facts needed to
understand these Mishnaic discussions are provided by the
following Scriptural passages. Dt. 14:22-26 and Lev. 27:30-31
deal in turn with the separation of second tithe and the law for

redeeming it. These laws are covered in Tractate Maaser Sheni's
first five units, the main bulk of the tractate. Lev. 19:23-25
concerns the restrictions placed upon produce of an orchard's
fourth year of growth, the topic of unit vi. Dt. 26:12-15,
finally, outlines the laws of removal and the confession the
householder recites upon carrying out the removal. These matters
are discussed in unit vii.

> (Dt. 14:22-26)   "You shall tithe all the yield of your
> seed, which comes forth from the field year by year.   And
> before the Lord your God, in the place which he will choose,
> to make his name dwell there, you shall eat the tithe of
> your grain, of your wine, and of your oil, and the first-
> lings of your herd and flock; that you may learn to fear the
> Lord your God always.   And if the way is too long for you,
> so that you are not able to bring the tithe, when the Lord
> your God blesses you, because the place is too far from you,
> which the Lord your God chooses, to set his name there, then
> you shall turn it into money, and bind up the money in your
> hand, and go to the place which the Lord your God chooses,
> and spend the money for whatever you desire, oxen, or sheep,
> or wine or strong drink, whatever your appetite craves; and
> and you shall eat there before the Lord you God and rejoice,
> you and your household."
> (Lev. 27:30-31) "All the tithe of the land, whether of
> the seed of the land or of the fruit of the trees, is the
> Lord's; it is holy to the Lord.   If a man wishes to redeem
> any of his tithe, he shall add a fifth to it."
> (Lev. 19:23-25) "When you come into the land and plant
> all kinds of trees for food, then you shall count their
> fruit as forbidden; three years it shall be forbidden to
> you, it must not be eaten. And in the fourth year all their
> fruit shall be holy, an offering of praise to the Lord.   But
> in the fifth year you may eat of their fruit, that they may
> yield more richly for you: I am the Lord your God."
> (Dt. 26:12-15)   "When you have finished paying all the
> tithe of your produce in the third year, which is the year
> of tithing, giving it to the Levite, the sojourner, the
> fatherless, and the widow, that they may eat within your
> towns and be filled, then you shall say before the Lord your
> God, 'I have removed the sacred portion out of my house, and
> moreover I have given it to the Levite, the sojourner, the
> fatherless and the widow, according to all thy commandments
> which thou hast commanded me; I have not transgressed any of
> thy commandments, neither have I forgotten them; I have not
> eaten of the tithe while I was mourning, or removed any of
> it while I was unclean, or offered any of it to the dead; I
> have obeyed the voice of the Lord my God, I have done
> according to all that thou hast commanded me. Look down
> from thy holy habitation, from heaven, and bless thy people
> Israel and the ground which thou hast given us, as thou
> didst swear to our fathers, a land flowing with milk and
> honey.'"

A. Maaser Sheni Before 70

A major point of the tractate first is argued by the Houses,
ii.A.2:7, 8A-C and 9F-H. They dispute whether coins used in the

purchase of second tithe are individually sanctified with the
status of that offering, or whether the coins simply represent
the value of the consecrated produce, yet have no abiding status
of consecration of their own. The Shammaites take the former
view. In a case in which consecrated and unconsecrated coins are
mixed,[2] they would hold that the individual must locate the
specific coins that had the status of second tithe. These
specific coins, they claim, retain the status of consecration of
the original second tithe produce for which they were exchanged.
According to the Hillelites, by contrast, in the case of a
mixture, the status of sanctification originally held by the few
coins now pertains to the batch as a whole. The householder need
simply collect the value in coins equal to that of the second
tithe-money that was lost. This constitutes a designation of
these newly collected coins to represent the original second
tithe-produce. This Hillelite view is important, for it may
stand behind the theory of sanctification found in this division
as a whole. In allowing the householder to choose certain coins
to be holy, the Hillelites hold that he determines that what he
picks will represent the holy share owed from the whole batch.
This action thus is comparable, for instance, to the designation
of produce to be heave-offering. This view of the transfer of
holiness dominates in the material before us (ii.B.2:9I-L,
ii.C.2:8D-E, ii.D.2:5), although, for the specific case at hand,
the Shammaite view appears as well (ii.D.2:6).

Other issues attributed to the Houses cannot be firmly
verified to the period before 70 and, in all events, do not play
roles in the unfolding of Mishnah's law. The Houses argue
whether produce that can be used either as food for humans or as
animal fodder normally is to be treated as an edible, such that
it is subject to the rules of uncleanness and the separation of
tithes (i.A.2:3B-D, 4F-J). Later authorities will simply assume
that, if known, the owner's intention regarding the use of the
produce determines whether or not it is to be treated as a food.
The Houses dispute whether or not produce of the fourth year of
growth of a vineyard is in all respects comparable to second
tithe (vi.A.5:3). vii.A.5:6H-J's dispute concerning whether or
not agricultural gifts that have been cooked are subject to
removal cannot be verified to the period before 70. Finally, the
list of ordinances attributed to Yohanan the High Priest does not
concern matters referred to elsewhere in the Mishnah, such that
its origin in Second Temple times cannot be authenticated.[3]

B. Maaser Sheni in the Time of Yavneh

The Yavneans' central concern is that the full value of produce designated second tithe will be transferred to the money for which it is sold, and that later the full value again will be received, when food is purchased and eaten in place of the original tithe. To make certain that none of the value is lost, Yavneans require that, in selling consecrated produce, the individual accept only coins that are properly minted, circulating and available to be used as payment at the time of the sale (i.B.1:2G). They further rule that the purchase of non-food items with second tithe-coins does not transfer to those items the status of consecration held by the coins (i.B.1:5A-C, 2:3A, 4A-E). The coins retain their status as second tithe and must still be used to purchase foods that can be eaten in place of the original tithe. While in line with the general Yavnean picture of the processes of sanctification, these rules are quite different from the Ushan ones which, as we shall see, hold that anything an Israelite intentionally purchases with consecrated coins takes on the status of holiness held by that money.

Aqiba introduces a point that is assumed throughout the Division of Agriculture. He states that, at the time of removal, one need not separate and remove heave-offering and tithes from produce that only later will become subject to those offerings. Aqiba holds, that is to say, that offerings are in no physical sense present in produce that is not yet subject to their separation (vii.B.5:8). This view is in line with the under-standing of Tractate Maaserot that agricultural gifts need not be separated at all from produce that is not yet processed and ready for consumption.

A final Yavnean pericope likewise introduces an idea that will be important in the development of the laws of agriculture. Yavneans rule that one who is away from home and, at the time of removal, cannot physically distribute the agricultural gifts he has gathered, validly may make an oral declaration designating those gifts for their rightful recipients (vii.B.5:9). Yavneans thus initiate for this special case a mode of designating heave-offering and tithes that, in Ushan times, will become a common place. Such designations are assigned by Ushans for use in the separation of heave-offering (Terumot, ii.C.3:5) and for accounting for agricultural gifts that may not have been separated from doubtfully tithed produce (Demai, iv.D.5:1, 2).

C. Maaser Sheni in the Time of Usha

The Ushan development of the Yavnean ideas is predictable on the basis of what we have seen in the Ushan strata of other tractates in this division. Ushans indicate that, as in the designation of heave-offering, the individual's intention is central in the valid consecration of second tithe. Proper intention, that is, determines whether or not produce one purchased with second tithe-coins actually takes on the status of second tithe (i.C.1:3, 4, i.D.1:5D-E, 6, 7, iii.C.3:12, 13). Unlike Yavneans, Ushans hold that, if purchased intentionally, non-edibles take on the status of second tithe. Ushans even hold that a householder's intention to consecrate something as second tithe is effective in a case in which an actual exchange of produce and coins is not carried out (iii.D.2:10, 3:3, 4).

Like other consecrated offerings, that which has the status of second tithe must be put to its normal use (i.C.2:1A-H, i.D.1:1, 2A-F). This assures that portions of the produce that normally would be eaten do not go to waste. Yet, as in Tractate Terumot, Ushans here are clear that once sanctified produce or coins are of insignificant value, they lose their status of consecration and again may be put to secular use (see iv.A.4:8G-I). The Israelite's attitude towards the holy determines whether or not it retains its consecrated status.

The long shank of this tractate, units iii-vi, covers topics not referred to by Yavnean authorities. Like the other Ushan materials in this tractate, these parallel the chief Ushan concern of Tractate Terumot for the period of time during which sanctified produce is protected in the hands of the Israelite, such that it might be subject to misuse. The point made by two of these discussions likewise is familiar. One concerns the case in which a householder finds produce and is not certain whether or not it is consecrated. Contrary to the view of Judah, v.C.4:10, Yose, v.C.4:11, and the anonymous rules, v.D.4:9, 12, hold that produce need be treated as consecrated only if the householder has good reason to believe that it is in fact holy. So long as there are any grounds for claiming that what he has found is not sanctified, he may in fact treat it as secular. The point, familiar from Tractate Terumot, is that the objective status of the produce--consecrated or secular--is of no real weight. What matters instead is the attitude towards the produce of the Israelite who finds it. This same view pertains to the question of the value at which produce in the status of second tithe is bought and sold (iv.D.4:1, 2, 6, 8A-F). This value depends upon the prevailing market at the time and place of the sale. Sanctified produce has no intrinsic value. Nor is its worth established by the high or low value it has at any given point. It is determined, rather, by what an Israelite would pay for it at the given moment if it were normal, secular food.

Ushans agree with the Shammaite-view of Tractates Demai and Shebiit, that each individual must take actions to prevent others from transgressing. Here they dispute the extent to which a farmer must protect from transgression passersby who might pick and eat produce ripening in a vineyard in its fourth year of growth (vi.C.5:1).

A large section of the Ushan materials concerns the Scriptural rule that produce in the status of second tithe may be sold only if the individual lives too far from the holy city easily to carry the produce itself. Ushans rule that, once produce in the status of second tithe has been brought into Jerusalem, it may not be brought out again or redeemed (iii.C.3:5). Since the householder had the opportunity to eat the produce in the holy city, the Scriptural conditions for redemption no longer pertain. This settled, Ushans dispute whether the same rule regarding redemption applies to coins in the status of second tithe that are brought into Jerusalem or to produce from which second tithe has not yet been separated that is carried into the holy city (iii.C.3:5, 6A-B, 6C-F, 6G-L). The issue, whether or not the Biblical prohibition applies in cases in which the householder can already use the second tithe in Jerusalem, remains moot and has no larger implications for the law of this tractate as a whole. The short Ushan discussions of the field or vineyard in its fourth year of growth (vi.C.5:1, 2, vi.D.5:4, 5), of the laws of removal (vii.C.5:6A-G, 14) and the apparently Ushan exegesis of the text of the confession read at the time of removal (vii.D.5:11-12) detail secondary, though relevant, aspects of the agricultural law.

II.   The History of Tractate Maaser Sheni

i.   The Use of Food and Coins that are Second Tithe

Yavneans know from Dt. 14:22-26 that produce designated as second tithe may be sold. The proceeds are brought to Jerusalem and used there to purchase food that is eaten in place of the original tithe. Yavneans wish to assure that in this process of sale and repurchase none of the value of the original second tithe is lost. They therefore rule that the original tithe may be sold only for well minted coins that currently are circulating (i.B.1:2G). The farmer surely will be able to use these in Jerusalem to buy food. Yavneans, second, rule that, in Jerusalem, the farmer may use the money only to buy edibles (i.B.1:5A-C, 2:3A). This assures that produce equal in value to the original tithe will be bought. These edibles, finally, must be eaten in their usual manner, so that none of the food goes to waste (see i.C.2:1A-H).

Ushans examine the application of the Yavnean rules in ambiguous cases. How, for instance, do we treat the container in which wine purchased as second tithe is sold? Ushans rule that this depends upon the intentions of the individual who makes the purchase. If he purposely purchased the container, it is consecrated as second tithe and must be exchanged for food to be eaten in Jerusalem (i.C.1:3-4). The individual's intentions have the same importance in a case in which the food he purchases has more than one normal use, such as oil that may be eaten or used as an unguent. Ushans rule that the oil must be put to the purpose for which it was purchased. The farmer's own attitude, that is, determines whether it is a food or a lotion (i.C.2:1A-H, i.D.1:5D-E, 6).[4]

A. Before 70

2:3B-D The House of Shammai say: Fenugreek which is heave-offering normally is treated as a food and is preserved in a state of cleanness. If it is to be put to some other use, it is allowed to become unclean. The House of Hillel say: It normally is not treated as a food, such that it is not preserved in cleanness. But if it is to be eaten as a food, it must be kept clean.

Fenugreek is an ambiguous type of food, for it may be eaten by humans, used as cattle fodder, or used as a shampoo. The Houses agree that if it is heave-offering, it may be put to any of its usual purposes. They simply dispute whether fenugreek more regularly is used as a food or as a non-edible. The dispute appears in this tractate because it supplies the facts that

underlie the Ushan
discussion at i.C.2:2.
Since the fact that heave-
offering-fenugreek may be
used as fodder likewise is
assumed at Terumot,
viii.D.11:9, probably an
Ushan rule, it is clear that
the facts of this dispute
were known by Ushan times.
Yet there is no evidence
that the material is so
early as Yavnean or pre-
Yavnean. Uncertainty in
Ushan times over the exact
nature of the Houses'
opinions--disputed by Meir
and Judah, T. 2:1b--gives
weight to the view that this
material does not derive
from Ushan times.[5]

2:4F-J Vetches in the status of   The issue is the same as in
heave-offering: The House of   the preceding entry, as
Shammai--They normally are treated   is the reason for this
as a food. The House of Hillel--   material's inclusion in
They normally are treated as fodder. Tractate Maaser Sheni.
Shammai says: They always are used Participation here of the
as a food and kept in cleanness.   Yavnean, Aqiba, as well as
Aqiba says: They never are treated the reformulation of the
as a food, and are allowed to   Houses-dispute by Ushans
to become unclean.   (Meir, Judah, Yose, T. 2:1c)
                                     gives strong evidence that
                                     this issue is, at earliest,
                                     Yavnean, and that the
                                     materials attributed to the
                                     Houses and Shammai are
                                     Ushan.

B. The Time of Yavneh
1:2G They do not exchange (=   The farmer must exchange his

deconsecrate) produce in the status of second tithe with poorly minted coins, coins that are not currently circulating or coins that one does not have in his immediate possession.

second tithe-produce for coins that will surely be accepted as legal tender in Jerusalem. This rule appears to be Yavnean. Dosa, a Yavnean authority, disputes one aspect of it, T. 1:4. It receives further development in Ushan times, with a discussion of the validity of coinage deriving from the period of the Bar Kokhba revolt, T. 1:6.

1:5A-C One who buys water, salt, unharvested produce or over-ripe produce with money in the status of second tithe--that which he buys has not acquired the status of second tithe.

This is the logical correlate of the preceding entry. Money in the status of second tithe must be used to purchase foods that are processed and fit for consumption. A basic concept of this tractate, there is no evidence that this notion, stated anonymously, is known before Yavnean times. Discussion of it appears at Usha, i.C.1:3-4, and iii.C.3:2. At T. 1:13b-14 Ushans cite Yavnean discussions concerning the permissibility of the purchase of specific types of produce.

2:3A Fenugreek that has the status of second tithe must be eaten as a food.

While fenugreek may serve as cattle fodder or shampoo, if it is in the status of second tithe, it must be consumed by humans. The principle, that second tithe must be eaten or otherwise

consumed by people, has its
full expression at Usha,
i.C.2:1A-H. I assume that
this anonymous rule is
Yavnean because the parallel
rule, for vetches, is firmly
assigned to a Yavnean
authority, in the following
entry.

2:4A-E Vetches in the status of
second tithe must be eaten when
sprouting, i.e., when they are a
food for humans. Later in their
growth they serve as cattle fodder.
If they become unclean: Tarfon--
Let them be eaten in small pieces,
which do not impart uncleanness.
Sages--Let them be exchanged for
coins, which can be used to
purchase clean produce.

The principle is the same as
in the preceding unit and is
attested to Yavneh by Tarfon.

C. The Time of Usha
1:3 The hide of an animal
purchased in Jerusalem with money
in the status of second tithe
remains unconsecrated. The sealed
jar in which wine is purchased
remains unconsecrated. The shells
of nuts purchased with second
tithe-funds are unconsecrated.
Unfermented grape-skin wine, which
is not yet ready for consumption,
may not be bought with money that
is second tithe.

In line with i.B.1:5A-C,
containers purchased
incidentally along with
foods are not deemed to
have the status of second
tithe. Ushans add their own
reason for this. The
containers remain
unconsecrated because the
farmer did not intend to
consecrate these things as
second tithe. If he did
have that intention,
i.C.1:4, even the non-
edible containers or shells
become second tithe and must
be exchanged for edibles.
The role of intention in

this and the following materials, the participation in this discussion of contemporaries of Rabbi (T. 1:9 and 12) and the logical relationship to Yavnean material indicate that these rules derive from no earlier than Ushan times.

1:4 If one purchases with consecrated money a wild animal as a sacrifice or a domesticated animal as ordinary meat--the hide is consecrated. If one purchases a jug of wine in a place in which it is possible to buy the wine without the jug, the jug is consecrated. Fruit purchased in a basket--the basket is consecrated.

Here the individual purposely uses consecrated money to buy inedibles--the wine jar or fruit basket as well as the skins of animals that are not fit for the offerings for which he purchased them. All that the individual has acquired is deemed consecrated. The jug, basket and animal hide must be resold so that food may be purchased in their place.

2:1A-H Produce in the status of second tithe must be used for its usual purpose, eating, drinking or anointing. One may not prepare it in a way which prevents its being used for its intended purpose, e.g., by spicing oil which was purchased for consumption as a food. One may spice wine, for it still will be used as a drink.

The principle that consecrated produce must be put to the purpose for which produce of its type normally is used derives from Yavneh (Terumot, viii.B.11:3). Expression of that principle for the specific cases given here appears to be Ushan, as the parallel at Terumot, viii.C.11:1 indicates. Note also the consideration of the purpose for which the individual purchased the oil. According to the

present rule, this determines
whether the oil is deemed an
unguent or a food. This
parallels the role of
intention at i.C.1:3-4.

2:1I-P If unconsecrated honey or
spices fall into wine in the status
of second tithe and increase its
value--when the farmer sells the
wine in order to bring the proceeds
to Jerusalem, the value of the
consecrated food is determined
according to its percentage in
the mixture. If one bakes dough
in the status of second tithe,
when he sells it, the total value
is deemed consecrated. General
principle: If an unconsecrated
ingredient is added, the value of
the second tithe is determined by
proportion. If no ingredient is
added, but only the individual's
labor, the total value is ascribed
to the second tithe.

The problem is to determine
what proportion of the money
that the farmer receives for
the spiced wine is
consecrated and must be
taken to Jerusalem. This is
explained in the general
principle, attributed at
T. 1:18 to the Ushan
authority, Yose. On the
basis of this attestation
and the dependence of these
materials upon i.C.2:1A-H,
we are on solid grounds in
assigning this to the Ushan
stratum.

2:2 Simeon: They may not anoint
in Jerusalem with oil in the status
of second tithe. Sages: They may
(+ debate).

Simeon and sages dispute
what i.C.2:1A-H took for
granted, that anointing is a
proper mode of consuming oil
in the status of second
tithe. Simeon presumably
wants the tithe to be used
only as a food, not as an
unguent.

D. Unassigned
1:1 Produce in the status of
second tithe may not be sold, given
as a pledge or used as a
counterweight. In Jerusalem it may

This states in different
terms the rules given at
i.B.1:2G and 1:5A-C.
Produce in the status of

not be traded for other produce in the status of second tithe. Produce in the status of second tithe may be given as a gift.

second tithe may be used only for its designated purpose, being brought to and eaten in Jerusalem. Since it is consecrated for this purpose, the farmer may not use it for his own benefit, e.g., by selling or trading it, or using it as a counterweight.

1:2A-F The rules of the preceding entry apply as well to tithe of cattle, a consecrated offering comparable to second tithe (Lev. 27:32-33). Priests may do whatever they wish with firstlings, which are not consecrated and which are the personal property of the priests (M. Bekh. 4:1).

These rules apply the principle of the preceding entry to two further types of tithes.

1:5D-E If, outside of Jerusalem, an individual unintentionally uses money in the status of second tithe to purchase produce--the transaction is null. If he did this intentionally, he must bring the produce to Jerusalem to be eaten as second tithe. After the destruction--the produce is left to rot.

Only what the farmer purposely purchases with money in the status of second tithe takes on a consecrated status. Parallel in principle to i.C.1:3-4 and, in the following entry, referred to by Judah, this principle appears to derive from Ushan times.

1:6 Same rule as M. 1:5D-E, phrased for case of purchase of a domesticated animal with second tithe funds.

Judah, T. 1:15, cites and qualifies this rule.

1:7 List of nine items that may· not be purchased with second tithe funds. If one purchases these

The point is the same as in the Yavnean rule, i.B.1:5A-C. Second tithe fund may be things, he must consume in their stead the same value in produce. General rule: Money in the status of second tithe may be used only for the purchase of things suitable for eating, drinking, or anointing.

used only for the purchase of consumables.

ii. Exchanging Coins for Coins

An issue disputed by the Houses is developed in the periods of Yavneh and Usha. This issue concerns whether coins in the status of second tithe are understood individually to be consecrated as that offering or whether the holiness of second tithe is diffused throughout the batch as a whole. This is an important question, for instance, in a case in which the second tithe coins are mixed with other, unconsecrated, coins. If each coin individually is deemed to be second tithe, the householder must recover the lost tithe by identifying exactly those coins that originally were received in payment for second tithe-produce. If the holiness of second tithe is diffused through a batch as a whole, the householder may replace the consecrated coins that were lost simply by picking out of the mixture the correct monetary value (ii.D.2:5, 6).

The Houses agree that, outside of Jerusalem, the householder may exchange second tithe-coins for coins of a better metal. This assures the easy transport and marketability of the second tithe-currency. The issue for the Houses is whether each coin changed must have as its counterpart a coin of better metal (= the Shammaites) or whether we judge matters by the character of the batch as a whole (ii.A.2:8A-C). Following the latter alternative, the Hillelites allow the exchange of silver and copper for silver. This view, that the status of second tithe adheres in the batch as a whole, is normative in the time of Yavneh (ii.B.2:9I-L), providing good evidence that consideration of this issue indeed began in the period before 70. Yet ii.C.2:8D-E presents an Ushan dispute on the specific issue referred to by the Houses, ultimately leaving in doubt the exact legal development of the matter before us.

A. Before 70

2:7 The House of Shammai: One should not exchange silver <u>selas</u>

The Shammaites prohibit the exchange, since gold coins

in the status of second tithe for
gold <u>dinars</u>. The House of Hillel
permit this. Aqiba: I exchanged
silver coins for gold <u>dinars</u> for
Gamaliel and Joshua.

rarely circulate and
therefore are not a common
medium of exchange. The
Hillelites ignore this
practical consideration and
allow the transaction,
because in it the status of
consecration is transferred
from a less desirable metal
to a better one. The
Hillelite view is attested
to Yavneh by Aqiba, cited
here in support of the
Hillelites' position. This
provides firm grounds for
assigning this material to
the period before 70.

2:8A-C The issue is the same as
at M. 2:7. The Shammaites allow
the farmer to exchange a batch
composed solely of copper coins for
silver <u>selas</u>. The Hillelites allow
the exchange even if a portion of
the batch to be exchanged already
is comprised of silver.

The basic theory is that
expressed by the Hillelites
in the preceding entry. An
exchange is allowed of
second tithe-coins of a base
metal for coins of a better
metal. The Shammaites now
agree to this, so long as
rare, gold coins are not
involved. They simply
required that the trans-
action improve the quality
of metal of each second
tithe-coin. The Hillelites
by contrast hold that the
status of second tithe
adheres to the batch as a
whole. Exchanging some
silver and some copper coins
for silver represents a move
to a better metal, and is
accordingly permitted.
Since it is parallel to the

theory of ii.A.2:7 and is
carried forward in Yavnean
and Ushan times (ii.B.2:9I-L;
ii.C.2:8D-E), we confidently
may assign this material to
the period before 70.

2:9F-H In Jerusalem the farmer may exchange silver coins in the status of second tithe for copper ones, which are more easily spent. The House of Shammai say: When he exchanges the silver, he must receive only copper coins. The House of Hillel say, he may take a silver coin of small denomination along with the copper.

The positions of the Houses
are consistent with their
views at M. 2:8A-C. The
Hillelites approve the
transaction, so long as it
results in the farmer's
having some coins of baser
metal than those he turned
in for exchange. Parallel,
in principle to the Houses'
views at M. 2:7-8 and
developed in Yavnean times,
ii.B.2:9I-L, we are on firm
grounds in assigning this
dispute to the period before
70.

B. The Time of Yavneh
2:9I-L The disputants before the sages, Aqiba and Tarfon accept the Hillelite position of ii.A.2:9A-C, so long as a specific percentage, under dispute here, of the coins that the farmer receives are copper or silver. Shammai: Let him deposit the _sela_ with a merchant and, over a period of time, consume its value.

Yavnean authorities, who
agree with the Hillelites,
explore a secondary problem.
They want the exchange to
result in some set advantage
to the farmer. Otherwise it
is prohibited. Shammai is
out of place, set in dispute
with Yavneans. His position
disagrees with those of both
Houses, for he does not
permit the use of second
tithe coins for anything
except the purchase of food.
Since this view does not

appear elsewhere in these
materials, it is impossible
to place it in the unfolding
of the law.

C. The Time of Usha

2:8D-E Meir: They do not exchange
silver and produce for silver.
Sages: They do.

The problem is a variation
on that addressed by the
Houses at ii.A.2:8A-C. Like
the Shammaites, Meir does
not want the silver in the
status of second tithe to
be exchanged for other
silver. Sages follow the
view of the Hillelites, who
permit the transaction so
long as it results in the
status of second tithe's
adhering in what is, all in
all, a more valuable
commodity. The particular
case is secondary to that
disputed by the Houses,
such that assignment, on the
basis of Meir's partici-
pation, to Usha is on
relatively firm grounds.[6]

D. Unassigned

2:5 If unconsecrated coins and
coins designated as second tithe
are mixed together--whatever he
collects first is deemed
consecrated, until he reaches the
value of the lost second tithe.
If he scoops up the coins all
at once, the proper proportion
of the mixture is deemed
consecrated as second tithe.

The status of second tithe
is not localized in the
specific coins to which that
status originally applied.
When those consecrated
coins are mixed with unconsecrated ones, the status of
the tithe therefore pertains
to the whole batch. Coins
that will carry the correct
value of the status of
second tithe may be chosen

at the farmer's own will,
either by selecting coins
one at a time or by setting
apart a portion of the
mixture. The underlying
assumption concerning second
tithe is that of the
Hillelites and ii.B.2:9I-L.

2:6 If an unconsecrated silver
sela is confused with a sela in
the status of second tithe, he
brings a sela's worth of copper
coins and declares the copper
exchanged for the original,
consecrated sela. He then chooses
the finer of the silver coins and
exchanges it for the copper. For:
they exchange consecrated silver
for copper only out of necessity
and must immediately exchange it
back again.

The problem is the same as
in the preceding entry, but
the solution now follows the
Shammaites, ii.A.2:8A-C.
The status of consecration
adheres to the specific
coin. The farmer therefore
cannot simply choose one
of the coins to be second
tithe. Rather, he
deconsecrates the coin--
whichever it might be--by
declaring it exchanged with
copper ones. Then he
immediately reverses the
process and declares one of
the silver coins to be
second tithe. Participation
in this discussion by the
Yavnean, Simeon b. Azzai
(T. 2:5), attests this item
(and probably the preceding
one) to early in the
unfolding of the law.
Continued discussion after
Usha, by Eleazar b. Simeon
and Rabbi (T. 2:7) indi-
cates however that the issue
first addressed by the
Houses was still not settled
by the end of the Mishnaic
period.

iii.   Buying and Using Second Tithe Produce in Jerusalem

If second tithe produce is brought into Jerusalem, it may not be removed again from the holy city (iii.c.3:5). Second tithe thus is viewed as analogous to a sacrifice which, once it is upon the altar, may not be taken down again. Ushan and post-Ushan disputes over refinements of this principle constitute the bulk of this unit (iii.C.3:6A-B, C-F, G-L and 3:9-11). The most important of these concerns the case in which produce from which second tithe has not yet been separated is carried through Jerusalem. Once the offering is separated, need it be returned to the holy city, or may it be redeemed and other produce brought in its stead? While placed in the mouths of the Houses, this issue depends upon, and therefore must be historically subsequent to, the basic Ushan rule upon which this unit rests.

The unassigned material contains a second important notion of this unit. It states that through a simple act of will the householder designates produce or coins to take on the status of second tithe. That is to say, there is no requirement of a physical act of separation or exchange of produce for coins. Therefore the farmer may leave second tithe-money with a shopkeeper and make a conditional designation, stating that certain produce to be taken from that shop in the future will be second tithe and credited against the coins on deposit. He likewise may designate his friend's produce to take on the status of his second tithe-coins. The exchange in the status of the food and money is effected even though no actual trade of food and coins occurs. Attentive to the powers of intention of the common Israelite and parallel to the notions of sanctification found in the Ushan stratum of Tractate Terumot, these materials appear to derive from Ushan times.

A.   Before 70
3:6C-F While reported in the names
of the Houses, this dispute derives
from the period of Usha. See
iii.C.3:6C-F.

3:6G-L Like the preceding entry,
this Houses' dispute, attested by
Simeon b. Judah, belongs to the
period of Usha or later. See
iii.C.3:6G-L.

3:7 As for a tree a bough of which hangs over the wall of Jerusalem-- only that part of the tree that is actually located within the walls of the city is deemed to be in Jerusalem. As for a shed that intersects the walls of Jerusalem-- The House of Hillel say: As in the case of the tree, only the part of shed that is located within the walls of Jerusalem is deemed inside the city. The House of Shammai say: The shed itself creates a new boundary, such that all of its contained space is deemed to be like Jerusalem itself.

This material is located here because of its topical relevance to the issue of iii.C.3:5 and 6. Yet this discussion is theoretically distinct from that of those other pericopae. They therefore do not serve as tests for the placement of this Houses' dispute in the unfolding of the law. (Cf., T. 2:12, a clearly Ushan construction, which rewrites M. 3:7's dispute in light of those Ushan and post-Ushan issues found at M.3:5-6.) In placing this pericope in the period before 70 we thus depend upon attributions alone. Cf., Haas in Neusner, Judaism, p. 297. See iii.D.3:8.

3:9 See iii.C.3:9

3:13 See iii.C.3:13

B. The Time of Yavneh

C. The Time of Usha

3:2 Money consecrated as second tithe may not be used to purchase produce in the status of heave-offering, for the heave-offering may only be eaten by a priest and, should it become unclean, may not be eaten at all. Simeon: Second tithe-money may be used for the purchase of produce in the status of heave-offering.

This material depends upon the Yavnean notion, i.B.1:5A-C (found also at Usha, i.C.2:1A-H), that coins in the status of second tithe may only be used to purchase edibles. M. 3:2 presents an ambiguous case. While the heave-offering is presently edible

by certain individuals, it
might become completely
inedible. Taking account of
what might happen in the
future, the anonymous rule
does not allow the purchase
of the heave-offering.
Simeon is concerned only
with the present state of
the food. It is edible and
therefore may be purchased
as second tithe. Assigned
to an Ushan authority and
developing ideas known both
at Yavneh and Usha, this
dispute is firmly placed in
the Ushan stratum.

3:5 Coins in the status of second
tithe that are brought into
Jerusalem may be brought out again.
Produce in the status of second
tithe which is brought into
Jerusalem may not again be taken
out of the city. Simeon b.
Gamaliel: Produce, like coins,
may be taken out again.

The produce is like a
consecrated offering.
Bringing it into Jerusalem,
which is where it must be
eaten, is comparable to
placing a sacrificial animal
on the altar, such that it
may not again be withdrawn.
Simeon b. Gamaliel rejects
the analogy between second
tithe and sacrificial
animals. Since the
principle that a sacrificial
animal may not be removed
from the altar is Yavnean
(see Neusner, Holy Things,
VI, p. 68), we are on
strong grounds in assigning
this development of that
principle to Ushan times.
The anonymous rule of this
pericope is further developed at iii.C.3:6A-B,
C-F and G-L.

3:6A-B Produce that is subject to the separation of tithes and that is brought through Jerusalem--when second tithe is separated from it, that tithe must be brought back to Jerusalem and eaten there. It may not be redeemed.

The issue is whether or not the anonymous rule of iii.C.3:5 applies to that portion of a batch of produce that eventually will be designated second tithe. The point here is that since the produce is already fully subject to the offering, it is as though the offering itself were in Jerusalem. In accordance with M. 3:5, once separated, that offering therefore cannot be redeemed, but must itself be brought back to the holy city and eaten there. This principle clearly is Ushan or later, for it depends upon and expands the Ushan M. 3:5. It is discussed after Ushan times by Simeon b. Judah, iii.C.3:6G-L, who, in the name of an Ushan, Yose, formulates a Houses' dispute on this issue.

3:6C-F If produce is brought through Jerusalem before it is subject to the separation of tithes--Shammaites: When it becomes subject and second tithe is separated from it, that tithe must be brought back to Jerusalem and eaten there. It may not be redeemed. Hillelites: The second tithe need not be brought back to Jerusalem for consumption. It may be redeemed.

This is a subtle refinement of the preceding entry. If, when the produce is in Jerusalem, it is not yet subject to tithes, do we treat the offering which later is separated from it as though it had been in the holy city, such that it may not be redeemed? The Shammaites say that we do. The produce that now comprises the second tithe

was physically in Jerusalem,
such that it should not have
been brought out of the city
(iii.C.3:5). Once the
second tithe is separated,
it must be brought back to
Jerusalem and eaten there.
The Hillelites by contrast
claim that since, when the
produce was in the holy
city, it was not yet subject
to the removal of second
tithe, we cannot treat the
second tithe that later is
separated as though it had
been in Jerusalem. It
therefore may be redeemed.
A refinement of the
preceding entry, this item
cannot derive from before
Ushan times. Note the
Hillelites' underlying
assumption that agricultural
offerings are in no sense
contained in produce from
which they have not yet been
separated.

3:6G-L Simeon b. Judah in the name
of Yose says: The Houses did ·not
disagree concerning produce that
was not subject to tithes while it
was in Jerusalem. For that case
both Houses take the position
assigned to the Hillelites at
M. 3:6C-D. Rather, they disputed
the case given at iii.C.3:6A-B,
in which the produce was subject to
tithes while it was in Jerusalem.
The Shammaites take the position
of the previous anonymous rule,

Simeon b. Judah offers a
different version of
M. 3:6C-F's Houses' dispute,
formulating it in terms of
the issue of M. 3:6A-B.

that second tithe that later is
separated may not be redeemed.
The Hillelites disagree.

3:9 Produce in the status of
second tithe which entered
Jerusalem and was rendered
unclean--The House of Shammai:
It is redeemed so that clean
produce may be purchased. But even
that which is redeemed must remain
within the holy city and be eaten
there (iii.C.3:5). The House of
Hillel say: The produce must be
redeemed and eaten outside of
Jerusalem (= Simeon b. Gamaliel,
iii.C.3:5).

While assigned to the
Houses, the present material
depends upon the Ushan
M. 3:5, such that it cannot
derive from before Ushan
times. The Shammaites hold
that even once the produce
is redeemed, it retains
certain traits of second
tithe and must be eaten in
Jerusalem. The Hillelites,
by contrast, are concerned
for the purity of the holy
city and therefore want the
unclean produce to be eaten
elsewhere. Note the
continued development of
this issue (in the names of
the Houses) at Usha and
later, by Meir, Judah and
Simeon b. Eleazar, T. 2:16.
The issue of this pericope
is further developed in the
following entry.

3:10 Produce purchased in
Jerusalem with coins in the status
of second tithe that becomes
unclean--let it be redeemed.
Judah: Like produce purchased with
second tithe-funds outside of
Jerusalem, it may not be redeemed.
It must be buried.

Produce designated second
tithe which becomes unclean
may be redeemed, M. 3:9.
The question is whether or
not this applies as well to
produce purchased in
Jerusalem with second tithe-
funds. The anonymous rule
states that it does. Judah
holds that it does not, for,
unlike the produce origi-
nally designated second

tithe, that which is
purchased with second tithe
funds never may be redeemed.
Developing the preceding
entry and assigned to an
Ushan authority, this
clearly belongs to the Ushan
stratum.

3:11 A deer purchased with money   Ushan authorities continue
in the status of second tithe   discussion of the issue
which died--bury it with its hide.   introduced at M. 3:10. The
Simeon: Redeem it. If it was   specific problem is the
purchased alive, was slaughtered   circumstances under which
and then became unclean--redeem   the rule for produce applies
it. Yose: Bury it. If one   as well to meat. The point
purchased it slaughtered and it   seems to be that a purchase
subsequently became unclean--like   of meat is comparable to a
produce purchased with second   purchase of other foods.
tithe-money which becomes unclean,   If, by contrast, at the
it is redeemed.   time it is purchased, the
                                            animal is not yet prepared
                                            as food, it is unclear
                                            whether or not it should be
                                            treated as produce. These
                                            cases, accordingly, are
                                            under dispute. On the basis
                                            of substance and cited
                                            authorities we are on firm
                                            grounds in assigning this
                                            pericope to the Ushan
                                            stratum.

3:12 If one sells wine in jugs   The point is exactly the
intending the jugs only as a loan,   same as that found at
those jugs do not take on the   i.C.1:3, on which basis this
status of second tithe. If his   pericope is placed in the
intention--to sell the jugs along   Ushan stratum. This
with the wine, or to simply loan   anonymous rule further
them--is not known, we judge the   provides the facts used in
case by whether or not the jugs   the following entry.

are sealed. Corked jugs take on
the status of second tithe;
uncorked ones do not.

3:13 Continuation of M. 3:12--If
the wine merchant has corked the
jug but changes his mind and
decides simply to loan it to the
buyer--Shammaites: He must pour
out the wine and then refill the
jug. Hillelites: It is sufficient
simply to uncork the jug. Then
it is not counted as part of the
sale and accordingly does not take
on the status of second tithe.
Simeon: He need simply say to the
buyer, "I sell you the wine without
the container."

The question of what happens
if the seller changes his
mind is a secondary development of the issue introduced
at i.C.1:3 and iii.C.3:12.
The participation in this
issue of the Ushan Simeon,
as well as of Simeon b.
Eleazer, T. 2:18, provides
good reason for assigning
this material to Usha. The
theories behind the Houses'
opinions also reveal
typically Ushan concerns.
While the Hillelites claim
that the physical state of
the container is
determinative, the
Shammaites are concerned
with the intentions of the
merchant throughout the
bottling process. These
intentions, they say, cannot
be reversed simply by
uncorking the jug. All of
the merchant's actions,
rather, must be informed by
his intention to loan, and
not sell, that container.

D. Unassigned
2:10 One who has some dependents
who are clean and some who are
unclean may deposit with a store-
keeper a sela in the status of
second tithe and declare that
whatever the clean dependents

The rule stresses the
metaphysical character of
sanctification. The farmer
may enact a conditional
designation of produce to be
second tithe, dependent

eat is second tithe while what
unclean ones eat is unconsecrated.

upon a future act. As a
result, in the present
case, the clean and unclean
persons could sit and drink
from the same jug of wine,
one of them drinking wine in
the status of second tithe,
the other drinking uncon-
secrated wine.

3:1 A farmer may not give a friend
produce in the status of second
tithe in return for his
transporting that produce to
Jerusalem. But he may offer to
share with the friend the second
tithe which the friend transports
to Jerusalem for him.

The point is the same as at
i.D.1:1, that produce in
the status of second tithe
may not be used in a
business transaction, yet
may be given as a gift.
Found as well in the Ushan
stratum of Shebiit, this
rule presumably derives from
Ushan times.

3:3 In Jerusalem an individual may
transfer the status of second tithe
from his coins to a friend's
produce. The friend consequently
eats his produce as second tithe,
while the first individual may
use the coins for whatever he
wishes, since they no longer are
in the status of second tithe.

The farmer may transfer the
status of second tithe from
money to produce without in
fact buying the produce and
even though the coins and
produce do not change hands.
All that matters is that the
correct value in produce
will be eaten as second
tithe, no matter who eats
it. Parallel in conception
to the preceding entry and
expressing the notion of
the transfer of holiness
found in the Ushan stratum
of Tractate Terumot, this
rule appears to be Ushan.

3:4 If a farmer has unconsecrated
produce in Jerusalem and money in

As in the preceding entry
the point is that the status

the status of second tithe in the
provinces, he may declare them
exchanged, such that the produce
now has the status of second tithe.
If the coins are in Jerusalem and
the food is in the provinces he
may do the same thing, provided
that he then brings the food to
Jerusalem to eat as second tithe.

of second tithe may be
transferred from coins to
produce even if there is no
"purchase."

3:8 Roofs of Temple buildings have
the same status as the ground over
which they are built. The inner-
space of chambers, however, is
deemed part of the domain to which
it is contiguous. If a chamber
opens on to two different domains,
one holy and one unsanctified, it
is deemed to have the status of
the actual ground over which it is
built.

This carries forward the
exercise of iii.A.3:7, now
for the case of Temple
property. Sustained
discussion of the issue of
this pericope in Ushan times
(T. 2:13-15) indicates that
this material probably
derives from late in the
development of the law.

iv.   Selling Produce in the Status of Second Tithe

Produce in the status of second tithe is redeemed at the
prevailing market price at the time and place of the redemption
(iv.D.4:1, 2, 8A-F). Payment of less or more than the current
value will leave the produce imperfectly redeemed (iv.D.4:6). If
less than the produce's value is paid, a portion of that produce
will retain its consecrated status. If more than the produce's
value is paid, some of the money received is not in the status of
second tithe. In this way, in the Ushan period, the processes of
sanctification and desanctification are tied to the human market
place. Holy produce is made a commodity, the value of which is
determined by and changes with the values of other, secular
foods. This is close to the theory of Tractate Terumot, that the
quantity of holy produce contained in any batch is determined by
the intentions and desires of the householder. So here, the
quantity of produce that must be eaten in Jerusalem in conditions
of holiness depends ultimately upon the monetary value the
Israelite ascribes to the foods that he buys and sells.

The secondary issue disputed in the Ushan stratum concerns whether or not the farmer must make an oral declaration indicating that he intends a sale of consecrated produce to comprise the redemption of that food. Yose states that the act of sale is sufficient and that no declaration need be made. Judah holds that the individual's intention must be explicitly indicated, through actions and corresponding words (iv.C.4:7). Judah thus disagrees with the preceding unit, which does not even require a concrete act of sale.

A. Before 70

4:8G-I The Houses dispute the amount of second tithe-money the farmer may choose to ignore and leave behind in Jerusalem by not purchasing and eating produce against its value.

The dispute appears here because it is ancillary to iv.D.4:1-6+8A-F, which discuss the value at which second tithe is bought and sold. The underlying theory, that commodities which the Israelite does not deem worthy of attention lose their status of consecration, is familiar from the apparently Ushan material at Terumot, viii.D.11:4-8. The present Houses' dispute too presumably derives from Ushan times. The issue does not occur elsewhere in this tractate.

B. The Time of Yavneh

_____

C. The Time of Usha

4:7 Yose: One who redeems produce in the status of second tithe need simply pay for that produce. He need not make a declaration that the purchase is an act of deconsecration. Judah: He must

Yose holds that an action-- paying for the produce or handing over a writ of divorce--is sufficient indication of the individual's intention to

make an explicit declaration.
Same dispute concerning a man's
informing his wife that she is
being divorced.

change the status of the
produce or woman. Judah,
by contrast, holds that
intention must be indicated
specifically, both by deed
and formal declaration.
Only then is it efficacious.
The issue of the oral
declaration also occurs in
the Ushan stratum of
Tractate Terumot, providing
a sound basis for the
placement of this pericope
in Ushan times.

D. Unassigned

4:1 One who carries produce in
the status of second tithe from
place to place and wishes to
redeem it, redeems it according to
the market price in his current
location. If the value is higher
than in the place in which he
began, still, the increase accrues
solely to the second tithe. The
farmer pays out of his own pocket
the cost of transporting the
produce.

The value of a consecrated
thing is determined on the
basis of the prevailing
market at the time and place
of the sale. The principle
that value added through the
farmer's labor does not
accrue to the second tithe
is known from i.C.2:1I-P.
The Ushan origins of that
notion, as well as the
discussion of this pericope
during Ushan times (Joshua
b. Qorha, T. 3:1a), indi-
cates that M. 4:1 too
derives from the Ushan
period.

4:2 They redeem produce in the
status of second tithe at the
lowest selling price of the
particular locale, i.e., the rate
at which shopkeepers buy. They
do not sell by an estimation of
value. If the value is known,

M. 4:2 appears to develop
the principle first set down
in the preceding entry.
While the produce is to be
sold for its market price,
it is to be priced
competitively. This

the valuation of one buyer is sufficient. If it is not known, three bids must be received.

competitive price is not determined privately by the buyer and seller, but on the basis of the prevailing market, just as M. 4:1 would lead us to expect. Dependent upon M. 4:1 and attested to Ushan times and later by Simeon b. Eleazar, T. 3:1b, Judah, T. 3:4a, and Judah and Simeon, T. 3:6, it is clear that these rules belong in the Ushan stratum.

4:3 If the farmer wishes to redeem his own second tithe with his own money, his bid of one _sela_ has priority over anyone else's bid of one _sela_. This is because someone who redeems his own produce with his own coins must add a fifth to the value. If the outside bidder offers more money, even if it is not so much as an added fifth, his bid has priority. The produce's owner pays the added fifth even if he had been given the produce as a gift.

A farmer who redeems his own tithe pays an added fifth, Lev. 27:31. Still, in determining which bid purchases the produce, we take into account purchase price alone. The highest bidder receives the produce, even if he pays less than the farmer himself would. Only in the case of a tie-bid do we take into account the added fifth that the farmer will pay. While the notion of the added fifth is Scriptural, there is no evidence that this formulation of the law is known before Ushan times or later, to which it is attested by Eleazar b. Simeon, T.4:2a.

4:4 They avoid paying the added fifth by giving the money to someone else who can redeem the produce

This carries forward the discussion initiated at M. 4:3. Like that entry it

for them. The individual who
performs the transaction must be
able to engage in business of his
own right. This disqualifies the
farmer's minor children and
Canaanite servants.

appears to derive from Ushan
times, to which it is
attested by Joshua b. Qorha,
T. 4:3, and Simeon b.
Eliezer, T. 4:7.

4:5 To avoid paying the added
fifth the farmer may give the
produce to a friend as a gift and
then declare that the produce is
redeemed with the farmer's own
coins.

This develops the rule of
M. 4:4 in light of the law
that produce in the status
of second tithe may be given
as a gift, i.D.1:1. While
there are no firm grounds
for placement of the latter
rule within the unfolding
of the law, on the basis of
M. 4:3-4, it appears that
this entry belongs in the
Ushan stratum.

4:6 If the purchaser took
possession of the second tithe
but did not pay for it before
its value went from one sela to two
selas, the purchaser has earned a
sela on the increased value of
the produce. But that additional
sela's worth of produce retains
the status of second tithe. If
the value of the produce went down
from two selas to one sela, only
one of the selas paid for the
produce is deemed to have the
status of second tithe. To avoid
confusion, the buyer pays the
second sela with a coin already
consecrated as second tithe.

The rule depends upon and
develops iv.D.4:1. What
happens if the value of the
produce changes between the
time that the purchaser
takes possession and the
time that the money is paid?
We rule that the quantity
of produce deconsecrated
depends upon the market
value of the produce when
payment is actually made,
regardless of the agreed
upon purchase price. This
rule surely is Ushan, for
it depends upon the Ushan
iv.D.4:1 and further is
attested to that period by
Simeon b. Gamaliel and
Ishmael b. Yohanan b.
Beroqah, T. 4:14c.

4:8A-F In Jerusalem coins in the   The point is the same as at
status of second tithe are spent   iv.D.4:1 and 4:6. The value
at their current market value. If   of the holy thing is
the individual has eaten against   determined on the basis of
some of the coin's value and then   market value at the exact
moves to a different area where the   time of the sale. Dependent
remainder is worth more or less,   upon and carrying forward
he must continue to purchase and   ideas developed in the Ushan
eat produce until the new value of   stratum, this rule
the coin has been spent.   apparently derives from
                                           Ushan times.

    v. Doubts Whether or Not Produce or Coins are Consecrated

        If we have fair reason to believe that produce, coins or
other objects that we find are consecrated, we assume that they
are holy and treat them accordingly. So Judah. Yose applies the
theory of Tractate Terumot. If there is any cause for doubt, we
need not deem the object, money or food to be sanctified.
Discussion of this issue occurs solely in Ushan times.

A. Before 70

    _____

B. The Time of Yavneh

    _____

C. The Time of Usha
4:10 One who finds a vessel in-   The inscription is ambiguous
scribed with the word "offering"--   for it may refer to the
Judah: If it is clay it is   vessel or its contents.
deemed unconsecrated, but what it   Judah resolves the ambiguity
contains is deemed an offering.   in light of people's normal
If it is metal, it is an offering   behavior. Since a clay
and what it contains is uncon-   vessel would not be
secrated. They said to him: dedicated to the Temple, the
People do not normally put uncon-   inscription must refer to
secrated things in sanctified   the contents. In the case
vessels.   of a vessel of high value,
                                           however, the inscription may
                                           apply to the vessel itself.

The anonymous reply takes
Judah's reasoning to its
logical conclusion.

4:11 Vessels with abbreviated
inscriptions are assumed to contain
produce in a status relevant to
the abbreviation, e.g., "T" for
tithe or "H" for heave-offering.
Yose: We always assume that the
vessels contain unconsecrated
produce, even if they are inscribed
with the full name of the offering.

The anonymous rule
corresponds to Judah's
position. Yose rejects the
whole notion that, in a case
of doubt, we treat produce
that we find as though it is
consecrated. The attri-
bution to Yose and the
parallel to ideas in the
Ushan stratum of Tractate
Terumot provide solid
grounds for assigning this
pericope to Usha. At T.
5:2 Meir joins in the
discussion.

D. Unassigned

4:9 Coins found in Jerusalem are
deemed to be unconsecrated, even
if they appear to be a collection
set aside for a special purpose.
This is the case unless a potsherd
inscribed with the word "tithe" is
found with them. In that case the
coins are deemed to be second
tithe.

This appears to mediate
between the positions of
Judah and Yose, v.C.4:10 and
11. In a case in which we
can be reasonably certain
that something is an
offering, it must be treated
as such. Otherwise, as in
the case of coins simply
found in Jerusalem, we
assume the object is secular.
I assume that this, like
v.C.4:10 and 11, is Ushan.

4:12 If one expects to find
consecrated coins in one corner,
coins he finds in a different
corner are deemed secular. If he
expects to find a certain amount
of money, but finds more, only the

This is essentially the same
principle that informs
v.C.4:10 and the preceding
entry, for it claims that
what reasonably can be
assumed to be consecrated is

expected amount is deemed
consecrated. If he finds less
than he expected, it all is deemed
consecrated.

so treated. This
commonality of principle,
along with the participation
in this discussion of Rabbi,
T. 5:7, provides firm
grounds for placement of
this unit in the Ushan
stratum.

vi. Produce of a Vineyard in its Fourth Year of Growth

Grapes from a vineyard's fourth year of growth are
comparable to produce in the status of second tithe in that they
are consecrated and must be brought to Jerusalem and eaten there.
This unit touches upon several distinct issues concerning this
produce. Since none of these issues is developed in more than
one pericope, they do not aid us in detailing the development of
the law. Available evidence, however, suggests that these
discussions occurred in the Ushan period. This applies to a
Houses' dispute (vi.A.5:3), which questions whether or not the
fourth year grapes are in all respects like produce in the status
of second tithe. It also pertains to the unit's unassigned
materials, which state that the farmer may redeem the grape
clusters before they are harvested (vi.D.5:4, 5). The unharvested grapes have a low market price, such that the farmer will
not have to carry a large amount of money to Jerusalem.

One issue attributed to Ushan authorities is familiar from
Demai, ii.A.3:1C-H and Shebiit, ii.A.4:2A-H, I-K and 5:8. It
concerns the individual's responsibility to protect someone else
from an unwitting transgression. The Shammaite's claim, that a
person is so responsible, underlies all of Tractate Demai's rules
as well as a good portion of M. Shebiit. Ushans here question
how this responsibility is to be extended to the owner of a
vineyard in its fourth year of growth. How he is to prevent
passers-by from taking and eating the produce is disputed at
vi.C.5:1.

A. Before 70

5:3 The produce of a vineyard in
its fourth year of growth--The
House of Shammai say: The added
fifth (Lev. 27:31) and law of

The Hillelites hold that
produce from the fourth year
of a vineyard's growth is
comparable to produce in the

removal (Dt. 26:12-15) do not apply. Single grapes and defective clusters must be left for the poor (Lev. 19:10). The House of Hillel say: The laws of the added fifth and removal do apply. The laws of single grapes and defective clusters do not apply.

status of second tithe. The Shammaites disagree. Each of the restrictions referred to here is Scriptural, and the only other reference to the issue of this pericope is at T. 5:17, where Rabbi and Simeon b. Gamaliel dispute the meaning of the position of the House of Shammai. Since this Houses' dispute is attested only in Ushan times, it seems unlikely that it dates back to the historical Houses.

B. The Time of Yavneh

——————————

C. The Time of Usha

5:1 Vineyards in their third or fourth years of growth are marked off so that passers-by will not pick the produce and eat it as though it were unconsecrated. Simeon b. Gamaliel: "They do this only in the Sabbatical year, when produce growing in the field is legally available for public use. Conscientious people set aside coins to serve to deconsecrate produce of the fourth year that a passer-by might pick and eat."

Produce from a vineyard in its first three years of growth is forbidden for use, Lev. 19:23-24, while that of the fourth year is consecrated and must be eaten in Jerusalem, Lev. 29:25. Simeon b. Gamaliel proposes a precaution that assures that even a passer-by who ignores all warnings and steals and eats grapes from the vineyard will not have transgressed. Assignment to Usha is on the basis of the attribution.

5:2 Grapes from a vineyard in its fourth year of growth were allowed to be redeemed only if they grew more than a day's journey from

The anonymous rule takes seriously Dt. 14:14-25's rule for the redemption of second tithe and applies it

Jerusalem. When produce became abundant, they ordained that all grapes of all fourth year vineyards could be redeemed. Yose: The rule was changed when the Temple was destroyed. When it is rebuilt it will revert to its original formulation.

to the case of the produce of a vineyard's fourth year. Dt. states that produce may be redeemed if God's chosen place, i.e., Jerusalem, is too far away for the farmer to carry it. Once produce became abundant, even a day's journey would have been impossible. Yose gives a different reason for the change in rule. Once the Temple was destroyed, con- secrated produce could not be eaten in the city. Under this circumstance, all farmers were allowed to redeem their fourth-year- grapes. Placement in the Ushan stratum depends upon the attribution to Yose and the participation in this discussion of Simeon b. Gamaliel and Simeon, T. 5:14.

D. Unassigned

5:4 To redeem produce from a planting's fourth year of growth that is as yet unharvested, he sets a basket of produce in front of three potential buyers and says, "How many such baskets are you willing to redeem for a sela, on condition that you harvest the produce."

This procedure permits the farmer to avoid investing his labor in produce the value of which he will have to consume in Jerusalem. Instead the individual has someone else harvest his field, such that he may bring to Jerusalem only the small amount of money he received for the unharvested crop. The notion that it is permitted to sell the produce cheaply, before the

harvest, is assigned to the
House of Hillel, T. 5:18-20.
The basic notion of this
pericope therefore may
derive from the period
before 70. The claim that
three bids are to be
received, however, repre-
sents an idea known, it
seems, only in Ushan times,
iv.D.4:2.

5:5 Continuation of M. 5:4--During
the Sabbatical Year one may not
deduct from the value of a fourth
year-crop the cost of harvesting.
In other years, if the fourth
year-crop is from an ownerless
field, it is redeemed at the cost
of harvesting alone. One who
redeems his own fourth year-crop
pays the added fifth.

In the Sabbatical Year,
harvesting is prohibited.
In that year, the crop of a
field in its fourth year of
growth therefore has the
same value as all other
unharvested produce, and it
must be sold at that price.
An ownerless crop can be
taken by anyone and therefore has no market value.
Its worth is only what it
costs to harvest it. That
is the value at which it is
redeemed. The final rule is
familiar from iv.D.4:3,
which repeats Lev. 27:31.
Like the rest of this construction, there are no
grounds for placing it
within the logical unfolding
of the law.

vii. The Law of Removal

The bulk of the unit presents an exegesis of the confession
that Dt. 26:13-15 states is recited by the householder when he
distributes to their proper recipients all of the agricultural
offerings he has separated. This exegesis is for the most part
independent of specific laws found in Mishnah, such that there

are no grounds for locating it in a specific historical period.
Only one rule of this unit is firmly placed within the unfolding
of Mishnah's law. This concerns the oral designation by which
the householder may distribute to their proper recipients agricultural gifts that are out of his physical reach (vii.B.5:9).
Such a declaration, which Yavneans hold is used in special
circumstances, in Ushan times becomes a regular aspect of the
separation of agricultural offerings.

A. Before 70

5:6H-J As for a cooked dish
containing produce in a consecrated
status--The House of Shammai say:
It is as though it already is
removed.

The principle under dispute
here is unclear, for no-
where else in Mishnah is
cooking held to destroy
consecrated produce or to
reduce its status as an
agricultural offering.
Since its principle is
unclear, I see no way of
determining the place of
this dispute in the unfolding of this tractate's law.

5:7 See vii.D.5:7.

5:15 Yohanan the High Priest did
away with the confession concerning
the removal, dismissed those who,
in the Temple, sang the song of
awakening and those who stunned
the sacrificial animals. Until
his day work was allowed on the
intermediate days of Passover and
Sukkot. In his time no one had
to ask which agricultural gifts
had been separated from doubtfully
tithed produce.

Yohanan's abolishing of the
confession is unknown to the
rest of this unit, which
assumes that it will be
said. I see no way of
authenticating the
attribution of this collection of ordinances to the
period before 70.

B. The Time of Yavneh

5:8 Judah reports: At first they
would notify people that the time

The notion that what is not
yet subject to tithes stands

of removal is approaching, so that
they should quickly remove
agricultural offerings from all
produce, even that which is not yet
subject to those gifts. Later
Aqiba taught that produce that is
not yet subject to tithes is
exempt from the law of removal.

completely outside of the
system of agricultural
restrictions is a
commonplace in this division
as a whole. There is no way
to test the assignment to
Aqiba of this particular
expression.

5:9 One whose produce is
unavailable to him at the time of
removal makes an oral designation
assigning the agricultural gifts
to their proper recipients.
Gamaliel and Joshua were traveling
on a ship and did this.

The notion that an oral
designation is used in the
designation and transfer of
agricultural offerings is
known in Ushan times,
iv.C.4:7, and at Terumot,
i.C.3:5. This pericope
perhaps represents an
earlier stage in the con-
sideration of the oral
designation, in which time
the designation was allowed
in situations in which the
householder could not
physically separate the
offering.

C. The Time of Usha
5:6A-G The removal is carried out
on the last day of Passover in the
fourth and seventh years of the
Sabbatical cycle. Heave-offering,
heave-offering of the tithe, first
tithe and poorman's tithe are given
to their proper recipients, priest,
Levite and poor person. Second
tithe and first fruits are
destroyed, since there is no time
to take them to Jerusalem, where
they properly are eaten. Simeon:
First fruits are given to the
priests, even outside of Jerusalem,
just like heave-offering.

The pericope repeats the
substance of Dt. 26:12, that
every third year agricultural
tithes are to be given to
their proper recipients.
Only Simeon's minor dispute
leads us to assign this
construction to Ushan times.
The basic concept however
might have been derived any
time that a Mishnaic master
chose to phrase Scripture's
rule in terms of Mishnah's
distinctive system of
tithes.

5:14 Dt. 26:15 states: <u>As you vowed to our fathers, to give them a land flowing with milk and honey.</u> Aliens or freed slaves, who do not have a portion of the land, may not recite the confession. Meir: Priests and Levites may not recite, for they did not acquire a portion of the land. Yose: They may recite, for they have the Levitical cities.

This is placed in the Ushan stratum on the basis of the attributions alone. While it appears as the conclusion of the extended exegesis at vii.D.5:11N-O, 12, 13, it is substantively and logically distinct from those other units. It therefore does not aid in placing those pericopae within the unfolding of the law.

D. Unassigned

5:7 After the destruction of the Temple--The House of Shammai say: At the time of removal, produce in the status of second tithe is redeemed. The House of Hillel say: It is all the same whether the second tithe is removed in the form of food or coins.

This dispute assumes the Houses to be active after the destruction of the Temple. The Shammaites, like Yose, vi.C.5:2, take seriously Dt.14:24-25's statement that a farmer who cannot carry second tithe to Jerusalem should redeem it. The Hillelites recognize that redeeming the produce does not solve the problem Scripture addressed. They therefore do not obligate the farmer to redeem the produce. Parallel to vi.C.5:2, this dispute presumably is the creation of the Ushan period. It self-evidently does not derive from before 70.

5:10 On the day of removal the farmers recite the confession, Dt. 26:13-15: <u>I removed all sanctified produce from my house;</u>

This shows each of Mishnah's tithes to be referred to by Scripture. Since the complete set of agricultural

I gave it to the Levite, and I
also gave it to the stranger, the
orphan and the widow, out of my
house. These references to those
who receive produce at the time
of removal indicate that all of
the agricultural gifts known to
Mishnah are subject to removal.

offerings discussed by
Mishnah was known by the
beginning of the Mishnaic
period, this exegesis may
have come at any point in
the unfolding of Mishnah's
law.

5:11N-O I have carried out the
law according to all the precepts
you commanded me. This means that
if he separated second tithe before
first tithe, he may not recite the
confession.

This depends upon Terumot,
i.D.3:6-7's description of
the correct order of the
separation of agricultural
gifts. Since that unit is
independent of all other
legal statements in the
tractate, it is impossible
to place it or this entry
within the unfolding of the
law.

5:11P-S I did not transgress your
precepts. This means I did not
transgress the restrictions upon
the separation of heave-offering
found at M. Ter. 1:5. I did not
forget anything means I did not
forget to praise you.

Dependent upon Terumot
i.B.1:5, the present
exegesis may derive from
Yavneh or Usha.

5:12 I did not eat of it while in
mourning. Nor did I separate
unclean produce from it. If he did
either of these things he may not
recite the confession. I did not
give any of its value for the dead
--to buy a coffin or shrouds--
and I did not give it--to other
mourners. I obeyed the Lord--I
brought it to the Sanctuary.
I did all you commanded me--I was
happy and made others happy with
the produce.

These rules derive from
Scripture and are not
discussed elsewhere in
Mishnah. It therefore is
impossible to place this
exegesis within the
unfolding of Mishnah's law.

5:13 Homoletical interpretation of   It is impossible to place
the end of the confession, Dt.   this exegesis within the
26:15: We did what you required   development of Mishnah's
of us, God, now you fulfill the   law.
promises you made.

III. Conclusion

The tractate explains how a status of holiness is transferred to and from objects in the secular world so as ultimately to be disposed of in Jerusalem, the locus of all holiness. The point that the tractate makes about these processes of sanctification and desanctification is that they depend upon the everyday workings of the Israelite economic system. The factors of supply and demand determine the value consecrated produce has at any given time and place. Normal procedures used in all sales establish who has purchased--and therefore desconsecrated--produce in the sanctified status of second tithe. These same procedures apply in Jerusalem to the purchase of produce to be eaten in conditions of holiness. The view of the tractate thus is that the processes of sanctification are under Israelite control. These processes correspond to the workings of the Israelite community's own, secular, economic system. Holiness is not conceived as an awful tremendum, the power of which transcends the control of the common Israelite. While, as we have seen, that which is holy is set apart and special, still, as Tractate Maaser Sheni shows, it comes into existence and is maintained as an ordinary facet of Israelite economic life. Holiness functions within the Israelite world like all other commodities produced upon the land of Israel, traded in the Israelite marketplace and eaten on the Israelite table. In this regard, in the materials before us, Mishnah's authors ask us to view secular economic processes from the perspective of the holy, as aspects of an economy of the sacred flowing between God and the people of Israel.

Only in one respect does holiness differ from the other market-goods to which Tractate Maaser Sheni finds it comparable. The difference is the requirement that, in trading or selling that which is holy, the Israelite recognize that he is engaged in a sacred act. He does this by formulating the intention to deconsecrate one object and to impart a status of sanctification to another. This requirement, familiar from Tractates Terumot

and Maaserot, serves to highlight the particular perspective that
the Division of Agriculture brings to its description of the
source and nature of holiness in the Israelite world. The
possibility of sanctification in the world ultimately depends
upon the presence of God, looking over and sanctifying Israelite
life. The deepest message of Mishnah, however, is that in doing
this, the divine will does not act of its own initiative or
because of its own, personal, desires. God acts, rather, in
response to the Israelite's own, human, determination to bring
holiness into the world. For Tractate Maaser Sheni, like the
other tithing tractates in this division, God is profoundly
passive. Only through the imposition of the Israelite's will is
holiness brought into the world, properly maintained and,
finally, disposed of in proper conditions of sanctity.

CHAPTER NINE

HALLAH

I. Introduction

At Num. 15:17-21 God commands that once Israelites are living in the land of Israel, they must separate from dough that they prepare an offering to the Lord. Mishnah's interest in this agricultural gift parallels its concern in Tractate Maaserot. The primary question concerns the conditions under which dough is subject to the separation of dough offering. The answers the tractate proposes likewise are familiar from materials we already have seen in the Division of Agriculture. Yavneans propose that liability to dough offering depends solely upon the class of grain from which the dough was made. So long as that dough is made from grain normally subject to leavening, dough offering must be separated from it. While not rejecting the Yavnean idea, Ushans bring to the law the perspective that marks their materials throughout the division. They hold that in cases of ambiguity and doubt, the Israelite's own perceptions of the character of the dough determines whether or not it is subject to the offering.

Specific legal concepts found in this tractate undergo no identifiable intellectual development. The vast majority of the tractate's rules derives from Yavnean times, and Ushans show no interest in the implications of the particular questions raised by the earlier generation. My depiction of the history of this tractate therefore depends upon the fact that the ideas presented by each generation of authorities correspond with the perspectives of Yavnean and Ushans elsewhere in this division. Before we turn to the specifics of these laws, however, let us bring to mind the Scriptural passage upon which the tractate rests.

> (Num. 15:17-21) The Lord said to Moses, "Say to the people of Israel, when you come into the land to which I bring you and when you eat of the food of the land, you shall present an offering to the Lord. Of the first of your coarse meal you shall present a cake as an offering; as an offering from the threshing floor, so shall you present it. Of the first of your coarse meal you shall give to the Lord an offering throughout your generations."

A. Hallah Before 70

The tractate's one dispute attributed to the Houses cannot be proven to derive from the period before 70 and, indeed, shows evidence of being a late creation (i.A.1:6A-F). The issue concerns whether or not the batter used in making certain types of dumplings is considered dough, such that it is subject to dough offering. The dispute assumes the Yavnean or post-Yavnean notion that all grains prepared like bread-dough are subject to dough offering, regardless of the purpose to which that dough ultimately will be put (see i.D.1:5, 7, and 6G-I).[1] Citation and explanation of the Houses' position by the late Ushan, Ishmael b. Yose, T. Hal. 1:1-2, lends further weight to the contention that the dispute is a late creation. This being the case, there is no evidence that work on the topic of dough offering began before Yavnean times.

B. Hallah in the Time of Yavneh

Yavneans are concerned with the concrete conditions under which dough becomes subject to the separation of dough offering. Their central idea is that this depends upon the physical character of the dough, leavened or not. As elsewhere, Yavneans here leave no room for consideration of the intentions and perceptions of the individual Israelite. They thus state that dough offering is separated from any dough made from those types of grain that can be leavened (i.D.1:1). Liability to dough offering is activated at the point at which the grain is made into dough. The dough remains subject to the offering even if it ultimately is used for some purpose other than the baking of bread (i.D.1:5, 7). Likewise, dough is subject to dough offering even if it is not in the class of produce that is subject to other agricultural tithes or if it actually has the status of a different agricultural gift (i.B.1:3). All that matters to Yavneans is the physical fact that grain has been made into dough. They only exempt from dough offering small quantities of dough (ii.B.2:3, ii.D.2:6), for these normally are not made into bread at all. Unlike Ushan legislation, which holds that such exemption depends upon an Israelite's perception that the produce is insignificant (see, e.g., Terumot, viii.D.11:4-8), the Yavnean law holds that this applies without regard to the Israelite baker's purpose or sense of the usefulness of the particular batch of dough.

C. Hallah in the Time of Usha

The few apparently Ushan rules found here repeat ideas familiar from other tractates in this division. They indicate that, at each point in the designation and separation of dough offering, the effects of the Israelite's actions are judged in light of the intentions and perceptions with which he carried out those actions. This is stated in general terms, i.D.1:9, by the rule that, since dough offering is designated for the exclusive use of the priest, its separation and handling are subject to the rules that apply to heave-offering. Other rules here make the same point. In cases of ambiguity, for instance, whether or not dough is subject to the separation of dough offering depends upon the perceptions of the Israelite who owns the dough. Only what the Israelite deems edible is subject (i.D.1:8). In the same way, dough made from a mixture of leavened and non-leavened grains is subject only if it tastes like dough made from grains that normally are subject to the offering (iii.D.3:7, 10).[2] The concern is not the actual edibility of the dough or the fact that it contains types of grains that, according to Yavneans, are subject. According to Ushans, rather, liability to dough offering, like liability to the other agricultural gifts, occurs only in response to the perceptions of common Israelites.

As in Tractate Demai, Ushans take up the distinction between those who observe the laws of cultic cleanness and those who do not. Normally, agricultural gifts may be given only to priests known to eat their foods in proper conditions of cleanness. Ushans rule that this does not apply to offerings separated from produce that might not have been subject to those particular gifts in the first place (iv.C.4:9). Since these offerings might not have a sanctified status, Ushans are not concerned that they be consumed by priests who are not careful to eat food under conditions of cultic purity.

II. The History of Tractate Hallah

i. What Dough is Subject to Dough Offering?

The main work of defining the conditions under which dough is subject to the separation of dough offering takes place in Yavnean times. First, Yavneans determine that only grains that may be leavened produce dough subject to the offering (i.D.1:1). This idea is developed in minor ways in post-Yavnean times.

Ushans hold that such doughs are considered bread in all other
legal contexts as well (i.C.1:2). That is hardly a major
contribution. An important point is found in the anonymous
materials. If the grain is treated like dough at any point in
its processing, the final product is subject to dough offering,
even if it is not bread (i.D.1:5). As is the case with other
agricultural offerings, the process by which the grain becomes
subject to dough offering is not reversible. Once it becomes
subject, it is not rendered exempt by the actions of a householder who decides not to make dough.

Second, Yavneans state that all dough from grains that are
leavened is subject to dough offering. This is the case even if
the grain already is in the status of a different agricultural
offering or if, because it is abandoned by its owner, it stands
outside of the system of agricultural laws as a whole (i.B.1:3).
As in the first Yavnean idea, the point here is that the
householder's actions in making dough are determinative. The
separation of dough offering supersedes all other agricultural
requirements.

Finally, Yavneans apply the considerations just enumerated
to the case in which grain is brought from outside of the land
into the land of Israel (i.B.2:1). Since the dough is produced
within the land, it is subject to the separation of dough
offering. This is so even though the grain itself is not subject
to other agricultural tithes. Yavneans dispute the rule for the
case in which grain grown in the land is made into dough outside
of the land of Israel. The issue concerns whether or not we take
into account the fact that the dough is subject to other tithes,
such that we might declare it subject to dough offering as well.
Ushans develop this concern in a secondary manner, indicating
what is assumed throughout this division, that only produce grown
within the land of Israel is subject to heave-offering and tithes
(i.C.2:2).

A. Before 70

1:6A-F The Shammaites declare m^{c}ysh   Since the considerations
dumplings exempt from the   that explain the Houses'
separation of dough offering but   views are unclear, it is
deem hlyth-dumplings liable. The   impossible to establish on
Hillelites hold the opposite   substantive grounds whether
position.   or not this dispute might

derive from early in the
development of the law.
The fact that the late
Ushan, Ishmael b. Yose,
T. 1:1-2, is involved in
explaining the Houses'
views provides evidence
that the dispute is a late
creation.[3] If the dispute
derives from pre-Yavnean
times, it is unclear why it
should attract no comment
for approximately one
hundred years.

B. The Time of Yavneh

1:3 Dough made from grain that was
in the status of an agricultural
offering, dedicated to the Temple,
abandoned or that had not reached
a third of its growth is subject to
dough offering. Eliezer: Dough
made from grain that had not
reached a third of its growth is
not subject.

The items described here are
exempt from tithes, for they
already have the status of
an offering, have not been
brought into the system of
tithes, or are not yet
deemed food. Liability to
dough offering is unaffected
by these facts. Eliezer
disagrees concerning
immature grain. It is not
deemed a food for purposes
of the tithing system.
Dough made from it likewise
should not be deemed a food
and should not be subject
to dough offering.[4]

2:1 Grain that is brought into the
land of Israel is subject to dough
offering. If it is removed from
the land--Eliezer declares it still
to be subject; Aqiba deems it
exempt.

The issue is the conditions
under which grain is deemed
to be "of the land of
Israel," such that it is
subject to the agricultural
restrictions. Eliezer
concentrates upon where the

grain is grown. Aqiba by
contrast holds that all
depends upon where processing occurs. The question of
what dough is subject to
dough offering is familiar
from the preceding Yavnean
discussion. This particular
issue receives minor
expansion at Usha, i.C.2:2.

C. The Time of Usha

1:2 Five types of grain, listed   This Ushan expansion of
at i.D.1:1, are deemed bread as   i.D.1:1 supports assignment
regards other aspects of the law   of that rule to Yavneh.
as well. Meir: One who vows to
abstain from eating bread abstains
from these (see M. Ned. 7:2).

2:2 Produce that grows in the hold   This develops the point of
of a ship in earth that was brought   i.B.2:1, considering the
from outside of the land of Israel   case of other agricultural
to the land is subject to tithes   tithes and restrictions.
and the restrictions of the seventh   Unlike the case of dough
year. Judah: This is the case   offering, in which liability
only if, at the time the produce   might be determined by
grows, the ship actually is   where the dough is made,
touching the shore of the land of   the applicability of other
Israel.   restrictions depends solely
                                            upon where the produce is
                                            grown. Judah requires that
                                            the produce grow not only in
                                            the territorial waters of
                                            the land, but right up
                                            against it, as though the
                                            ship were part of the holy
                                            country.

D. Unassigned

1:1 Loaves of bread made from   Grains that can be leavened wheat, barley, spelt, oats and rye are subject to the separation of dough offering and to other rules that apply to grains.

produce dough subject to dough offering.[5] This is attested to Yavnean times by Yohanan b. Nuri, T. 1:1. It is assumed and developed at Usha by Meir, i.C.1:2. See also i.B.1:3.

1:4 Dough from species of produce that do not leaven and dough prepared in manners other than those in which bread normally is made are exempt from dough offering.

This continues the preceding exercise of definition. It therefore appears to be Yavnean.

1:5 Continuation of M. 1:4--If the dough is prepared like bread dough at any point in its processing, it is subject to dough offering, no matter into what it ultimately is made.

The dough becomes subject as soon as it is prepared as bread dough. Once liability takes effect, it does not matter what takes place subsequently or what had happened previously. It remains subject. Exploring an ambiguity in the Yavnean definitions, this item too appears to derive from Yavneh, to which it is attested by i.D.1:6G-I, below.

1:6G-I Loaves of thank-offering and wafers of a Nazarite, both of which go to the priest, are exempt from dough offering if an individual prepares them for his own use. If they are made to sell, they are subject.

This parallels the Yavnean discussion at i.B.1:3, and is attested to Yavneh by Ilai, T. 1:6, who cites Joshua, Eliezer and Eleazar b. Azariah. If the loaves are anyway consecrated for the priest, there is no sense in separating dough offering. If the wafers, by contrast, are not consecrated for the priest

until some time after they
have been made (e.g., when
they are sold), then, having
once become subject to
dough offering, they remain
so, just as i.D.1:5 has told
us.

1:7 A baker who made dough for
use as leaven to distribute to
customers must separate dough
offering.

This repeats the principle
of M. 1:5 for a concrete
case. The fact that the
baker will not make bread is
of no account. Since he
has made a bread dough, he
must separate dough
offering.

1:8 Dogs-dough that shepherds will
eat is deemed a food for humans as
regards all matters of law. If
they will not eat it, it is not
deemed a food, except that it is
subject to uncleanness (see M.
Ter. 8:6).

What is or is not to be
deemed a food is determined
by people's perception of
it to be edible or not
edible (= Terumot,
viii.D.11:5-8, all Ushan).
This common Ushan notion is
attested to Usha by Judah,
T. 1:7.

1:9 The rules that apply to the
separation and handling of heave-
offering apply to dough offering
as well.

Since both offerings go to
the priest, many of the same
rules apply to each. The
present list contains items
known in M. Ter. to derive
from Yavnean and Ushan
times.

ii. The Separation of Dough Offering

Of the unit's two central points, one is familiar from the
tractate's preceding materials. Whether or not grain produces
dough that is subject to dough offering depends solely upon that
grain's ownership at the time the dough is made. If, when the
dough is made, the grain is owned by an Israelite, that dough is

subject. This is the case whether or not the grain was
previously owned, or even grown, by a gentile (ii.B.3:6).

The second issue is how we handle grain that is unclean,
such that the offering separated from it may not be eaten by the
priest. A Yavnean rule suggests processing the grain in quantities of less than a qab, which are not subject to the offering
at all (ii.B.2:3; see ii.C.2:4, ii.D.2:7). Aqiba rejects this
notion, not wishing the individual to avoid the responsibility to
separate dough offering (ii.B.2:3). At Usha, Eliezer offers a
different solution, rejected by anonymous sages. As in Tractate
Terumot, he holds that the householder may separate an agricultural offering from unclean produce on behalf of clean produce,
since, in doing so, the individual simply intends to give the
priest produce he may eat (ii.C.2:8). Eliezer also responds to
the rule that less than a qab of dough is exempt from dough
offering (ii.C.2:4). He states that if the householder should
treat these small quantities as a single batch, they are in all
events subject to the offering.

A.   Before 70

_____

B.   The Time of Yavneh

2:3 A naked woman may cut off a   Aqiba does not want the
portion of her dough to be dough   dough made in small
offering, for she can cover   portions, since these would
herself. A man may not. If the   be exempt from the
grain is unclean, he should prepare   separation of dough offering
dough in portions of less than a   all together. This issue is
qab. Aqiba: Dough offering may   continued by Eliezer,
be separated from unclean dough.   ii.C.2:4.

2:5 Joshua: One who sets aside   The point already has been
dough offering while it is still   made in i.B. Only dough is
in the form of flour has done   subject to dough offering.
nothing. Both that flour and   This notion is firmly
the batch it came from still are   assigned to Yavnean times.
subject.

3:6 If a man became a proselyte,   This same theory is
dough in his possession that   exemplified several times at

already is prepared remains exempt from dough offering. Dough that is not completely prepared will become subject upon the completion of its preparation. Aqiba: Processing is deemed complete only at the point at which the dough forms a crust in the oven.

ii.D.3:2-5. Whether or not dough will be subject to the offering depends upon its ownership at the exact point its processing is completed. Its previous status, or what might happen to it afterwards, are of no weight. This is placed in the Yavnean stratum on the basis of Aqiba's comment.

C. The Time of Usha

2:4 Dough prepared in portions of only one qab is exempt, unless the portions wholly adhere one to another. Eliezer: If they are placed in a basket, they join together and become subject to dough offering.

Eliezer holds that what counts is not the loaves' being physically attached, but, rather, the person's intention in treating them as a single batch, indicated by the fact that he places them together in the basket.

2:8 Eliezer: Dough offering may be separated from clean dough on behalf of unclean dough. Sages forbid.

Eliezer's view is the same as what is assigned to him at Terumot, i.C.2:1.

D. Unassigned

2:6 Five quarter qabs of dough are subject to dough offering. Less than this is not subject.

This basic rule is assumed by ii.B.2:3 and iii.B.4:4, providing firm grounds for assigning it to Yavneh. Note that it occurs at M. Ed. 1:2 in the name of the Ushan, Yose, who disputes this issue with the Houses (!).

2:7 Dough offering separated from dough to be used for one's personal consumption should comprise one-

The basic issue of how much produce is to be separated as an offering is known

twenty-fourth of the batch. If
it is dough for the market, one-
forty-eighth suffices. This same
amount is sufficient for unclean
dough. If one purposely rendered
the dough unclean, he must separate
one-twenty-fourth, just as from
clean dough.

before 70 (see Terumot,
ii.A.4:3). This provides
some evidence that the
present rule might be early.
Specific reference to the
householder's intention in
rendering the dough unclean
is, however, a sign of the
late development (see also
Terumot, iii.D.5:9). Since
there are no other
references in M. Hal. to the
figures given here, it is
impossible firmly to place
these rules in the unfolding
of the law.

3:1 They may snack on wheat-dough
without separating dough offering,
until it has been rolled out. With
barley dough, they may snack until
it is kneaded into lumps.

The issue is at what point
in its processing the flour
and water are deemed dough.
Aqiba, ii.B.3:6, attests
and rejects the specifics
given here.

3:2 If her dough became mixed with
heave-offering before it was rolled
out, it is not subject to dough-
offering. If after it was rolled
out, it is subject.

That which has the status of
heave-offering is not
subject to dough offering,
since it in all events goes
to the priest. If it
already was dough and
subject to the offering when
the mixture occured,
however, dough offering
still must be separated.
Like the preceding rule,
this one disagrees with
Aqiba concerning when the
processing of dough is
deemed completed.

3:3   Same point as M. 3:2 made for   The theory again is that of
cases in which dough in various   ii.B.3:6, such that this
stages of processing is dedicated   should be Yavnean.
to the Temple and then redeemed.

3:4   Theory of M. 3:3 repeated for   This must be dated to the
case of produce normally subject   Yavnean stratum, for it
to tithes that is dedicated to the   shares the theory of M. 3:3.
Temple. The produce becomes
subject unless, at the point at
which liability normally would be
incurred, it is actually owned by
the Temple.

3:5   Dough an Israelite prepares   If at the point at which the
for a gentile is exempt from dough   dough would have become
offering. If the gentile gave the   subject it was owned by the
Israelite the dough as a gift, it   gentile, it never becomes
is exempt or subject according to   subject. This is the same
the rule given at ii.B.3:6.   point made in the preceding
                                             entries.

iii.   Mixtures

We know from the preceding unit that quantities of less than
a qab of dough are not subject to the separation of dough
offering. Yavneans here state that, should several small
quantities of the same kind of dough, owned by a single individual, come into contact, they join together to comprise the
quantity from which the offering must be separated (iii.B.4:1).
Yavneans further address a point of ambiguity deriving from this
rule (iii.B.4:4, 5). If the two quantities of dough are from
different years of the Sabbatical cycle, an offering may not be
separated from one on behalf of the other (Terumot, i.B.1:5).
Ishmael, Aqiba and anonymous authorities therefore dispute
whether or not dough offering may be separated. The unit's
assigned materials provide several secondary and undeveloped
rules concerning mixtures. Of note are iii.D.3:7, which states
that the status of a mixture of exempt and subject grain is
determined on the basis of taste (see Terumot, vii.C), and
iii.D.4:6, which states that, in cases of doubt, the restriction
which normally prohibits the separation of clean dough as dough

offering for unclean dough does not apply (cf., Eliezer, ii.C.2:8).

A. Before 70

B. The Time of Yavneh

4:1 Two individual qabs of dough owned by two different women, which touched one another, remain exempt from dough offering. If they belonged to the same person, they become subject if they are of the same kind of flour.

To be subject to dough offering the requisite quantity of dough must be in one batch, owned by a single person and must all be of the same kind of flour. This is assigned to Yavneh on the basis of the continuation of the pericope, which follows.

4:2 What types comprise a single kind? Wheat and spelt, barley and wheat. Yohanan b. Nuri: Any of the five kinds (referred to at i.B.1:1) join together.

Since only the five kinds are subject to dough offering in the first place, Yohanan rejects the whole issue raised by M. 4:1. Assignment to this stratum is on the basis of the attribution. It is supported by further discussion of a comparable issue in the entry which follows.

4:4 A qab of this year's dough adheres to a qab of last year's dough--Ishmael: Take dough offering from the point of junction. Sages: Dough offering should not be separated. Aqiba: One may validly separate dough offering from only a qab of dough. Sages: One may not.

We know from Terumot, i.B.1:5, that an offering may not be separated from produce of one year on behalf of produce of a different year. The two qabs of dough therefore do not join together. Ishmael and Aqiba make a single point. The dough offering

may be separated from the
individual qabs, even though
they comprise less than the
minimum volume of dough
established by ii.B.2:3 and
ii.D.2:6. Sages disagree.
Since we do not have the
minimum quantity, dough
offering may not be
separated.

4:5 Positions of Aqiba and sages
exemplified in a further case.

C.   The Time of Usha

———————

D.   Unassigned

3:7 Dough prepared from wheat-   Part of the mixture is
flour and rice-flour--if it has the   subject to dough offering;
taste of grain, it is subject to   part is exempt. Its overall
the separation of dough offering.   character is determined by
                                        taste, a notion familiar
                                        from Terumot, vii.C.
                                        Expressing a theory current
                                        in Ushan times, this anony-
                                        mous rule too presumably
                                        derives from Usha.

3:8-9 A mixture of dough from   The point is familiar from
which dough offering has been taken   Terumot, i.B.1:5. Produce
and dough from which dough offering   that is not subject to an
has not been taken--they should   agricultural offering cannot
separate dough offering from a   serve as the required
different, fully subject batch.   portion for produce that is
                                         subject.

3:10 Case and theory comparable   Like M. 3:7, above, this can
to M. 3:7.   come from no earlier than
                                         Ushan times.

4:3 That which is not subject to   This adds to the Yavnean
dough offering does not serve to   definition of what
join together two quantities of   constitutes a batch of dough
dough which, if of sufficient   subject to dough offering.
quantity, would be subject.

4:6 In a case of doubt whether or   This minor development of
not dough offering already has been   ii.C.2:8 belongs at Usha.
separated, clean dough may be   The notion that the
designated as dough offering on   restrictions that normally
behalf of that which is unclean.   apply are not operative
                                          in the case of doubtfully
                                          tithed produce is a
                                          commonplace in this
                                          division.

iv.   Produce Grown Outside of the Land of Israel

This closing appendix 1) discusses the status of land leased
by an Israelite in Syria (iv.B.4:7, 8), 2) explains the rules
that apply to the bringing to the Temple of offerings separated
outside of the land of Israel (iv.D.4:10-11), and 3) includes a
list of types of offerings that, because they are of impaired
status, may even be given to priests who are not trusted to
observe the rules of Levitical cleanness (iii.C.4:9). The unit
does not appear to contain an over-arching legal theory. Nor are
its materials developed so as to allow secure placement within
the unfolding of the law.

A.   Before 70

_____

B.   The Time of Yavneh
4:7 Land leased by an Israelite in   Eliezer holds that produce
Syria--Eliezer: The produce is   grown on land held in Syria
subject to tithes and the   by an Israelite is
restrictions of the seventh year.   comparable to produce grown
Gamaliel: It is exempt. Eliezer: in the land of Israel
In Syria one portion of dough   itself. Gamaliel disagrees.
offering is separated. Gamaliel:
Two portions (one of which goes to

a priest, the other of which is
burned).

C. The Time of Usha

4:9 List of offerings which may   Judah's view appears again
be given to any priest, even if he   at Bikkurim, iii.C.3:12F-G.
is not trusted as regards matters   There is a question whether
of cleanness. Aqiba includes   or not vetches will be
vetches in the status of heave-   eaten by humans at all
offering. Judah forbids first   (Terumot, viii.D.11:9),
fruits.   which accounts for Aqiba's
                                           position. While discussion
                                           of the larger issue of
                                           this pericope began in the
                                           Yavnean period, it appears
                                           still to have been moot in
                                           Ushan times.

D. Unassigned

4:10-11 List of figures who   This construction appears to
brought offerings from outside of   be late, since several of
the land of Israel, at the wrong   the restrictions it assumes
time, or in the wrong form, and   are known only in Ushan
the Temple priests did not accept   times.
them. They did accept first
fruits from an Israelite's land in
Syria.

III. Conclusion

Yavnean materials comprise the great majority of the
tractate.[6] These Yavnean laws repeat for the topic of dough
offering the legal perspective we have identified in the Yavnean
strata of other tractates. In this view, the liability of
produce to the separation of agricultural gifts is determined on
the basis of the botanical classification of the food and in
light of the physical actions of the Israelite who handles the
produce. In the present case, Yavneans thus state that dough
offering must be separated whenever bread dough is made from
types of grain that can be leavened. In the typically Yavnean
perspective, this is without regard for the Israelite's underlying intention to make bread or even to use the dough as food.

To the extent that the Yavnean material both sets the tractate's issues and provides the greatest bulk of its assigned traditions, this tractate, more than any other in the Division of Agriculture, must be deemed a Yavnean creation. Its place in the system of agricultural law as a whole, parallel in topic to Tractate Maaserot and covering the role of human actions in rendering produce susceptible to sanctification, indeed is established by the Yavnean materials. As we have seen, the Ushan materials that appear here share the legal perspectives found in Ushan laws throughout this division. Yet it is unclear why, for the case of this particular tractate, Ushans did so little work in developing the apparently substantial body of Yavnean law they inherited. What Ushans tell us about dough offering is predictable. The paucity of rules they provide is not and, so far as I can see, has no ready explanation.

The several Ushan rules that occur here develop in typically Ushan directions the theme of the tractate established at Yavneh. Eliezer in particular is active, holding that the householder's own perspective determines what batch of dough is subject to dough offering in the first place and that his intentions in separating the offering itself define whether or not the separation is valid. The tractate's anonymous rules as well repeat ideas commonly found in the mouths of Ushans. These rules state that, in cases of doubt, the perceptions and intentions of Israelites must be taken into account. These determine what is subject to dough offering and, once the offering has been separated, define permitted and forbidden modes of handling the consecrated produce. This Ushan point, derived directly from Tractate Maaserot and Terumot, is that the desire of Israelites for the produce of the land determines the liability of the produce to the separation of the offerings mandated by God. God again is shown to demand a share only as a reflex of Israelites' own desires to use the fruit of the land of Israel. While God is the ultimate source of all holiness, specific portions of produce become susceptible to sanctification and are actually sanctified only in response to the actions and intentions of common Israelites.

CHAPTER TEN

ORLAH

I. Introduction

Lev. 19:23 states: "When you come into the land and plant all kinds of trees for food, then you shall count their fruit as forbidden; three years it shall be forbidden to you, it must not be eaten." To allow observance of this commandment, Tractate Orlah 1) clarifies what are to be classified as fruit trees, 2) defines what produce of such trees comprises their fruit and 3) indicates whether or not an old tree that is uprooted and replanted is deemed a new growth, so as again to be subject to the three-year restriction. Finally, 4) several rules discuss neutralization and the loss of forbidden status of orlah-produce.

Yavnean and Ushan deliberations on these topics reflect the legal perspectives already identified in these periods. The few Yavnean rules show concern for the botanical characteristics of the tree and its produce. Since a tree that is uprooted and replanted begins to grow anew, Yavneans deem it again subject to the restriction of orlah. This is the case unless a root had remained in the ground during the time that the tree was being transplanted. Yavneans thus disregard the Israelite's perception to be planting the tree as a new growth or simply to be moving an old tree. Ushans, by contrast, do judge matters in light of the intentions of the Israelite who plants a tree. They hold, for instance, that only a tree planted purposely for its fruit is subject to the restriction of orlah. If the tree is planted for lumber or as a fence, by contrast, it is not classified as a fruit tree at all. Even in its first years of growth an Israelite may, therefore, eat its produce.

The particular laws given here on the topic of orlah are not surprising in light of the other Yavnean and Ushan legislation found in this division. Viewed as a whole, however, the tractate is note-worthy. Concerned with basic matters of definition, the rules on orlah just reviewed lack a single, generative, issue such as characterizes other tractates in the Division of Agriculture. Furthermore, these rules on the topic of orlah comprise no more than half of the tractate's laws. The rest of the tractate discusses tangentially related matters, concerning

323

the status of mixtures of forbidden and permitted produce. Yet even this question, of what determines the character of a mixture, is not answered in the materials before us.[1] It therefore is impossible to locate an overriding point of the tractate as a whole. Unlike the other tractates in this division, Tractate Orlah lacks an identifiable problematic or even a single topical theme.[2]

In Tractate Orlah, Mishnah's formulators thus address a topic about which they have little of importance to say. This negative conclusion regarding the specific tractate before us is in line with a fact that is clear from the review, found above in Chapter One, of the Division of Agriculture as a whole. The topics considered in this division have been chosen because of their importance within Scripture's tithing law, not because in each case Mishnah's framers had on hand distinctive or even sustained statements on them. Mishnah's formulators recognized Lev. 19:23's importance for those individuals who desired to consume their food under divinely mandated conditions of sanctity. The tractate therefore was created. As a result, we have before us a collection of materials that barely may be called a tractate at all. This is, rather, a set of loosely connected chapters on tangentially related topics, only in part discussing the very area of law that, in the first place, called for their compilation.

A. Orlah Before 70

The one dispute attributed to the Houses makes use of ideas known, in Tractate Terumot, to derive only from the period of Usha. These concern whether or not forbidden produce that leavens or flavors permitted produce renders that permitted produce forbidden for consumption (ii.A.2:4-7). In light of its dependence upon late ideas, the dispute cannot be authentic to the early period. Since this one entry in any case does not concern the particular topic of orlah-produce, we can state confidently that Mishnah's treatment of that topic begins only in Yavnean times.

B. Orlah in the Time of Yavneh

The three basic issues discussed at Yavneh determine the direction that deliberation of the topic of orlah will have in this tractate as a whole. Yavneans, first, define a new tree, subject to the restrictions of orlah, as one that has freshly been planted. If an old tree is uprooted and replanted, it again becomes subject to the restrictions of orlah. This is not the case if, while the tree is uprooted, a single root still connects it to the ground. Since this tree can continue to survive without being replanted, it is deemed the same, old tree (i.B.1:4). Even when it is completely replanted, it is not subject to the restrictions that normally apply to a tree in its first three years of growth.

Eliezer and Joshua dispute whether the restrictions of orlah apply to all edible products of a tree or only to the primary fruit (i.B.1:7D-I). Eliezer follows the view commonly found in his name. He takes no account of the Israelite's attitude but, instead, deems all of the tree's edible products to be forbidden. Joshua, as expected, takes into account the Israelite's perspective, and he therefore exempts a tree's secondary products from the restrictions of orlah. Ushans, as we shall see, accept Joshua's view and develop it to its most striking conclusion (i.C.1:1, 7A-C).

One Yavnean item, unrelated to the specific topic of this tractate, forms the basis for an extended Ushan discussion of mixtures of more than one type of forbidden produce in a large quantity of permitted food. The specific Yavnean issue remains moot at Usha. This concerns whether or not we attribute dough's being leavened to heave-offering, even if unconsecrated leaven may in fact have acted upon the dough (ii.B.2:11-12, 13).

C. Orlah in the Time of Usha

While following the same basic theory of what constitutes a new tree as is found at Yavneh, Ushans add their own, distinctive perspective. They define a fruit tree, subject to the restrictions of orlah, as a tree that Israelites purposely plant in order to use its fruit. A tree planted for lumber or as a fence is not subject to the restrictions of orlah, even if it does, incidentally, produce fruit (i.C.1:1). In such a case Israelites may in fact eat the fruit of that tree during its first three years of growth. In the Ushan view the tree's classification and status within the law is not determined by botanical genus but by the Israelite's attitude towards it and perception of its primary purpose.

Ushans are clear that, like heave-offering, orlah-produce
that is mixed with unconsecrated food loses its forbidden status.
The mixture as a whole then may be consumed (i.C.1:6). Yet here
again the perceptions of the Israelite are central. Meir, for
instance, holds that orlah-produce already subject to processing
by an Israelite no longer is rendered permitted through
neutralization (ii.C.3:1-2, 6-8). Having come under the
Israelite's careful attention and desires, the produce has
intrinsic and irrevocable value. It never may be deemed an
insignificant portion of the mixture and, therefore, is not
subject to neutralization.

The Ushan discussion of neutralization accounts for the
presence here of other materials concerning mixtures of two or
more types of forbidden produce and permitted food. As in the
Yavnean stratum, the question of the status of the three-part
mixture remains moot (ii.C.2:10, 14, ii.D.2:15-16). Ushans
clarify only one situation. If heave-offering leaven and
unconsecrated leaven, both sufficient to leaven dough, are mixed
with unconsecrated dough, that dough's rising is to be attributed
to the heave-offering (ii.C.2:8). As a result the dough is
forbidden for consumption by non-priests. Ushans dispute whether
or not this is the case if it can be proven that the
unconsecrated leaven, and not the heave offering, accounts for
the dough's rising (ii.C.2:9). Unaccountably, in these cases the
theory that in matters of doubt we avoid an impairment of status
(see e.g., Terumot, iv.C.7:5-7) is not applied.

II. The History of Tractate Orlah

i. Trees and Fruit Subject to the Laws of Orlah

If a tree is uprooted and replanted, it is deemed a new
growth, such that its fruit is forbidden under the laws of orlah.
If the uprooted tree remains attached to the ground by even a
single root, it is not deemed a new growth and, therefore, does
not revert to the status of orlah. This basic theory of what
constitutes a new tree is known in Yavnean times, i.B.1:4. Its
line of reasoning is developed by Ushans, who determine that
shoots, which grow from the tree into the ground, are not
comparable to roots. If an uprooted tree is connected to the
ground by a shoot, both the tree and that shoot (which depends

upon the tree for sustenance) are considered new growths and
subject to the restrictions of orlah (i.C.1:5).

Yavneans ask whether or not the restrictions of orlah apply
to edible portions of the tree (e.g., sap) other than the primary
fruit (i.B.1:7D-I). The issue, moot at Yavneh, is resolved by
Ushans, who determine that the restrictions of orlah apply only
to the tree's primary fruit (i.C.1:7A-C). It is only in respect
to that fruit that Israelites classify the tree as a "fruit
tree." Ushans add a further important point to this discussion.
They state that the tree's fruit is forbidden under the
restrictions of orlah only if, when he planted it, the individual
intended the tree for fruit (i.C.1:1, 2). If the tree was
planted for lumber or as a fence, its fruit is not forbidden
under the laws of orlah. In the Ushans' conception, again,
whether or not a tree is deemed a "fruit tree" is determined not
by its genus and species but by the perceptions of the individual
who plants it.

A.   Before 70

_____

B.   The Time of Yavneh

1:4 A tree that is uprooted but a root remains in the ground remains exempt from the restrictions of orlah. Simeon b. Gamaliel in the name of Eleazar b. Judah of Bartotha: The root must be as thick as a stretching pin.

Since the tree can continue to survive from the single root, it is not deemed a new growth which would be subject to the restrictions of orlah (i.D.1:3). The particular concern expressed here is developed at i.C.1:5, in the name of Meir. This supports placement of the present rule in the Yavnean stratum.

1:7D-I Milk curdled with the sap of an orlah-tree is forbidden. So Eliezer. Joshua: It is permitted. If the milk is curdled with the sap of unripe-figs from an orlah tree, it is forbidden.

Eliezer and Joshua dispute whether the restriction of orlah apply to all edible parts of the tree (Joshua) or to the fruit alone (Eliezer). The dispute is

resolved in Ushan times,
i.C.1:7A-C, where there is
agreement that the laws of
orlah apply only to the
fruit.

C. The Time of Ushah

1:1 A tree planted for lumber or   The individual's intention
as a fence is exempt from the   to use the tree either for
restrictions of orlah. Yose: If   food or for some other
half of the tree is designated as   purpose determines whether
a fence or for lumber, that half   or not it is subject to the
is exempt.   restrictions of orlah. This
                                           typically Ushan notion is
                                           attested to Ushah by Yose,
                                           here, and by Simeon b.
                                           Gamaliel, T. 1:1.
                                           Discussion continues in the
                                           following item.

1:2 A tree planted for public use   These items are gray areas:
is subject to orlah. Judah   they are planted for fruit,
exempts. A tree planted in the   but not in the normal manner
public domain, in a boat, or which   of the land's owner planting
sprouts by itself, as well as trees   the tree for his own use.
planted by gentiles and robbers is   The anonymous rule holds
subject to the restrictions of   that it does not matter who
orlah.   plants the tree or who will
                                           eat the fruit. So long as
                                           the tree will be used for
                                           food, the restrictions
                                           apply. Judah holds that
                                           unless the planter intends
                                           the tree to produce fruit
                                           for his own use, the law
                                           does not apply. Developing
                                           the idea introduced at
                                           M. 1:1, and attested by
                                           Judah, this is firmly placed
                                           in the Ushan stratum.

1:5 If an old tree is uprooted and a sunken shoot remains, both the tree and the shoot become subject to orlah. Grafting does not render that which is grafted subject to orlah. Meir: This is the case only if it is grafted to a healthy place on the vine, such that the graft lives off of the vine and not from its own shoots in the ground.

Developments of the principle known from i.B.1:4 and i.D.1:3 are attested to Usha by Meir. The point is that we follow the status of the root. So long as it is viable, a new tree has not been planted. Once the original root breaks off, or if it is not healthy, any shoots or grafts are considered new growths.

1:6 A sapling subject to the restrictions of orlah and one subject to the laws of Diverse Kinds that were mixed--one may not pick the fruit. If he did, the forbidden status is neutralized in two hundred and one pieces of permitted fruit. Yose: It is neutralized even if the individual purposely created the mixture so as to neutralize the forbidden fruit.

This problem of neutralization is assigned to the Ushan stratum on the basis of the attribution to Yose. I cannot explain why, in this case, he is unconcerned with the intentions of the individual who picks and mixes together forbidden and permitted fruit.[3]

1:7A-C Parts of the tree other than its fruit are not subject to the restrictions of orlah, but are forbidden under the laws pertaining to the use of a tree in idol worship. Yose: The budding berry is included under the laws of orlah, because it is a fruit.

The point is cognate to that of i.C.1:1. Only fruit of a tree comes under the laws of orlah. This appears to develop the Yavnean dispute found at i.B.1:7D-I. Along with the attribution to Yose, this gives us firm grounds for placement in the Ushan stratum.

D. Unassigned

1:3 An uprooted tree which can live off of the earth surrounding its roots is not again subject to

An act of planting creates a new tree if, without it, the tree would die. This is the

the restrictions of orlah. If it
cannot live from the earth around
its roots, when replanted it is
again subject to orlah.

most basic phrasing of the
point found both in Yavnean
and Ushan times (i.B.1:4,
i.C.1:5).

1:8 Defective grapes, grape pips,
grape skins and their wine, pomegranate shells and fruit pits are
forbidden under the laws of orlah
but are permitted under the laws
of the fourth year. Fallen unripe
fruit is forbidden under both
restrictions.

These items are parts of
fruit. Therefore, even
though they are not
themselves eaten, they are
forbidden under the laws of
orlah. The prohibition of
the fourth year, however,
applies only to what
actually is food. Of these
items, that prohibition can
apply only to unripe fruit,
which may be edible and can
be used to manufacture wine.
Developing for ambiguous
cases the list of items
introduced at i.C.1:7A-C,
this law can derive from no
earlier than Ushan times.

ii. Mixtures of Permitted and Prohibited Produce

Forbidden produce imparts its own status to permitted food
with which it is mixed, to which it imparts flavor or which it
leavens. The issue here, which remains moot at Yavneh and Usha,
is what happens when inconsequential amounts of food subject to
different restrictions together flavor or leaven permitted food
with which they are mixed.[4] Both Yavneans and Ushans dispute
whether two different kinds of forbidden food jointly render
forbidden the produce they leaven, or whether, since neither
alone could have any effect upon the produce, their joint effect
likewise is null. This issue reaches its clearest statement and
most protracted discussion--but not its resolution--in Ushan
times. Against the anonymous view, Simeon consistently holds
that types of produce subject to different prohibitions never
join together. So long as a type of forbidden food is not itself
sufficient to flavor or leaven permitted produce with which it is
mixed, it likewise has no effect in combination with produce

subject to a different restriction. Unfortunately this rather interesting debate over the nature of forbidden status is not resolved in the materials before us and does not provide sufficient facts for reconstruction of the ideology that underlies each viewpoint.

A. Before 70

2:4-7 Forbidden produce that leavens or flavors permitted produce renders that permitted produce forbidden. The House of Shammai: If it was unclean, it also conveys uncleanness to the produce that it flavors. House of Hillel: Uncleanness is conveyed only if there is an egg's bulk of unclean produce. Dositheus of Kefar Yatmah: I heard a tradition from Shammai the elder which agrees with the Hillelite view. + Long explanation of anonymous rule.

The Shammaites hold that leavening or flavoring and imparting uncleanness go hand in hand. The House of Hillel deem these different processes to be distinct and unrelated. The rules for the flavoring and leavening of permitted food by forbidden food first were worked out in Ushan times, Terumot, vii.C.10:1, 3, 8, 11A-D. It therefore is unlikely that the rules and dispute given here go back to the period before 70.[5] This particular question does not appear elsewhere in Mishnah.

B. The Time of Yavneh

2:11-12 Heave-offering leaven and common leaven together fall into dough. Neither of them alone is sufficient to leaven the dough, but together they do so. Eliezer: The status of the dough is determined by which leaven fell in last. Sages: The dough is not forbidden unless the heave-offering alone is sufficient to leaven it. Yoezer of the Birah reports in the name of Gamaliel the elder: The dough is forbidden only if the

An issue reported in the name of pre-Yavnean authorities is still moot at Yavneh. Sages view (= Gamaliel the elder), that forbidden leaven renders dough forbidden only if it causes it to rise, is assumed and developed at Usha, ii.C.2:8, 9. This gives us good reason to assign this to the Yavnean period. There are however

heave-offering is sufficient.

no substantive grounds for
placing this idea in the
period before 70 (see
ii.A.2:4-7 and cf., Neusner,
Pharisees, I, pp. 344-345).

2:13 Vessels which one greased
with clean and then unclean oil,
or vice versa--Eliezer: The status
of cleanness of the vessel is
determined on the basis of the oil
used first. Sages: Last.

The theoretical issue is the
same as in the preceding
entry: Is the status of a
mixture determined by the
element that is added first
or last? Here the argument
revolves around the facts
of the case, that is,
whether the first or the
last oil will exude from the
leather (T. Ter. 8:15). The
similarity of issue and the
appearance of Eliezer give
us good grounds for placing
this at Yavneh.

C. The Time of Usha

2:1 Heave-offering, heave-offering
of the tithe, dough offering and
first fruits are neutralized in
one hundred and one parts of
produce. Orlah-produce and Diverse
Kinds are neutralized in two
hundred and one parts of produce.
Simeon and Eliezer dispute whether
or not quantities of orlah and
Diverse Kinds combine to render
produce forbidden. Eliezer states
that they do only if together they
also impart flavor to the mixture.
Simeon holds that they do not under
any circumstance.

The pericope makes use of
the figures for
neutralization known already
in Yavnean times (Terumot,
iii.B.4:7) and advances the
issue through the dispute
between Eliezer and Simeon.
Since this is surely the
Ushan Simeon b. Yohai, the
issue as a whole is placed
here in the Ushan stratum.
The same position attributed
to Simeon here appears in
his mouth at ii.C.2:10.

2:8 Leaven of common produce and
leaven of heave-offering, each

This is a subtle extension
of the principle given at

sufficient to leaven dough, are
mixed with unconsecrated dough.
The dough is deemed forbidden, as
though it had been leavened by the
heave-offering.

ii.A.2:4-7 and i.B.2:11-12.
That which is leavened by
heave-offering takes on the
status of that offering.
M. 2:8 is attested to Usha
by Simeon, in the rule which
follows.

2:9 Situation like that of
M. 2:8--if the unconsecrated leaven
already has leavened the dough when
the heave-offering leaven is
added, that dough still is rendered
forbidden. Simeon: It remains
permitted.

The principle of the
preceding is extended even
further. Even though the
dough was already leavened,
the heave-offering is
deemed to affect it, such
that it takes on a
sanctified status. Simeon
disagrees, claiming that
the heave-offering could
have had no effect.

2:10 Condiments subject to
different prohibitions join to
render forbidden the food they
flavor. Different condiments
subject to a single prohibition
likewise render forbidden
produce they flavor. Simeon
disagrees.

The issue is whether types
of produce subject to
different sorts of
prohibitions combine to
render other produce
forbidden. Simeon states
that they do not, comparable
to the position in his name
at ii.C.2:1.

2:14 Leaven of heave-offering and
of Diverse Kinds fall into dough.
Neither alone is sufficient to
leaven it, but together they do.
The dough is forbidden to non-
priests but permitted to priests.
Simeon: It is permitted to both.

This is a rephrasing of the
issue of ii.C.2:10. The
anonymous view holds that
the different forbidden
things combine and render
the dough forbidden to non-
priests. From the priest's
point of view, the heave-
offering-leaven has no
effect on the dough. The
leaven of Diverse Kinds

alone could have had no
effect and, as a result, the
dough remains permitted to
priests. Simeon's view is
just as at M. 2:1 and 2:10.

3:1-2 A garment dyed with dye from   The issue is whether the
orlah-fruit is burned. If it is   rule for neutralization
mixed with other garments--Meir: (ii.C.2:1) applies only to
All are burned. Sages: It is   the orlah-fruit itself or
neutralized in two hundred and one   also to a product made with
parts. Same dispute for case of   that fruit. This secondary
a single forbidden thread woven in   problem of neutralization is
a garment.   firmly placed in Ushan times
                                       on the basis of its
                                       substance and the
                                       attribution to Meir.

3:6-8 Same problem as at M. 3:1-2   The issue of the preceding
for case of bunches of fenugreek   entry is expanded to include
that are Diverse Kinds. Meir: the typically Ushan notion,
the mixture is not neutralized   phrased here by Meir, that
because the items, sold by a count,   what the householder
remains discrete. Sages: That   perceives as distinct--
theory applies only to six specific   because he is careful to
items listed by Aqiba (+ Aqiba's   sell or maintain it in
list of six and an additional   discrete and correctly
item).   counted amounts--cannot be
                                       neutralized. Sages claim
                                       that this is not the theory.
                                       Aqiba simply ruled that
                                       certain extremely special
                                       types of produce never
                                       are neutralized from a
                                       forbidden status they hold.
                                       We have here both the
                                       inception of a rule at
                                       Yavneh and its development
                                       and re-interpretation at
                                       Usha.

D. Unassigned

2:2 Heave-offering in a mixture
serves to neutralize orlah-produce
in that same mixture and orlah-
produce in the mixture serves
to neutralize heave-offering +
example using figures given at
ii.B.2:1.

In making up the quantity of
produce in a mixture
sufficient to neutralize
heave-offering, orlah
produce counts as
unconsecrated food. This
problem is derivative of the
rules for neutralization
given at M. 2:1. It
presumably derives from
Ushan times, although it may
be Yavnean.

2:3 Same point as at M. 2:2--
orlah-fruit neutralizes Diverse
Kinds and vice versa.

Considerations for placement
of this rule are the same as
above.

2:15-16 Same issue as in the
preceding entry, but for cases of
seasonings that are heave-offering
mixed with seasonings that are
Diverse Kinds (M. 2:15), and for
flesh of Most Holy Things and
flesh that is Refuse or Remnant,
which are cooked with permitted
foods (M. 2:16).

This is Ushan, just like
ii.C.2:1, 2:10 and 2:14.

2:17 Flesh of Most Holy Things
and flesh of Lesser Holy Things are
cooked with ordinary flesh. Even
if each alone would have been
neutralized, together they render
the mixture forbidden to those
who are unclean.

Here the two types of
prohibition are the same,
such that even Simeon will
agree that the prohibited
meats join together to
render the dish forbidden
to those who are unclean.
Carrying forward the
problem of ii.C.2:14 and
ii.D.2:15-16, this belongs
to the Ushan stratum.

3:3 Garments in which forbidden hair or wool are woven must be burned.

These objects are not subject to neutralization, which accounts for the difference between this rule and that of ii.C.3:1-2. Developing the theme of that other pericope, this entry too presumably derives from Ushan times.

3:4-5 Food cooked in an oven fired with the shells of orlah-fruit must be burned. If the food is mixed with other, permitted, food, its forbidden status is neutralized in two hundred and one parts.

The food takes on the status of the fuel with which it is cooked. Neutralization then applies, as to any other orlah-produce. There is no evidence that this secondary issue derives from earlier than Ushan times. It parallels the Ushan rule at Terumot, vii.D.10:4, yet gives an opposing ruling. The question of the effect of cooking fuel upon that which it heats apparently remained moot late in the formation of the law.

3:9 Doubts concerning the status of produce: In the land of Israel they are adjudicated stringently. In Syria they are adjudicated leniently. The restrictions of orlah apply inside of the land of Israel as halakah. The restrictions of Diverse Kinds apply outside of the land of Israel as a rabbinic enactment.

This anonymous rule is unrelated to what has preceded in the tractate, such that there are no grounds for placing it within the unfolding of Mishnah's law.

III. Conclusion

Tractate Orlah, a compendium of materials on several different topics, differs from each of the other tractates in the Division of Agriculture. These other tractates are generated by

a single, encompassing question, pertinent to their chosen subject of discourse. As a result, these other tractates appear to
be protected essays that make a discernable point about their
topic. Tractate Orlah, by contrast, neither makes an identifiable point nor, for that matter, has a single, sustained topic.

Tractate Orlah does however have a unifying theme that
deserves recognition. For in taking up this particular theme,
the tractate accords with the norms of Mishnaic inquiry--both in
the Division of Agriculture and throughout Mishnah. Tractate
Orlah concerns the classification of ambiguous objects, that is,
ones that fall between two or more different legal categories.
More than anything else, the tractate's materials concern how to
determine the status of a thing that is equally like two
different classes of objects. The old tree that is uprooted and
replanted, and products of a tree that may or may not be deemed
its fruit are classic examples of objects that elude clear-cut
classification. This concern for ambiguous cases is highlighted
in the long section of the tractate concerning mixtures.

In consistently turning to such gray areas in the law,
Tractate Orlah fits firmly within the larger program of inquiry
that characterizes the Division of Agriculture and Mishnah as a
whole. As Neusner has shown (Judaism, pp. 256-270), Mishnaic
discourse in general addresses a narrow range of questions to
each of the diverse topics it chooses to discuss. In his words,
"The Mishnah presents a homogeneous set of inquiries, consistently asking the same sorts of questions, about gray areas,
doubts, excluded middles without regard to the subject matter at
hand or the topics of the material under analysis" (p. 256). In
this respect, the most untypical tractate in the Division of
Agriculture, in terms of its diverse agendum of topics, turns out
to be very typical of Mishnah as a whole, in terms of its single
theme.

Tractate Orlah provides an example either of an unsuccessful
Mishnaic tractate, or perhaps, of an unfamiliar theory of the
concerns around which a tractate should be organized. The former
conclusion seems the more likely. For while the questions asked
by the tractate's authorities indeed are predictable, they are
adduced without reference to an underlying topical issue that
could have produced a legal statement of interest and importance.
For unlike in the other tractates in this division, in Tractate
Orlah the major issues under discussion remain moot throughout

the development of the law. This precludes identification of a Mishnaic theory of orlah or, for that matter, of mixtures in general.

The apparent reason for this is not far below the surface. The Ushans who are responsible for the vast majority of Tractate Orlah's materials recognized the centrality of Lev. 19:23 for Israelites determined to eat their food according to the standards of holiness established by Scripture. Yet they really had very little interest in the deeper implications of the topic of orlah as a concern unto itself. They were, perhaps, constrained to talk about this particular agricultural restriction. Doing so without regard to a particular message that might be portrayed through the pertinent legislation led, however, to the anomolous tractate just considered.

CHAPTER ELEVEN

BIKKURIM

I. Introduction

The tractate's first unit lists the prerequisites for separating first fruits and reciting the Scriptural confession. The third unit describes, in a narrative passage, the actual procedures through which this offering is designated, separated and carried to the Temple in Jerusalem, where it is presented to the priests. Constructed almost exclusively of Ushan materials, these two units thus supply all the Israelite needs to know in order to designate and dispose of first fruits. Concerned primarily with the mechanics of this operation, they provide few issues of legal interest or theoretical importance within the Division of Agriculture as a whole. As is the case for Tractate Orlah, while Mishnah's authorities deemed it important to discuss this Scriptural offering, they did not produce an agendum of issues deeper than the surface question of what the Israelite must do to fulfill the requirement described in Scripture.

The tractate's middle unit contains a series of comparisons of rules that apply to each of the several agricultural offerings referred to in the Division of Agriculture. Irrelevant to the specific topic of first fruits, this material would, however, comprise a fitting conclusion and summary for this division as a whole. It is unclear why it has been redacted between the tractate's two units on laws of first fruits, instead of in the more apt position at the end of the tractate.[1]

Before turning to the substantive development of the tractate's law, let us review the Scriptural passages that provide the facts upon which Mishnah's rules depend.

> (Ex. 23:19) "The first of the fruits of your ground you shall bring into the house of the Lord your God."
> (Num. 18:8, 13) Then the Lord said to Aaron, "And behold, I have given you whatever is kept of the offering made to me, all the consecrated things of the people of Israel... The first ripe fruits of all that is in their land, which they bring to the Lord, shall be yours; every one who is clean in your house may eat of it."
> (Num. 26:1-11) "When you come into the land which the Lord your God gives you for an inheritance, and have taken possession of it, and live in it, you shall take some of the first of all the fruit of the ground,

339

which you harvest from your land that the Lord your God
gives you, and you shall put it in a basket, and you
shall go to the place which the Lord your God will
choose to make his name dwell there. And you shall go
to the priest who is in office at that time, and say to
him, 'I declare this day to the Lord your God that I
have come into the land which the Lord swore to our
fathers to give us.' Then the priest shall take the
basket from your hand, and set it down before the altar
of the Lord your God. And you shall make response
before the Lord your God, 'A wandering Aramean was my
father; and he went down into Egypt and sojourned
there, few in number; and there he became a nation,
great, mighty, and populous. And the Egyptians treated
us harshly, and afflicted us, and laid upon us hard
bondage. Then we cried to the Lord the God of our
fathers, and the Lord heard our voice and saw our
affliction, our toil and our oppression; and the Lord
brought us out of Egypt with a mighty hand and an
outstretched arm, with great terror, with signs and
wonders; and he brought us into this place and gave us
this land, a land flowing with milk and honey. And
behold, now I bring the first of the fruit of the
ground which you, O Lord, has given me.' And you shall
set it down before the Lord your God, and worship
before the Lord your God; and you shall rejoice in all
the good which the Lord your God has given to you and
to your house, you, and the Levite, and the sojourner
who is among you."

A. Bikkurim Before 70

The tractate contains no materials assigned to authorities
who lived before 70. Nor does the logic of the development of
the law indicate that any of the ideas of the tractate, other
than those taken from Scripture, derive from earlier than Yavnean
times.

B. Bikkurim in the Time of Yavneh

Yavneans refer to three diverse areas of concern, leaving it
to Ushans to provide the larger framework within which the laws
of first fruits will be systematically expounded. Basing their
considerations upon Scripture, Yavneans establish when in the
agricultural year the Israelite may bring first fruits and recite
the accompanying confession (i.B.1:6G-K, i.D.1:3E-H). They
dispute whether or not Trans-Jordan was part of God's gift of
land to the Israelites, such that first fruits may be brought
from there (i.B.1:10). Finally, Yavneans ask whether or not the
decorations with which farmers adorn the baskets of first fruits
being brought to the Temple are comparable in status to the first
fruits themselves (iii.B.3:9).

C. Bikkurim in the Time of Usha

Ushans explore the conditions under which an individual may bring first fruits and recite the confession, delineate the procedure for the actual designation of the first fruits, and describe the procession in which the fruits are carried to Jerusalem, presented in the Temple and in which the confession is recited by the farmer. Within this account two issues of interest arise. Anonymous law holds that in order to bring first fruits, the individual must own the land upon which the produce grew (i.C.1:1-2, 6A-C, 6D-F, 7, 11). In this view the recitation's statement, "The first fruits of the ground which you, Lord, have given me" (Dt. 26:10) refers literally to a specific Israelite's ownership of the land, at the particular moment at which the confession is recited. Judah, by contrast, holds that these matters of day-to-day economics within the Israelite community are not at issue. The confession, he says, thanks God for giving the land of Israel as a whole to all of the people of Israel. In this view, the question of who presently owns an area of land is not a factor in determining the right of individual Israelites to bring first fruits and recite. Even those who do not own land may do so.

The second issue of Ushan concern is familiar from Tractate Demai and elsewhere in this order. Judah states that the farmer may give first fruits only to priests who are scrupulous regarding matters of purity. The anonymous law disagrees, holding that, like other Temple offerings, first fruits are divided among all of the priests serving in the Temple. It therefore does not matter that the farmer gives his first fruits to one priest and not another. Ultimately all the priests will share in them equally (iii.C.3:12F-G). While the materials before us offer no resolution to this issue, it is important to note that, as we have found elsewhere in this division, the notion that observance or non-observance of the purity laws divides the people of Israel into distinct groups occurs only in the Ushan period.

The middle unit of this tractate compares and contrasts the rules that apply to the several agricultural offerings referred to in the Division of Agriculture as a whole. Synthesizing a wide range of facts familiar from other tractates, these materials come at the end of the formation of the law.

II. The History of Tractate Bikkurim

     i. Bringing First Fruits and Reciting the Confession

     Yavnean authorities delineate the periods of the year during
which Israelites are permitted to bring first fruits to the
Temple and to recite the confession. These rules derive from
Scripture. Ex. 23:16 links the bringing of first fruits to the
harvest festival of Pentecost. Yavneans therefore agree that
from this festival and until Sukkot (that is, during the harvest
months) the individual may bring first fruits and recite the
confession (i.B.1:10). After Sukkot and until Hanukkah, first
fruits still may be brought. Yet Yavneans dispute whether during
this later period, which no longer comprises the harvest months,
the confession may be recited (i.B.1:6G-K). A second Yavnean
issue also remains moot. This concerns whether or not
Trans-Jordan was included in God's original gift of land to the
people of Israel, such that first fruits may be brought from its
area (i.B.1:10).
     Ushans address basic questions regarding the right to bring
first fruits. Scripture states that these are brought in
recognition of God's having given the land to the people of
Israel (Dt. 26:1-2). Certain Ushan authorities therefore hold
that only an individual who owns the land upon which the produce
grew may bring first fruits. Judah disagrees. He holds that
reference is not to God's having given specific plots of land to
individual Israelites, but to his having turned over to all of
the people of Israel collective possession of the land as a whole
(i.C.1:1-2, 6D-F, 11). In Judah's view the individual may bring
first fruits and recite whether or not he owns the specific plot
of land upon which the fruits grew.

A. Before 70

     _____

B. The Time of Yavneh
1:6G-K From Pentecost until Sukkot   The recitation is made only
one both brings first fruits and   during the months closest to
recites the confession. From   the festival of the harvest.
Sukkot until Hanukkah, one may   But late ripening first
bring first fruits but may not   may be brought even after

recite. Judah b. Betehra: He
both brings and recites.

that period of time. Judah
b. Bethera permits the
recitation whenever one
brings first fruits.

1:10 They bring first fruits and
recite from Pentecost until Sukkot
They bring the best of the produce
of the land of Israel, including
olives used for oil that grow in
Trans-Jordan. Yose the Galilean:
They do not bring first fruits from
Trans-Jordan, for it is not "a
land flowing with milk and honey"
(Dt. 26:15).

The unit both repeats
material stated in the
preceding entry and
introduces material that
will be fully developed at
Usha. We therefore have
good grounds for assigning
it to this stratum. Yose
rejects fruit from Trans-
Jordan, claiming that that
land was not included in
Israel's inheritance from
God.

C. The Time of Usha
1:1-2 Individuals whose trees grow
part on their own property and
partially on adjacent property do
not bring first fruits from that
which grows on the adjacent
property. Judah: They do bring.
Sharecroppers, tenant farmers and
those who hold property that is
not rightly theirs do not bring
first fruits. Because Scripture
states: You shall bring the first
of the fruits of your land
(Dt. 26:2).

The anonymous rule holds
that first fruits may be
brought only by an
individual who grows
produce on his own land. As
the citation of Scripture
indicates, this view
understands first fruits to
be an offering thanking God
for giving over to
Israelites ownership of
specific parcels of land.
Judah disagrees, holding
that this offering
celebrates Israelite
possession of the land in
general. Placement is on
the basis of the attribution
to Judah, paralleled at
i.C.1:11.

1:4-5 A proselyte brings first fruits but does not recite the confession, for he cannot say: "I have come into the land which the Lord swore to our fathers to give us" (Dt. 26:3). Executors, agents, slaves, women, people of doubtful sex and androgynous people bring first fruits but do not recite, for they cannot say, "The first fruits of the ground which you, Lord, have given me" (Dt. 26:10).

The Ushan construction begun at i.C.1:1-2 continues and is further attested to Usha by Eliezer b. Jacob, who refers to a secondary issue within this pericope. This entry presents a subtle development of M. 1:1's claim. Here the individuals do own the land upon which the first fruits grow. But, because of their secondary status within the Israelite community, they still cannot refer to the land as having been given to them. They comprise a gray-area within the law, such that they are allowed to bring first fruits (insofar as they meet i.C.1:1-2's qualifications) but may not recite the confession. Further discussion is by Ushans, Judah and Yose in the name of Meir, T. 1:12.

1:6A-C If he buys two trees but not the property upon which they grow, he brings the first fruits but does not recite. Meir: He recites, for a purchase of two trees includes the land.

By holding that he brings first fruits at all, the anonymous rule disagrees with i.C.1:1-2. Meir is consistent with that other rule. The purchase automatically includes the land, such that the individual both brings and recites.

1:6D-F After the first fruits are harvested, the tree dies and is cut down. He brings the first

Once the land does not support trees, it is not the sort of agricultural land fruits but does not recite. Judah: He does recite.

from which first fruits are brought at all. Therefore the anonymous rule holds that the individual--no longer a landowner in the usual sense--may not recite. Judah, who holds (i.C.1:1-2 and 11) that ownership of land is not even a requisite for bringing first fruits, disagrees and holds that the recitation is made.

1:7 If after he separated first fruits he sold the field, he brings them but does not recite. The one who purchases the field may bring first fruits from a different kind of produce growing in that field, but not from the same kind. Judah: Even from the same kind he brings and recites.

The situation is comparable to that of the preceding entry. Since, at the time that he brings the first fruits, the individual does not own the land, he does not recite. The real issue is the status of the new owner. The anonymous rule judges his rights and responsibilities from the perspective of the field. There can be no more first fruits of a kind that already produced first fruits. Judah, by contrast, judges matters from the point of view of the owner. That which grows grows under his ownership is the first fruits of his field, such that he may bring them and recite. Placement here depends upon the attribution to Judah and the secondary character of the issue, comparable to that of i.C.1:6A-C and D-F.

1:11 One who purchases three trees
on the land of his fellow brings
first fruits and recites. Meir:
Even if he buys only two trees.
Judah: Even sharecroppers and
tenant farmers, who do not own the
land, bring first fruits and
recite.

A purchase of three trees
includes the land (M. B.B.
5:4), such that the
individual meets the
requirements of i.C.1:1-2
and may both bring first
fruits and recite. Meir
agrees with the principle
but disagrees concerning
the required number of
trees. Judah disputes the
whole notion that one need
own the land in order to
recite. See i.C.1:1-2.

D. Unassigned

1:3A-D Only the choicest fruits,
which represent the fertility of
the land, are brought as first
fruits (see Dt. 8:8).

This appears to be Yavnean.
The notion that first fruits
are brought only from the
seven types of produce for
which the land of Israel is
noted is known by Yavnean
authorities, iii.B.3:9. The
eligibility of two specific
types of produce is
discussed by Eliezer and
Simeon b. Gamaliel, T. 1:15.

1:3E-H First fruits are not
brought before Pentecost, for
Scripture refers together to
Pentecost and first fruits
(Ex. 23:16).

The question of when first
fruits are brought occurs at
i.B.1:6G-K and i.B.1:10.
Along with those pericopae,
this too presumably is
Yavnean.

1:8-9 If he separated first fruits
and they were stolen, lost or
became unclean, he brings other
produce in their stead but does not
recite. The substitutes are not
subject to the stringencies that

The priests must in all
events receive their due.
The substitute produce is
not however really first
fruits, such that the
recitation may not be made.

normally apply to first fruits. If
the produce became unclean in the
Temple courtyard he scatters it on
the ground and does not recite.
+ Scriptural prooftext.

The land owner's
responsibility ends once he
reaches the Temple-court.
He may not recite, since he
has not actually offered
first fruits. But he need
not bring a replacement
offering. The larger notion
of a replacement offering is
first known in the Yavnean
stratum of Terumot,
iii.B.5:2. This development
of that idea is attested to
Usha by Judah, T. 1:5.

ii. Comparisons of Different Agricultural Offerings

A series of apparently Ushan and post Ushan constructions compares and contrasts the rules that apply to the several agricultural offerings referred to in this division. This unit thus synthesizes facts that we already know. It does not provide its own, new, ideas.

A. Before 70

B. The Time of Yavneh
2:6 A citron tree is like a tree
as regards the laws of orlah, the
fourth year and the seventh year.
Gamaliel: The citron tree is like
a vegetable in that it is tithed
according to the year the fruit is
harvested. Eliezer: No. It is
like a tree and the fruit is tithed
in accordance with the year in
which it ripens.

The rule is placed in the
Yavnean stratum on the basis
of the attributions to
Gamaliel and Eliezer.

C. The Time of Usha
2:2 Second tithe and first fruits
are like each other but unlike
heave-offering: They must be

See Maaser Sheni, vii.D.5:12
and vii.C.5:6A-G. Along
with the attribution to

eaten in Jerusalem; they may not
be eaten by a mourner (Simeon
permits); they are subject to
removal; in Jerusalem they are not
subject to neutralization; and
what grows from them is forbidden
(Simeon permits).

Simeon here, these parallels
provide good reason for
placing this discussion in
the Ushan stratum.

2:8-11 A koy is in certain respects
like a wild animal, in some ways
like a domesticated animal, in
certain ways like neither + long
list of examples. Eliezer glosses.

The material in this list
derives from sources in each
of the strata of Mishnah's
law. The construction must
be Ushan, such that I assume
that the reference here is
to an Ushan Eliezer. T.
2:1 supports this assumption,
citing both Eliezer and the
late authority, Yose b.
Judah.

D. Unassigned

2:1 Heave-offering is like first
fruits: Non-priests are culpable
for eating them; they are the
property of priests; they are
subject to neutralization; and
they must be eaten in a state
of cultic cleanness.

The rule for neutralization
derives from Yavnean times,
Terumot, iii.B.4:7. The
other rules are clear from
Scripture itself. This
comparison therefore can
derive from Yavnean times
or later.

2:3 Heave-offering and first tithe
are like each other but unlike
first fruits: They render
forbidden produce on the threshing
floor; they have prescribed
quantities; they must be separated
from all produce, whether or not
the Temple stands; and they are
separated by sharecroppers and
tenant farmers.

Various facts used in this
pericope are known before 70
(Terumot, ii.A.4:3), at
Yavneh (Terumot, i.B.1:1)
and only as late as Ushan
times (Bikkurim, i.C.1:1-2).
This construction as a whole
therefore could not have
been created before the time
of Usha. Discussion occurs
at Usha, with Simeon, Yose
and Simeon b. Judah, T. 1:7.

2:4 First fruits are unlike heave-   The facts known here derive
offering and tithe: They are   from Yavneh (Terumot,
designated from unharvested produce; ii.B.4:5) and probably Usha
an entire field may be designated   (Bikkurim, i.D.1:8-9). This
as first fruits; one must replace   construction therefore
them if they cannot be offered;   appears to be Ushan.
and offering them requires a peace
offering, singing, waving and
staying over night in Jerusalem.

2:5A-D Heave-offering of the tithe   The basic facts derive from
is like first fruits: It is taken   Usha (Terumot, i.C.2:1).
from clean produce for unclean, and
it is taken on behalf of produce in
a different location.

2:5E-G Heave-offering of the tithe   The facts given here are
is like heave-offering: It renders   assumed throughout the
forbidden produce on the threshing   Division of Agriculture.
floor, and it has a prescribed
quantity.

2:7 Human blood is like that of a   The rules for blood, found
domesticated animal in that it   at M. Makh. 6:4-5, derive
renders seed susceptible to   from Ushan times. This
uncleanness (Lev. 7:26, 11:34,   comparison therefore belongs
M. Mak. 6:4). It is like the blood   no earlier than the Ushan
of a reptile in that people who eat   stratum.
it are not subject to extirpation
(Lev. 11:29ff., M. Mak. 6:5).

iii. Separating First Fruits and Bringing Them to the Temple

    The unit describes the process through which first fruits
are designated (iii.C.3:1), carried to the Temple in Jerusalem
(iii.B.3:9, iii.C.3:2-6) and handed over to the priests
(iii.C.3:12F-G). These concerns are almost exclusively products
of the Ushan period. There is no evidence that they made use of
earlier rules concerning how these rites were to be carried out.
Indeed Ushans dispute the one important issue of this unit. This
concerns whether, like heave-offering, first fruits are the

property of the single priest, to whom the householder turns them over, or whether, like a Temple offering, they are to be divided among all the priests (iii.C.3:12F-G).

A. Before 70

B. The Time of Yavneh

3:9 Simeon b. Nanos: The land-owner may decorate the first fruits with any produce he wishes. Aqiba: He may decorate them only with the seven kinds from which the first fruits themselves are brought.

Placement here is on the basis of the attributions to Yavnean authorities and the parallel at i.D.1:3A-D, which indicates that the first fruits themselves are designated only from the seven kinds.

C. The Time of Usha

3:1 How do they separate first fruits? He marks the first ripening fruit in his field and designates it as first fruits. Simeon: When the fruit is picked it must be designated again.

Assignment to Usha is on the basis of the attribution alone.

3:2-6 Long narrative description of the ritual of bringing first fruits to Jerusalem. Discussion of the processional, of the manner in which the fruits were to be processed, of the baskets in which the fruits were brought, and of the procedure for reciting the confession. Judah disputes this latter rule.

Placement in the Ushan stratum is on the basis of the participation of Judah. There is no evidence that this description was known before Judah's day.

3:10 Simeon: Three categories of produce make up the offering of first fruits: The first fruits, the supplement and the decorations.

Discussion of the decorations begins at Yavneh, iii.B.3:9, and is continued here. Along with

+ Rules for each category of produce.

the substantive development, placement here is on the basis of the attribution to Simeon.

3:12F-G Judah: Israelites may give first fruits only to priests who are scrupulous in matters of cleanness. Sages: They give the first fruits to any member of the priestly guard, and the fruits are divided among the priests, as are other holy things of the Temple.

Judah maintains that the first fruits are the personal property of one particular priest to whom they are given. Anonymous sages state that they are the property of all priests. Placement in the Ushan stratum is on the basis of attribution alone.

D. Unassigned
3:7 The law was that anyone who could should read the confession without assistance. When people became embarrassed and refrained from bringing first fruits, sages ordained that the priests should lead everyone through the reading.

There are no grounds for placement of this unit within the logical unfolding of the law.

3:8 The rich bring their first fruits in baskets of silver and gold, the poor in wicker baskets. The baskets belong to the priests.

Derivative of an issue introduced at iii.C.3:2-6, this rule derives from Ushan times.

3:11 Under what circumstances did sages say that the supplement of first fruits has the same status as the first fruits themselves?

Discussion of the supplement, begun at Usha, iii.C.3:10, is continued here. This rule belongs in the Ushan stratum.

3:12A-E First fruits are the personal property of the priests, to do with as they please, using them either as a food or to pay debts.

There are no substantive grounds for placing this rule within the unfolding of Mishnah's law.

III. Conclusion

Tractate Bikkurim proposes to detail the mechanics of the separation of first fruits and to describe the processional in which the offering is carried to the Temple in Jerusalem. In this regard the tractate is parallel in concern to Tractate Peah, which describes how poor offerings are designated and transmitted to the poor, and to the introduction to Tractate Terumot, which describes the designation and separation of heave-offering. Unlike these other tractates, which detail the metaphysical aspects of the consecration of produce to be an agricultural offering, Tractate Bikkurim concentrates primarily upon matters of ritual. Indeed, in describing this Temple ritual, its concluding section, set in narrative form, is particularly effective.

At the same time, the tractate's narrative form and interest in details of ritual must not be allowed to disguise an important fact. This is that, like Mishnah Orlah, Tractate Bikkurim has no generative problematic. It lacks the single issue of mind that, in other tractates in this division, allows Mishnah's authorities to develop generalized, theoretical perspectives upon the rights and obligations of Israelites in relation to God, the land upon which they live and the food that they eat. While Tractate Bikkurim fills in details left open by Scripture, it does not leave the framework of Scripture's own law so as to describe, as Tractates Terumot and Peah do, the deeper processes through which produce comes to have the status of a sanctified agricultural offering.

Like Tractate Orlah, Tractate Bikkurim thus provides evidence that decisions regarding what topics should be included in the Division of Agriculture preceded the actual work done on those topics. Tractates Orlah and Bikkurim appear in this division, creations of the Ushan period,[2] despite their failure to produce important statements of law comparable to those found in their companion tractates.

PART III

THE HISTORY OF MISHNAH'S DIVISION
OF AGRICULTURE

CHAPTER TWELVE

BEFORE 70: MISHNAH'S DIVISION OF AGRICULTURE
IN THE TIME OF THE TEMPLE

I. Introduction

Examination of sayings that, with some degree of reliability, may be said to derive from the period before 70 tells us little about the state of the agricultural law while the Temple stood or about the beginnings of a rabbinic theory of agriculture. These sayings, all of which appear in the mouths of the Houses of Hillel and Shammai, are episodic and fragmentary. Seen as a whole they do not mark the inception of the discussions that, in the periods of Yavneh and Usha, lead to the creation of a Mishnaic system of agriculture. Examined individually, moreover, none of the facts that they present constitutes the underlying proposition upon which a tractate of Mishnah is based and which that tractate's later authorities worked fully to expose. In the Division of Agriculture, the role of authorities who flourished before 70 thus is in two different respects minor. First stands the simple fact that these individuals contribute very little to the law. In their names we find only a few, in all but one case, trivial statements. Second, and much more important, the few comments that these authorities do provide neither encapsulate Mishnah's system as it develops in later periods nor even enter that system as important components.

Before turning to the implications of these facts, let us examine in detail the materials that have been shown to derive from the period before 70. This will show clearly the exact content and nature of the earliest stratum of Mishnaic law in the Division of Agriculture. This description, like the ones in the two chapters that follow, depends of course upon the analyses found in Chapters Two through Eleven. In those chapters I isolated within each tractate's several thematic units the materials that derived from before 70, Yavneh and Usha.[1] Now I go back and draw together in a single description the materials pertinent to each of these three strata. The result is a cogent picture of the state of legal thinking in each of Mishnah's formative periods.[2] This picture provides an answer to the

355

central questions of 1) when the law of agriculture emerged as a full and integral system and 2) of the character of that law as a systematic whole.

With the purpose of this and the two following chapters clear, I turn to the Mishnaic evidence for the long centuries in which the Temple stood and in which priests and Levites, the designated recipients of Mishnah's agricultural gifts, had concrete authority. The evidence, as I already have stated, is disappointing. Examined as a whole, the materials assigned to the period before 70 do not represent a stratum of Mishnah's law at all. They are too episodic to be held in themselves to comprise a system of agriculture. Even viewed simply as a corpus of facts they are negligible, for in all but one possible case they have no weight in the later development of the law.

II. Agriculture Before 70

The materials from before 70 are arranged according to the five principal themes covered in the Division of Agriculture as a whole. Under two of these themes authorities from before 70 provide no contribution at all. In two other categories, the Houses argue matters of definition, left open by Scripture and for the most part rejected in later Mishnaic authorities' development of these topics. Only in one instance might a Houses' dispute presage an issue of importance later on. In this case, the position of the House of Hillel, that holiness pertains to a batch of second tithe as a whole but not to specific coins within that batch, may stand behind the conception of holiness developed in Yavnean times.

A. Producing Crops under Conditions of Holiness

In order to produce crops under conditions of holiness, the Israelite must be careful not to sow together within a single field or vineyard different species of produce or plants. This much is known from Lev. 19:19 and Dt. 22:9-11. In the period before 70 the Houses clarify Scripture's rule. They define exactly what constitutes a vineyard subject to the Biblical restrictions, delineate the area surrounding the vines that is deemed integral to the vineyard, and determine the conditions under which, because of the great amount of empty space found within the vineyard, a second kind may be planted there (Kilaim, iii.A.4:1-3, 5, 6:1). To the extent that Yavneans continue along

this same line of questioning, the Houses materials do engender
continued discussion concerning the growing of crops under
conditions of holiness. Yet, as we shall see in our review of
the Yavnean materials themselves, even their repertoire of
definitions does not provide the notions, distinctive to Mishnah,
that account for the principal rulings on this theme and that
lead to the development of Tractate Kilaim as a whole. Only in
the Ushan period does a distinctive rabbinic theory of how
Israelites assure that they produce their crops under conditions
of holiness emerge.

The Houses dispute whether or not an individual may, in the
Sabbatical year, sell tools that might be used in forbidden field
work (Shebiit, ii.A.4:2A-H, I-K, 5:8). While not leading to
important developments within Tractate Shebiit, this ethical
issue of importance in the deliberations, in Tractate Demai, of
the question of how Israelites are to assure that they eat their
food under proper conditions of sanctity (see below).

B. Conditions under which Produce Becomes Subject to
    Sanctification.
    This theme receives no attention in the period before 70.

C. Designating Produce to be an Agricultural Offering
    The period before 70 produces no ideas that, in the times of
Yavneh and Usha, are formed into a theory of how Israelite
farmers designate produce to have the holy status of an
agricultural offering. The only pertinent dispute, at Terumot,
ii.A.4:3, concerns the quantity of produce that the individual
must separate as heave-offering. As we have seen, this notion,
that the householder should measure out a specific quantity of
produce to be heave-offering, is explicitly rejected by later
authorities.

D. The Care and Handling of Holy Produce
    The House of Hillel (Maaser Sheni, ii.A.2:7, 8A-C, 9F-H)
holds that a status of holiness pertains to a batch of coins as a
whole but not to the individual coins in that batch. Therefore,
should second tithe-coins be mixed with unconsecrated ones, the
householder need simply separate out the correct value in money,
paying no attention to which coins originally were sanctified and
which were unconsecrated. This opinion may stand at the root of

the theory of the care and handling of holy produce first worked out in the Yavnean stratum and greatly expanded in Ushan times. This view holds that by separating a portion of a batch to be an offering, the householder designates that portion to be holy and leaves the rest of the batch totally unconsecrated. In the present case, in choosing certain coins to replace the lost offering, the householder effectively transfers to the money he sets aside the status of consecration previously spread throughout the batch. The Hillelite view, that is, holds that the Israelite may designate as holy whatever coins he desires, such that which coins previously were sanctified is irrelevant. The Hillelite view thus presents a basic proposition that could allow for the development of later authorities' transactional understanding of holiness.

E.   Eating Food under Conditions of Holiness

The one verifiable Houses' dispute on this theme (Demai, ii.A.3:1C-H) does not stand behind developments of the Yavnean and Ushan periods. The Shammaites' claim, that each person is responsible to prevent another from transgressing, does however provide an ethical consideration important in a general way to the law of Tractate Demai. The main point of the tractate is that people must tithe all food that they give away, lest the recipient transgress by eating it untithed. This is a concern only in light of the Shammaite view, that by allowing the other's actions, the produce's original owner also is culpable. This consideration does not however generate any of the tractate's specific laws. In fact, both of the Houses hold opinions that contradict the Ushan theory that accounts for the tractate as a whole, that one must tithe all that leaves his possession. By contrast, both the Shammaites and the Hillelites believe that, if it is known that the recipient will tithe, the produce's original owner need not do so. Continued acceptance of that view would have precluded the creation of Tractate Demai.[3]

The other item on this theme assigned to the Houses does not appear to be authentic to the period before 70. The Shammaites (Demai, v.A.6:6) hold that olives may be sold only to individuals trusted to process them in cleanness. This reflects the much later, Ushan, definition of the haber, a person who does not sell food to anyone not trusted as regards tithes and the laws of cleanness. The Hillelite position, which holds that the individual may give away or sell olives without tithing them, is out of phase with the law of the tractate as a whole, for it demands that one tithe all produce that leaves his possession. If it is old, then it represents a notion of the tithing laws rejected by Yavnean times (see Sarason, Demai, p. 226).

III. Conclusion

Authorities from the period before 70 contribute little to the Division of Agriculture. The smattering of facts they provide does not in itself present an identifiable ideology regarding the character or meaning of the agricultural laws. These facts are not even sufficient to allow practical implementation of Scripture's tithing restrictions. Nor do these facts, when viewed individually, provide the starting point for later deliberations on any of the Division of Agriculture's particular themes. Only a single opinion from the period before 70 even enters the system of agriculture in an important way, the Hillelite statement that coins in the status of second tithe are not deemed individually to be sanctified with the status of that offering. Yet even in this case, the relatively minor character of the Hillelite view must be stressed. Its importance is a function of the peculiar way Yavneans interpreted it and of the notions of sanctification that appear to have been created from it. Standing alone, the Hillelite opinion does not constitute even a basic datum of its own period, for it is under dispute by the Shammaites. In all, if we had the materials from the period before 70 alone, we could in no way predict the character of the system of agricultural laws as it develops at Yavneh and Usha. Nor could we even imagine how, during the years when the Temple stood, the Scriptural requirements to separate agricultural offerings were carried out.

This is not to claim that, prior to the completion of the Mishnaic Division of Agriculture, Scripture's tithing laws were not implemented. Historical sources from the time of Scripture itself and through the Second Temple period make it clear that Jews tithed. The point, rather, is that, whatever tithing practices did exist in the earlier periods, so far as the evidence of the Mishnah indicates, these were not taken up by the rabbis and made components of their own legislation. As we have seen in detail, the Division of Agriculture is almost totally the creation of Yavneh and Usha and contains little material that can be shown to derive from before the destruction of the Temple. Out of the division's 569 entries, only 40 (7%) are even attributed to authorities who lived before 70. The vast majority of these assignments, we have seen, are pseudepigraphic.

These facts, provided by close scrutiny of the specific materials preserved in Mishnah, are striking. For contrary to what these materials would lead us to believe, other evidence makes clear that, during the time of the Temple, agricultural tithes were a central topic of concern. In this regard I need only refer to the Pharisees, whom later rabbinism claims as its forbears. They comprised a table fellowship, distinguished from the rest of the people of Israel by their observance of restrictions concerning cultic cleanness and separation of tithes.

The importance, in the period before 70, of agricultural law further is shown by facts internal to the Division of Agriculture. For a wide gulf distinguishes the agricultural laws available in Scripture from the set of restrictions and practices assumed within all strata of Mishnah's law. This corpus of assumed facts indeed contains the very identification and definition of the distinctive set of agricultural gifts upon which this division focuses. These gifts are not defined clearly in Scripture, but depend upon a rather elaborate interpretation and reconciliation of the Hebrew Bible's several tithing passages.[4] This means that, at some point prior to the inception of the discussions later redacted in the Mishnah, unidentified individuals carefully read Scripture and, on its basis, delineated a set of agricultural tithes. While clearly dependent upon Scripture's relevant rules, their work in laying out specific offerings represents a synthesis of passages that, in Scripture, derive from distinct and in part contradictory sources. This work of synthesis therefore should not be taken for granted.

On the one hand it thus appears that, in the time of the Temple, certain individuals were concerned with agricultural restrictions and indeed carried out important work in developing Scripture's injunctions. Yet except for definitions of the offerings themselves, Mishnah's later authorities neither preserved nor, so far as we can tell, availed themselves of any significant laws they may have inherited concerning the separation and disposition of heave-offering and tithes. These matters were worked out in full by Yavnean and Ushan authorities.

Both in its component parts and as a whole, the Division of Agriculture is the creation only of the time after the destruction of the Temple.

Short of denying that the Pharisees followed tithing taboos, or of assuming that, after the destruction of the Temple in 70, all knowledge of past ritual practice was lost, only one explanation appears reasonably to account for the facts before us. This explanation is that the rabbinic movement itself chose not to take up the extant legislation of Pharisees or Temple-priests and, in the first centuries, made little claim to continue their traditions. The reason for this choice may have been the early rabbinic movement's own lack of power and concomitant inability to speak in the name of others who actually held authority in the Israelite community. Or it could have been the simple desire of the early rabbis themselves to develop the agricultural law along lines dictated by their particular social and religious perspectives. Only later, based upon their own growing strength, did rabbinic authorities dare to rewrite their own history and to claim as their ancestors the Pharisaic group, remembered for its power and piety.

These suggested reasons for the lack of firm foundations of the Division of Agriculture in the period before 70 are, of course, only guesses. We have imperfect knowledge of what the Pharisees represented, of the ideals they held and of the rituals they actually performed.[5] Our understanding of the goal--political or religious--of early rabbinism likewise is imperfect. The significance of the absence of a Pharisaic legacy in the Division of Agriculture--the context within which we should most expect to find exactly that legacy--must therefore be narrowly defined. This absence means that later rabbinic claims of a continuity between rabbinic legislation and the traditions of Temple times and before are in fact a rewriting of rabbinic legal history. This revisionist history reflects, we must assume, the desire of a maturing rabbinic movement to legitimate its own rather recent origins. This was accomplished by tying them in with the group most remembered for piety and, as Josephus tells us, political control. The facts of the matter, however, appear clear. The evidence of the Division of Agriculture indicates that Mishnah's tithing laws are a creation of rabbis living at Yavneh and primarily at Usha. Contributions to the law from individuals living while the Temple stood are few and far

between. Those that are found, moreover, have no important
implications for the law as it develops in the document before
us.

The implication of the late origins of the Division of
Agriculture is that its notions of the meaning of the agricultural laws, the nature of sanctification and, through these
topics, the meaning of Israelite existence after the destruction
of the Temple and the failed Bar Kokhba revolt, comprise a
distinctively rabbinic statement.   These ideas reflect the human
situation of individuals who attempted to start a new Jewish life
after the destruction of the Temple.   These rabbis chose to turn
directly to Scripture as an independent source of authority, and
not to those priests or other individuals who might have
preserved the actual rules and practices of the time of the
Temple.[6]   Unlike what later rabbinic literature would like us to
believe, then, the evidence internal to the Division of
Agriculture proves that this division is a creation of Yavneh and
Usha, not the final development of an unbroken and ongoing chain
of tradition the character of which was conceived and set while
the Temple stood.

CHAPTER THIRTEEN

FROM 70 TO 140: MISHNAH'S DIVISION OF AGRICULTURE
IN THE PERIOD OF YAVNEH

I. Introduction

With the destruction of the Temple in 70, questions
concerning the cultic life of the people of Israel will have come
dramatically to the fore. The sacrificial cult had previously
constituted the central place in which God's sanctity was
revealed and called upon. Holiness was made present in the
actions of the priests. They laid on hands, thereby designating
animals to be consecrated, and then offered them up as holy gifts
to heaven. God's sanctity further had been located in the Holy
of Holies, the connecting point of the umbilical cord between
heaven and earth. While the Temple stood, it and its cult
comprised for the priestly and scribal circles from which
rabbinic Judaism springs[1] the central proof that God filled the
people and land of Israel with holiness. After 70, these people
mourned the loss of the structure that, until then, had proven
that God's promise to make of Israel a holy nation indeed had
been fulfilled.

Certainly the people looked back upon what once was and
thereby maintained hope for the future. They continued to have,
for one thing, access to the Temple mount itself. The site was
open to Jews, and the people did go there.[2] Yet this access
presumably was as discouraging as it was reassuring. For the
Romans' appropriation of the Temple tax meant that, for the
foreseeable future, the Temple would not be rebuilt. The
continued existence of the priestly cast too served as a reminder
of God's authority and presence. Yet with the cult destroyed,
the priests had no concrete function in the sanctification of
Israelite life. Like the site of the Temple, the priesthood
could be no more than a symbol of the holiness that once had
abided in the land.

The work of Yavneans in the Division of Agriculture reflects
and in two ways attempts to resolve the problems left by the
destruction of the Temple. The vacuum left by the cessation of
the cult was filled by the creation, at Yavnean hands, of a fully
expressed system of agricultural offerings. In the Yavnean
period, unlike in the time before 70, we find a clear formulation

363

of the facts and procedures that allow the separation of the
tithes required by Scripture. The important point is that,
within the Yavnean's understanding, separating and paying these
offerings represents a cultic act by which Israelites designate
produce to be holy and then present this holy produce to God,
through the tithes' recipients on earth. Delineation of the mode
of separating these holy offerings thus constitutes an important
step in assuring that, even with the Temple destroyed, the
effects formerly ensured by the cultic life of the Israelite
nation will continue, through the actions of common Israelites
who farm and eat the produce of the land.

The Yavnean notion that Israel's cultic life is transformed
through the actions of common Israelites depends upon the Yavnean
understanding that, in tithing their produce, Israelites do more
than simply pay taxes to priests and Levites. Yavneans
understand the separation of heave-offering and tithes, rather,
to constitute a procedure through which Israelites pay off God's
lien upon produce grown on land that he owns and gave as a
special gift to the Israelite nation. Produce designated for
God, in this view, is by definition holy. In separating
agricultural offerings and presenting them to God's representatives, Israelites engage in an economy of holiness comparable
to that which once existed in the Temple. The Yavnean material
thus makes the deep statement that, despite the loss of the
Temple, the holiness that once filled the people and land of
Israel still is present and subject to control. Even with the
cult destroyed, the processes through which objects in the
Israelite world are made holy continue. The ultimate meaning of
this claim is that the loss of the Temple and its cult, as well
as the continued rule of the Romans, do not change the most basic
fact of Israelite existence. God still rules over and sanctifies
the people and land, of Israel. His presence and rule are
underscored by the claim that Israelites still must pay God for
the use of the land, and that these payments have a consecrated,
status, comparable to that of the sacrifices once offered in the
Temple.

In laying out their agricultural rules, Yavneans accomplish
two concrete things. First, they provide the details of a
working system of agricultural law. They describe exactly how
produce comes to be subject to the separation of agricultural
offerings, indicate how those offerings are to be maintained in

the householder's own domain, and determine how they are to be disposed of in the hands of their proper recipients.

Second, in legislating these facts and details, Yavneans provide more than a simple catalog of mundane procedures. Rather, the details of the tithing system serve Yavneans--as they will serve Ushans--as a context in which to reply directly to the issue central in their day. This is the question of the modes through which the holiness once found in the Temple cult could now be located outside of the Temple. Yavneans, that is to say, provide a theology of sanctification meant, in the period immediately after the destruction of the Temple, to explain how holiness still could be found and manipulated in the Israelite world.

II. Agriculture in the Time of Yavneh

Before turning to the specifics of the Yavnean laws, let us review their understanding seen whole. The Yavneans' claim, simply put, is that all produce grown upon the land of Israel is subject to sanctification. The reason for this is that the produce grows upon land the ultimate owner of which is God, who like all land owners must be given a share of the crop that grows on his property. As should be clear, produce designated as God's share is holy, insofar as it belongs to God. It may only be consumed by those designated to eat it, primarily priests and Levites, who are God's cultic representatives on earth, and the poor, who have a special claim upon God for food. In order to prepare food for consumption at their common tables, Israelites must therefore separate the required agricultural gifts. This separation comprises an act of sanctification on the part of the Israelite, who, by choosing produce to be the holy offering, releases the rest of his food for common consumption.

This rather straightforward Yavnean schema has two important implications for our understanding of the Yavnean notion of holiness. The first is that, according to Yavneans, the presence of sanctification in the world is a result of the continuing presence and concern of God. Only that which grows upon God's special land--and thus with God's blessing--may, in the first place, be designated to be holy. Holiness' existence therefore does not hinge upon any actions or deeds of Israelite farmers or householders. They determine what specific portion of the crop is to represent God's share, such that it is sanctified. But they do not have the power to designate as holy other things, which are not already owed to God. Notably, holiness, in this view, continues without regard to the existence of the Temple and quite separately from the political and economic facts of who at any given time controls the land of Israel as a whole or owns a specific plot of property within that land. This is stressed by the Yavnean understanding that even crops of fields owned by gentiles are subject to tithes.

The second implication is that, for Yavneans, Israelites' power over holiness is confined to those physical actions through which they separate a portion of their crop, thereby designating it as the share owed God, and then transfer that share to the offering's proper recipients. Surely there may be intermediate stages, in which the status of holiness will be moved from the original offering into different produce or coins, as in the case of second tithe. In these cases, however, as in the original designation of the offering, the Israelite's power is confined to transferring, through physical actions, the status of holiness from one object to another. The crop's bond to God allows sanctification in the first place. Sanctity's attaching to any particular produce is the result of the physical action of an Israelite who chooses food for the Levite, priest, poor or for consumption in Jerusalem.

In stating that non-priests select the portion of the crop to be holy and physically separate that portion from the rest of the food, Yavneans appear to make the non-priest an important actor in the process through which holiness is manipulated. As we shall see in our review of their specific laws, however, Yavneans are clear that, in this process, the Israelite does no more than to play a secondary part. The potential for sanctification exists whether or not Israelites will that certain produce should be holy, and, indeed, without regard for whether or not they consider the food edible or otherwise worthy of holiness. In the same way, Yavneans hold that, in determining whether or not the Israelite validly has separated an offering, that individual's own perceptions and desires play no role. What matters, simply, are the physical rules by which tithes normally are set aside. These determine what the Israelites may and may not do, without regard for the specific circumstances within which an individual separates the required agricultural gifts. Year after year the land yields its holy crop. God's lien upon

it must be released in ways that are preset and unvarying.
Israelites thus are only actors in a play that they did not write
and do not themselves direct. What they personally think or want
has no effect upon the holy. They have the power only to follow
a script outlining prescribed and unchanging actions. In this
Yavneans take up and continue the Bible's priestly perspective.

In order to make clear the overriding theory of the Yavnean
materials, I now review the specific laws that Yavneans promul-
lgate. Then we may turn to the meaning of these laws within the
context of Judaism immediately after the destruction of the
Temple.

A. Producing Crops under Conditions of Holiness

Yavneans describe preset and unvarying conditions adherence
to which represents the Israelites' conformity to God's ideal,
set out in Scripture, for the production of crops under
conditions of holiness. The central point for Yavneans is that
these prescriptions apply without respect to the circumstances of
the individual Israelite farmer or the intentions and perceptions
that he brings to the planting and harvesting of his field.
Yavneans, that is, do not take into account the fact that, while
carrying out what might be construed as a forbidden action, the
individual actually has in mind some different, permitted,
purpose. In the same way, Yavneans do not mind if, in doing what
is permitted, the farmer should appear to transgress. To their
thinking, all that matters is the concrete effects of the
farmer's deeds, not the intentions with which he performs them
nor the appearances that his actions create.

In light of this attitude, Yavnean materials on this theme,
found in Tractate Kilaim, develop the work of definition first
begun in the period before 70. Yavneans, that is, define in
detail the field within which only a single kind of produce may
be planted (Kilaim, ii.B.2:10, 3:3, 4, 6). Yet unlike the prior
authorities, Yavneans make clear the theory that underlies this
work of definition. They state that the original lay-out of a
field determines what may and may not be planted in it.
Subsequent changes or the way that a field appears at any given
moment are not taken into account in determining how the field
may be planted in a single agricultural year (Kilaim, iii.B.4:8).
This rule emphasizes the Yavneans' belief that there is a preset
order in the world, unaffected by the actions or understandings

of Israelites who year-to-year farm their land in accord with their own changing needs and desires. (See also Kilaim, iii.B.5:7, 6:4.)

This same perspective accounts for the Yavnean law in Tractate Shebiit, which concerns permitted and forbidden agricultural activities during the Sabbatical year. Yavneans disregard the appearance the farmer projects when, in the seventh year, he works his field. Nor are they interested in the intended results of his labor. What counts to Yavneans, rather, is whether or not, in concrete terms, that which he does promotes the growth of the seventh year crop (Shebiit, ii.B.3:10, 4:6). Any work that promotes this growth is forbidden. If, however, what the farmer does has no effect upon the crop of the seventh year, it is permitted.

This same objective understanding of the restrictions against growing crops in the seventh year appears to stand behind Ishmael's refusal to extend the restrictions of the Sabbatical year back into the sixth year of the seven year cycle (Shebiit, i.B.1:4I-K). Work done in the sixth year may indeed effect the crop of the seventh. Yet, in physical terms, these actions have not been carried out in the Sabbatical year. Ishmael therefore holds that they do not fall under Scripture's ban upon working the fields in the seventh year. Ishmael thus is careful to rule according to the letter of Scripture's law, just as other Yavneans consistently judge actions only on the basis of whether or not their concrete results are contrary to what Scripture demands. Only Yose the Galilean, Shebiit, ii.B.4:6, departs from the perspective that informs the vast majority of the Yavnean material on this theme. He holds that an Israelite's actions are holy--sanctioned by God--only if they appear to other Israelites to be permitted. According to Yose, the farmer therefore may do nothing that appears to be forbidden, even if it is in fact a permitted activity. Yose's minority opinion, as we shall see, paves the way for the overall perspective that Ushans bring to this topic.

B. Conditions under which Produce Becomes Subject to
    Sanctification

The four Yavnean rules on this topic make the basic point that is developed in the Ushan discussions of this theme. Produce becomes subject to the separation of agricultural

offerings at the point at which it will be used in a regular
meal. This is when an individual brings the food into his home,
for it is there that he normally eats his meals. With this as
the basic proposition, Yavneans question other conditions under
which the produce will become subject to consecration as an
agricultural gift. They ask, for instance, whether or not a
courtyard is comparable to a home (Maaserot, iv.B.3:5A-D, 3:9).
This is determined on the basis of the physical characteristics
of that courtyard. A more interesting Yavnean question concerns
seed crops, which will not be eaten at all. Yavneans state that
these are not subject to tithes, for they are not a food
(Maaserot, vi.B.4:5E-H). They further dispute whether an
ambiguous crop's status as a food depends only upon whether it is
edible at all or whether we must ask as well if people normally
eat it (Maaserot, vi.B.4:6). These basic definitions of what is
a food and subject to tithes differ from the Ushan materials,
which, in cases of ambiguity, consistently take into account the
Israelite's own intention to eat, or not to eat, the particular
commodity.

    Tractate Hallah, which describes the conditions under which
grain becomes subject to dough offering, is primarily a Yavnean
tractate. The point that it makes as a whole is no different
from what we already have seen in the Yavnean stratum of Tractate
Maaserot. Tractate Hallah holds simply that dough offering must
be separated from any grain that is leavened (Hallah, i.B.1:3,
i.D.1:1). This is without regard to whether or not the baker
intends actually to use the dough for bread. The individual's
actions in making dough take precedence over his intentions, for
instance, to use that dough as leaven and not to bake it at all.
Only small quantities of dough are exempt from dough offering,
for they are too insignificant to be termed food (Hallah,
i.B.2:3, ii.D.2:6). This too is the case, Yavneans hold, without
regard to the attitude of the particular Israelite who owns them
and who may indeed intend to use the small bits of food in making
a meal. They become subject only if the bits are thoroughly
combined so as to form a single batch of at least a qab.

C.   Designating Produce to be an Agricultural Offering

    Yavnean authorities hold that Israelites' manipulation of
the holiness held by agricultural gifts is subject to rules like
those that govern the handling of tangible materials. This

Yavnean notion is revealed clearly in Tractate Terumot. Yavneans there hold that, validly to designate heave-offering, the householder must physically separate produce as that offering. Since what the householder does with one batch has no physical effect upon produce in a different batch, Yavneans prohibit the separation from one amount of produce of the heave-offering required for a different batch. Moreover, to be combined into a single batch, all of the produce must be in the same status regarding year of growth, susceptibility to the offering and ownership (Terumot, i.B.1:5, 2:1). Only such homogeneous produce combines into a single entity for purposes of the separation of heave-offering. In light of the requirements of physical separation, Yavneans rule that an Israelite may not designate all of a batch of produce to be heave-offering (Terumot, ii.B.4:5). Ushans, as we shall see, likewise require the householder to distinguish his share from that which becomes the offering. Their reason for this however is quite different from the simple one found in the Yavnean stratum.

The majority of Yavnean discussions concerning the designation of produce to be agricultural offerings do not reveal sustained theories of the matter. They concern basic facts and definitions. Yavneans dispute whether or not grape clusters in a vineyard can be deemed defective, such that they belong to the poor, if they all have the same, albeit unusual, shape (Peah, v.B.7:7). The issue is whether we define a defective cluster on the basis of a single standard, applied to all fields, or on the basis of the norm in each individual field. Yavneans resolve an issue left open by the Houses, agreeing that to be deemed a forgotten sheaf, the sheaf must be completely forgotten by the farmer and his agents (Peah, iv.B.6:6). If someone might remember the sheaf in the field, it may not, in the meantime, be taken by the poor. For the case of first fruits, Yavneans supply the facts of when in the year these offerings may be brought to the Temple and the recitation made (Bikkurim, i.B.1:6G-K, i.D.1:3E-H). They dispute whether or not the decorations used on the baskets of fruit take on the consecrated status of the first fruits themselves (Bikkurim, iii.B.3:9). In all of these areas, Yavneans thus define the basic character of agricultural offerings and delineate the terms of their separation.

In one final issue, Yavneans argue what is clear throughout the Ushan stratum of this division. Yavneans know that _peah_ must

be left unharvested at the rear of the field. The question
concerns what defines a field, whether geographical considerations or the perspective of the farmer who chooses to plant
and harvest his property in one manner and not another (Peah,
i.B.2:3-4, 3:2). Yavneans, that is, dispute whether or not the
attitude of the farmer should be taken into account in
determining where peah is to be left. In this context, certain
Yavneans thus move beyond the common Yavnean notion that the
farmer's intentions and perceptions do not matter. These
authorities presage the Ushan view, which deems the Israelite's
attitude always to be determinative.

D. The Care and Handling of Holy Produce
    The theory of holiness found in the Yavnean materials
concerning the designation of produce as an agricultural offering
controls as well Yavnean notions of the proper care and handling
of consecrated produce in the secular world. Yavneans, that is
to say, answer the question of what happens when holy and secular
produce are mixed together by taking into account the physical
character of what has happened, without regard for the
perspectives or intentions of the individuals involved.
    This Yavnean ideology is most prominent in Tractate
Terumot's discussions of what happens when heave-offering is
mixed with unconsecrated produce, planted in place of secular
seed or cooked with common food. In the first example, in which
heave-offering and unconsecrated produce are mixed together
(Terumot, iii.B), Yavneans hold that if there is much secular
produce, the holy charge is dissipated, such that the batch as a
whole may be eaten by a non-priest. If, however, there is a
large quantity of consecrated produce, it renders all of the
mixture forbidden to non-priests. This occurs mechanically,
without regard to the householder's sense of what happened or
even, according to Joshua, to his ability to locate and recover
the holy offering.
    The holy status of heave offering seed is maintained by the
crop that grows from that seed (Terumot, vi.B.9:4). This is
because Yavneans see the seed as an integral part of the crop
that grows from it. Cooking heave-offering with unconsecrated
food, by contrast, does not impart a status of consecration to
the secular produce. If the heave-offering can be removed from
the dish, it has no physical impact upon that with which it was

cooked. For that reason, it is accorded no metaphysical effect either. The secular food still may be eaten by a non-priest (Terumot, vii.B.10:11E-H). For the cases of both of these types of mixtures, the Yavnean rules differ considerably from later Ushan law, which determines the status of the mixture on the basis of the attitude of the Israelite who planted the heave-offering seed or cooked his own food with the priest's share. As we have come to expect, the Yavnean materials do not evidence this concern for the perceptions or intentions of the Israelite farmer or householder.

Interest in the physical characteristics that define the proper maintenance of consecrated food occurs as well in the Yavnean deliberations concerning second tithe. Tractate Maaser Sheni discusses proper modes of transferring, through ordinary business transactions, a status of consecration to and from objects in the secular world. In working out the facts of how these transfers are made, Yavneans, like Ushans, hold that the normal rules of economics apply. The central point, derived from Yavnean legislation, is that, in transferring a status of second tithe from produce to money and *vice versa*, the individual must be certain that the correct value of the original second tithe is preserved. The Israelite may neither increase nor decrease the quantity of holy substance through accepting an amount of money or food that is not commensurate with the value of the original second tithe given in exchange. Yet unlike later Ushans, Yavneans greatly limit the Israelite farmer's ability to transfer the status of holiness from one object to another (Maaser Sheni, i.B.1:5A-C, 2:3A, 4A-D). No matter what he intends to do, Yavneans hold that he cannot validly consecrate as second tithe non-food items, which never were envisioned by Scripture as having that status. Ushans by contrast hold that Israelites consecrate with the status of second tithe any object that they intentionally exchange for consecrated second tithe coins or produce.

In one important dispute, Eliezer and Joshua (Terumot, iv.B.8:1-3 and v.B.8:8-11) argue the role of the intentions of the Israelite in assuring that holy offerings are properly maintained. We know that under normal circumstances the Israelite must care for heave-offering by protecting it in cleanness and by making certain that he does not eat it in place of his own secular food. Eliezer argues that these restrictions apply mechanically, without regard to the particular circumstances in which the Israelite might come to eat or impart uncleanness to heave-offering. In all cases the Israelite is culpable for tampering with the holy. In this view, Eliezer represents the common Yavnean perspective, that holiness is controlled by a preset and unvarying standard of behavior, unaffected by the circumstances, concerns or intentions of the individual Israelite. Joshua, by contrast, holds that culpability may be determined only in light of what the Israelite thought he was doing in the instance at hand. He thereby foreshadows the Ushan conception that the rules of holiness are largely reflexes of the Israelite's own perceptions of what is right and wrong. Exposition of this view, that an Israelite's rights and responsibilities are functions of his own analysis of what should or should not be done, is absent from the Yavnean stratum as a whole, yet, as we shall see, represents the central focus of the Ushan materials in the division.

E. Eating Food under Conditions of Holiness

     In their few statements on this theme, Yavneans rule leniently concerning the consumption of food that may not have been properly tithed. They permit householders to serve possibly untithed produce to poor people who eat at their table (Demai, ii.B.3:1A-B). They are not even certain that, in order to prepare for consumption possibly untithed food, the Israelite householder must remove all of the doubtfully separated offerings (Demai, iii.B.4:3). Finally, they allow an Israelite to purchase and eat food without tithing at the word of people who are not themselves trusted to tithe that which they sell or serve (Demai, iii.B.4:1). These leniencies reveal a general lack of Yavnean concern to prevent the Israelite from eating produce that might not have been completely tithed. While, as we have seen in the other thematic units just discussed, Yavneans show great interest in the physical acts by which Israelites separate agricultural offerings, they are not equally concerned with the social issues and concerns created by the determination of certain individuals only to consume produce under conditions of holiness. This is an important contrast to the Ushan materials, which require that the individual account for <u>all</u> of the required offerings and which define a separate group within the people of Israel distinguished by its consumption of produce under strict conditions of holiness.

Yavneans legislate proper observance of the restriction against eating the fruit of a tree or vine in its first three years of growth (orlah) by defining what is deemed a new tree subject to that restriction (Orlah, i.B.1:4). Yavneans continue the work of definition by indicating that the restriction applies only to the tree's primary fruit but not to secondary products that derive from it (Orlah, i.B.1:7D-I). Again, the individual's intention to use part of the tree as food does not come into play, only the botanical definition of what constitutes that particular tree's primary "fruit".

Yavneans supply the basic rule governing the consumption of heave-offering and other consecrated offerings (Terumot, viii.B.11:3). To assure that none of the holy food will go to waste, the heave-offering must be processed in the manner normal for produce of its type. This concern for maintaining the full value of holy produce is familiar from the Yavnean deliberations on the proper care and handling of second tithe. It also is in line with the Yavnean view that what counts is the normative definition of what is food, not the particular individual's desire to use a certain portion of the produce in a particular way.[3]

III. Conclusion

The Yavnean materials make the strong claim that even though the Temple-cult has ceased, the holiness that once filled the land of Israel continues to be present. Yavneans make this claim by designing a system of tithing that assures that, just as when the Temple stood, the people will live a life of holiness and will return to its proper recipients the portion of their crop that represents God's share of the food of the land of Israel. In developing their tithing law, Yavneans deny the significance of the events of history that have destroyed the Temple and left the Romans in control of the land of Israel. Despite these occurrences, Yavneans claim that God still rules over the people and land of Israel.

Their particular understanding of the processes of sanctification and desanctification takes us deeper into the Yavnean mentality. As we have seen time and again, Yavneans hold that, in the creation and disposition of holiness, the Israelite plays only a mechanical role. The potential for holiness, they say, is a result of God's rule over the land of Israel. Produce becomes subject to the separation of tithes in accordance with the natural calender of ripening and consumption, unaffected by a particular individual's preparation of a meal, for instance, using unprocessed food or sitting outside of his own home. The transfer and maintenance of holiness within the world too follows preset and unvarying laws. These do not reflect the desires of Israelites who, under particular circumstances, act as they think is correct. Holiness rather is manipulated through physical acts of transfer. What counts accordingly are the concrete actions but not the intentions of Israelites. The permissibility of specific modes of growing, tithing and eating food thus depends not upon the Israelite's sense of what is proper but upon laws of holiness that are applied to all cases without variation.

Particular to the Yavnean theory of agriculture thus is the conception of a preexistent order and law, imposed by God upon the world and independent of the emotions and intentions of individual Israelites who act within changing circumstances. This order is found by Yavneans in the geographical character-istics that, they say, define a field, just as it is found in the physical actions that Yavneans say determine how the Israelite may and may not treat holiness. Foremost in these Yavnean ideas is the perspective that Israelites do not create their own world but, rather, that they face a world already created and ordered. Within this world their own individual responsibilities and abilities are preordained and unvarying.

This Yavnean understanding of the world presents a strong statement that, with the destruction of the Temple, nothing essential has changed for the Israelite nation. The rule of God still is complete. It leaves no room for, nor is it affected by, the ideals or desires of individual Israelites. While the Temple stood, the cult had presented a clear image of the requirements of holiness existing in unchanging order. In the Division of Agriculture, Yavneans describe rules of holiness that, while applied outside of the Temple, work according to this same ideal. The change in historical situations has neither increased the powers of individual Israelites nor rendered the laws of God relative. As when the Temple stood, Yavneans see God's rule to be concretized through the preset and unchanging laws that control the processes of sanctification and desanctification.

It will take Ushan authorities, working after the failed Bar Kokhba revolt, more than two generations after the destruction of the Temple, to recognize the extent to which the spiritual situation of the Israelites indeed has changed. If the Temple, the physical sign of God's presence, is gone, and the priesthood, the earthly representation of the Lord's dominion, is without concrete function, then a new measure for cultic activity must be determined. As we shall see in the following chapter, this is the task that Ushan authorities in the Division of Agriculture take upon themselves. In this way they take clear steps to develop and complete the nascent system of tithing created in the Yavnean period.

CHAPTER FOURTEEN

FROM 140 TO 170: MISHNAH'S DIVISION OF AGRICULTURE
IN THE PERIOD OF USHA

I. Introduction

Ushans inherit from Yavneans a basic framework of law
describing how Israelites are to grow, harvest and eat their food
under conditions of holiness. Through these topics Yavneans
legislated on a complete range of issues concerning use of the
land of Israel in the production of food. They taught how
Israelites are properly to plant and till the fields, designate
and separate the required agricultural offerings, maintain these
holy gifts in the secular world and, finally, eat these gifts as
well as the produce from which they were taken.

In developing these topics, Yavneans established the
concerns and issues of each of the tractates in the Division of
Agriculture. They further created a nascent system of
agricultural law, comprised of this division as a whole. Before
Yavnean times, that is to say, neither a theory of what a code of
agricultural law as a whole should discuss nor even the topical
concerns of any single tractate was in hand. By the end of
Yavnean times, by contrast, the character of the Division of
Agriculture was set. The system of agriculture as a whole thus
emerged at the hands of a single generation of authorities. In
response to the exigencies of their own time, they created a set
of individual laws and, through them, a system of holiness that
responded to the theological crisis of their day.

This Yavnean system of agriculture does not however
represent the final or even overriding meaning of the Division of
Agriculture as it comes finally to stand before us. For this
Mishnaic division is not a creation of those Yavneans who first
conceived it. Both in content and form it comes to being at the
hands of the final generation of Mishnaic authorities. Surely,
as we have now seen, Yavneans determine the topical structure of
this division.[1] Yet, at the hands of Ushan legislators, the work
conceived at Yavneh is given a new and, I shall argue,
distinctively Mishnaic meaning. At the hands of the Ushans, that
is to say, the Division of Agriculture comes to have a meaning

peculiar to Mishnaic law and quite different from previous
Yavnean and Scriptural legislation on the topic of agriculture.
Ushans reject the central Yavnean claim, which denies the
power and importance of the thoughts and desires of common
Israelites. Throughout the material before us, Ushans, rather,
stress a single point. The Israelites themselves are central in
determining what is holy and what is secular, what is sanctioned
by God and what is forbidden. These determinations are made
through reference to the perceptions and purposes that individual
Israelites bring to their actions in cultivating crops upon the
land of Israel, in harvesting the produce, in separating
agricultural gifts and, finally, in eating the food of the land.
In this Ushan view, what is holy is that which appears to
Israelites themselves to be special and therefore set apart. To
be holy--sanctioned by God--means, in the Ushan view, to be
sanctioned by Israelites.

Through these ideas Ushans replace the Yavnean notion of
holiness as a quality imposed upon the world by God and
manipulated only through physical actions, almost as though it
were itself a physical entity. They hold instead that holiness
is a reflex of the ideals and attitudes of Israelites themselves.
With only minor limitations, Israelites may impose a status of
sanctification upon whatever they desire. Their conformity to
the requirements of the holy life, further, is determined through
reference to their own intention to abide by what they understand
to be God's will. Surely, like Yavneans, Ushans hold that God
represents the source of all holiness. Yet Ushans depict in God
a profound passivity. In sanctifying Israelite life, God acts
solely in response to the Israelites' own desires and
intentions. In determining the permissibility of an Israelite's
actions, God judges what physically has been done only in light
of the individual's perceptions and purpose.

In their larger message, Ushans repeat exactly what Yavneans
before them had believed. Despite the destruction of the Temple,
cultic sanctification continues in the Israelite world. It is
found now in the hands of common Israelites, who separate from
their produce the holy offerings required by God. The underlying
claim is that God remains the proprietor of the land of Israel.
Like all landlords God must be paid a share of the produce, the
payment for use of the land. At its deepest level, Mishnah's
concern that Israelites make this payment is an insistence that,

despite what earthly events seem to indicate, God remains lord over the land of Israel. Agricultural tithes therefore must be separated and paid. And yet, as we have seen, while the underlying motivation behind the system of agricultural laws remains the same for Ushans as for Yavneans, then still, Ushans institute a profound change in their understandings of the specifics of the laws that express that motivation. To these specifics we now turn.

II. Agriculture in the Time of Usha

Ushan legislation concentrates upon the proposition that the thoughts and perceptions of common Israelites determine the significance of their actions. It follows that, in the Ushan view, God's law of holiness functions primarily as a reflex of the attitudes of Israelites themselves. What Israelites desire to do and that which they perceive others as doing determine the status and meaning of their actions. Israelites' intentions properly to plant their fields, for example, assure that Diverse Kinds of crops will be considered separate. Their own purposes in carrying out field labor in the Sabbatical year determines whether or not, in that year, forbidden work has been carried out. Once food is ripened, it becomes subject to the separation of tithes as a reflex of the Israelites' own desire to use the crop as food. The required offerings, finally, may be separated from this food and maintained in safety only if the Israelite householder is intent upon properly guarding the sanctity of these holy offerings.[2]

The ideas reviewed here reveal the Ushan notion that the chain of events through which food reaches the Israelite table in holiness depends upon the intention of Israelites to observe God's law. From their vantage point after the failed Bar Kokhba revolt, Ushans recognize that, unlike the original Yavnean claim, things really have changed dramatically from the time when the Temple stood. Perhaps cultic sanctification still exists. Yet Ushans reflect upon the fact that the Temple, the traditional locus of sanctification, no longer stands and that, accordingly, the priests who previously represented God's power in controlling holiness have no concrete function. In this circumstance, Ushans institute the basic changes in perspective that we have seen. If the Temple no longer showers the people with holiness, then instead, through their own actions and deeds, the people

themselves must bring holiness into the world and assure that it
properly is maintained. For Ushans, unlike Yavneans, the common
Israelite thus becomes the center and focus of the system of
agricultural laws. Israelites are made to take responsibility
for directing the earthly drama of sanctification. God, the
ultimate source of holiness, acts only in response to the call of
his holy people. In this way, in the period after the failed
revolt, those people come to represent the primary statement that
God's holiness still exists in the world.

This Ushan perspective rejects the Yavnean claim that
Israelites confront an already ordered world, and that holiness,
consequently, is manipulated only through concrete actions that
transfer its status according to unvarying, physical laws.
Ushans hold instead that the presence of holiness on earth is a
reflex of Israelites' own perceptions that certain objects are
set aside and special. God, in this Ushan view, is passive,
accepting as holy whatever Israelites themselves determine to be
worthy of consecration. Ushans thus come to claim that what is
holy is that which Israelites themselves decide should be holy.
Holiness is a function of Israelites' own ideals for the proper
production and consumption of food. This central point of the
Ushan rules appears in each of the Division of Agriculture's five
topical sections, to which we now turn.

A. Producing Crops under Conditions of Holiness

Like their Yavnean counterparts, Ushan authorities know from
Scripture that growing produce in holiness requires 1) keeping
separate from each other different species of plants and 2) not
tilling the fields in the Sabbatical year. Unlike Yavneans,
however, Ushans propose that compliance with these restrictions
is achieved when Israelites perceive their own actions in tilling
the soil, planting seed and harvesting crops to be in accord with
Scripture's demands. Ushans, this is to say, ignore the preset
and unvarying definitions by which Yavneans determine proper
action. Instead they hold that what counts is the Israelite's
personal intentions and attitudes. Adherence to the requirement
to keep different species apart, for instance, depends upon the
farmer's own sense that he has not mixed together different
kinds. It is reflected as well in the fact that, when looking at
his field, other Israelites can perceive the different types
growing in it to be separate from each other. The Ushan point

thus is that God sanctions and deems holy that which Israelites themselves understand to accord with the order in which the world originally was created. Unlike the Yavnean view, which claims that holiness is achieved through observance of set and unchanging rules, this Ushan perspective states that the Israelite's own perceptions of what he has done and his concomitant desire to bring God's blessing upon his fields account for the holiness of the produce of the land. This is the case without regard for the actual facts of how one plants his fields or goes about his agricultural work.

The facts are made clear throughout the Ushan strata of Tractates Kilaim and Shebiit. Since I have dwelled upon these ideas in my reviews of each of these tractates, consideration of them here is brief. In Tractate Kilaim, first, Ushans indicate that whether or not different species of produce growing together comprise a forbidden mixture is determined by the Israelite who sows these plants or who observes them growing in a field. Only what Israelites perceive to be a mixture is considered forbidden (Kilaim, ii.C.2:1-2, 7, 9, 3:1). Indeed, types of plants that comprise Diverse Kinds, such that they may not be planted together, are defined not by botanical categories but on the basis of the individual plant's appearance (Kilaim, i.C.1:1-3). Diverse Kinds, that is, are defined as what appear to Israelites to be closely related but different species.[3] Determination of Diverse Kinds does not depend upon those facts of botany known to the rabbis. In the same way, a vineyard to which the restrictions of Diverse Kinds apply is defined as that which people generally term a vineyard. Formal definition is rejected (Kilaim, iii.C.5:1; contrast the Houses, iii.A.4:1-3, 5, 6:1). Finally, even a farmer who actually grows together Diverse Kinds is not automatically culpable. Only an individual who intentionally maintains the mixture has transgressed and thereby rendered all of the produce forbidden for consumption (Kilaim, iii.C.7:4-5, iii.D.5:6, 7:6). An Israelite has committed no sin if his actions were not intended.

The theme referred to here is expressed throughout the Ushan stratum of Tractate Shebiit. Ushans there claim that Israelites may not carry out actions through which they _intend_ to enhance the growth of produce during the Sabbatical year or by which they _appear_ to others to be promoting that crop's development. Actions that the farmer does not intend to benefit the crop or which do not appear to others to be forbidden are, by contrast, permitted. As in Tractate Kilaim, the concrete effects of the farmer's labors are not at issue so much as are individual Israelite's perceptions of what they are doing. In the Ushan view, Israelites grow produce and maintain their fields in holiness when, in their own minds, they have complied with God's intentions for the use of the fields of the land of Israel.

B. Conditions under which Produce Becomes Subject to
   Sanctification

   Israelites' desire to make use of the land of Israel in the production of food and, later, their intent to take that food and use it for their own purposes trigger the restrictions of the tithing system. In the Ushan view, that is, the requirement that Israelites tithe and, moreover, their very ability to designate produce as sanctified are functions of their own actions in planting and harvesting. God takes an interest in and demands a share only of food for which Israelites have indicated their own desire. This desire is shown by the fact that the Israelites purposely cultivate the produce upon the land of Israel and that they later harvest it for consumption, storage or processing (Maaserot, i.C.1:1, 2-3, 4). What grows wild, by contrast, is not subject to tithes, even if the Israelite desires it as food. Since its growth was not subject to the intentions and desires of an Israelite, it never becomes subject to sanctification as an agricultural gift.

   In the Ushan view, even food that stands within the system of tithes--having been cultivated by Israelites--may not actually be tithed until the Israelite takes it for his own personal possession, either to eat it or to use in a business transaction. God's demand for a share of the produce, that is to say, is understood to be a reflex of the Israelite's own desire to make use of the   produce of the land of Israel. In light of this perspective, the majority of Ushan materials in Tractate Maaserot details the conditions under which Israelites are deemed to have acquired produce for their own use, such that they must tithe (Maaserot, iii.C.2:4A-C, v.C.4:3). While the specifics of these rules need not detain us, their larger implications for the Ushan notion of holiness must be clear. Ushans hold that only objects subject to the Israelite's particular care and use may be designated as holy. Like Yavneans, Ushans hold that God's lien upon food renders that food susceptible to sanctification. Unlike Yavneans, Ushans view God as playing a profoundly passive role in the actual processes through which that lien takes effect, such that the food becomes subject to consecration. Only in reaction to the deeds and desires of common Israelites does God determine that produce grown upon the land of Israel may be or, later, must be designated as an agricultural gift.[4]

The rules in Tractate Hallah that appear to be Ushan express this same view. Unlike the Yavnean materials, which claim that all leavened dough is subject to the separation of dough offering, Hallah, i.D.1:8 claims that the offering need be separated only from dough that Israelites themselves deem significant as food. The second pertinent rule concerns mixtures of subject and exempt types of dough (Hallah, iii.D.3:7, 10). Dough offering need be separated from these only if they have the taste of dough that is subject. The dough's being susceptible to sanctification thus depends upon the Israelite's own perception of whether or not it is the type of dough from which the offering normally is separated. The actual fact that it contains produce usually subject to the offering is not, in itself, determinative.

C. Designating Produce to Be an Agricultural Offering

Tractate Terumot describes in detail the procedures through which the Israelite householder sets aside produce to be the consecrated heave-offering. Ushans state that the designation depends primarily upon the intention of the individual to impose upon a certain quantity of produce a status of sanctification. What the householder separates, that is to say, takes on the status of heave-offering only if, in removing it from the larger batch, the individual 1) properly formulates the intention to consecrate that produce (Terumot, i.C.1:1) and 2) makes concrete that intention through corresponding words (Terumot, ii.C.3:5). A separation of produce performed without properly formulated and expressed intention leaves both that which was separated and the batch from which it was taken in the status of untithed food. The householder's unintended actions are null.

The centrality for Ushans of human intention is proven by their claim that individuals deemed to have no understanding (e.g., imbeciles and minors) and therefore no powers of intention may not validly separate heave-offering (Terumot, i.C.1:1). Ushans even go so far as to rule that a designation of heave-offering that does not conform to the formal requirements established in Yavnean times still may be valid. This is the case so long as the householder carried it out with proper intention (Terumot, i.C.2:2, 3). In all then, the Ushan view holds that, on the basis of thoughts and deeds, not physical actions, Israelites control what produce and how much of it will become holy.

In Tractate Peah, Ushans describe in detail how produce becomes the property of the poor as peah, gleanings, forgotten sheaves and defective clusters. On the surface, these processes are different from the ones through which heave-offering and tithes are designated. This is because, unlike the latter offerings, which are set aside by the householder and given to specific priests and Levites, poor gifts are comprised of produce that is abandoned and left for the poor to collect without interference from the field's owner. Here, then, the house-holder's intention does not come into play in choosing specific produce to be an offering. Instead, produce becomes the property of the poor when it falls outside of the intentions of the farmer, because he leaves it unharvested, because, during the harvest, it falls from his sickle, or because, after the harvest, he forgets to come and collect it in the field.

These differences, which reflect Scripture's own description of what produce constitutes poor gifts, mask important similarities Ushans draw between the designation of these poor tithes and the separation of heave-offering and the Levitical tithe. In the case of poor gifts, as in that of the other agricultural offerings, the processes through which the designation occurs begin with the farmer's actions in harvesting his field. The rights of the poor, like the rights of priests and Levites, constitute a reflex of the farmer's own demand for the ripened produce of his field (Peah, i.C.1:3C-E). This applies even in the case of defective grape clusters which, quite early in their growth, are known by their shape to belong to the poor. Even so, God's lien upon the produce, and with it, the preemptive right of the poor to their share begin only when the farmer perceives his crop to be valuable as food, such that he begins the harvest. This act of harvesting signals the farmer's desire for his crop and, concomitantly, the designation of the poor's share (Peah, v.C.7:5, 8). In the same way, in the case of peah, Ushans hold that the farmer's own attitude towards his land determines exactly which produce must be left unharvested for the

poor. While agreeing with Yavneans that the produce in the rear
of the field is to be left as peah, Ushans hold that what
constitutes the rear of the field is determined not by
geographical boundaries or other physical characteristics but by
the Israelite's own perceptions of the land, indicated the way in
which he chooses to plant and harvest his property (Peah,
i.C.3:4, 5). As does Tractate Terumot, Tractate Peah thus
describes the designation of agricultural gifts to be dependent
upon the intentions and desires of Israelite householders. They
determine when produce may become an agricultural gift and, in
certain cases, which produce and how much of it is to comprise
that gift.

In Tractate Bikkurim, Ushans provide a full, narrative,
description of the ritual through which first fruits are
identified, designated and carried to the Temple in Jerusalem,
where they are presented to the priests (Bikkurim, iii.C). The
presence of this topic in the Ushan stratum emphasizes the active
role of Ushan authorities in defining how specific ceremonies
will be carried out in a perfected Temple-cult. These materials,
however, reveal no theoretical stance concerning the processes
through which produce takes on the status of an agricultural
offering.

D.   The Care and Handling of Holy Produce
Once heave-offering or other agricultural gifts have been
designated and separated a new set of problems occurs. So long
as the consecrated gifts remain in the Israelite's secular
domain, they are liable to be used to some purpose other than
their proper one, consumption by priest or Levite. The
agricultural gift may, for instance, be mixed or cooked with the
Israelite's own food, might be eaten by the non-priest or even
planted as seed. Recognizing the potential for these
occurrences, Tractate Terumot in particular asks of the
culpability of the Israelite who in one way or another mishandles
consecrated produce. As we should expect on the basis of what we
have seen in other Ushan deliberations, these authorities rule
that culpability depends upon the intentions and perceptions of
the householder who allows the heave-offering to be mixed with
his own food, eaten as secular produce or planted as seed. In
this way Ushans move beyond Yavnean thought, which determines
culpability solely on the basis of the physical character of the

Israelite's actions. Unlike Yavneans, Ushans hold that the Israelite has committed sacrilege only if he intentionally did wrong. Israelites' own perceptions of what they do thus determine the significance of their actions.

This Ushan theory appears in several important examples in Tractate Terumot. One concerns a case in which a bin of heave-offering and a bin of common produce are confused, so that it is not known which contains the consecrated heave-offering. If two different people eat the produce in the bins, neither is culpable. Each may claim to have eaten the unconsecrated food (Terumot, iv.C.7:5-7). The indisputable fact that one of them has certainly eaten consecrated produce is not taken into account. So long as both individuals perceive themselves not to have transgressed, Ushans deem neither of them to be culpable.

Perceptions again are brought into play in a case in which an Israelite plants heave-offering as seed. Yavneans, we recall, deem the individual invariably to be culpable, so as to be forced to cultivate a consecrated crop (Terumot, vi.B.9:4). Ushans, by contrast, take into account the intentions of the individual who misused the heave-offering. If he did so intentionally, he must suffer the consequences of his deed by continuing to cultivate the field seeded with heave-offering. He thereby loses both the use of his field and the ultimate enjoyment of the crop, which has a consecrated status. If however the individual unintentionally planted the seed, he may plow it up (Terumot, vi.D.9:1). While he may not make personal use of the heave-offering he planted, he likewise is not held to have transgressed so as to be made to suffer for that which he unintentionally did. As in the previous example, Ushans thus hold that only through their intentions do Israelites encroach upon the holy, just as it is only through their powers of intention that they designate produce to be sacred in the first place.

Yavneans, we recall, reject the notion that heave-offering imparts a sanctified status to produce with which it is cooked (Terumot, vii.B.10:11E-H). So long as the heave-offering itself can be removed from the dish, the rest of the food retains its unconsecrated status. Ushans (Terumot, vii.C.10:1, 3), by contrast, are concerned that, if the heave-offering imparts flavor to the unconsecrated dish, the individuals who later eat that food will perceive themselves as benefitting from the priestly ration. Ushans therefore hold that any time heave-offering imparts its flavor to unconsecrated food, the dish as a whole must be deemed heave-offering. This does not apply only if the heave-offering ruins the flavor of the other food, such that the Israelites do not desire its taste. Then they may ignore the fact that the food was cooked with heave-offering. Even the concrete flavoring power of the heave-offering thus is not always determinative. The real concern of Ushans focuses upon the Israelite's own personal likes and dislikes.

The Ushan view that holiness is a reflex of the attitudes and perceptions of Israelites is evident in the two rules of Tractate Maaser Sheni pertinent to this theme. In the case of second tithe, the Israelite exchanges the original tithe for coins. These he carries to Jerusalem for use in purchasing produce to be eaten in place of the original, sanctified, offering. While this is the only proper use of the second tithe-money, Ushans hold that anything that the Israelite intentionally purchases with the coins--including inedibles-- takes on the status of second tithe (Maaser Sheni, i.C.1:3, 4, i.D.1:5D-E). Only an unintentional purchase is invalid. Ushans thus give Israelites full power over what will and will not become holy. This view differs substantially from the Yavnean perspective, which restricts the Israelite's power of consecration to foods and coins, which were envisioned by Scripture itself to have the status of second tithe.

The second pertinent rule of Tractate Maaser Sheni is comparable to the case in which it is not clear which of two bins contains heave-offering. Here an individual who finds coins that might have the sanctified status of second tithe is permitted to treat them as secular. This is so unless he is quite certain that the money does in fact have a consecrated status (Maaser Sheni, v.C.4:11, v.D.4:9, 12). The point, as before, is that so long as the Israelite perceives an object not to be consecrated it is deemed for all practical purposes actually to be secular. This view highlights the Ushan notion that, rather than a physical state, sanctification is a reflex of the attitude of Israelites themselves.

E. Eating Food under Conditions of Holiness

Israelites may only consume foods from which all of the required agricultural offerings have been separated. So far as they are in a position to do so, they must also assure that foods others eat have properly been tithed. These notions, which describe the requirements for Israelites' eating of their food under conditions of holiness, come to full expression in the Ushan stratum of Tractate Demai. Indeed, as we have seen, the very creation of Tractate Demai as a systematic essay begins with the particularly Ushan notion that Israelites must tithe both what they eat and all foods that leave their possession.

In light of these central concerns, Ushans define membership in a group that is set apart from the rest of the people of Israel by its observance of tithing and purity laws (Demai, ii.C.2:2, 3, 4, 3:3E-G, 4, 5, 6). These rules detail first and foremost the restrictions that apply to individuals who wish to assure that all foods they eat have properly been tithed. This is accomplished by establishing firm grounds for determining who may be trusted to state that they have tithed food they are about to sell (Demai, iii.C.4:7), as well as by setting up procedures for the tithing of produce about which there is a doubt whether or not it already has properly been tithed. In light of the requirement that Israelites take responsiblity to tithe that which others will eat, considerable attention also is paid to defining the circumstances under which Israelites must in fact separate agricultural gifts from produce that leaves their possession (e.g., Demai, v.C.6:1, v.D.6:7, 8-9, 10, 11). Through these rules Ushans state that the ability of any Israelite to eat food under conditions of holiness is a reflection of the responsibility accepted by other Israelites properly to prepare food for consumption. Sanctification of Israelite life thus is made to depend upon the human concerns of mutual trust and responsibility among people working together to build a holy society. In describing a distinct group of individuals who observe all of the tithing laws, Ushans recognize that, within Israelite society as a whole, the rabbinic movement's larger program will not have immediate success.

Tractate Orlah provides two more ideas pertinent to this theme. Each of these carries forward the overriding Ushan proposition that the laws of holiness are applied in response to the intentions and actions of common Israelites. The larger point of the tractate is that, as Lev. 19:23 states, Israelites may not consume the fruit of a tree or vine in its first three years of growth. Ushans however narrow this injunction to apply only to trees or vines that Israelites intentionally plant for their fruit (Orlah, i.C.1:1). A tree planted, for instance, as a fence is not viewed as a "fruit tree" and therefore is exempt from this restriction. The Israelite's attitude towards the tree and not its botanical characteristics thus determine the status of the fruit. Ushans note that, as in the case of heave-offering, produce of the first three years of growth of a fruit tree is rendered permitted if it is neutralized through being mixed with a large amount of permitted produce (Orlah, i.C.1:6). In the Ushan view of Meir, however, neutralization applies only to orlah-produce that has not been processed (Orlah, ii.C.3:6-8). Once householders process food, they are careful to sell or maintain it in discrete and correctly measured quantities. It always is perceived as separate from other food with which it is mixed. Neutralization therefore no longer applies to it. Ushans here again view the Israelite's own attitude and intention to be central in determining the status of food. Holiness does not come into being and disappear in accordance with an unvarying set of physical laws but, rather, on the basis of the concerns and perceptions of the common Israelite.

III. Conclusion

The theory of holiness presented in the Ushan materials holds that, through their intentions and perceptions, human beings define the boundaries of the sacred. On the basis of their own will, Israelites determine the proper conditions for planting and growing food in holiness. They establish what produce may and may not become holy, and they determine the specific conditions under which holiness actually comes to pertain to particular quantities of produce. Israelites even are envisioned as controlling the processes through which consecrated produce returns to the secular. What is important is that, in assigning these powers, Ushans claim that the character of the physical actions of the Israelite generally is not of central concern. This is the case except to the extent that those actions reveal the individual's intentions and desires. For the point of the Ushan stratum as a whole is that, through their will, Israelites determine what foods are to be treated as holy. In the same way, in the Ushan view, Israelites improperly handle or wrongly use holy produce, so as to be culpable for sacrilege, only if they actually perceive themselves to have done what is wrong. Whether or not an individual actually misuses holy

produce is not so much of concern as are his own perceptions of
what he has done. Finally, the ability of Israelites to eat
their food under conditions of holiness is seen to depend upon
the actions of the community as a whole which must, according to
Ushans, be intent upon preparing food for consumption in
accordance with the proper rules of holiness.

Through these laws Ushans reveal their view that God blesses
and sanctifies all that Israelites themselves deem worthy of
sanctity and want to be holy. Holiness does not continually
emanate from God and behave in accordance with unchanging norms
and physical laws. It comprises, rather, a reflection of the
Israelite's own will. In this Ushan view, to be sanctioned by
God, so as to be holy, actions must appear to the Israelites
themselves to accord with the divine will. No preset and
unvarying laws determine right and wrong, holy and profane.
Through their own conscious efforts, rather, Israelites build a
society conceived in holiness.

The implication of this Ushan perspective is that common
Israelites play a central role in giving meaning to their world
and in lending significance to mundane and ordinary things.
Israelites, Ushans hold, face a disorderly world in which their
actions are accorded no preordained significance. Inherently
they are neither right, nor wrong, holy nor profane. Instead,
Israelites themselves must define what is consistent with God's
larger plan for the world. They do this through their personal
intention to sanctify their production and consumption of food.
That intention determines the status and meaning of every action
Israelites carry out. Israelites thus impose order and meaning
upon the world. In the Ushan view this order, defined by the
ideals and perceptions of common Israelites, is identified as the
objective, God-ordained, order in the world. Common Israelites
therefore represent the measure of holiness on earth. Human
thought and action defines what does and does not accord with the
divine will. Israelites have the central role in designing, not
just implementing, God's plan for a perfected--and therefore
holy--world.

The extent to which the Ushan view differs from that found
in the Yavnean materials in the Division of Agriculture should
already be clear. As our review of the Yavnean laws indicated,
Yavnean authorities understand the world to contain a preset and
unvarying order to which Israelites must conform. It is left for

us now to see the extent to which the Ushan perspective likewise takes initiatives unforeseen in the Biblical sources that stand behind the legislation in the Division of Agriculture.

Mandelbaum, A History of the Mishnaic Law of Agriculture: Kilaim, points out Scripture's own understanding of the significance of the agricultural restrictions concerning Diverse Kinds. His discussion of the meaning within the Priestly Code of these particular laws serves both to explain Scripture's understanding of holiness in general and to contrast that understanding with the view of the Ushan materials we now have reviewed. I therefore cite Mandelbaum's discussion at length (pp. 3-4). In the following, Mandelbaum refers to the meaning of Lev. 19:19: "You shall keep my statutes. You shall not let your cattle breed with a different kind; you shall not sow your field with two kinds of seeds; nor shall there come upon you a garment of cloth made of two kinds of stuff."

> [A] study of the context of the rules in the Holiness Code of Leviticus yields important knowledge of P's views of the laws of diverse-kinds. Leviticus 19 consists of a list of rules headed by the command You shall be holy; for I the Lord your God am holy (Lv. 19:2). According to the catalogue's redactor, then, observance of the laws of diverse-kinds, like observance of the other rules of the catalogue, makes Israel holy. The laws are therefore interpreted in the context of the priestly understanding of the relationship between order and holiness. By examining this relationship we shall be able to put into perspective Mishnah's divergence from the views of Scripture.
> In the view of the priestly circles which stand behind P, order is a precondition of holiness. This notion is clearly reflected in P's account of the creation (Gn. 1:1-2:4a). P describes the making of a well ordered, hierarchical world. Each type of creation is brought forth in order of ascending importance, with (among living things) plant life first (Gn. 1:11-12). All living things, furthermore, were created each according to its kind (Gn. 1:11-12, 21, 24-25). Creation is thus an act of ordering, the purpose of which is to make the world perfect and thus prepare it to be made holy. The actual act of the sanctification of the world then takes place on the Sabbath (Gn. 2:1-3). The point of P's laws in Leviticus, then, is to prevent the confusion of those classes and categories which were established at the creation. P thus commands man to restore the world from its present condition of chaos to its original orderly state, and so to make the world ready once again for sanctification.
> Although Mishnah takes up P's general interest in order, it clearly diverges from P's view that the task of man is to restore the original order of creation. For, as we have already stated, Mishnah claims that it is man, and not a set of already established rules, who decides what is orderly and what is confused.

While concerned specifically with the restrictions of
Diverse Kinds, Mandelbaum's comments have clear implications
regarding the other agricultural restrictions. For as we have
seen throughout the Division of Agriculture, Ushans' main claim
is that, in all matters related to Israelites' agricultural
activities, their own perceptions and intentions are central in
imparting meaning and significance to their world. The
continuation of Mandelbaum's discussion, which concerns the
meaning, in the years after the Bar Kokhba revolt, of the Ushan
claims for the centrality of human intention, likewise is
instructive for our present purposes. Again, therefore, I cite
Mandelbaum's comments (pp. 4-5) at length.

> Mishnah's divergence from P becomes even more
> interesting when one takes into account the historical
> context of the two documents. Both P and Mishnah take shape
> in the aftermath of historical catastrophes. P was compiled
> during and after the exile which followed the destruction of
> the First Temple, while Mishnah was redacted primarily after
> the failure of the Bar Kokhba rebellion (132-135 A.D.), a
> disaster which erased the Jews' last hope of regaining and
> rebuilding the Temple. It is thus noteworthy that both P
> and Mishnah respond to these similar historical
> circumstances with an interest in restoring order to a world
> which to them appears to lie in utter confusion. It is
> striking, therefore, that these two documents should
> disagree concerning the nature of the order which they
> intend to restore. What is important to P is that the world
> would be returned from its present condition of confusion to
> its original, ordered state, as God had created it. P thus
> responds to the crisis it perceives by calling for a return
> to an unchanging, perfect world. By contrast, Mishnah
> underlines man's power to impose order upon the world, a
> capacity which is unaffected by historical events. In spite
> of the occurrence of catastrophes and disasters, man retains
> the ability to affect the world around him through such
> ordinary activities as sowing a field. While P has man
> confront confusion by reconstructing the ideal order of
> creation, Mishnah regards man as imposing his own order upon
> a world in a state of chaos, and so, in effect, as
> participating in the process of creation.

Mandelbaum's comments point to the important relationship
between the historical context in which Ushans worked and the
perspective on the world that their law presents. The Division
of Agriculture comes into being and speaks at a time in which the
earthly signs of God's power and dominion are gone. The Temple
is destroyed and the land of Israel remains in the hands of
foreigners, with little hope for its return to Israelite
sovereignty. Like Yavneans, Ushans reject the possibility that
these earthly events mean that God, and God's holiness, have
departed from Israel. Yet unlike Yavneans, Ushans are not so

naive as to claim that nothing has changed from the time that the Temple stood. The Temple and its cult once projected upon the earth an image of a God-ordained order. With these things destroyed, Ushans locate a new locus for order and holiness. They do this by concentrating upon the people of Israel themselves, claiming that they have the power to create a world of sanctity.

For Ushans, Israelites who perform commanded actions--separating tithes, planting their produce in accordance with Scripture's demands--do not simply adhere to God's plan for the world. To the contrary, in performing these mitzvot, Israelites themselves create a world envisioned as that desired by God. In the Ushan perspective, the authority of God thus is severely mediated by Israelites' own power. For Israelites determine what God sanctions and prohibits, often doing so in direct contradiction to what Scripture's passages seem to make clear.

The Ushan notion of the religious importance of human lect is familiar from later developments in rabbinic intel-thinking. These state explicitly that, having been recorded in Scripture, God's revelation now is subject to human evaluation and interpretation. Its meaning is determined only through Israelites' own thinking, safe from God's intercession into the human realm. Human investigation and reason, not even God's active signaling of what he desires, charts the proper course for commanded behavior.[5]

Within the context of Scripture's thought, this rabbinic perspective is unexpected and perhaps absurd. For according to it God loses to the Israelites themselves the exclusive authority that, in Scripture, he demands as creator and Lord. Ushans certainly agree with Scripture that the validity of their legal system is a function of the existence of God, who chose Israel and commanded that nation's activities. What is new and important, rather, is the Ushan claim that definition of conformity to these norms is in the hands of Israelites who, through personal evaluation and application, determine the exact form that adherence to the mitzvot should take. In rabbinic times, Israelites become the center and focus of the system of holiness that, previously, had depended only upon God, priest and Temple.

Within this system, Ushans thus describe common Israelites as an abiding symbol that the cultic sanctification that existed in the time of the Temple still exists in the world. This means that God still rules over and consecrates the people and land of Israel. In the Ushan view, God does this in response to the intentions and perceptions of those Israelites who work to plant, harvest and eat their food in holiness. Through these actions the people have the ability themselves to create a world of sanctity. Through their intention and perceptions they thus may deny those devastating events of history that have taken from them the concrete signs of God's power that once were found in their midst.

PART IV

CONCLUSIONS

CHAPTER FIFTEEN

CONCLUSIONS

The analysis of the formation of each of Mishnah's tractates, found in Chapters Two through Eleven, provided a picture
of the context and overarching concern of this division as a
whole. Chapters Twelve through Fourteen then summarized the
contributions to that whole of specific generations of rabbinic
authorities. In the concluding chapter, accordingly, I first
list this study's results that pertain to the Division of
Agriculture as a redacted whole. Then I examine what the
historical development of that law teaches about the growth of
nascent rabbinic Judaism.[1]

I. The Division as a Whole

1) The chapters that preceded have shown that the materials
in this division have no identifiable context or significance
prior to their inclusion in Mishnah. The Division of
Agriculture, that is, is not simply a collection of random laws,
deriving from Israelite antiquity and transmitted to Mishnaic
rabbis who, in turn, formed them into the tractates that stand
before us today. Mishnah's legal system, rather, forms a cogent
whole, an independent creation of individuals who, in the first
centuries, conceived and carried out a new and unique program of
legal inquiry. The Division of Agriculture indeed contains both
the basic ideas that instigate the growth of Mishnah's law and
the clear signs of development in legal thinking that led finally
to division as we know it. Were we to claim that the law as a
whole, or even significant parts of it, were the creations not of
Mishnah's rabbis but of Israelite antiquity, it would be
difficult to explain the basic level of initial inquiry found in
the Yavnean stratum or the fact that almost all of the Ushan
materials take up questions first posed by Yavneans. This means
that, even if Mishnah's rabbis did inherit certain laws or
concepts from the Second Temple period, their own work in
developing and structuring these materials is so new and
innovative as completely to efface all signs of the original
inheritance. Let me explain.

In the period before 70 little is reported concerning the law of agriculture. What is discussed concerns basic issues of definition. This indicates Mishnah's authorities' preference to turn directly to Scripture as an independent source of authority, rather than to cite tithing practices as they actually were carried out in Second Temple times. This same basic level of inquiry is taken up by those authorities who live after the first war with Rome. Yavnean authorities define basic terms and outline the central ideas needed to create an operational system of tithes. In doing this, Yavneans assume as fact only the small amount they inherited from pre-70 rabbinic traditions and ideas taken directly from Scripture, the document believed by all the people of Israel to contain the revealed word of God. There is no evidence that these authorities depended upon other traditions from Second Temple times. As in the preceding generation, those who worked after the Bar Kokhba revolt assume as fact only the laws created in the Yavnean period or taken directly from Scripture. They do not refer to laws that appear to have developed in the long period from the conclusion of Scripture until the beginning of the rabbis' own work. For the first time in this stratum, further, we find extended discussion of the notion, central to Mishnah, that all matters of law are judged in light of the intentions and perceptions of common Israelites. Depending upon and building the corpus of laws first legislated at Yavneh, there again is no evidence that this central notion of this division is the product not of the Ushan period but of Israelite antiquity.

Ability to identify both a starting point, in the period before 70, in thinking about the law of agriculture in general and to point out a developing agendum of concerns and attitudes towards the law indicates that the Division of Agriculture represents a creation of the first centuries, not an inheritance of ancient laws that Mishnah's authorities simply collected and placed in sequence. The Division of Agriculture is the creation of those individuals who Mishnah itself cites as the authors of its laws.[2]

2) Conclusions regarding the temporal provenance of Mishnah's law apply to the anonymous material just as to the laws and statements attributed to named authorities. Analysis of the logical unfolding of the law indicates that anonymous rules generally depend upon legal considerations or facts known to

originate with specific, named authorities. These anonymous statements therefore cannot derive from earlier than the period of those named sources, whose ideas they take up and expand. In the vast majority of cases, in fact, the anonymous materials parallel or even develop Ushan concerns. This shows that the anonymous law derives from late in this division's development. These findings are contrary to what past students of the early rabbinic literature claimed. On the assumption that Mishnah embodies laws from prior to the first centuries, many of these scholars believed that the anonymous materials had to be among the most ancient found in Mishnah.[3]

3) In the Division of Agriculture, Mishnah's authorities present a careful essay designed to facilitate application of the agricultural law. The division, that is, is not a random collection of topics and facts but a systematic treatment of all topics relating to Israelites' planting, harvesting, and eating of produce of the land of Israel.[4] Decisions concerning what this division should talk about therefore seem to have come before the actual work of legislation begun even at Yavneh. As a result, by the end of the Yavnean period, all of the topics and concerns that would interest Mishnah's rabbis were in hand and had received some consideration. Yavneans seem to have instigated the predominant interest of this division with the issue of sanctification, an interest taken up and developed to its logical conclusion in Ushan times. This overriding interest in sanctification perhaps explains why this division includes tractates on agricultural gifts that are sanctified, but not on the central gift--first tithe--that has an unconsecrated status.[5]

4) Along with the narrowly defined topical concerns of the Division of Agriculture, it is striking to recall the extent to which authorities in each of Mishnah's formative periods explore a single, theoretical issue within the set of topics under consideration. The Yavnean material as a whole details matters of definition. Ushans then take up the role of human motivation and of extenuating circumstances. This means that this division is the creation of groups of individuals who, in each period, worked together upon a carefully conceived program of inquiry.[6]

5) A theology unique to Mishnah, in contrast to the ideals of Scripture, develops in the period following the Bar Kokhba revolt. Ushans formulate notions of sanctification that significantly distinguish Mishnah's ideology from that of Scripture.

They do this by advancing the theory that Israelites' motivations and intentions determine what is holy and what is secular, what is permitted and what is forbidden. The Ushans thus move far beyond the Yavnean theory--implicit in Scripture itself--that powers of holiness devolve upon God in heaven and upon the priests on earth, and that holy and profane, right and wrong are determined by laws external to individual Israelites.

6) The preceding comments highlight the fact that, in the formation of post-destruction Judaism, the Bar Kokhba revolt, and not the destruction of the Temple, signifies the major watershed in the history of rabbinic law. The fact should not be entirely surprising. Historians have pointed out the significance of the failed Bar Kokhba revolt as the turning point in the attitude of Rome towards the Jews and in the Jews' own perceptions of their place within the world and their condition as a nation. Clark, p. 273, for instance, points out that, after the first war with Rome, the "official attitude towards the Jews had been surprisingly lenient. No measures of reprisal or repression were taken and no hindrances were put in the way of Jews' exercising their religious customs either in the land of Israel or elsewhere." Clark (p. 275), Smallwood (p. 346) and Schurer-Vermes-Millar (vol. 1, pp. 521-22), note further that, in this period, the Jews even had access to the Temple mount. Clark even argues that Jews could have--and perhaps did--continue the sacrificial cult in this period, a fact that Josephus (Ant. iii, 224-36) and other sources seem to suggest.

The effects of the Bar Kokhba revolt were decidedly more devastating, as Schurer-Vermes-Millar point out:

> The whole of Judaea was practically a desert. Fifty forts were destroyed and 985 villages, 580,000 Jews fell in battle and those who succumbed to illness or starvation were uncounted. ... In Jerusalem the plan conceived already before the war was put into effect; the city was turned into a Roman colony with the name Aelia Capitolina. To ensure the permanence of its purely pagan character, Jews still residing there were driven out and gentile colonists settled in their place. From then on no Jews were permitted enter the city area; any Jew seen there was punished with death. [The city's] constitution was that of a Roman colony... The image of a pig is said to have been carved on the southern gate of the city, facing Bethlehem. The main cult of the city was that of Jupiter Capitolinus, to whom a temple was erected on the site of the former Temple of the Jews. ... Besides Jupiter, the following deities of the city are represented on coins: Bacchus, Serapis, Astarte and the Dioscuri (pp. 553-55).

In light of these historical facts, we need not be surprised that in the period after the failed Bar Kokhba revolt, we find the important theoretical developments of this division and, indeed, the final formulation of the Mishnah as a whole. This period represented the first point after the destruction of the Temple at which all live expectation for the re-institution of the Temple cult seems surely to have died.

II. The History of the Mishnaic Law of Agriculture

The preceding six points delineate the character of the Division of Agriculture as a historical document of the first centuries. With these facts in hand, we turn now to conclusions 1) regarding the character of Mishnah's law of agriculture in each of its formative periods and 2) concerning the overall development of Mishnah's rabbis' legal thinking.

Before 70 and in Yavnean times, Mishnah's authorities concerned themselves with basic questions of definition. They gave concrete measurements that define a field, delineated which field labors may or may not be performed in the Sabbatical year, outlined for the case of each tithe and agricultural offering the quantity of produce to be taken and indicated how the offering is to be set aside. In this way these authorities, predominantly in the period of Yavneh, established the parameters of the agricultural law and delineated exactly what is expected of the individual Israelite.

A single theory of law informs these materials. Yavneans consistently offer definitions that exclude attention to the motivations or perceptions of the Israelites themselves. The reasons or perceptions that lead an individual to act, that is to say, have no bearing upon the permissibility of that behavior. The status of a deed, rather, depends solely upon the character of the concrete actions through which it was carried out. It does not matter to Yavneans why an Israelite collects stones in his field during the seventh year. The fact is that, in doing so, he makes possible the cultivation of that land, which is not allowed during the Sabbatical. The actions therefore are forbidden. This is the case even if the individual actually wants only to build a stone fence, a deed that itself is permitted. Along these same lines, Yavneans define physical entities in light of their shape and form, with no regard to the use to which Israelites intend to put them. A field, for

Yavneans, is demarcated by geographical boundaries, by hills, streams or trees that set off one area of land from the adjacent lots. In this perspective the farmer's own actions in choosing to reap one area as autonomous are immaterial. Geographical boundaries, not the farmer's use of the land, determines where on his property the farmer must set aside peah.

As I detailed in Chapter Thirteen, these ideas reveal the Yavneans' understanding of the existence of a preset order in the world, of an objective reality separate from any individual's perceptions of how things are or should be. Correct acts are those that conform completely to the ideal. Behavior, not intention, counts. The result of the action, not its underlying motivation, is determinative.

In turning to the Ushan materials, we found a clear and consistent development of the Yavnean ideal. Ushans analyze all actions in light of the intentions of the individuals who perform them and of the perceptions of those who witness and interpret them. The permissibility of field labor in the seventh year therefore depends upon the Israelite's intentions in carrying out the work. So long as the individual does not intend to break the rules of the seventh year and so long as he works in a way that prevents others from assuming that he proposes to break the law, that which he does is permitted. In the same way, the effectiveness of the individual's actions in separating heave-offering depends upon the intention with which the separation is carried out, not upon the character of the physical actions by which the deed is accomplished. And finally, Israelites' own perceptions define what is orderly and distinct or disorderly and mixed together, so as to be permitted or forbidden under the laws of Diverse Kinds.

Unlike Yavneans, Ushans recognize no order in the world other than that imposed by Israelites who, through their own intentions and perceptions, give meaning to their activities in planting, tilling and harvesting produce on the land of Israel.

Study of the law of agriculture thus reveals a clear development from the earlier to the later period. The Yavnean period's concern for the facts of the matter is transformed, in the Ushan generation, to an interest in the human elements of action and perception, to a concern for the circumstances under which an individual does something and to an interest in the perceptions others have of what that individual has done.

Yavneans examine only the physical character of any activity. Ushans concentrate upon motivation and extenuating circumstances. The implications of this development for our understanding of Mishnaic law must now be explored.

III. The Development of a Legal System

Legal development of the character I have identified in the Division of Agriculture is not unique to that document. In particular, scholars of the medieval period have pointed out similar developments in medieval law.[7] In these developments, inattention to motive and circumstances gives way, in the growth of the legal system, to a set of laws that take carefully into account the human elements that explain specific actions. For the case of medieval law, this development is described by Charles M. Radding, "Evolution of Medieval Mentalities: A Cognitive-Structural Approach." Radding's description of the growth of medieval law clarifies what we have seen in Mishnah's Division of Agriculture. I therefore cite Radding's description in full:

> [In the period preceding the twelfth century] monks and patrons alike believed that piety demanded only the observance of a precise daily routine, and as late as the eleventh century they considered the performance of liturgical ritual to be the essence of monastic dedication.
> The confusion--perhaps one should say interchangability--of intention and behavior is also evident in secular law. In the Leges Henrici Primi of 1114-18, drawn primarily from Anglo-Saxon codes, the compiler discussed homicide--in scattered fashion through many different sections--without differentiating among intentional slayings, deaths caused by negligence, and those resulting from unavoidable fault. Generally, the penalty for homicide was owed "in circumstances in which a man cannot lawfully swear that a person was not through his agency further from life or nearer to death." The compiler included cases that seem strange to us: "If anyone sends for a person and the latter is killed while coming; if anyone, when summoned to a place by a person, suffers death there; if anyone, being brought to witness a public execution of a wild beast or a madman, incurs some injury at their hands; if anyone entrusts a horse or other thing to a person and thence some harm befalls him." The explanation of these rules, according to the compiler, was the maxim qui inscienter peccat, scienter emendet: who unknowingly commits a wrong knowingly shall make ammends...
> Few questioned these legal or monastic practices for the six centuries before 1050. After that time, however, these rules and assumptions were increasingly challenged and discarded: the law described in the Leges Henrici Primi virtually disappeared in the half century following its compilation; the Cistercians abandoned oblation [that is, the previously widespread custom in which young children,

unable to commit themselves to life as monks, were in all
events turned over to be raised in monastaries] around 1100
and it was moribund well before the Fourth Lateran Council
finally prohibited it in 1215. In each case change was
directed towards greater concern with the interior aspects
of human nature. Because monasticism and law could only
function with the support of medieval elites, these shifts
also indicate changes in the collective mentality of
European society (pp. 578-579).

The development of attitudes towards culpability in medieval
law exhibits the same pattern of growth found in the Division of
Agriculture. In both legal systems an early view that ignores
motivation gives way to a later understanding that takes the
human element to be central. While the materials before us in
Mishnah do not refer to homicide, the example of oblation does
show how close in character is the shift Radding describes to the
development in the laws before us. Since oblates had not, of
their own accord, chosen to become monks, "high standards of
asceticism or spirituality was hardly possible in their case" (p.
578). Later medieval law rejected the formalism inherent in such
individuals' performance of their liturgical responsibilities,
deeming priestly ministrations performed without proper intention
to be invalid. This is reminiscent of Ushan authorities'
insistence that, to be valid, the designation of heave-offering
must be carried out by an individual who has formulated the
intention to consecrate that which he separates as the priest's
share. Both the later Mishnaic law and the medieval legal
thinking to which Radding refers thus come to consider as invalid
any actions performed without proper consciousness.

In light of the parallel in medieval law, interpretation of
Mishnah's legal developments is shown to be a problem of explaining in general terms the reasons for growth of this character in
obviously unrelated cultural, religious and political
environments. Radding states the interpretative problem clearly:

These trends in mental attitudes have been examined by
many historians--among them Fredrich William Maitland, Dom
David Knowles, Marie-Dominique Chenu, R. W. Southern, and,
most recently, Colin Morris--but none has succeeded in
giving an adequate account and many have retreated to vague
generalities. Sometimes the matter has simply been
sidestepped by indefinite references to "social and economic
change." Another approach has related the new ideas in law
and religion to an intellectual renaissance of the eleventh
and twelfth centuries, on the theory that the innovations
were connected with the wider use of reason in human
affairs. But more intellectual activity does not
necessarily mean different thoughts. Equally plausible is
the argument that dissatisfaction with old attitudes

stimulated the growth of scholarly debate. The changes also have been attributed to the new institutions of the twelfth century... (pp. 579-580).

The problem as Radding sees it is the difficulty of proving a connection between a shift in mental attitudes and vague changes in social, political and intellectual environment that could, after all, lead to a variety of different legal or philosophical responses. Radding therefore does not search for specific factors within the mileu of the eleventh and twelfth centuries that would explain the legal growth that he describes. Instead, he turns to the work of cognitive psychologists in order to show the extent to which both the earlier and later attitudes found in these legal systems represent central stages in the growth of human thinking. The point for Radding is not to prove that the development from lack of interest in intention--that is, moral realism--to a concern for the human elements that explain action occurs in all civilizations. Radding hopes, rather, to show that both types of thinking are usual for people in general, such that we should not be surprised to find them alone or in historical juxtaposition. Radding's inquiry again instructs us as we explain the rabbinic legal system. We therefore continue to follow his argument.

> Piaget pointed out that the lack of interest in intention exhibited in primitive law resembles the attitude toward rules--called "moral realism"--that is typical of children in all societies. According to Piaget, moral realism has at least three features: (1) the belief that any act that shows obedience to a rule is good and that any act that does not conform is bad; (2) the rule is not to be taken as something to be judged and interpreted but as something that is given, already made and external to the mind, so that the letter and not the spirit of the rule is obeyed; and (3) acts are evaluated in terms of their conformity with the rule and not according to the motive that prompted them (p. 582).

The notion that authority and doctrine are exterior to the individual's mind, such that they must be taken literally and uncritically begins to change when children reach the age of about ten. Then, to use the example of their attitudes towards play, they see rules not as "sacred and untouchable," but as validated by agreement of all players.

> "In short," as Piaget put it, "law now eminates from the sovereign people and no longer from the tradition laid down by the Elders." ... This less rigid attitude toward rules is founded on an increased ability to understand the other person and to cooperate on the basis of mutual development of subjective responsibility: "When the child is accustomed to act from the point of view of those around

him, when he tries to please rather than obey," then "he will judge in terms of intentions. So that taking intentions into account presupposes cooperation and mutual respect" (p. 583).

The two stages Piaget points out in attitudes towards law and authority resemble the stages in the development of the law of the Division of Agriculture. The Yavnean perspective, which views Scripture's restrictions as preset and unaffected by circumstance, equals the attitude of younger children, who judge matters in terms of the letter of the law and the concrete effects of action, not on the basis of the perceptions or intentions that lead to the specific behaviors. In the same way, the Ushan perspective is comparable to that of older children and adults, who look for the intent of the law and who determine the morality of an action in light of its conformity with that intent.

The preceding descriptions are not intended to argue that the evolution of culture and society parallels the growth of thought in individual human beings. I do not mean to say, that is, that phylogeny recapitulates ontogeny. Radding is careful to note that psychological theory can be applied to individual people alone, but not to societies as wholes. "Societies do not possess a consciousness similar to that of an individual and capable of maturing" (Radding, p. 595). Indeed, the notion that the growth of cultures necessarily parallels that of human beings is clearly disproven by the fact that in many known instances of growing legal and cultural systems, the growth that we have seen in Mishnaic law and which Radding has pointed out in medieval society is lacking. He notes, for instance, that "the history of late Roman culture might show a reverse trend--from communitarian to authortarian conceptions of morality" (p. 595). In the same way, the Hebrew Bible which the rabbis read so closely itself contains important distinctions between intentional and unintentional acts, for instance, in providing special rules for manslaughter (Num. 35:9-20) or in noting, Lev. 22:14, that certain rules apply only to an individual who unintentionally eats a holy thing. The approach to the law represented here was largely rejected at Yavneh, except for the specific cases about which Scripture already had spoken and for the uncharacteristic views of certain Yavneans, e.g., Joshua, at Terumot, iv.B.8:1-3. The parallel pointed out between the medieval developments analyzed by Radding and what we have seen in Mishnah therefore cannot be construed to claim a normative development, such that all societies are expected to grow in the same way that moral sensibilities arise in children.

The lesson taught by the parallel in the growth of moral thinking in children and the development of the Mishnaic law of Agriculture must therefore be narrowly defined. This parallel teaches first and foremost that both the Yavnean and the Ushan approaches to the law are natural within individual human beings and therefore are expected within the conglomerates of individuals that comprise societies. Finding, first at Yavneh and then at Usha, a predominance of a certain mode of thought furthermore points to the close correspondence between the mentalities of individuals who live in a common social, cultural and political environment. The shared perspectives on law indicates the extent to which rabbis, first at Yavneh and then at Usha, developed a communal intellect and common ethical perspective.

At the same time it is important to recognize the rarity--and therefore significance--of large scale shifts in group mentality. "Usually, of course, one generation, through its interactions with the next, educates it into the same ways of thinking, just as the intellectuals and leaders of the twelfth century--by the institutions they created and the questions they posed, and the students they taught--assured that their concerns would be those of subsequent generations" (Radding, p. 595). In light of this, historical context--in terms of social, political and economic growth--must certainly be brought into play to help to explain such large scale developments as we have seen, for instance, in Mishnah. For in an extremely short period of time, Mishnah's masters shifted entirely from one pattern of legal thinking to a quite different one.

In light of this consideration, Chapters Thirteen and Fourteen have located within the historical context of Mishnah's own own time reasons for the shifts that we have seen. This approach, which takes seriously the political context in which Mishnah's rabbis worked, is familiar from recent studies of each of the individual tractates in the Mishnaic Division of Agriculture. These too have pointed out a connection between the destruction of the Temple, in 70 C.E., the failed Bar Kokhba revolt, of 135, and the formation, within Mishnah as a whole, of a system of law that focuses upon the power of individual Israelites.[8] My own comments concerning Tractate Terumot (The Priestly Gift in Mishnah, p. 7) illustrate this approach to the interpretation of Mishnah.

> To make the claim of God's continuing presence, the tractate ... focuses upon the actions and responsibilities of the Israelite who sets aside and protects the priestly due. By describing these actions and responsibilities, it makes the powerful point that even with the Temple gone, cultic sanctification remains. This means that God himself still rules over the people and land of Israel. He moves in response to the intentions and perceptions of Israelites who separate the offering which he mandated. This message is poignant. For as is clear, with the Temple destroyed and the Land defiled, these intentions and perceptions were all that remained to deny the events of history and affirm God's Lordship.

The present study's evidence for the historical growth and development of the legal thinking found in Mishnah allowed a careful nuancing of the theory just summarized, so as to take into account the perspective of Mishnah's Yavnean authorities. Chapter Thirteen suggested that we take seriously the fact that, in the period immediately following the war in 70, Israelites expected the imminent rebuilding of the Temple and the return of the sacrificial cult. Life thus was expected soon to return to exactly as it had been before the destruction. This explains the apparent insistence of Yavneans that nothing is changed from the time when the Temple stood. Yavneans, that is, continue to see a preset and hierarchical order in the universe, as was represented by the presence in their midst of the Temple and the God ordained cult that was carried out in it. Only with the Bar Kokhba revolt, the first point at which the lively expectation for the Temple's being rebuilt could not be maintained, did the circumstances ripen for new theological developments. These placed common Israelites at the center of Israelite theology by claiming that, through their own perceptions and intentions, Israelites impose meaning upon a world otherwise seen to be in a state of chaos.

This approach to understanding Mishnah suggests an important avenue for future consideration, for it begins to answer the basic questions that historians must ask concerning the relationship between social and legal developments and the larger historical contexts in which those developments occur. At the same time, specific methodological problems must be outlined, putting clearly into perspective the stature of this initial interpretive suggestion. These problems result from the

character of the written evidence upon which we depend for our
only access into the philosophical and social world of Mishnah's
authors. For the rabbis themselves work hard to hide all
evidence of the effect outside events and individual
personalities might have had on their work. We therefore know
almost nothing about the character of individual rabbis. Their
philosophies, further, are revealed to us only through their
legal work, which itself never explicitly indicates the
underlying reasons for specific statements or laws. Since the
very goal of the rabbis who created the Mishnah was to efface all
sign of historical background and individual philosophy,
attempting to interpret Mishnah in light of the political
background of its own day presents a serious methodological
problem. William Green, "Reading the Writing of Rabbinism"
states the methodological problem clearly.

> The obsession of the Mishnah with halakot pertaining to
> the Temple at a time when it must have been clear that the
> cult was gone forever certifies that the document speaks of
> a world that no longer existed.   The disjunction of the
> Mishnah's interests and the evidence of the historical
> record, therefore, contributes a fundamental component to
> the understanding and interpretation of the document as a
> whole.   It establishes beyond a doubt that the substance of
> the Mishnah is not mimesis, but fiction, and this knowledge
> helps to direct our assessment of its preoccupations and
> ultimate purposes. But the broad political context does not
> explain the details of the text, nor does it show how these
> two events [that is, the destruction of the Temple and the
> Bar Kokhba revolt] affected the form of the document. The
> danger of reading a text primarily against this sort of
> background is that limited and particular data, fragments of
> the historical record, may be used to explain too much, to
> constitute the single reference point for understanding.
> The assumption, for instance, that the Mishnah is designed
> principally and primarily as a strategy of rectification in
> the aftermath of the two wars carries in its wake the
> inevitable tendency to seek out its elements of structure
> and stability and to ignore its traits of disorder,
> ambiguity, and inconsistency (pp. 194-195).

Green, for the case of early rabbinism, and Radding, for the
medieval materials he discusses, agree concerning the importance
of interpreting legal and mental developments such as we have
seen in Mishnah on the basis of the concrete world from which the
documents derive. They warn us however that, in Green's words,
"In creating the various contexts against which the rabbinic
literature can be understood and interpreted, we need to begin
with epistemological modesty; we cannot push too far beneath the
surface before we have thoroughly mapped the terrain on the basis
of the most detectable landmarks" (p. 203).   As its primary

purpose this study has indeed set out to delineate the basic
concerns and facts of the Division of Agriculture. This mapping
of the terrain provided a clear picture of the issues confronted
in the Division of Agriculture, as well as a careful evaluation
of the specific perspective upon the law of each generation of
rabbis. This evaluation led to a historical reconstruction that
makes use of the central intellectual landmarks provided by the
Division of Agriculture.

Yet, as Green makes clear, the evaluations carried out here
teach first and foremost about the cognitive world of the rabbis
themselves, a world revealed in the specific concerns they
address and in the legal theories that they develop. In this
regard, the most important result of this volume is the
recognition of the growth, within this division, of the earlier
legal absolutism, which characterizes Yavnean thinking, into the
relativist perspective of Ushan legislation. This growth points
to the developing agendum of early rabbinic Judaism, a Judaism
that, by the end of the second century, centered upon the powers
of the human intellect and will to define and give meaning to the
world.

This conclusion regarding the internal legal focus of this
document parallels the conclusion drawn by Green from the formal
traits of the Mishnah as a whole. He states:

> [T]he Mishnah may be envisioned as a kind of primal
> list, mastery of which determined competence and credibility
> in rabbinic society. But the absence in its list of
> explicit hypotaxis suggests that expertise involved learning
> each single pericope, each separate unit, one after another.
> It also implies that in rabbinic discourse attention will be
> directed not to a picture of the whole but to details of the
> distinct components of the list themselves. Because their
> autonomy is never nullified and because they are not
> formally bound to one another, the elements of Mishnaic
> lists are capable of virtually endless comparison and
> contrast, of nearly infinite combination and recombination,
> in a system that maximizes the possibilities for ingenuity
> (pp. 202-203, emphasis added).

Ingenuity, indeed, is what the Division of Agriculture, and
with it the rest of Mishnah, is about. For in this document,
rabbinic masters envision a society in which each individual's
intellect will work towards creating a perfected world, conceived
by humans and yet believed to be in the holy image of God. While
awaiting realization of this dream, these rabbis, powerless
within their own nation, work at the elaborate puzzle that
constitutes Mishnah. Their highest value is seen both in their
internal intellectual life and in their legislation. This value

consists of using the mind to determine what God demands and so to participate directly in the processes of revelation and, ultimately, redemption.

NOTES

NOTES TO INTRODUCTION

[1]My delineation of the thematic units of the tractates of the Division of Agriculture makes use of recent commentaries to these tractates, referred to later in this introduction. These have indentified the cogent thematic organization of the tractates, showing them to be essays that develop a specfic line of inquiry. See [Avery-]Peck, pp. 7-21; Brooks, pp. 19-31; Essner, pp. 106-107; Haas, pp. 3-8; Havivi, pp. 151-153; Jaffee, pp. 6-13; Mandelbaum, pp. 5-17; Newman, pp. 22-30; Sarason, pp. 10-18; and Wenig, pp. 50-52.

[2]In this volume, discrete legal statements are cited by 1) title of tractate, 2) numeric designation of thematic unit, 3) letter designation of the period to which the rule is assigned, and 4) designation of chapter and paragraph within Mishnah. Designation of historical provenance is as follows: A = Before 70; B = Yavneh; C = Usha; D = Unassigned (i.e., anonymous). Kil., iv.C.8:3 thus refers to Mishnah Tractate Kilaim 8:3, which is an Ushan rule found in the tractate's fourth thematic unit (on diverse kinds of animals, as the Table of Contents indicates).

[3]These discussions are formatted in two columns. The left column contains a restatement of the law under consideration. In the right hand column I indicate the theoretical basis for the law and specify the grounds for assigning it to the particular period in the development of the tractate's rules.

[4]This idea is formulated along the same lines by Neusner, Purities, Part XXII, p. 271, note 1.

[5]See Neusner, Purities, Part XXI, in particular, pp. 234-46 and 298-302.

[6]Discussion of the anonymous rules is placed after my consideration of the Ushan materials. This is the case even for the few anonymous rules that are determined to belong in the Yavnean stratum. I have chosen to discuss the anonymous rules of each thematic unit as a corpus so as to make clear the less certain character of their assignment to specific levels in the formation of the law. Placement after the Ushan rules turns out in all events to be appropriate, since the vast majority of the anonymous materials appears to derive from Ushan times or later.

[7]See, for instance, Jacob Brull, Mabo LaMishnah, p. 34, cited by G. Porton in J. Neusner, ed., The Modern Study of the Mishnah, p. 86. The same view, that certain anonymous rules derive from the Second Temple period or earlier, is expressed by Guttman, p. 145, Albeck, Mabo, p. 76, and Urbach, "Mishnah," p. 94.

[8]Attempts to identify a specific legal agendum or perspective attached to an authority are complicated by the wide range of issues a single rabbi might discuss in the context of a small number of statements. The common theoretical underpinnings of opinions assigned to authorities from a single period likewise

413

makes it difficult to distinguish the specifics of any rabbi's thought.

[9]On occasion, a Yavnean will, in dispute with other Yavnean authorities, express an opinion that becomes common only later, in Ushan times. In such cases we see the beginning of the development of later ideas. Yet this does not provide insight into the development of the law at Yavneh, since we are not able to determine exactly when the Yavnean minority opinion developed. A good example of this is at Terumot, iv.B.8:1-3, where Joshua takes up a legal perspective that becomes normative only later, in Ushan times.

[10]On the theory of exegesis that stand behind these recent commentaries see, in particular, Jaffee, pp. 13-22.

NOTES TO CHAPTER TO ONE

[1]Tractates Peah, Maaser Sheni, Bikkurim and parts of Tractates Terumot and Hallah.

[2]The primary locus of this issue is Tractate Demai. Tractate Maaserot along with parts of Tractate Hallah describe how Israelites may be certain to tithe when required.

[3]The concerns listed here are taken up in Tractates Kilaim, Orlah and Shebiit, respectively.

[4]The basis for these ideas obviously occurs in Scripture, as I point out in detail in Section III of this chapter.

[5]See Newman, p. 15, and below, Chapter Five, note 1.

[6]See Mandelbaum, pp. 1-4.

[7]God provides the land of Israel and therefore has a lien upon the crops that the land produces. Payment of this lien, in the form of heave-offering and tithes, releases the food for consumption by Israelites. It should be clear that God's lien upon the produce, and not any intrinsic status of holiness, accounts for the prohibition against Israelites' making a meal of untithed food. This is explained by Sarason ("Zeraim," pp. 87-89 and p. 94, n. 17), who points in particular to the (Ushan) rules of Tractate Terumot, which even allow the householder to fulfill the liability to tithing of one batch by separating heave-offering and tithes from a different batch. I make the same point in The Priestly Gift in Mishnah, p. 3.

[8]For a general introduction to the Greco-Roman literary sources on agriculture and farming, see White, Farming, pp. 14-46. A detailed discussion of farm economy in the ancient world is found in Finely, pp. 95-122. See also Frank, Economic Survey of Ancient Rome. Vol. V. Roman Italy and the Empire. Unfortunately, Mishnah's reticence concerning the actual operation of farms makes even general correlation of the rabbinic material with the facts supplied by Finely impossible.

[9]Matthew 23:23-24, Luke 11:42. While expressing the same attitude, the issue of Jesus' picking on the Sabbath (Matthew 12:1-6 and parallels) is not relevant here, since it concerns work on the Sabbath, not agricultural taboos.

[10]On this and following see White, <u>loc. cit.</u>

[11]A detailed comparison between the Mishnaic system of agriculture and Greco-Roman agricultural rites and taboos is not possible because of the lack of a detailed study of the Greco-Roman materials. Such a study has not been carried out presumably because of the diverse nature of the sources for pagan agricultural customs. Most information derives from inscriptions, along with occasional references from writers such as Cato, who, in detailing proper estate management, suggests the proper prayers for different points in the agricultural year. Important for our purposes is the fact that, within Hellenism, the upper class Roman writers tended to have religious beliefs substantially different from those of the common practitioners of agricultural rituals. In the rabbinic context, by contrast, we find the intellectual class involved in the development of these ritual practices.

[12]Evidence of this is collected by Feliks, <u>Agriculture</u>. As Feliks shows, what little agricultural realia is revealed in the Mishnah (and in particular in the Talmudim) appears to conform to contemporary norms of farming and food production. One notable parallel is the equal importance of the threshing floor in Greco-Roman and Mishnaic law. In the Greco-Roman system, the crops are there divided between the crown and the peasants, and tax claims are there paid (Rostovtzeff, p. 280). Comparably, in Mishnaic law, tithes normally are paid at the threshing floor. In the Greco-Roman system, the importance of the threshing floor relates to its easy accessibility by tax officials. Mishnah, however, sees a very different significance to the threshing floor, specifically, its marking the point at which the food first is made ready for consumption. It therefore is not clear what significance can be made of the superficial similarity between the two legal systems.

[13]The following is intended to apply to the earliest period in the formation of rabbinic Judaism, represented by the documentary evidence of the Mishnah. I take it as a given that later documents' claims about rabbinism reflect the situation of those documents' own period, but not necessarily that of earlier times.

[14]Lieberman, "How Much Greek in Jewish Palestine?" makes this same point on different grounds. He points out the certain familiarity of the rabbis with Greek language and philosophical ideas. Yet he carefully delineates the overall autonomy of the rabbis, who pursued their own programatic issues and who did not frequently adopt Greek philosophical theory or even technical language.

[15]I count a total of 68 verses, scattered in nineteen passages. The majority of these passages contain only one or two verses. The overall total of verses is raised considerably by the single, long passage at Dt. 26:1-15, which discusses the liturgy for the presentation of first fruits and for Scripture's "year of tithing." The relevant passages from Scripture are discussed in my introductions to each of the tractates of this division.

[16]As I stated above, note 4, many of Mishnah's basic understandings derive from Scripture. The point here, to be supported in detail in the following summary of the contents of this division, is that Mishnah's framers use Scripture's laws in ways not envisioned by Scripture at all.

[17]In light of the unsystematic nature of Scripture's tithing laws, scholars have not reached a consensus concerning their origin or significance. The problem arises with the attempt to locate in Scripture a unitary system of agricultural offerings (see e.g., Oppenheimer, "Terumot"). This leads to claims of a dual focus of the tithing law, upon piety, on the one hand, and taxation, on the other (see MacCulloch, Guthrie). As Sarason, Demai, pp. 3-10, points out, however, the Deuteronomic and Priestly sources contain two distinct theories of tithing. The former holds that the separation of tithes acknowledges God's ownership of the land of Israel and expresses gratitude for the land's fertility. The latter holds that the tithes go to the Levites and Aaronide priests as their pay for serving in the Temple. (This same duality between piety and taxation is found, notably, within the Roman system of tithes and tribute. See Rouse.) Mishnah's authorities take Scripture's diverse statements and in part conflicting definitions of specific offerings and derive from them a unitary and focused set of laws concerned with the sanctification of Israelite life.

[18]Scripture's references, obviously, are the source of Mishnah's knowledge that certain offerings are consecrated. But again, Mishnah's authorities find in this fact an importance unforeseen by those who stand behind Scripture's rules.

[19]This point is developed by Neusner, Judaism, pp. 270-283. For the case of tractates in this division, see Newman, pp. 15-20, Brooks, p. 35, Mandelbaum, pp. 2-4, Avery-Peck, pp. 2-6 and Jaffee, pp. 4-5. For the role of human intention in the Division of Agriculture as a whole, see below, Chapter Fourteen and Conclusions. My characterization of the state of legal thinking in the period before 70 and at Yavneh appears in Chapters Twelve and Thirteen.

[20]The ideas summarized here are detailed in full in the introductions to each of the tractates, Chapters Two through Eleven.

[21]See Davies, pp. 15, 17-19.

[22]See below, Chapter Five, note 1.

[23]This one Mishnaic chapter contains almost all that the Division of Agriculture has to say about the normal transfer of agricultural gifts to a priest. Even it, however, focuses primarily upon the circumstances under which Israelites need not maintain these gifts for the priest at all and cases in which they may even consume parts of the gifts themselves. This focus is indicative of the concern of the division as a whole. This concern, as I said, is the role of the common Israelite in manipulating holiness. In light of this central concern, the Division of Agriculture, much like the rest of Mishnah, has little interest in the concrete rights of priests and Levites.

NOTES TO CHAPTER TWO

[1]That is, by contrast to first tithe, which, like poor offerings, is not consecrated, yet is not the subject of a tractate. See Chapter Seven, note 2, and Chapter Fifteen, note 5.

[2]The fact that such items as gleanings are not in the status of tithe at all until the poor take them is shown by the fact that, at the end of the harvest season, rich and poor alike may enter the fields and take any produce that remains, even if it had been left by the farmer for the poor.

[3]Note however that at Usha as well there are several enigmatic disputes on this issue, such that the legal development is not so clear here as we might desire.

[4]I do not believe that this is an over-interpretation. Surely Ushans here agree with what is explicit in Scripture, that gleanings and peah must be collected by the poor themselves. But in making this claim, they reject the alternative approach raised in the Yavnean period and phrase in particularly Ushan terms the requirement that the poor person actually "harvest" the produce and not simply lay claim to it.

[5]I see no way to explain the appearance for this particular rule of a legal precedent involving authorities from the period of the Houses, a percedent that indeed claims that the law at hand was given to Moses at Sinai. If it is, simply, pseudepigraphic, designed to lend credence to later rabbis' legal claims, it is unclear why the same device does not appear with any frequency in the document before us. At the same time, the specific legal ideology expressed here clearly belongs in the later period, such that it cannot be assumed to reveal facts about the legal perspective of those who lived while the Temple stood.

[6]Concerned with the question of whether or not, in applying the law, we take into account mitigating circumstances, this dispute is comparable to the issue argued by Eliezer and Joshua, Terumot, iv.B.8:1-3. It therefore appears that the central issue of this division, fully exposed in Yavnean times and settled in the period of Usha, did receive minor consideration before 70.

[7]The lack of interest in this issue may itself be considered evidence of its authenticity in the mouths of the Houses, there being no obvious context in which later authorities would have assigned such an idea to earlier ones. Even if it should be authentic, the fact that we have only one dispute on this topic makes it difficult to develop from it an understanding of the significance of the deeper legal issues it addresses.

[8]There is no evidence however that Gamaliel and sages are familiar with the specific positions assigned to the Houses at iv.A.6:1D-6:3. This makes it difficult to assign the Houses' opinions to the period before 70. See Brooks, Chapter Six, note 20 (p. 193).

[9]Brooks adduces both of the explanations given here, the former in the body of his comment to M. 7:7 (p. 132) and the latter in a footnote, in which he cites MR (p. 197, note 19).

NOTES TO CHAPTER THREE

[1]The Ushan legal developments possibly work to rectify the larger rabbinic claim, to speak in the name of all of the people of Israel, with the actual powerlessness of the early rabbinic group. By setting those who tithe above the rest of the people and by suggesting that the haber is responsible for the salvation

of the Israelite nation as a whole, Tractate Demai perhaps offered the rabbinic estate a sense of power that the rabbis' actual position in society denied. Coming in Ushan times, this development would have marked the point at which the rabbis first realized that their larger program for the nation as a whole was not soon to be accepted. Unfortunately, lack of evidence concerning the structure and attitude of rabbinic leadership in the first centuries, as well as our lack of a clear picture of the rest of Israelite society, prevents this sociological explanation from leaving the realm of speculation. On the problem of extracting a social description from rabbinic documents, see Green, "Rabbinism," pp. 195-99.

[2]Cf., Oppenheimer, "First Tithe." Oppenheimer claims that the law of tithing found in the Division of Agriculture existed as a complete system so early as the time of Ezra and Nehemia. He therefore pushes the conflict between the haber and the am haares back into Second Temple times. See the following note.

[3]Oppenheimer, op. cit., pp. 77-80, shows in detail that the terms neeman and haber refer to members of religious and social groups distinct from the rest of the Israelite people. He fails, however, to prove his central claim, that these groups existed primarily in the time of the Second Temple. While such groups may well have existed in that period, the sources concerning the haber and the neeman derive from no earlier than Ushan times.

[4]The parallel dispute between the Hillelites and Shammaites, at Shebiit, ii.A.4:2A-H, I-K and 5:8, further supports placement of this issue in the period before 70.

[5]All produce grown upon the land of Israel is subject to the separation of heave-offering and tithes, whether it is grown by an Israelite, gentile or Samaritan. The theory, found throughout the Division of Agriculture, is that ownership of property within the land of Israel by a non-Israelite is null. The land still is deemed to be Israelite property and, as part of the gift of God to the people of Israel, produces crops subject to tithes. Certain authorities, however, hold that produce separated by gentiles does not take on the status of agricultural gifts. This is because the gentile is not understood to have benefitted from God's gift of land and therefore does not himself owe God a share of the crop. See Chapter Six, note 9.

[6]Unfortunately there is no way of testing Sarason's suggestion, Demai, p. 226, that the Hillelite view might, "echo ... an earlier, subsequently discarded, conception of tithing practices." Cf., Neusner, Judaism, pp. 287-88.

[7]I elaborate upon this conclusion, as it relates to the Division of Agriculture as a whole, in Chapter Twelve.

NOTES TO CHAPTER FOUR

[1]This perhaps depends upon the same theory as the rules for neutralization (see Chapter Six, note 5). The particular application of this theory is totally in line with Ushan law in general, for it chooses to ignore what is known to be in the mixture and to take account only of the appearance of the grown crop.

[2]The theory obviously is the same as at ii.C.2:1-2, discussed in the preceding note.

[3]The theory of the present entry is however quite different from that of M. 2:10. While Yavneans require a minimum area of six by six handbreadths for the planting of one kind, Ushans allow the planting of six kinds in that same space.

[4]Mandelbaum, in Neusner, Judaism, p. 288, states: Both in this dispute and in that of M. Kil. 4:5 the Houses attest the concept of the area of tillage, i.e., the distance which must separate climbing plants from plants of other kinds. It appears, then, that two major conceptions of the tractate, the autonomous "field" and the area of tillage, were known to the Houses, and so may originate before 70. It is equally important to remember, however, that the Houses are generally concerned with fundamental definitions of areas or structures involved with the planting of different kinds. It is very clear, then, that the Houses stood near the beginning of the law of diverse kinds.

[5]The redactional conflation of M. 6:3, 4 and 5 superficially obscures the very different issues found within the Yavnean M. 6:4 and the other, Ushan, pericopae. Mandelbaum, p. 219, is careful to take this into account, noting that at M. 6:4 Ishmael does not address the question of the barren tree at all. By contrast, Mandelbaum cites Maimonides' interpretation. By reading the unit as an integral whole, Maimonides is forced to explain Ishmael's position with the claim that the sycamore tree (which bears a fig like fruit) is deemed partly like a barren tree and partly like a fruit tree.

[6]See above, note 1.

[7]I find no firm grounds for explaining why, in this case, Scripture's rule is taken literally while, for the case of Diverse Kinds of animals, unit iv, Scripture's narrow restriction is broadly expanded.

[8]31 out of the tractate's 81 units (39%) bear Ushan attributions, compared to only 13 entries (18%) with Yavnean names. Only eight of the tractate's 28 anonymous rules appear to derive from prior to Ushan times.

NOTES TO CHAPTER FIVE

[1]Newman, p. 15, suggests that the land of Israel is understood to have human qualities, such that, "like the people of Israel and their God, it too experiences fatigue and requires a period of repose." Neither Scripture nor Mishnah, however, understands the Sabbath and Sabbatical year legislation to derive from a psychological or physical need for a period of rest. As Scripture makes explicit, rather, the model for these observances is God's act of creation, in which God completed his work on the seventh day. Israelites too must therefore set aside their work on the seventh day and in the seventh year. The reason is not fatigue, but the necessity of following on earth the pattern established in heaven.

[2]On the implementation of the Sabbatical restrictions in the first centuries, see Safrai, "Sabbatical."

[3]See D. Hoffman, Sefer Devarim, I, pp. 232-48, and S. R. Driver, A Critical and Exegetical Commentary on Deuteronomy, p. 178, cited by Newman, p. 215, note 6. These exegetes argue that the financial obligations are cancelled precisely because, during the Sabbatical year, debtors do not have their usual income from farming.

[4]This accounts for the placement of these materials in the Division of Agriculture in the first place. Scripture spells out its Sabbatical restrictions in the context of its discussions of festivals and other sacred times, such that this tractate could, alternatively, appear in the Division of Appointed Times.

[5]According to this tractate, Israelites even determine when the restrictions of the Sabbatical year take effect. For Mishnah prohibits the farmer from performing field work at the end of the sixth year, insofar as, through that work, the farmer may enhance the crop of the following year. As Newman, p. 18, explains:
> By taking into account the deeds of Israelite farmers and their long-term impact upon the land, Mishnah moves beyond the strictly calendrical conception of the Sabbatical year presented in Leviticus. That is, while the priestly writer assumes that the Sabbatical year begins at a fixed time, determined only by the succession of the seasons and years, in Mishnah's view, Israelites too play a role in determining when the restrictions of the Sabbatical year begin to take effect.

[6]Newman, p. 215, note 1, argues that only Lev. 15:1-7 served as the basis for the law of this tractate. Newman's weightiest reason for this view is that the central point of the short passage at Ex. 23:10-11 is that each seventh year the land must lie fallow so as to produce food for the poor of the people of Israel alone. Mishnah by contrast assumes that in the seventh year all of the people of Israel may eat whatever grows on its own (cf., Judah, M. 9:8).

[7]Simeon's opinion here is anomolous since, throughout this tractate, Ushans seem quite content to place determination of what is permitted and forbidden in the hand of each individual. Indeed, ii.C.3:1-2 uses the point at which the ground dries up, as well as other criteria that differ from field to field, to determine other matters of Sabbatical law.

[8]At iii.A.5:4 the same underlying issue disputed here by Yose and Aqiba occurs in the mouths of the Houses. The Shammaites have the view of Yose. This same view is normative in the Ushan period. If the Houses' dispute is authentic, discussion of this issue was initiated before 70 and remained moot in Yavnean times. Since neither of the two pericopae in question develops the specific concern of the other, however, there are no grounds for establishing the authenticity of the attribution to the Houses.

[9]The presence here of Judah does not seem to me to preclude the conclusion that this issue is authentic in the period before 70. Judah claims simply that in this case the Shammaites rule leniently and the Hillelites stringently (see M. Ed. 5:1). But insofar as the issue raised by the Houses is found at Yavneh

(iv.B.9:9) and is not subject to Ushan consideration, there is no reason to discount the authenticity of this entry.

[10]So Albeck and Jastrow, p. 444, s.v., hzq. Newman and Danby by contrast translate "physically assist." The Division of Agriculture as a whole refuses to recognize as valid ownership by a gentile of property in the land of Israel. Since the gentile's land is under the Sabbatical restrictions, I see no reason that an Israelite should be permitted physically to work it. By contrast, the notion that polite encouragement may be given the gentile, who is not himself subject to the law, fits in with the theme of ii.D.5:6, 7 and 9, which permit Israelites to help others so long as by doing so they do not themselves engage in a transgression or definitely aid the other in committing one. This translation also is in line with the conclusion of the present pericope, which notes that, in general, Israelites should greet gentiles so as to encourage good relations with them.

[11]Eliezer here is not attentive to the circumstances under which the individual received the produce. In this regard, his view is parallel to what is assigned to his name at Terumot, iv.B.8:1-3, and elsewhere in this division.

NOTES TO CHAPTER SIX

[1]Yavneans, for instance, do not allow the separation from one batch of the heave-offering required of a different batch since what the individual does with the one heap of produce has no physical effect upon the other, distinct batch. This same approach is found in Yavnean materials in Tractate Maaser Sheni, which deem the redemption of second tithe to be valid only if the householder physically exchanges the second tithe produce and coins. Sarason is correct ("Zeraim") that this division as a whole does not view holiness as a physical property of certain produce. Still, as we shall see in detail, Yavneans do limit the Israelites' powers over consecration to the transferring of that status in ways comparable to the manipulation of physical entities.

[2]The same perspective appears in the Ushan stratum of Tractate Maaser Sheni, which holds that a status of holiness may be transferred from produce to coins or vice versa even if there is no sale of the one for the other and even if the transfer occurs between objects located in different cities.

[3]On this passage see Eissfeldt, pp. 81-83, and Snaith, pp. 266-267. Sarason, Demai, pp. 6-8, discusses the problem of the origin, within the Biblical sources, of Mishnah's tithes and other agricultural offerings. Further grounds for Mishnah's identification and description of heave-offering in particular is at Neh. 10:37a, which refers to offerings of "the first of our coarse grain, and our contributions (terumatenu), the fruit of every tree, the wine and the oil."

[4]Mishnah is concerned only with the designation and separation from the produce of God's share. It has no comparable interest in the actual payment to the priest of this produce, a topic on which the Division of Agriculture offers no legislation. While the division certainly expects the produce to go to its rightful recipient, its own interests, in the role of the

Israelite in the processes of sanctification, lead it to ignore the concern for the maintenance of the priesthood that, in Scripture, is central.

[5]Sarason, "Zeraim," pp. 95-96, suggests that the rule for neutralization "recalls Aristotle's notion of 'predominance,' viz., that 'if one component is predominant in bulk,...then the mixture results in fact in a change in the weak component into the predominant one'" (citing Sambursky, p. 12). Note however that even a small amount of heave-offering, slightly more than one percent of a batch, imparts its own status to the produce with which it is mixed. So the issue for the rabbis, unlike Aristotle, is not the relative bulk of each component in the mixture but some other, less tangible criterion. The same rabbinic view of mixtures, with the same divergence from the Aristotelian theory, occurs at Kilaim, ii.C.2:1-2 and v.D.9:1. In those cases the mixture is classified as that which the crop or fabric that results from it appears to be.

[6]Since the mixture contains produce of different kinds, the heave-offering is recognizable and remains distinct from the unconsecrated food. For this reason neutralization does not apply.

[7]This rule, which corresponds to the Yavnean legal perspective, indeed seems to have been known in Yavnean times. See iv.B.6:6.

[8]This must be an Ushan Eliezer, for, while agreeing with the theory of those materials, he has the opposite view of the Yavnean Eliezer b. Hyrcanus, cited at iv.B.8:1-3, who refuses to judge matters on the basis of the intentions of the individuals involved. There is no evidence that the question of separating heave-offering from clean and unclean produce arose before Ushan times.

[9]Simeon's position, that what is separated by a gentile is not valid heave-offering, takes into account the fact that gentiles did not receive portions of the land of Israel as part of God's gift of land to the Israelites. The gentiles therefore are not themselves indebted to God for allowing use of the land and, accordingly, cannot validly designate agricultural gifts which, in the first place, are payment for the use of the land granted by God. The issue does not arise for Samaritans, who are understood in certain respects to share in the people of Israel's covenant with God.

[10]In light of the involvement in the preceding entries of the Yavnean Eliezer b. Hyrcanus, I assume that we deal here too with that authority.

NOTES TO CHAPTER SEVEN

[1]In light of these questions, Tractate Maaserot serves as a prolegomenon to Tractates Peah, Terumot, Maaser Sheni and Bikkurim, which detail the processes through which the several offerings referred to here are physically separated and maintained. Except for the irrelevant fact of the ordering of the tractates, I find no basis for Albeck's claim that Tractate Maaserot comprises a "continuation" of Tractate Terumot (Zeraim, p. 217).

[2]While Albeck (Zeraim, p. 217) notes, as I do, that Tractate Maaserot concerns all of Mishnah's agricultural dues, he cites Num. 18:21-24 as the single Scriptural passage pertinent to the tractate (p. 216). Since that passage describes the Levitical tithe (Mishnah's first tithe), in citing it Albeck presumably takes seriously the name of Mishnah's tractate. While that passage, along with all of Scripture's tithing laws, has general relevance for the materials before us, it has no direct implications that would account for Albeck's prominent placement of it.

[3]As Jaffee, p. 1, notes, Scripture focuses upon the needs of the individuals who receive the agricultural offerings it describes. Beyond stipulating that the tithes are to be paid, however, it does not elaborate how or when in the growth and processing of the produce this is to be done.

[4]This is shown in detail by Jaffee in Neusner, Judaism, pp. 293-296.

[5]This idea appears to derive from Yavnean times. See iv.B.3:5A-D.

[6]Interest in the question of what the individual intended to do by separating one of the offerings provides further grounds for placement in the Ushan stratum.

[7]The Eliezer cited here has a very different legal perspective from that assigned to the Yavnean Eliezer b. Hyrcanus, who, in Tractate Terumot and elsewhere, refuses to take into account intentions or extenuating circumstances. See, e.g., Terumot, iv.B.8:1-3.

[8]T. Maaserot 3:14 appears to be wrong in assigning to Aqiba the rule stated here anonymously (so Primus, p. 78, who reconstructs an original Aqiban statement) and in citing Rabbi's position in the name of sages.

[9]Note as well the participation in this discussion of Simeon b. Gamaliel, T. 3:13, who reports that the Houses concur in accepting this rule. The Houses' statement itself appears to be a creation of Simeon's own day.

NOTES TO CHAPTER EIGHT

[1]Even the limits of the Israelite's ability to designate as holy (e.g., the item must be food and cultivated) largely depend upon his own perception. We have seen this, for instance, in Tractate Terumot's notion that Israelites themselves determine what is or is not in the status of food, without reference to an objective standard of edibility. Within the materials before us, further, Israelites even are accorded the power to render non-food items sanctified.

[2]The Houses argue their positions through a slightly different factual situation, discussed in detail in unit ii. To facilitate exposition, I have applied the Houses' theories to the case given here.

[3]Cf., Oppenheimer, Am Ha-Aretz, pp. 34-35, and Lieberman, Hellenism in Jewish Palestine, pp. 139-143.

[4]Within the Yavnean and Ushan strata of this unit, only two
rules contain attributions, i.B.2:4A-D and i.C.2:2. In order to
allow the reader to follow the development of the unit's legal
theories, I therefore have listed the anonymous materials
according to the periods from which they appear to derive,
instead of placing them in category D., the unassigned materials.
Placement of these rules depends upon the law's logical
development and is supported by attestations found in Tosefta.

[5]On this and the following entry, see Haas in Neusner,
Judaism, pp. 296-297.

[6]In light of the Yavnean interest in this same issue, it
does not appear as though this Ushan replay of a Houses' dispute
signals the Ushan origins of that dispute. At the same time, I
see no reason why, in this case, an issue apparently settled in
Yavnean times is reopened at Usha. The dispute therefore remains
enigmatic.

NOTES TO CHAPTER NINE

[1]See Havivi, in Neusner, Judaism, p. 299, who writes:
[A]t the heart of the dispute lies the question of the role
of human intention as made manifest by action. In this
specific case, what is discussed is how the preparation of
dough comes into play as a factor in determining liability
to or exemption from [dough] offering. Since the
philosophical question of intention and action is taken up
at Yavneh and thoroughly explored only at Usha, it seems
likely that the Houses' dispute is pseudepigraphic, deriving
from the post-70 era.

[2]See Chapter Six, note 5.

[3]Ishmael states that at issue is the order in which the
flour and water are added in the creation of each type of
dumpling. Ishmael thus sees the issue as comparable to that of
i.D.1:4, that is, whether or not the dumpling has been made in a
manner in which bread normally is prepared. Ishmael's view
accounts for Havivi's interpretation of the dispute, cited above
in note 1.

[4]I assume that this is Eliezer b. Hyrcanus, since, as at
Terumot, iv.B.8:1-3, and elsewhere in this division, he takes
account only of the concrete fact of the matter, that the grain
is not a food, and not the extenuating circumstance, that the
individual went ahead and made bread out of it anyway.

[5]In explaining this list, Havivi, p. 178, note 12, cites H.
E. Jacob, Six Thousand Years of Bread (N.Y., 1944), who states
that historically only six grains have been used in bread making.
Excluding maize, Mishnah's list is identical to Jacob's.

[6]Eleven out of the tractate's 37 entries (29%) are attrib-
uted to Yavneans, compared to only five pericopae (13%) bearing
Ushan names. Ten of the twenty anonymous rules appear to be
Yavnean. Only 6 of those rules are firmly placed in Ushan times.

NOTES TO CHAPTER TEN

[1]Note by contrast the theory of mixtures found in Tractates Terumot and Kilaim, which claim that in most cases, the Israelites' own perceptions of the status or character of the mixture determines how that mixture is treated under the law. See, e.g., Terumot, iv.C.7:5-7.

[2]Essner, p. 105, states, "The tractate has no problematic; no generative principle shapes the way the tractate approaches its subject matter. Indeed, it is difficult to speak of a 'tractate' at all, if by tractate we mean a systematic approach to a single subject."

[3]Terumot, iii.D.5:9, a rule assigned to the Ushan stratum, is clear, by contrast, that an individual's purposeful actions designed to neutralize heave-offering are void and leave the whole mixture in the status of heave-offering.

[4]The Yavnean position here is consistent with that found in Tractate Terumot, vii.B, which states that heave-offering has no effect upon unconsecrated produce that it flavors. Yavneans here do however assume that heave-offering leaven imparts the status of heave-offering to unconsecrated dough that it causes to rise. Yavneans apparently take seriously the change in the physical appearance of the dough caused by the heave-offering.

[5]See Neusner, Judaism, pp. 299-300.

NOTES TO CHAPTER ELEVEN

[1]A final chapter, M. Bik. 4:1-5, is found in standard printed editions of Mishnah, but is not authentic to the document. Omitted as well by Albeck, I have not included it in this discussion of the tractate. Since its contents have nothing to do with the law of agriculture, regardless of its origins, it need not detain us here.

[2]Only six of Tractate Orlah's 37 units and six of Tractate Bikkurim's 35 units are assigned to Yavnean names.

NOTES TO CHAPTER TWELVE

[1]For reasons that should be clear by now, in setting out the strata in the formation of the law, we must be content to differentiate among the periods of before 70, Yavneh and Usha. A complete explanation of the reason for this and of the methodology that allows assignment of specific laws to the pertinent periods is found in the Introduction.

[2]As I indicate in the Introduction, the role of later formulators and redactors in choosing for transmission and giving linguistic form to antecedent materials means that we cannot claim to know all that the authorities discussed and believed, let alone how they would have formulated their ideas for transmission. On the basis of the preserved materials, however, we are able to evaluate the larger legal perspective of those who preceded Mishnah's final redactions, insofar as that perspective is revealed in the rather consistent pattern of legal concerns and methods found in each generation's assigned statements.

[3]The basic premise that led to the creation of Tractate Demai--that one must tithe all that leaves his possession--is Ushan. In the view of earlier authorities, that one normally tithes when he is about to eat produce himself, the problem of doubtfully tithed food does not arise at all. On the Ushan origin of Tractate Demai, see the introduction to Chapter Three.

[4]The Scriptural foundations for Mishnah's set of agricultural offerings are detailed by Sarason, Demai pp. 2-10. Sarason shows how two "broad theories of tithing" found in Scripture yield Mishnah's unitary set of agricultural tithes and restrictions.

[5]See Neusner, From Politics to Piety: The Emergence of Pharisaic Judaism. After careful evaluation of the early Christian and Jewish sources concerning the Pharisees, Neusner, p. 143, concludes in part that: "The historical Pharisees of the period before 70 A.D. have eluded us. Our inquiry time and again brings us to the problems of the history of ancient Judaism after the destruction of Jerusalem."

[6]See Neusner, Holy Things, Part VI, p. 225.

NOTES TO CHAPTER THIRTEEN

[1]See Neusner, Judaism, pp. 230-250.

[2]See Smallwood, p. 346 and Schurer-Vermes-Millar, Vol. 1, pp. 521-522.

[3]This stands in clear contrast to the Ushan idea, found in the final chapter of Tractate Terumot, that what the Israelite deems worthy as food retains its consecrated status, while that which is perceived as waste becomes unconsecrated and may, accordingly, be eaten by anyone who wishes to do so.

NOTES TO CHAPTER FOURTEEN

[1]This is not meant to ignore the fact that authorities in the Ushan period and later determined which Yavnean materials would be included in this document and which would be excluded. Clearly, Yavneans may have legislated on a variety of topics that simply were not chosen for inclusion here. Important, however, is the fact that Yavnean legislation existed for each of the topics Ushans themselves choose to talk about. In this regard, the direction and concern of the division is set in the earlier period.

[2]Tractate Demai adds the further notion that each Israelite is personally responsible for all other Israelites' adherence to the law, such that the community of Israel as a whole should come to embody the ideals proposed by Mishnah's framers. The specific law of Tractate Demai simply takes into account the fact that the responsibilities Mishnah's authors wish to impose will not soon be accepted by the majority of the people.

[3]See Mandelbaum, p. 3.

[4]See Jaffee, pp. 3-6.

[5]The famous story at b. B. M. 59b makes this point explicitly, describing Joshua's citation of Dt. 30:12 ("It is not in heaven...") to reject supernatural proof of a legal point Eliezer claims is revealed law. Note that, while cited in the names of early authorities, there is no evidence that this story circulated before Talmudic times, when it is first cited. Note too that Joshua attributes to his prooftext a meaning hardly intended by Scripture. Dt.'s point is that the law already has been given and is available on earth, fully explained, for all easily to follow. Contrary to Joshua's claim, it does not indicate that, having been given, the law is subject to human, but not divine, interpretation.

NOTES TO CHAPTER FIFTEEN

[1]Since my results derive from a statistically significant percentage of Mishnah's materials, it is not surprising that they parallel the results of Neusner's studies of the five other divisions of the Mishnah. I refer in particular to his conclusions regarding the late provenance of the anonymous materials and the origins of Mishnaic law in rabbinic authorities' independent reading and evaluation of Scripture, not in their transmission of known laws and customs or their turning to priests or other individuals who may have preserved the practices carried out in the time of the now destroyed cult. In terms of its larger focus upon the powers of the common Israelite in defining the order and meaning in the world, this division fits entirely within the frame of Mishnaic discourse Neusner describes in his Judaism: The Evidence of the Mishnah.

[2]This understanding of the Division of Agriculture as a creation of the first centuries has important implications as we turn, in the second section of the conclusions, to the meaning of the rabbinic system of tithing within its own historical context.

[3]See the works cited above, Introduction, note 5.

[4]For ease of reference, the chapters in the body of this book are arranged according to the order of the tractates in manuscripts and printings of the Mishnah. See, however, the introduction to this volume, in which I list the tractates according to their contribution to the topical unfolding of the division as a whole.

[5]Treatment of poor tithes, which are not consecrated, occurs in this division as a function of the discussion of how specific produce comes to have the special status of an agricultural gift such that, for instance, it is not itself subject to the separation of other offerings. Poor gifts form an intersting part of this discussion, insofar as their designation, unlike that of all other offerings, depends upon two individuals, the householder--as usual--but also the poor, who complete the designation of the offering by finishing the harvesting and gathering of the food. First tithe, by contrast, is subject to no special rules regarding its designation and further is not even itself totally exempt from the separation of agricultural offerings, since the Levite must separate from it heave-offering of the tithe, for the priest.

[6]As noted above, Chapter Fourteen, note 1, the work of redactors, who chose which materials would be preserved in this document, obviously contributes to the impression that Mishnah's authorities as a group worked from the start upon a carefully conceived program of inquiry. However this might be, it remains clear that, throughout the topically diverse materials found in this division, an overriding theory of agriculture is formulated. This means that, whatever the specific role of redactors in organizing and formulating Mishnah's materials, the raw traditions with which they worked themselves evidenced a great degree of internal consistency.

[7]A complete list of sources is found in the bibliography in Radding.

[8]See Jaffee, pp. 3-6, Mandelbaum, pp. 3-4, Brooks, pp. 35-36 and Newman, pp. 17-20.

GENERAL INDEX